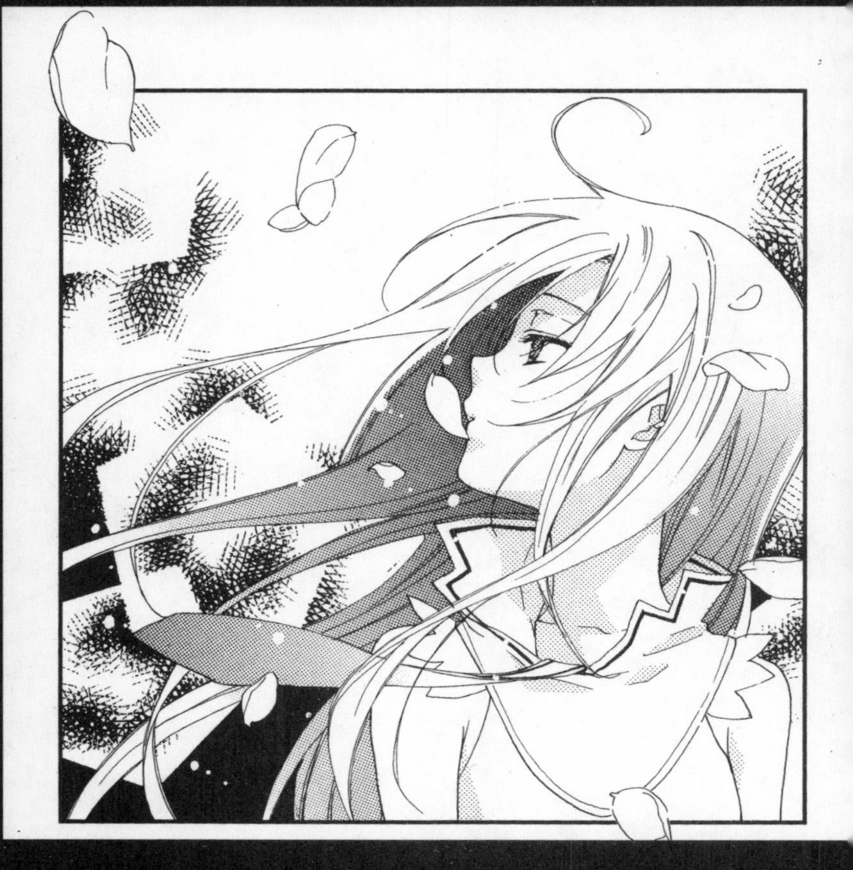

vol. 3

Ballad of a Shinigami

By Asuka Izumi
Original story by K-Ske Hasegawa

CONTENTS

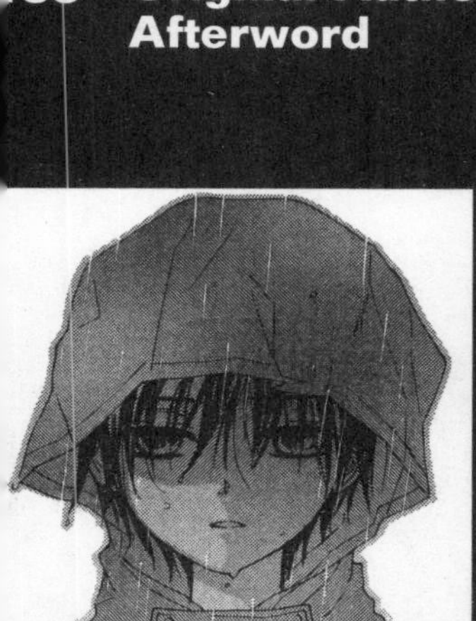

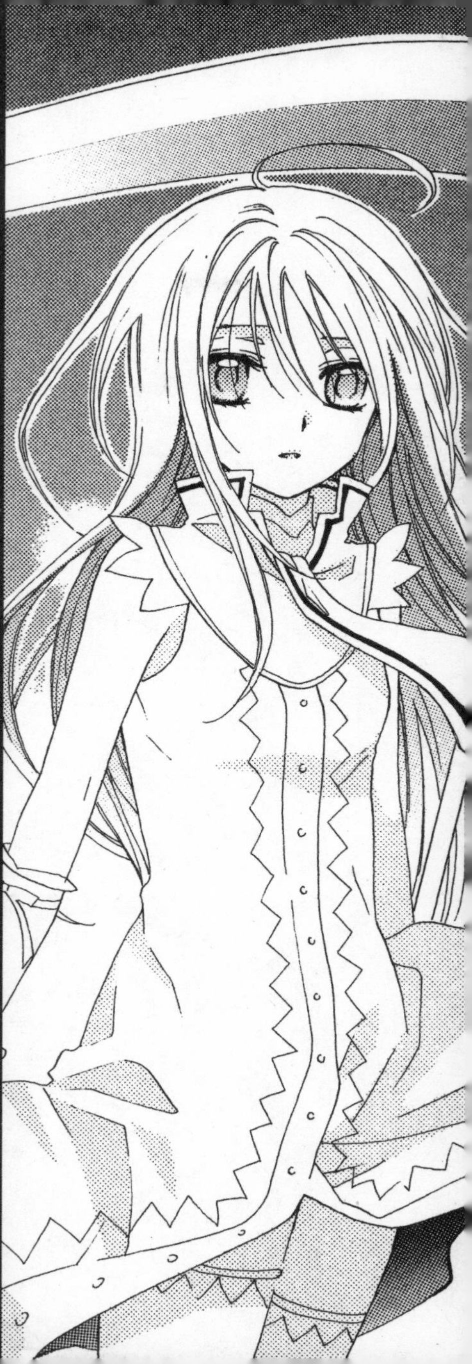

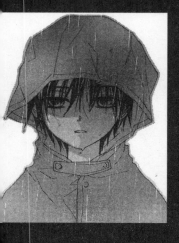

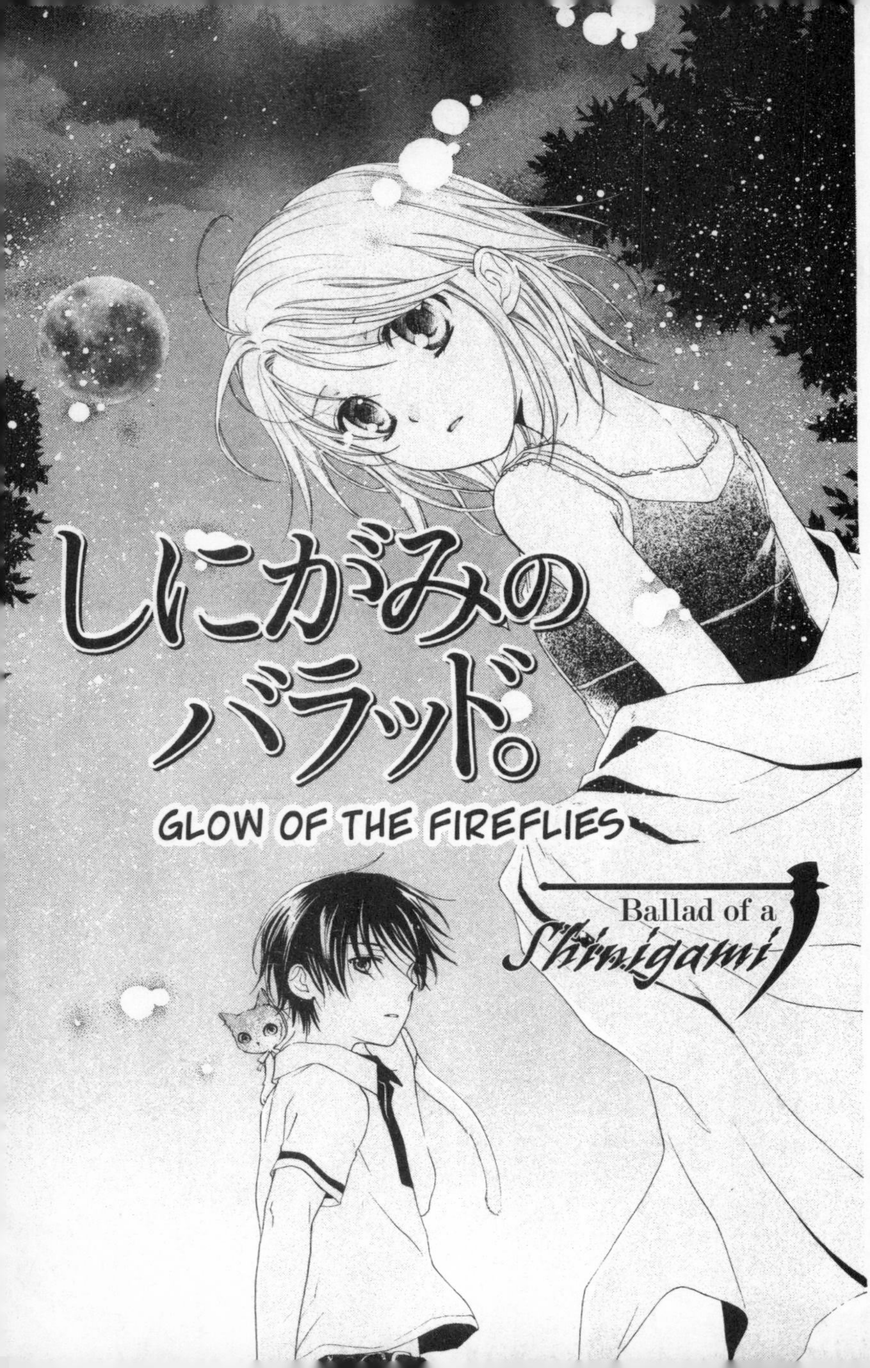
しにがみのバラッド。
GLOW OF THE FIREFLIES
Ballad of a Shinigami

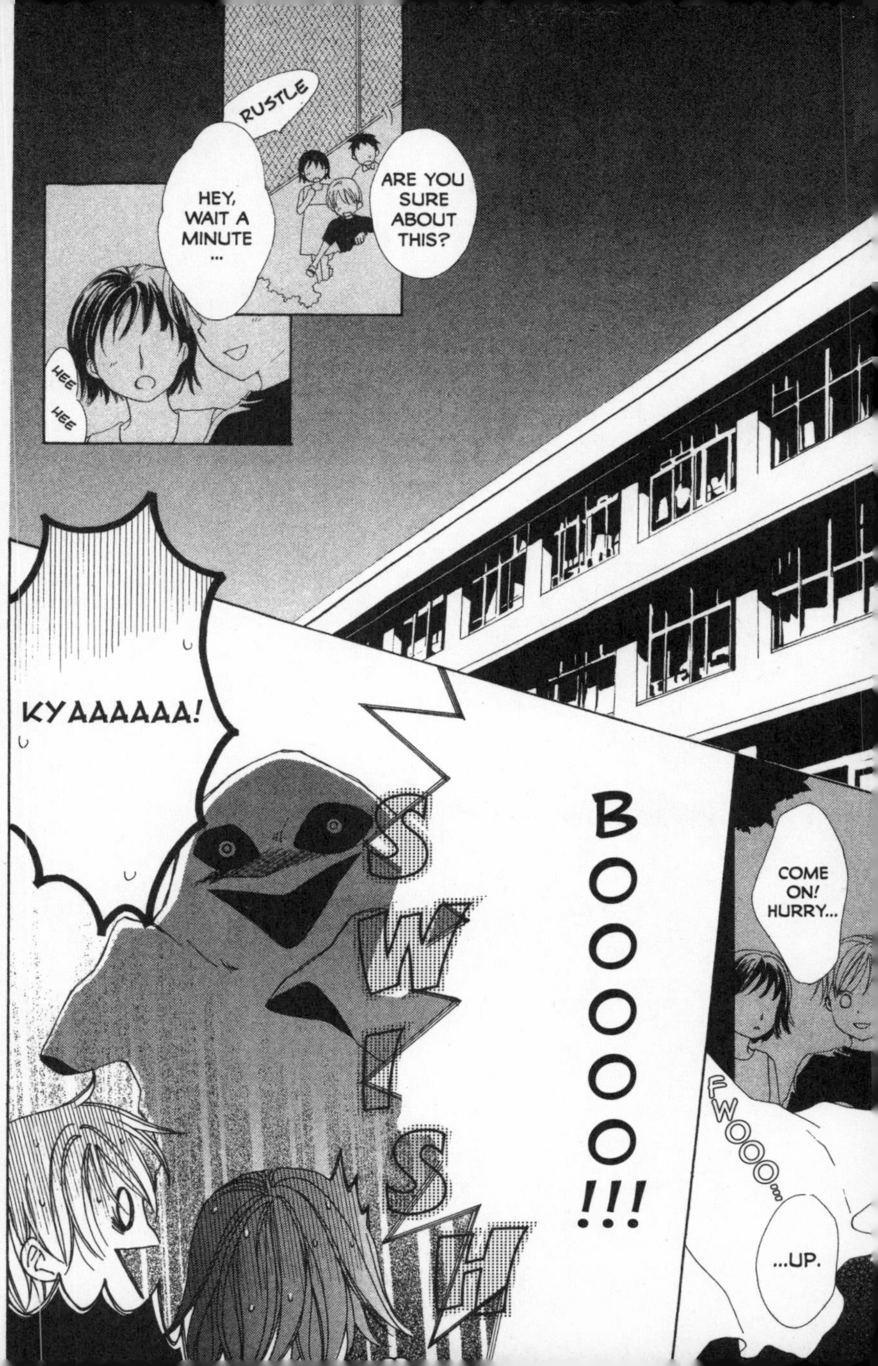
ARE YOU SURE ABOUT THIS?
RUSTLE
HEY, WAIT A MINUTE ...
HEE HEE
COME ON! HURRY...
FWOOO...
...UP.
BOOOOO!!!
SWISH
KYAAAAAA!

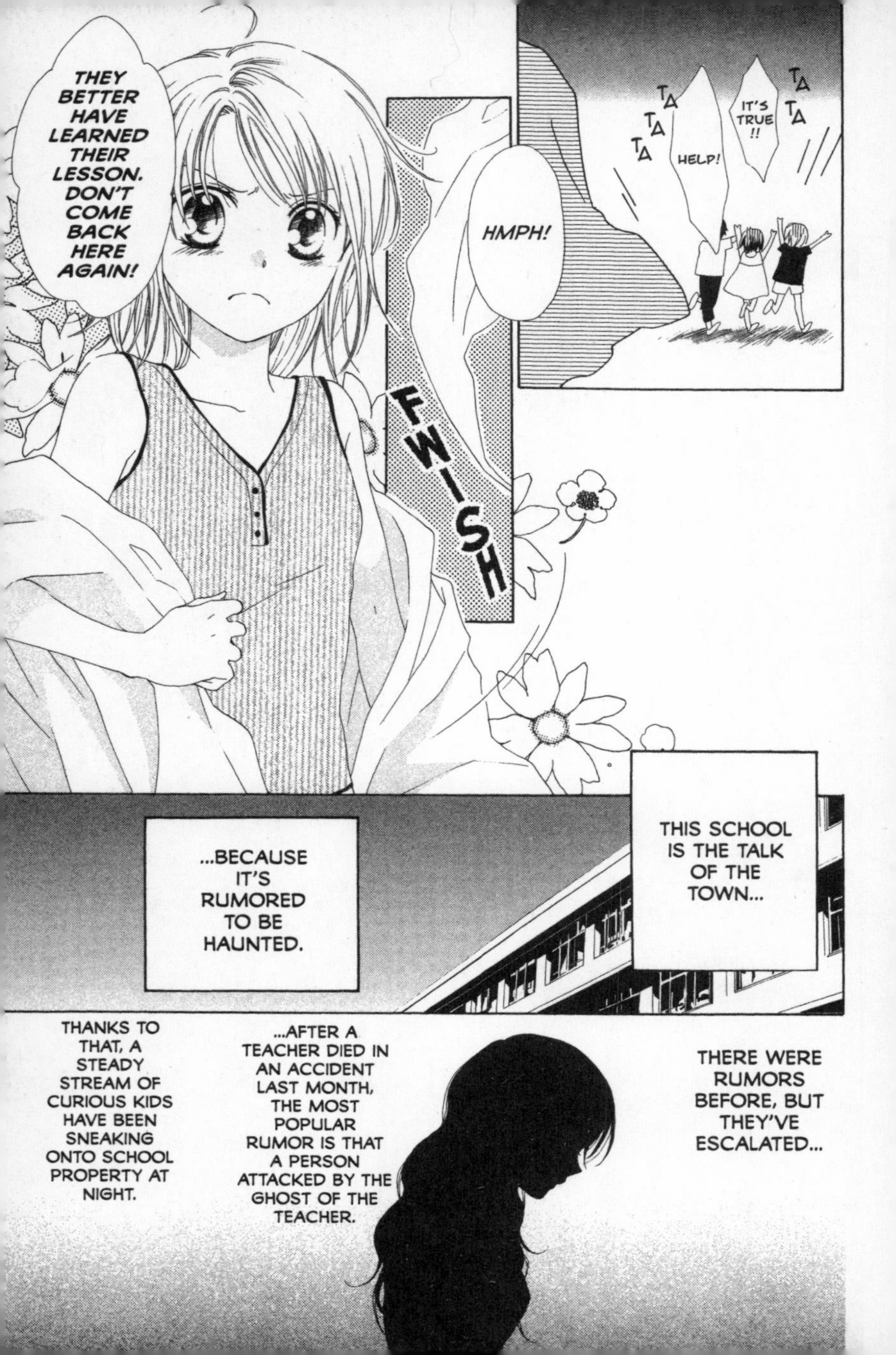
TA TA
IT'S TRUE!!
TA TA TA
HELP!
HMPH!
FWISH
THEY BETTER HAVE LEARNED THEIR LESSON. DON'T COME BACK HERE AGAIN!
THIS SCHOOL IS THE TALK OF THE TOWN...
...BECAUSE IT'S RUMORED TO BE HAUNTED.
THERE WERE RUMORS BEFORE, BUT THEY'VE ESCALATED...
...AFTER A TEACHER DIED IN AN ACCIDENT LAST MONTH, THE MOST POPULAR RUMOR IS THAT A PERSON ATTACKED BY THE GHOST OF THE TEACHER.
THANKS TO THAT, A STEADY STREAM OF CURIOUS KIDS HAVE BEEN SNEAKING ONTO SCHOOL PROPERTY AT NIGHT.

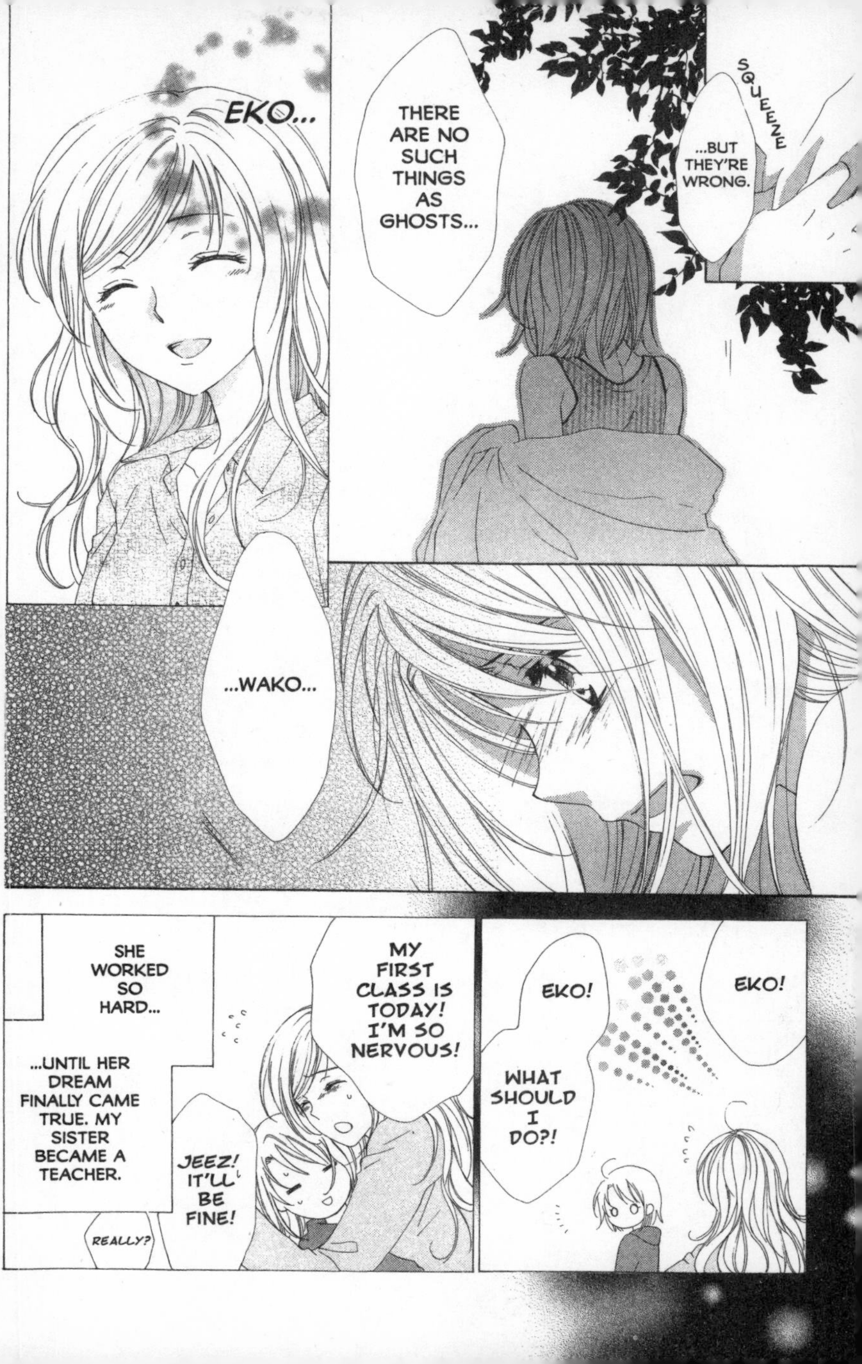
THERE ARE NO SUCH THINGS AS GHOSTS...
SQUEEZE
...BUT THEY'RE WRONG.
EKO...
...WAKO...
EKO!
EKO!
WHAT SHOULD I DO?!
MY FIRST CLASS IS TODAY! I'M SO NERVOUS!
JEEZ! IT'LL BE FINE!
REALLY?
SHE WORKED SO HARD...
...UNTIL HER DREAM FINALLY CAME TRUE. MY SISTER BECAME A TEACHER.

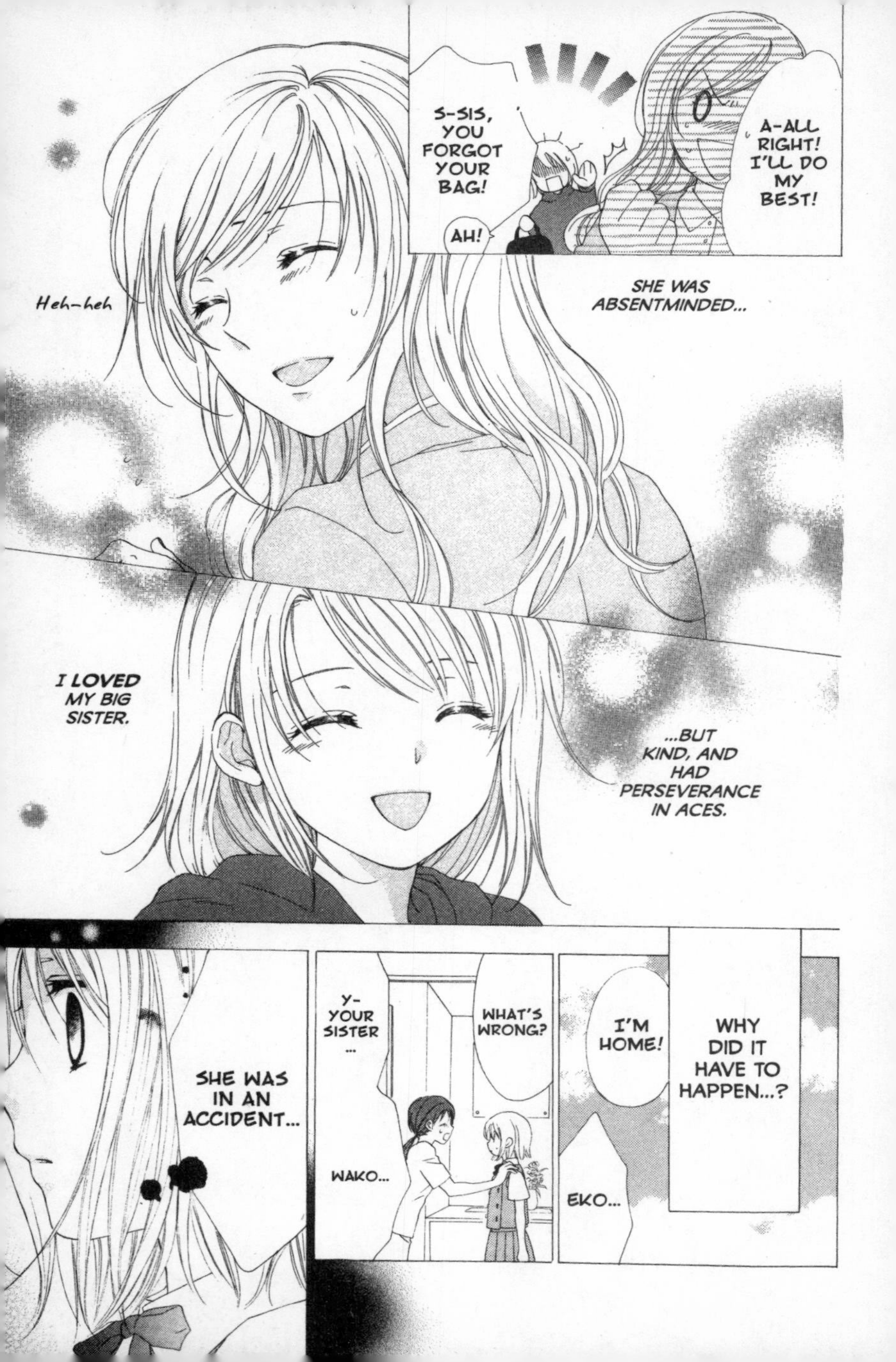
A-ALL RIGHT! I'LL DO MY BEST!
S-SIS, YOU FORGOT YOUR BAG!
AH!
SHE WAS ABSENTMINDED...
Heh-heh
...BUT KIND, AND HAD PERSEVERANCE IN ACES.
I LOVED MY BIG SISTER.
WHY DID IT HAVE TO HAPPEN...?
I'M HOME!
EKO...
WHAT'S WRONG?
Y-YOUR SISTER...
WAKO...
SHE WAS IN AN ACCIDENT...

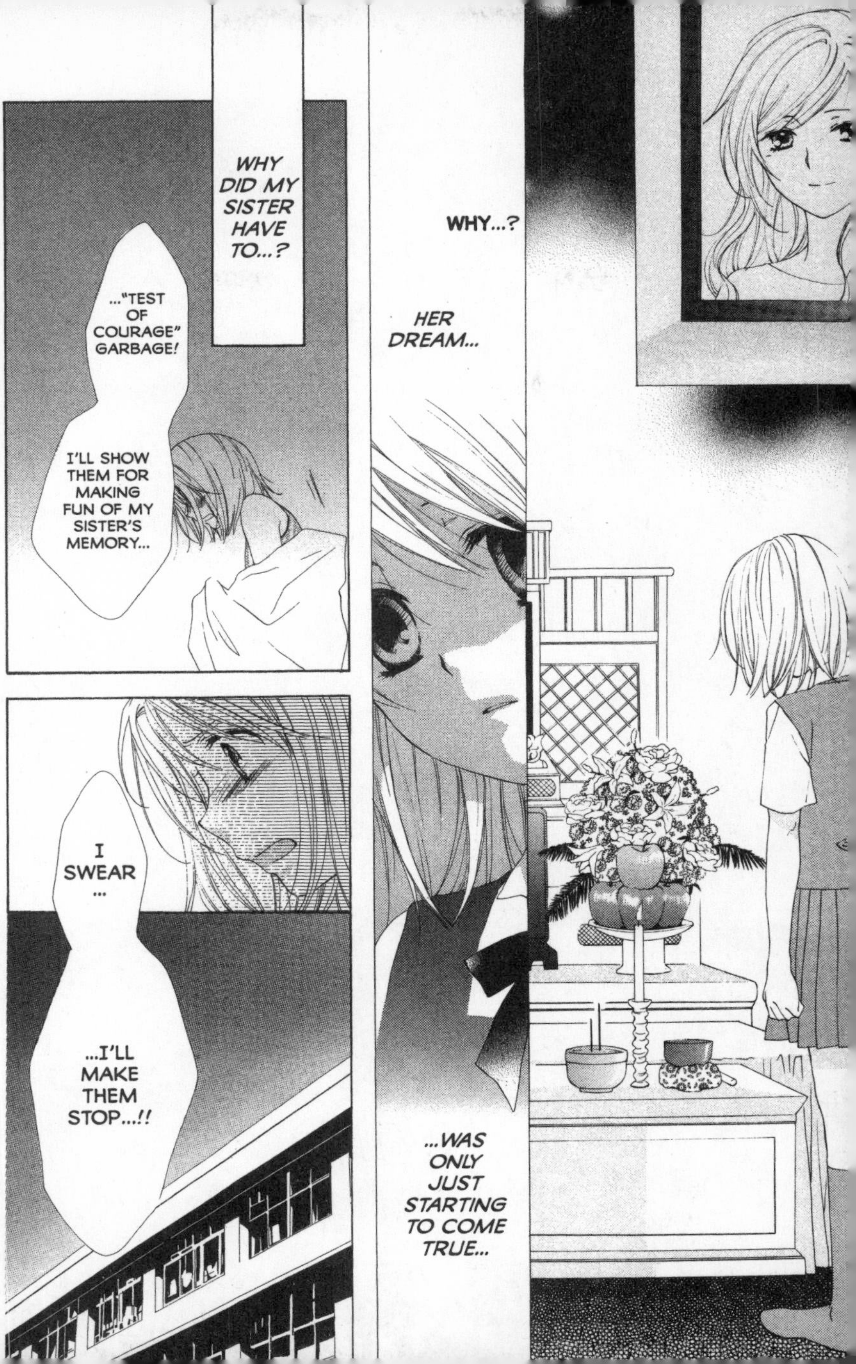

WHY...?
HER DREAM...
...WAS ONLY JUST STARTING TO COME TRUE...
WHY DID MY SISTER HAVE TO...?
..."TEST OF COURAGE" GARBAGE!
I'LL SHOW THEM FOR MAKING FUN OF MY SISTER'S MEMORY...
I SWEAR...
...I'LL MAKE THEM STOP...!!

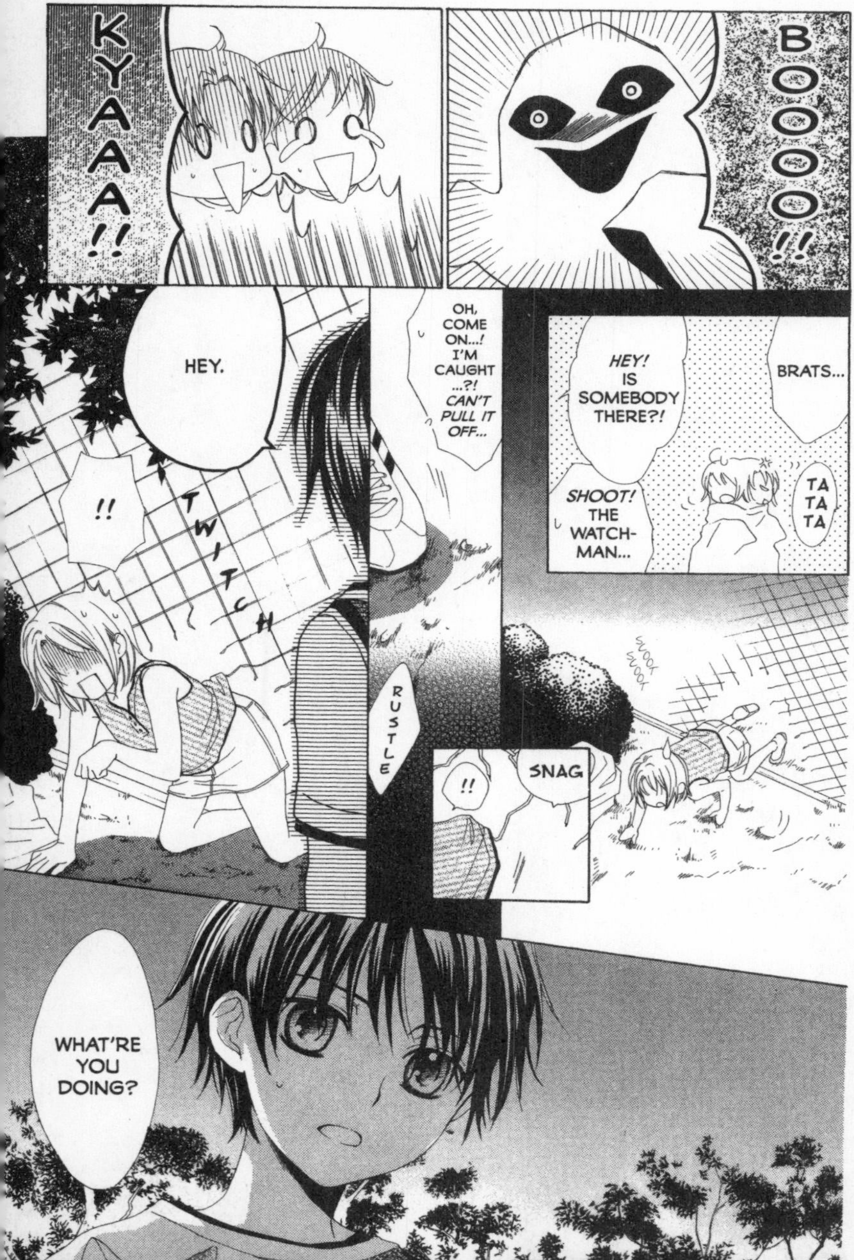
BOOOOO!!
KYAAAA!!
BRATS...
HEY! IS SOMEBODY THERE?!
SHOOT! THE WATCHMAN...
TA TA TA
SLOOK SLOOK
SNAG
!!
OH, COME ON...! I'M CAUGHT...?! CAN'T PULL IT OFF...
RUSTLE
HEY.
!!
TWITCH
WHAT'RE YOU DOING?

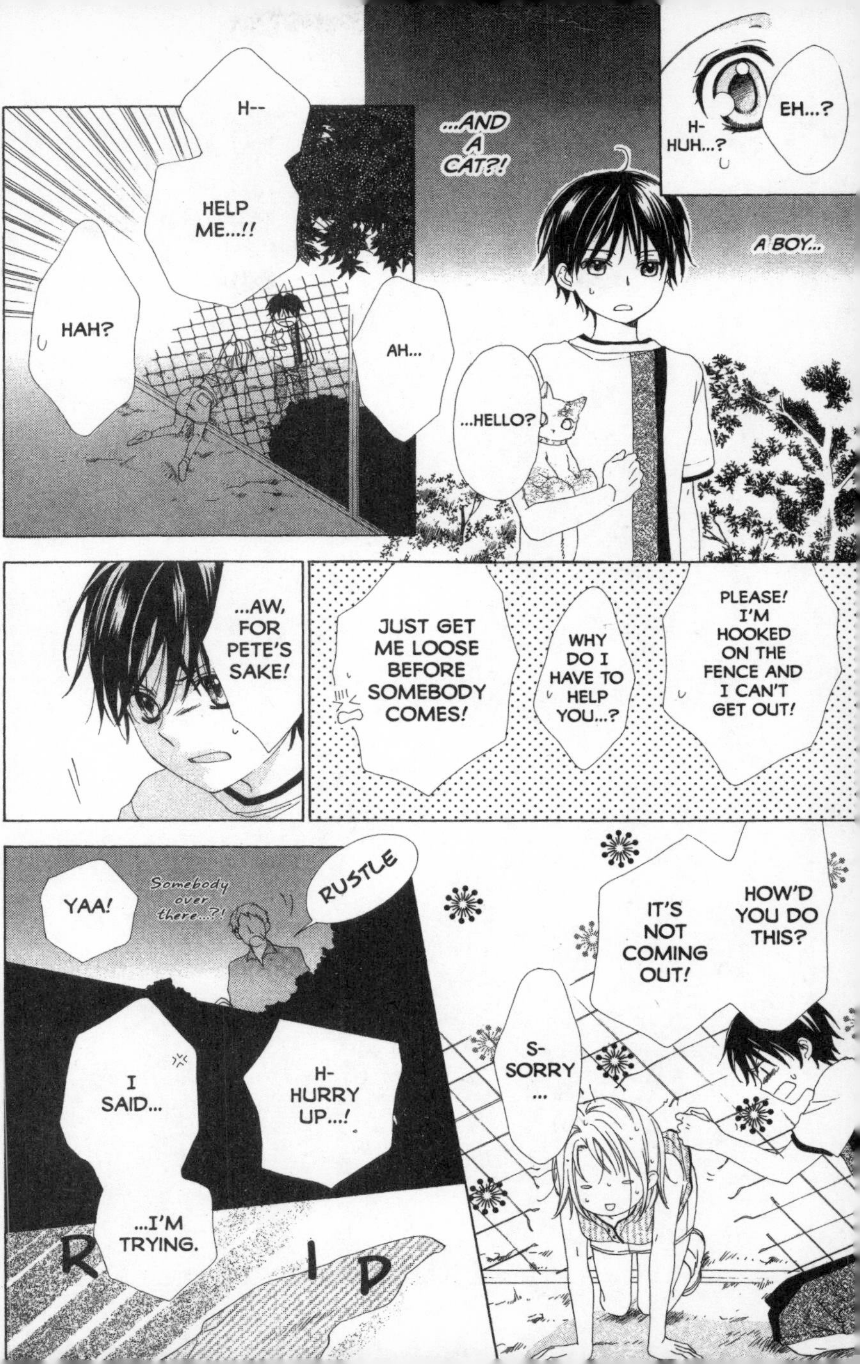
EH...?
H- HUH...?
A BOY...
...AND A CAT?!
...HELLO?
H--
HELP ME...!!
AH...
HAH?
PLEASE! I'M HOOKED ON THE FENCE AND I CAN'T GET OUT!
WHY DO I HAVE TO HELP YOU...?
JUST GET ME LOOSE BEFORE SOMEBODY COMES!
...AW, FOR PETE'S SAKE!
HOW'D YOU DO THIS?
IT'S NOT COMING OUT!
S-SORRY...
RUSTLE
Somebody over there...?!
YAA!
H-HURRY UP...!
I SAID...
...I'M TRYING.
RIP

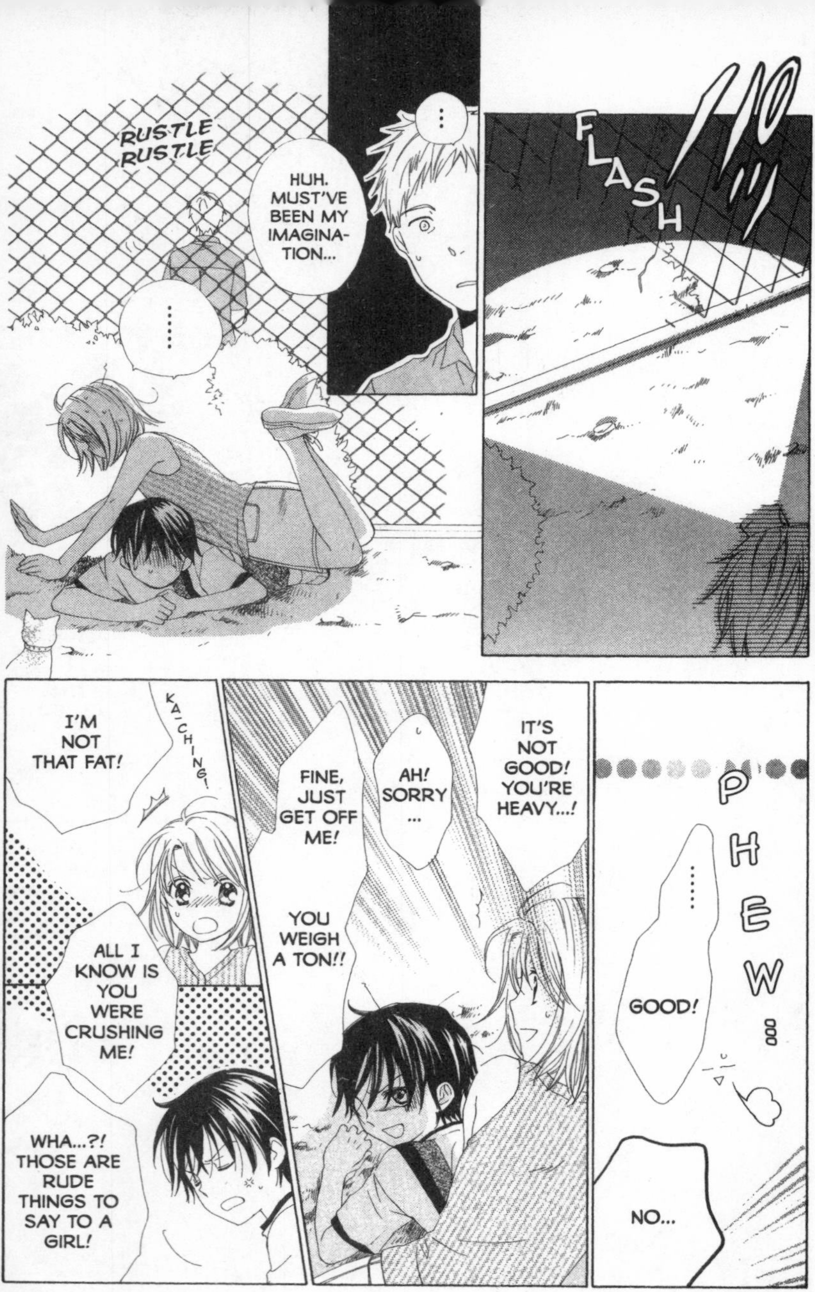
FLASH
...
HUH. MUST'VE BEEN MY IMAGINATION...
RUSTLE RUSTLE
......
PHEW..
......
GOOD!
NO...
IT'S NOT GOOD! YOU'RE HEAVY...!
AH! SORRY ...
FINE, JUST GET OFF ME!
YOU WEIGH A TON!!
KA-CHING!
I'M NOT THAT FAT!
ALL I KNOW IS YOU WERE CRUSHING ME!
WHA...?! THOSE ARE RUDE THINGS TO SAY TO A GIRL!

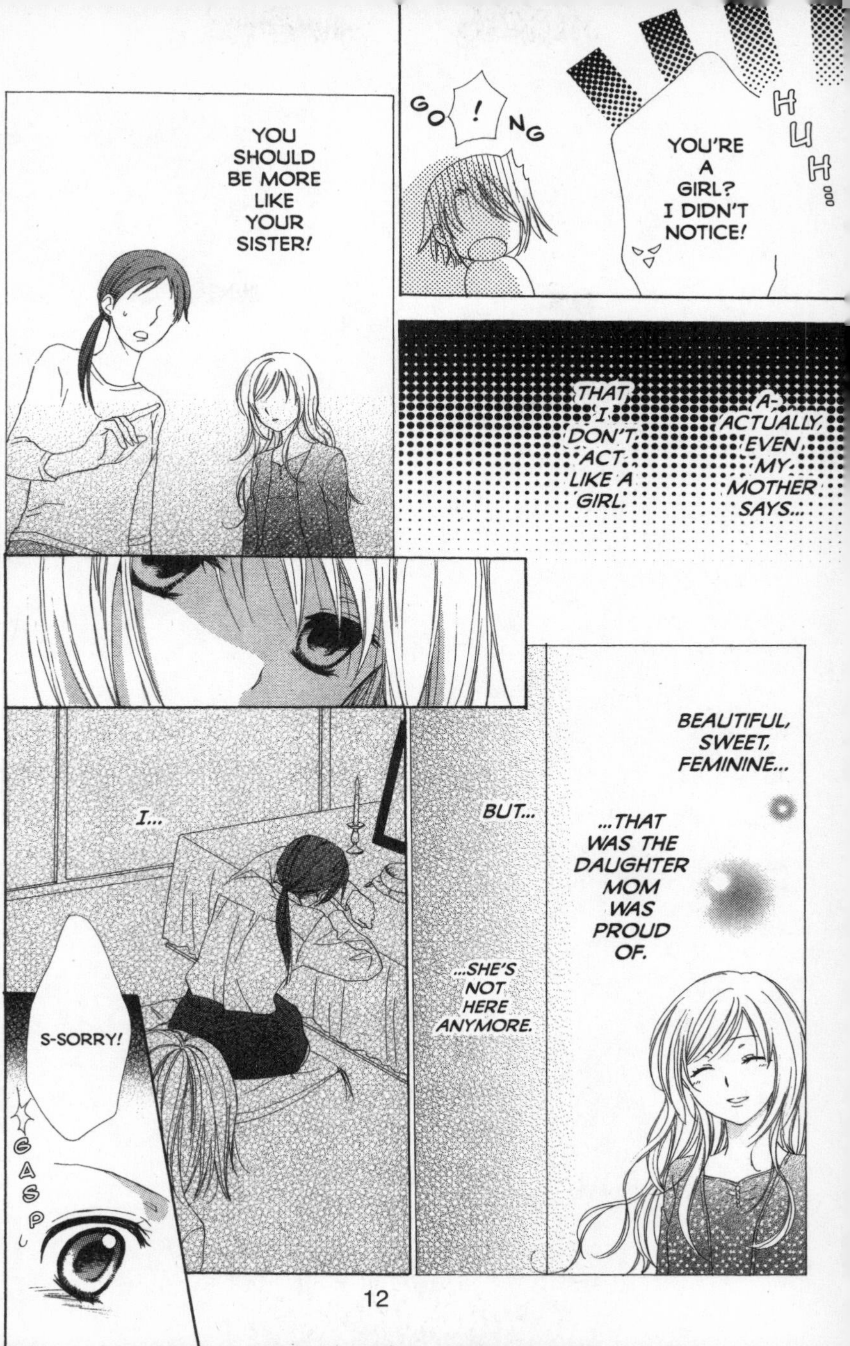
HUH...
YOU'RE A GIRL? I DIDN'T NOTICE!
GO ! NG
A-ACTUALLY, EVEN MY MOTHER SAYS...
THAT I DON'T ACT LIKE A GIRL.
YOU SHOULD BE MORE LIKE YOUR SISTER!
BEAUTIFUL, SWEET, FEMININE...
...THAT WAS THE DAUGHTER MOM WAS PROUD OF.
BUT...
...SHE'S NOT HERE ANYMORE.
I...
S-SORRY!
GASP

1

✽ ✽ ✽ ✽ ✽

HELLO, NICE TO MEET YOU.

I'M ASUKA IZUMI. THIS IS VOLUME 3!

I'M THRILLED BECAUSE THIS IS MY FIRST-EVER THIRD VOLUME! PRIOR TO THIS, VOLUME 2 WAS AS FAR AS I GOT! THANK YOU.

AS IN THE PREVIOUS VOLUMES, I'M GOING TO USE THESE COLUMNS TO SHOWCASE MOMO-SAN IN VARIOUS OUTFITS.

SEE YOU AT THE END OF THE VOLUME!

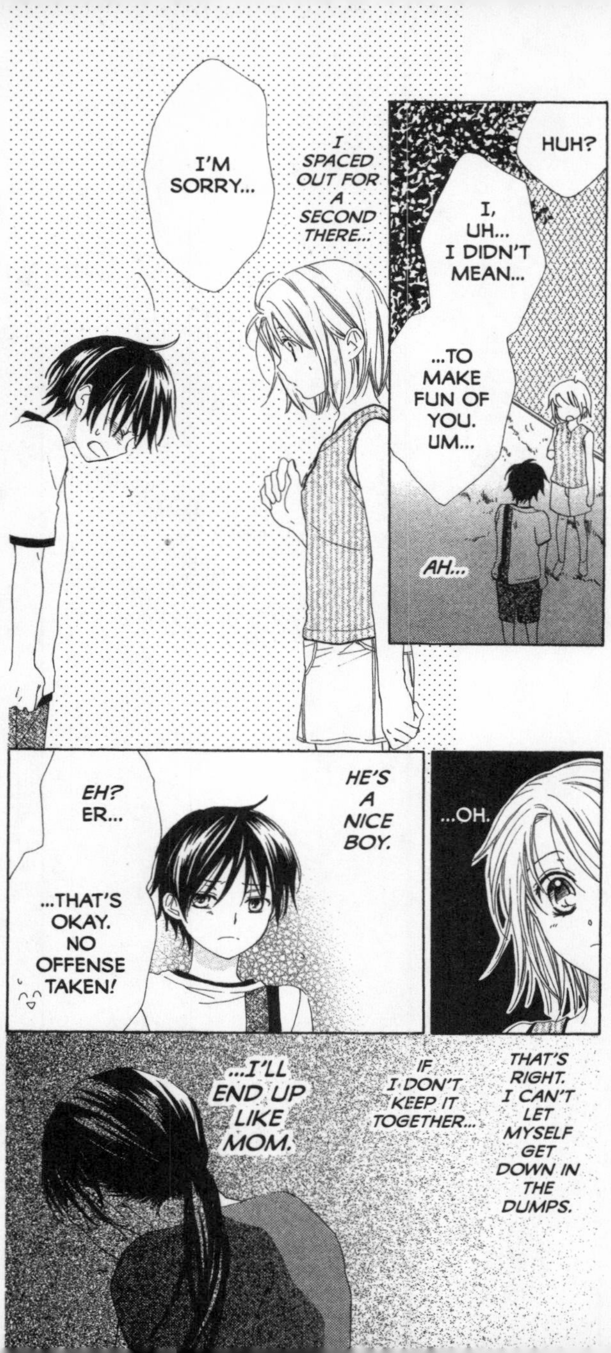

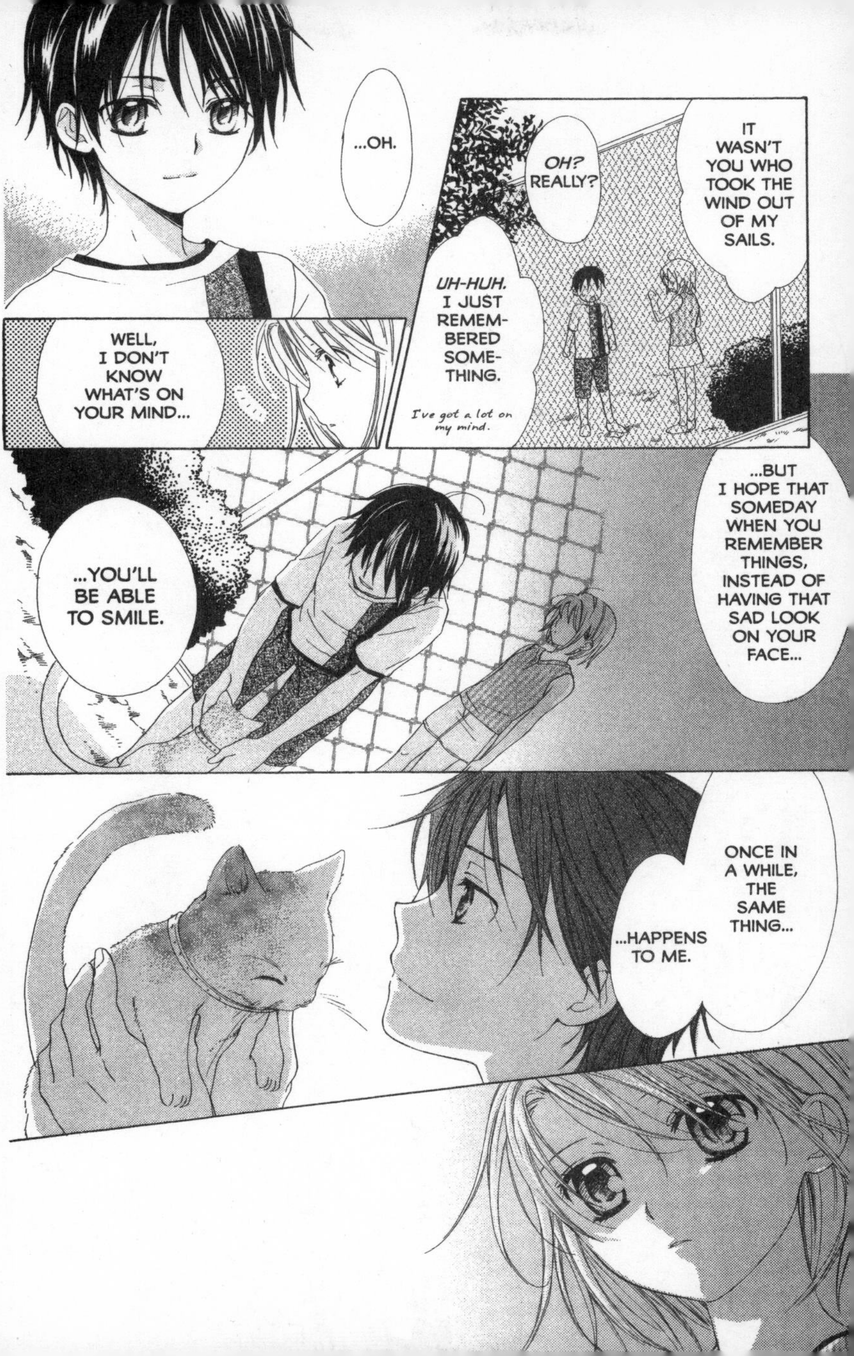
IT WASN'T YOU WHO TOOK THE WIND OUT OF MY SAILS.
OH? REALLY?
UH-HUH. I JUST REMEMBERED SOMETHING.
I've got a lot on my mind.
...OH.
WELL, I DON'T KNOW WHAT'S ON YOUR MIND...
...BUT I HOPE THAT SOMEDAY WHEN YOU REMEMBER THINGS, INSTEAD OF HAVING THAT SAD LOOK ON YOUR FACE...
...YOU'LL BE ABLE TO SMILE.
ONCE IN A WHILE, THE SAME THING...
...HAPPENS TO ME.

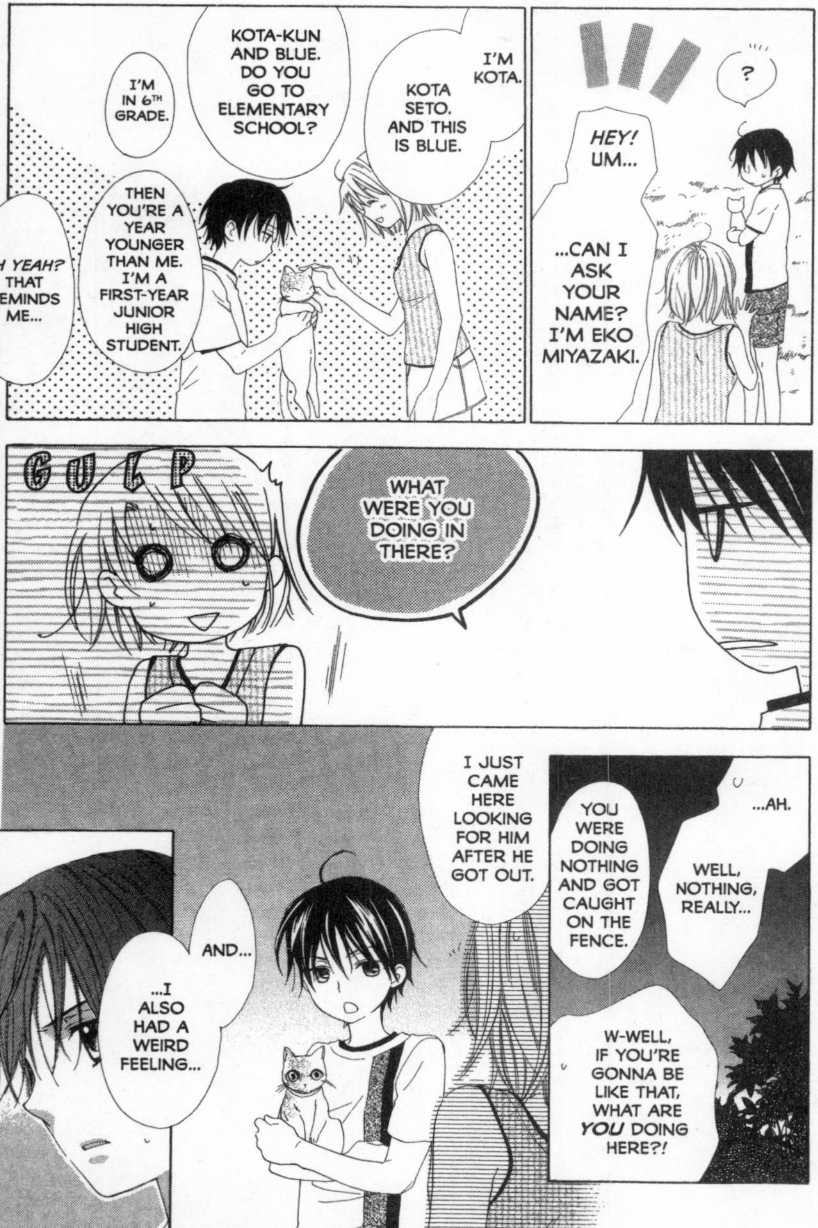
?
HEY! UM...
...CAN I ASK YOUR NAME? I'M EKO MIYAZAKI.
I'M KOTA.
KOTA SETO. AND THIS IS BLUE.
KOTA-KUN AND BLUE. DO YOU GO TO ELEMENTARY SCHOOL?
I'M IN 6TH GRADE.
THEN YOU'RE A YEAR YOUNGER THAN ME. I'M A FIRST-YEAR JUNIOR HIGH STUDENT.
OH YEAH? THAT REMINDS ME...
WHAT WERE YOU DOING IN THERE?
GULP
...AH.
WELL, NOTHING, REALLY...
YOU WERE DOING NOTHING AND GOT CAUGHT ON THE FENCE.
W-WELL, IF YOU'RE GONNA BE LIKE THAT, WHAT ARE *YOU* DOING HERE?!
I JUST CAME HERE LOOKING FOR HIM AFTER HE GOT OUT.
AND...
...I ALSO HAD A WEIRD FEELING...

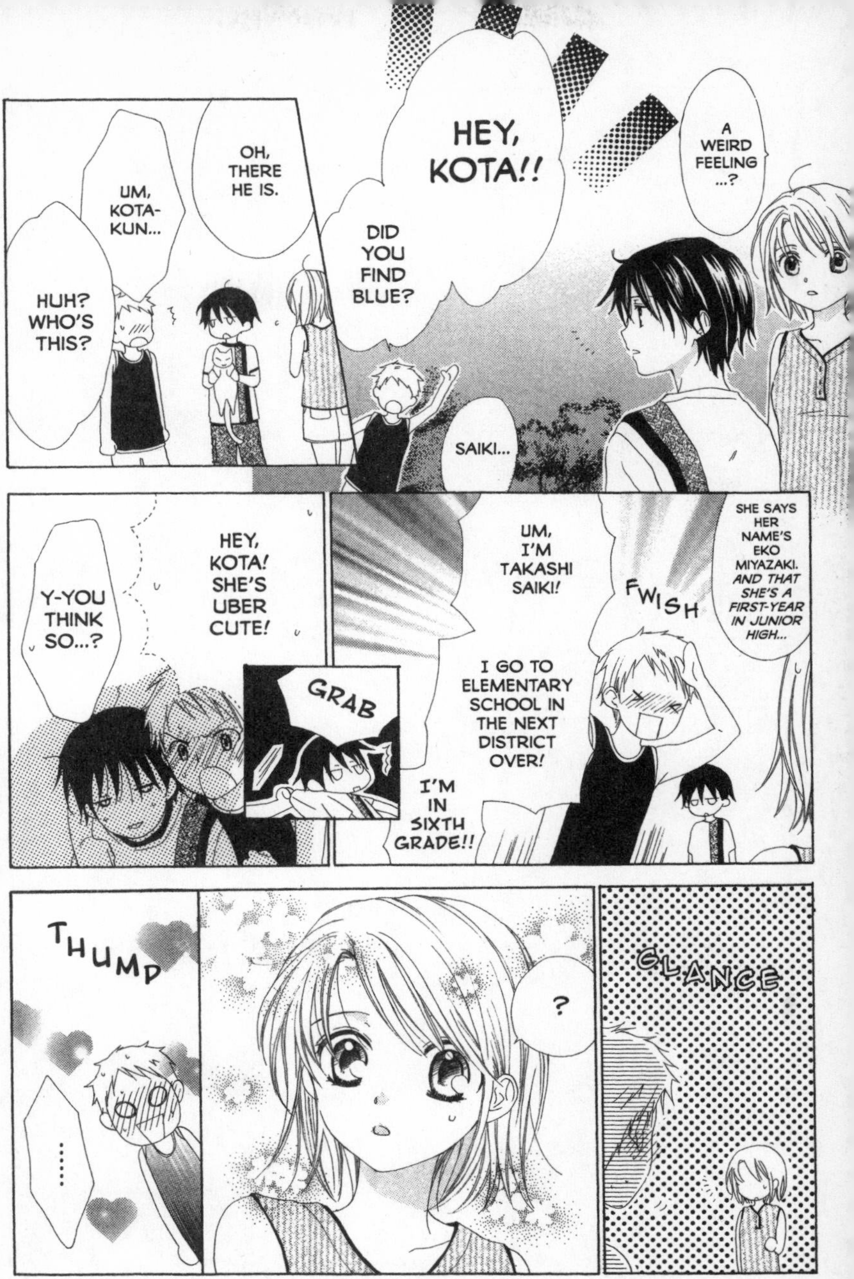
A WEIRD FEELING ...?
HEY, KOTA!!
DID YOU FIND BLUE?
SAIKI...
OH, THERE HE IS.
UM, KOTA-KUN...
HUH? WHO'S THIS?
SHE SAYS HER NAME'S EKO MIYAZAKI. *AND THAT SHE'S A FIRST-YEAR IN JUNIOR HIGH...*
FWISH
UM, I'M TAKASHI SAIKI!
I GO TO ELEMENTARY SCHOOL IN THE NEXT DISTRICT OVER!
I'M IN SIXTH GRADE!!
GRAB
HEY, KOTA! SHE'S UBER CUTE!
Y-YOU THINK SO...?
GLANCE
?
THUMP
......

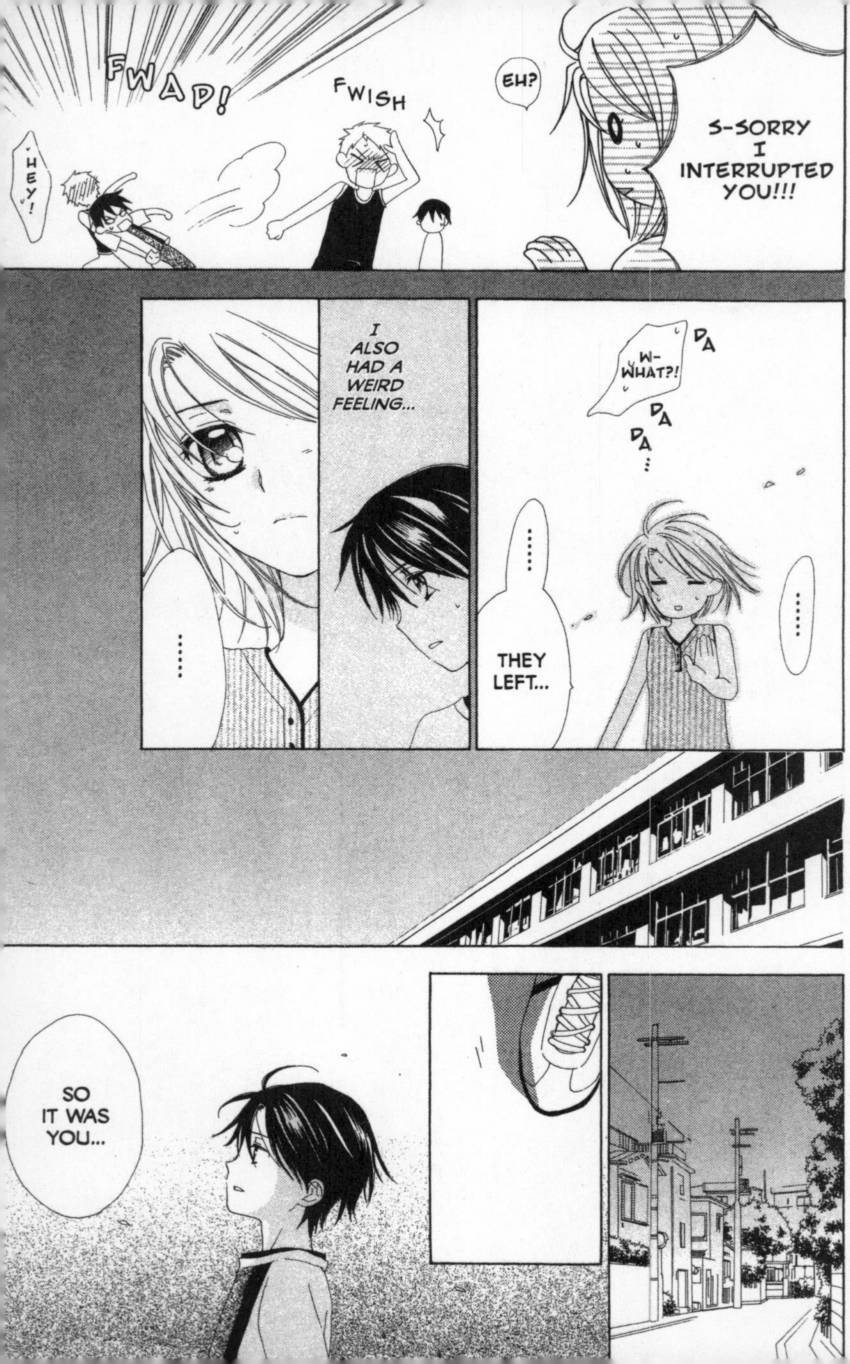
S-SORRY I INTERRUPTED YOU!!!
EH?
FWISH
FWAP!
HEY!
W-WHAT?!
DA DA DA...
......
THEY LEFT...
......
I ALSO HAD A WEIRD FEELING...
......
SO IT WAS YOU...

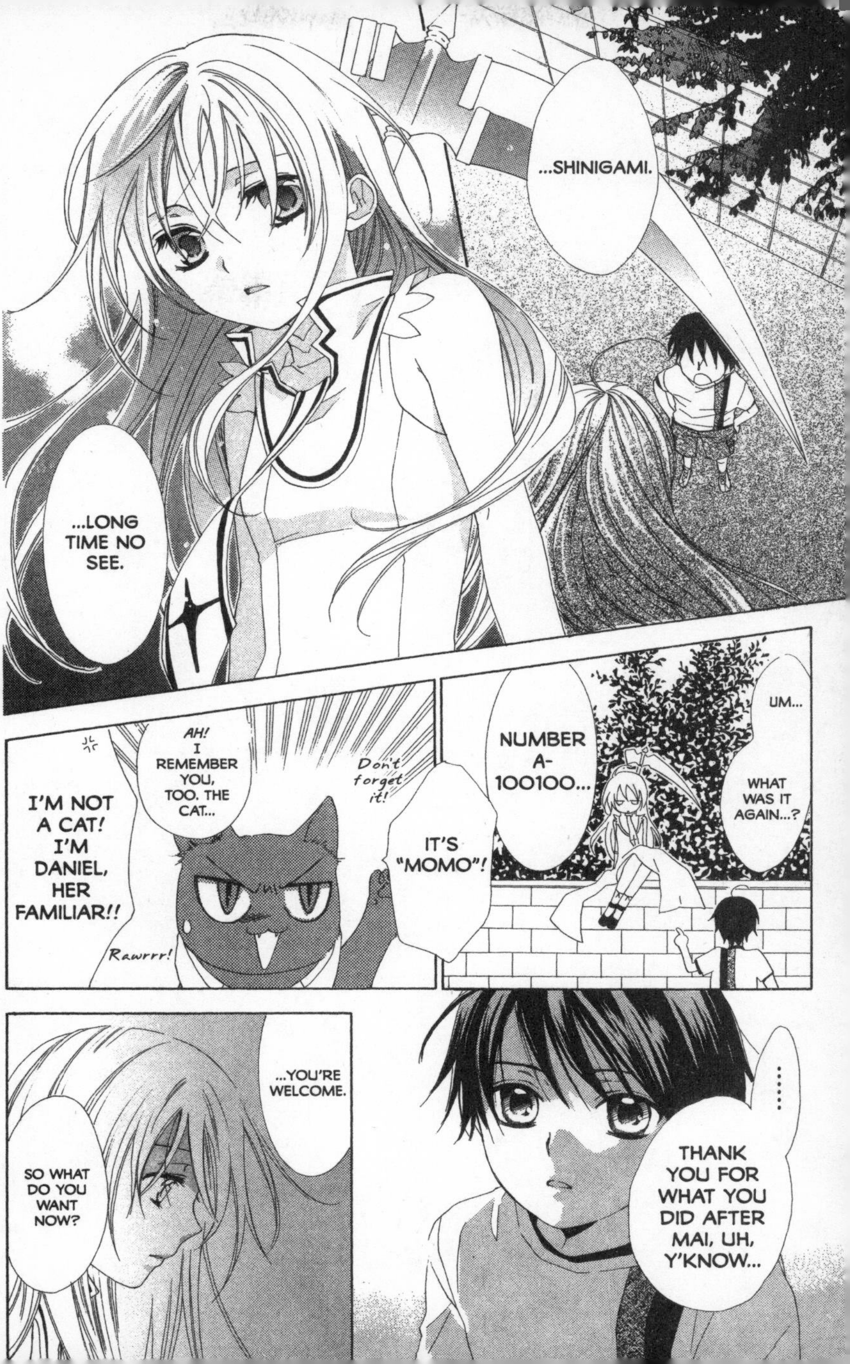
...SHINIGAMI.
...LONG TIME NO SEE.
UM...
WHAT WAS IT AGAIN...?
NUMBER A-100100...
IT'S "MOMO"!
Don't forget it!
AH! I REMEMBER YOU, TOO. THE CAT...
I'M NOT A CAT! I'M DANIEL, HER FAMILIAR!!
Rawrrr!
......
THANK YOU FOR WHAT YOU DID AFTER MAI, UH, Y'KNOW...
...YOU'RE WELCOME.
SO WHAT DO YOU WANT NOW?

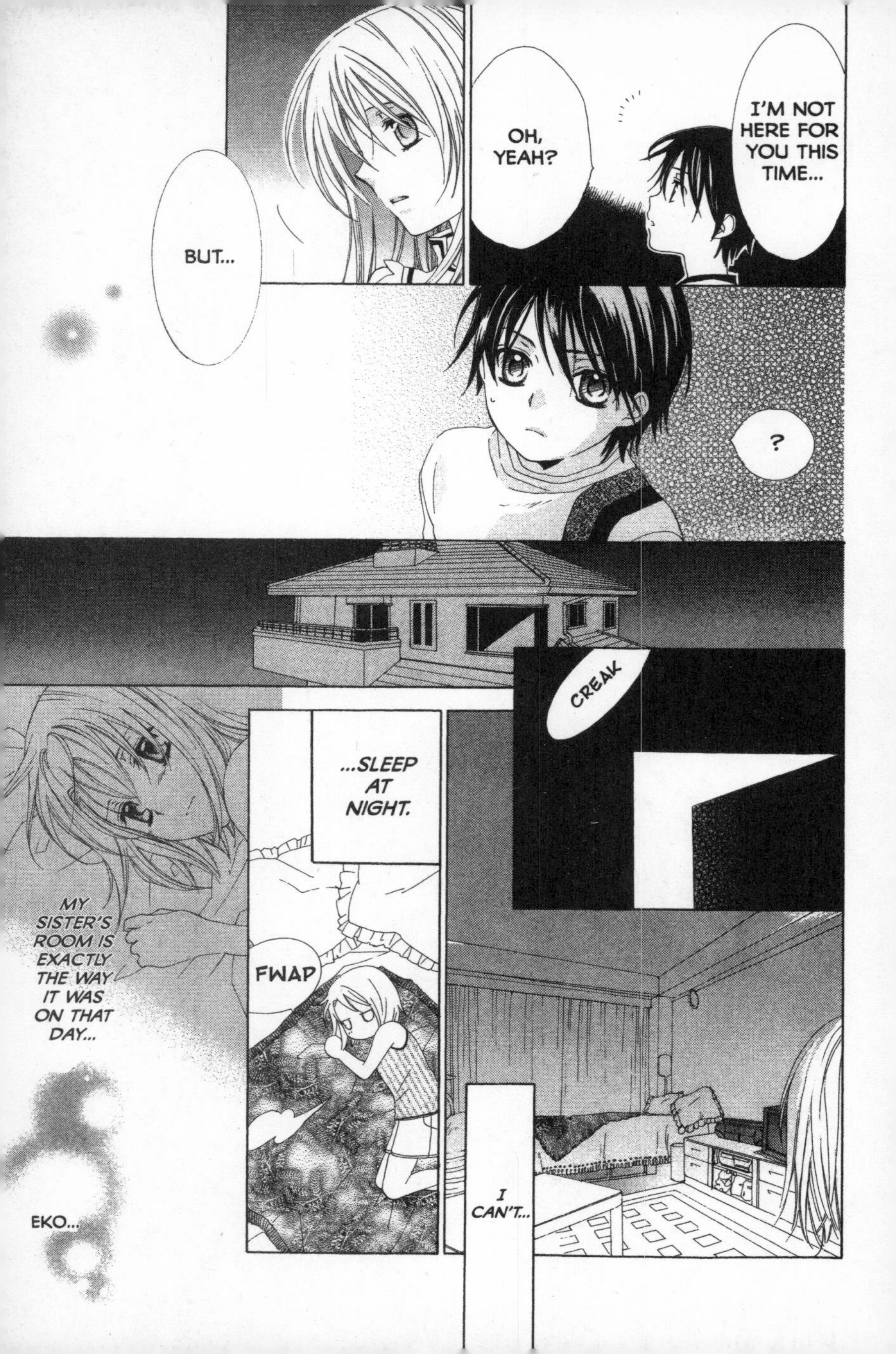
I'M NOT HERE FOR YOU THIS TIME...
OH, YEAH?
BUT...
?
CREAK
I CAN'T...
...SLEEP AT NIGHT.
FWAP
MY SISTER'S ROOM IS EXACTLY THE WAY IT WAS ON THAT DAY...
EKO...

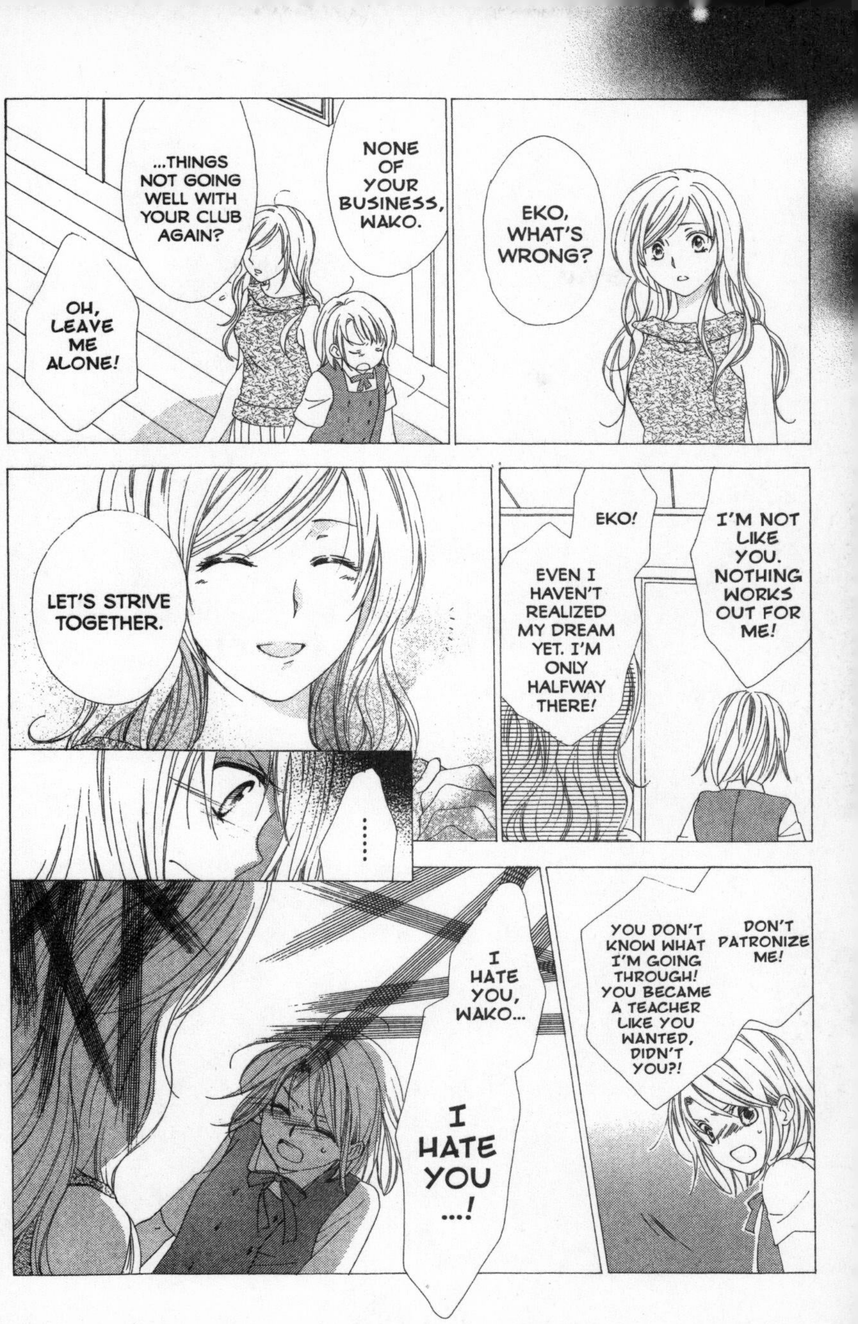
EKO, WHAT'S WRONG?
NONE OF YOUR BUSINESS, WAKO.
...THINGS NOT GOING WELL WITH YOUR CLUB AGAIN?
OH, LEAVE ME ALONE!
I'M NOT LIKE YOU. NOTHING WORKS OUT FOR ME!
EKO!
EVEN I HAVEN'T REALIZED MY DREAM YET. I'M ONLY HALFWAY THERE!
LET'S STRIVE TOGETHER.
......
DON'T PATRONIZE ME!
YOU DON'T KNOW WHAT I'M GOING THROUGH! YOU BECAME A TEACHER LIKE YOU WANTED, DIDN'T YOU?!
I HATE YOU, WAKO...
I HATE YOU ...!

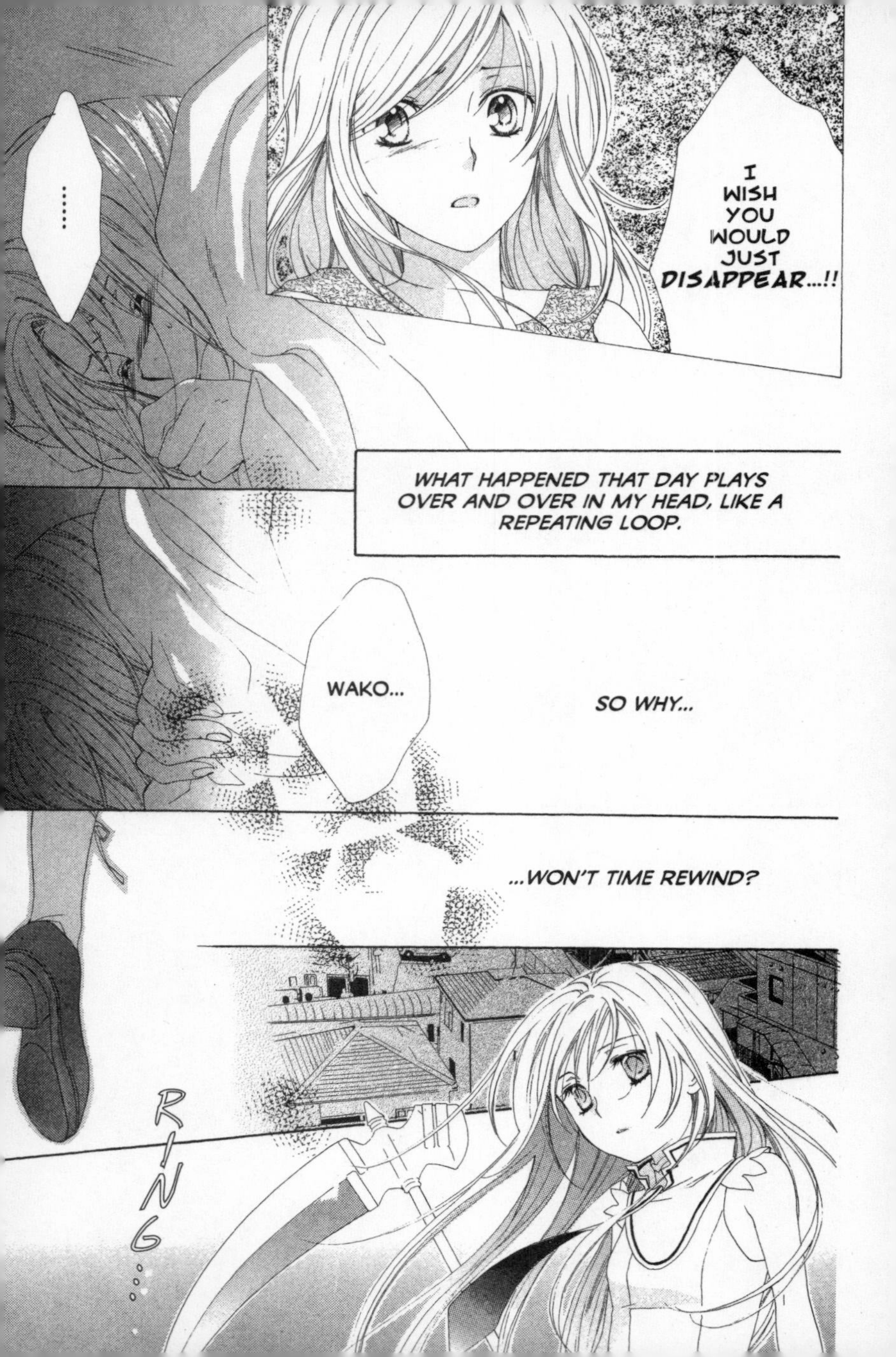
I WISH YOU WOULD JUST DISAPPEAR...!!
......
WHAT HAPPENED THAT DAY PLAYS OVER AND OVER IN MY HEAD, LIKE A REPEATING LOOP.
WAKO...
SO WHY...
...WON'T TIME REWIND?
RING...

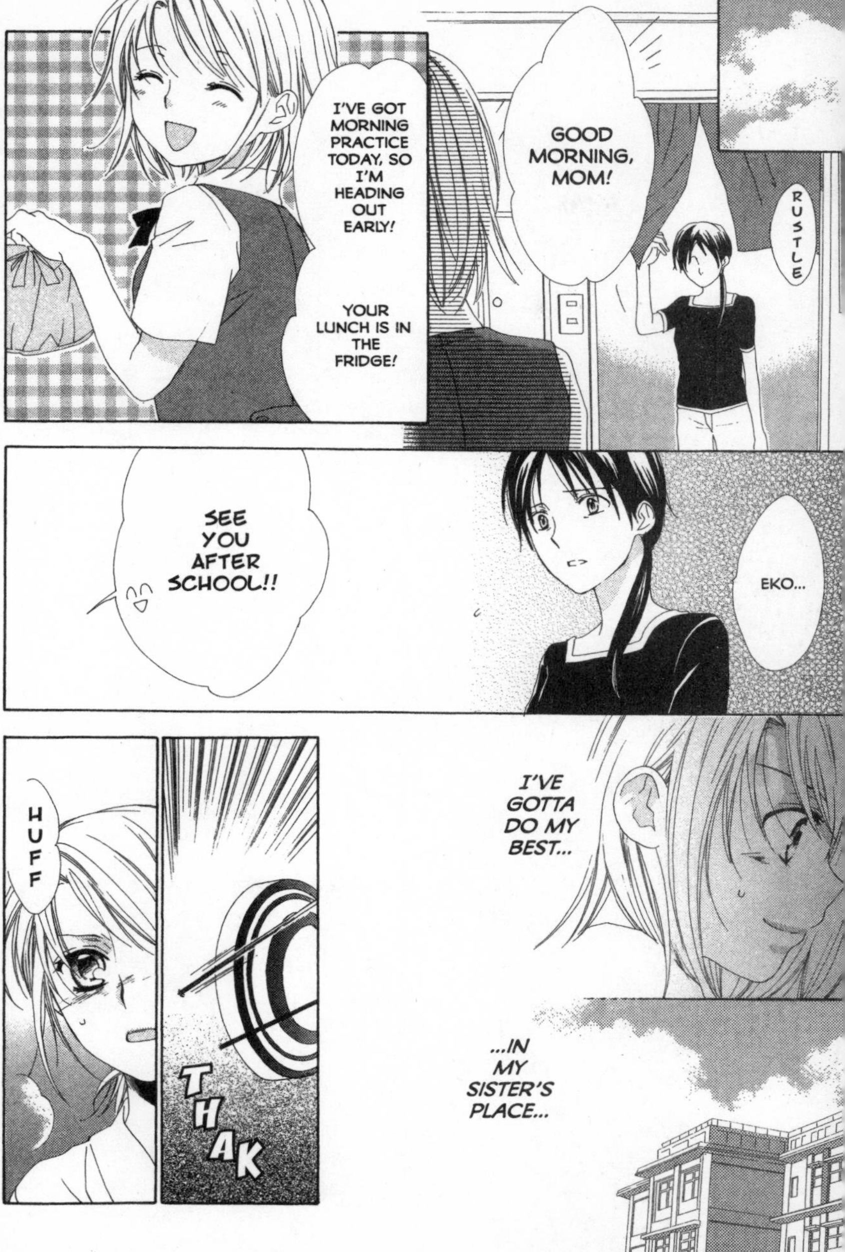

GOOD MORNING, MOM!
RUSTLE
I'VE GOT MORNING PRACTICE TODAY, SO I'M HEADING OUT EARLY!
YOUR LUNCH IS IN THE FRIDGE!
EKO...
SEE YOU AFTER SCHOOL!!
I'VE GOTTA DO MY BEST...
...IN MY SISTER'S PLACE...
THAK
HUFF

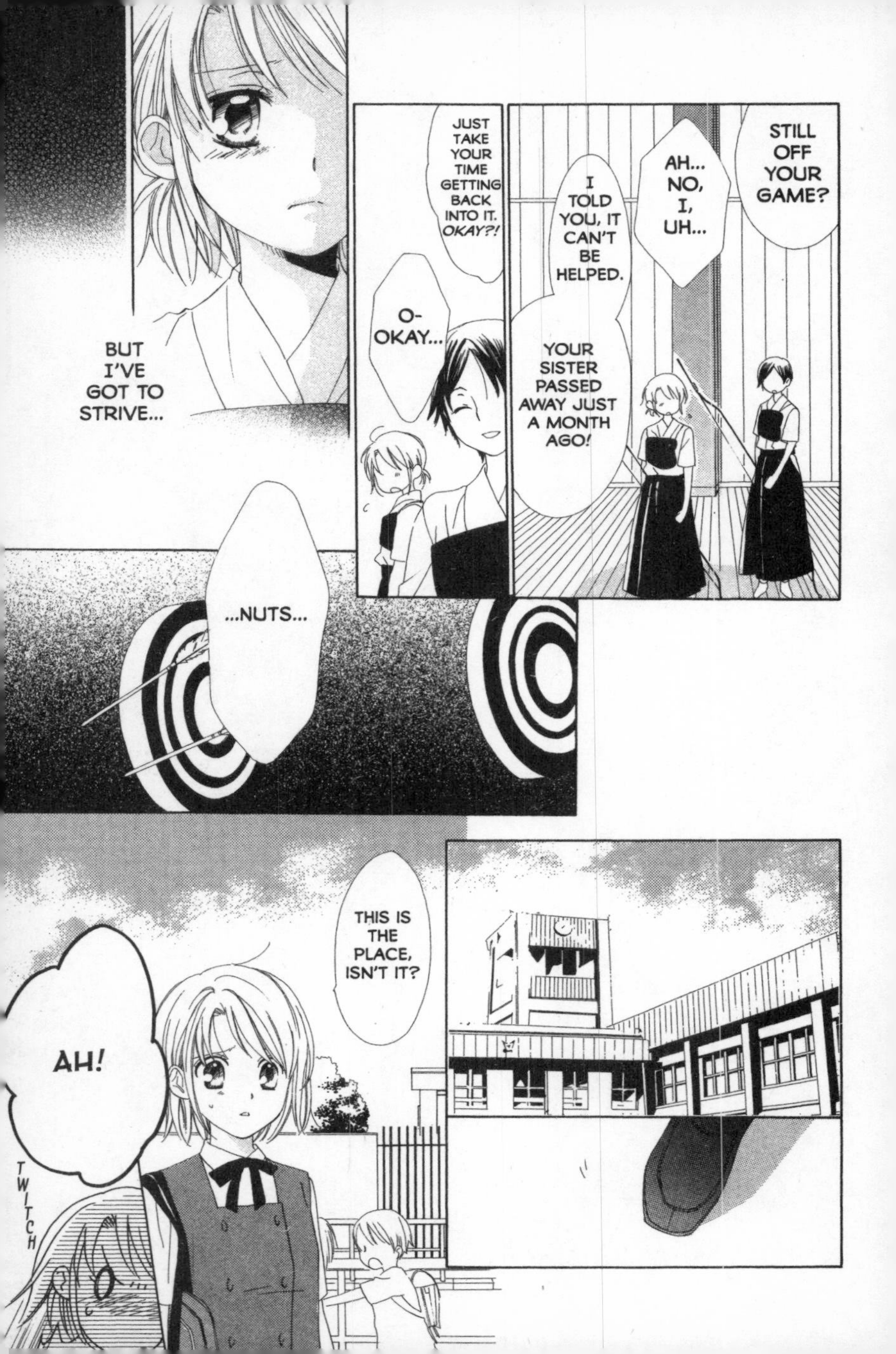
STILL OFF YOUR GAME?
AH... NO, I, UH...
I TOLD YOU, IT CAN'T BE HELPED.
YOUR SISTER PASSED AWAY JUST A MONTH AGO!
JUST TAKE YOUR TIME GETTING BACK INTO IT. *OKAY?!*
O-OKAY...
BUT I'VE GOT TO STRIVE...
...NUTS...
THIS IS THE PLACE, ISN'T IT?
AH!
TWITCH

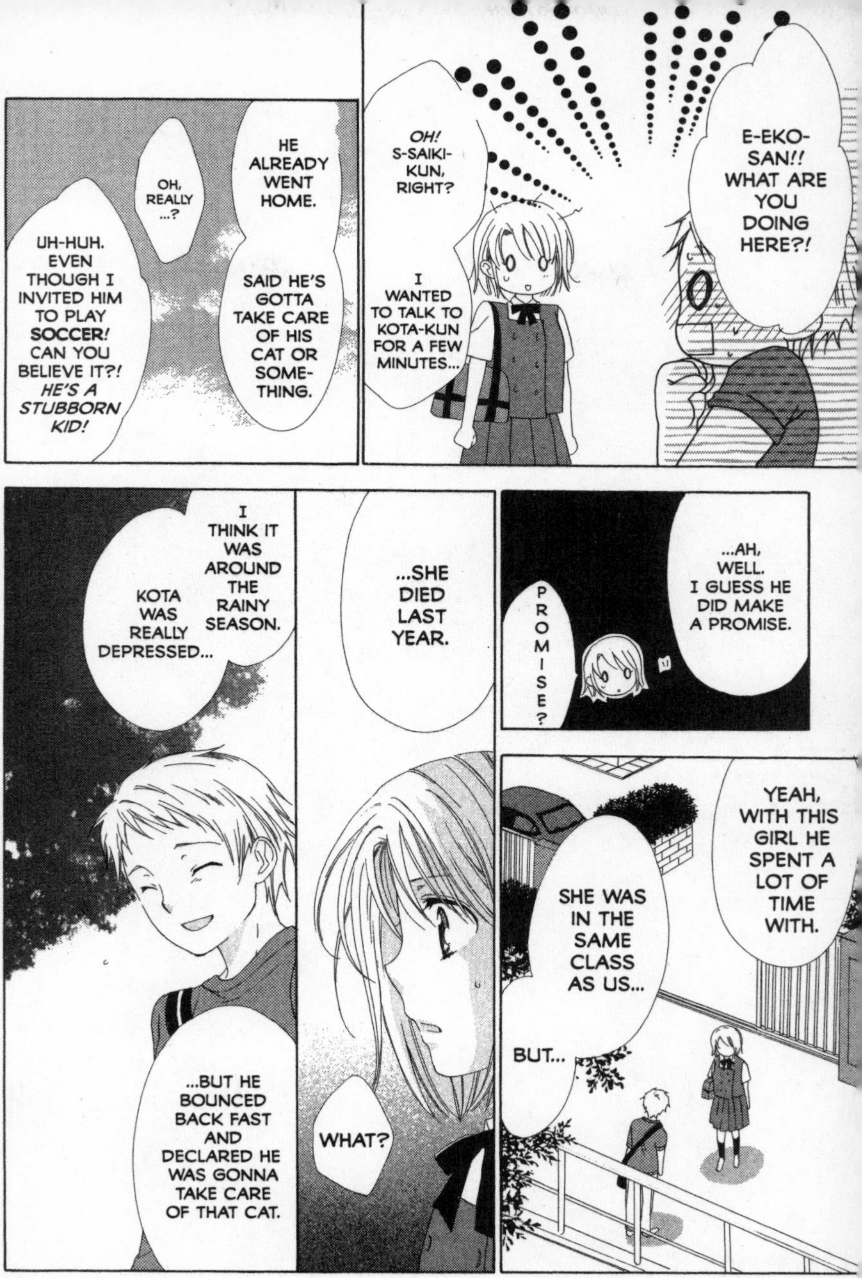
E-EKO-SAN!! WHAT ARE YOU DOING HERE?!
OH! S-SAIKI-KUN, RIGHT?
I WANTED TO TALK TO KOTA-KUN FOR A FEW MINUTES...
HE ALREADY WENT HOME.
OH, REALLY ...?
SAID HE'S GOTTA TAKE CARE OF HIS CAT OR SOME-THING.
UH-HUH. EVEN THOUGH I INVITED HIM TO PLAY **SOCCER**! CAN YOU BELIEVE IT?! *HE'S A STUBBORN KID!*
...AH, WELL. I GUESS HE DID MAKE A PROMISE.
PROMISE?
YEAH, WITH THIS GIRL HE SPENT A LOT OF TIME WITH.
SHE WAS IN THE SAME CLASS AS US...
BUT...
...SHE DIED LAST YEAR.
WHAT?
I THINK IT WAS AROUND THE RAINY SEASON.
KOTA WAS REALLY DEPRESSED...
...BUT HE BOUNCED BACK FAST AND DECLARED HE WAS GONNA TAKE CARE OF THAT CAT.

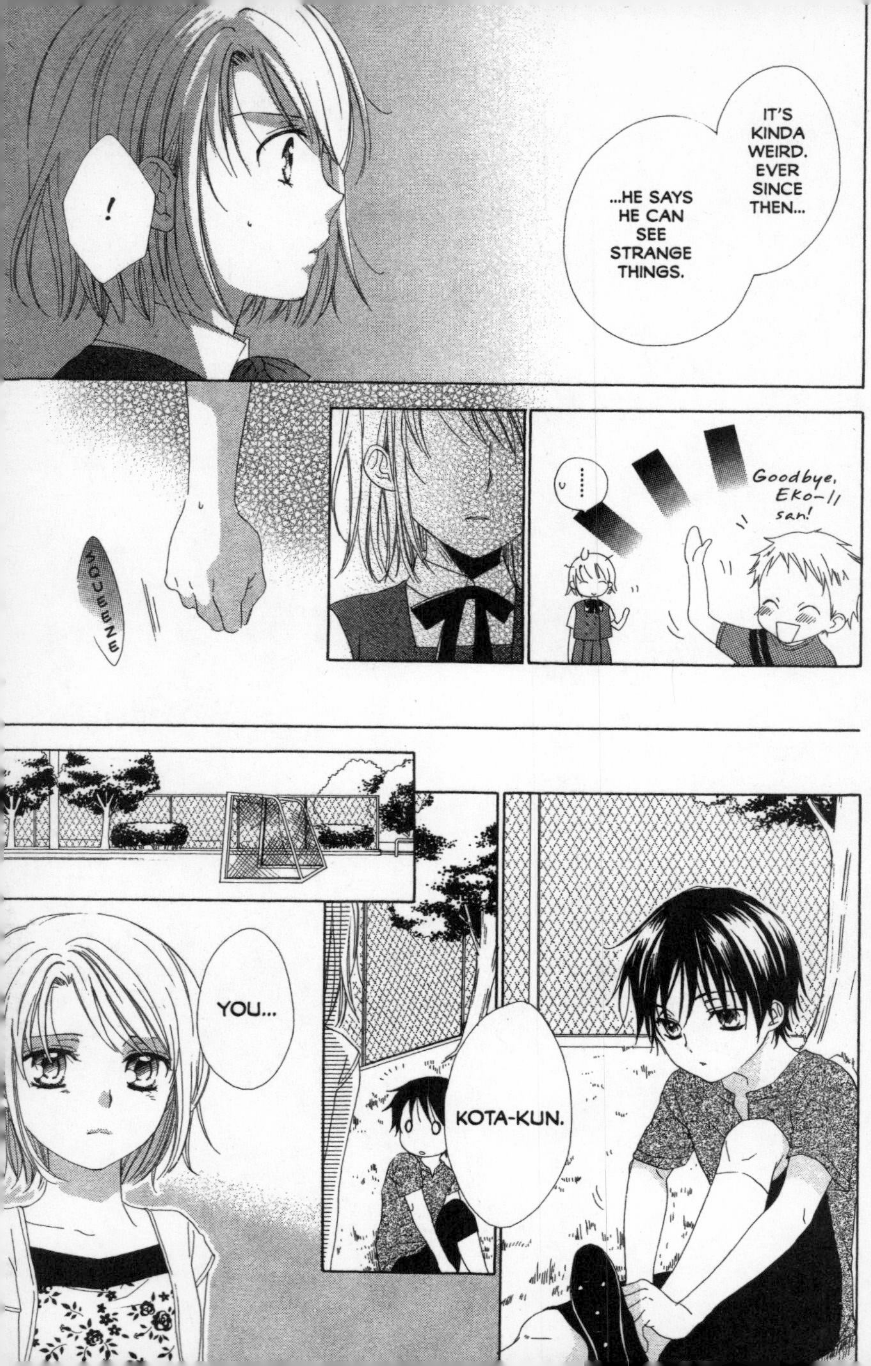
IT'S KINDA WEIRD. EVER SINCE THEN...
...HE SAYS HE CAN SEE STRANGE THINGS.
!
Goodbye, Eko-san!
......
SQUEEZE
YOU...
KOTA-KUN.

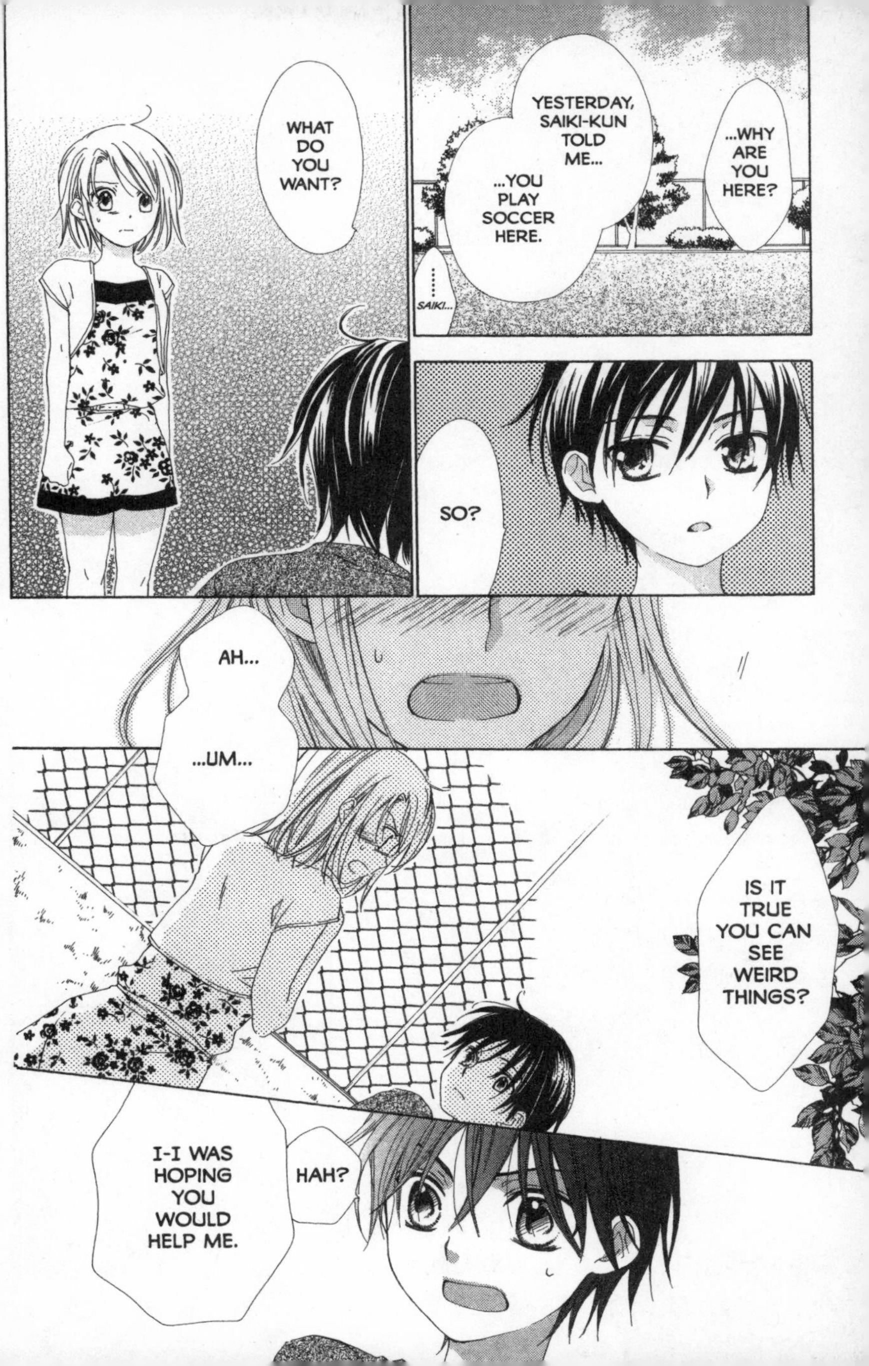
...WHY ARE YOU HERE?
YESTERDAY, SAIKI-KUN TOLD ME...
...YOU PLAY SOCCER HERE.
......SAIKI...
SO?
WHAT DO YOU WANT?
AH...
...UM...
IS IT TRUE YOU CAN SEE WEIRD THINGS?
HAH?
I-I WAS HOPING YOU WOULD HELP ME.

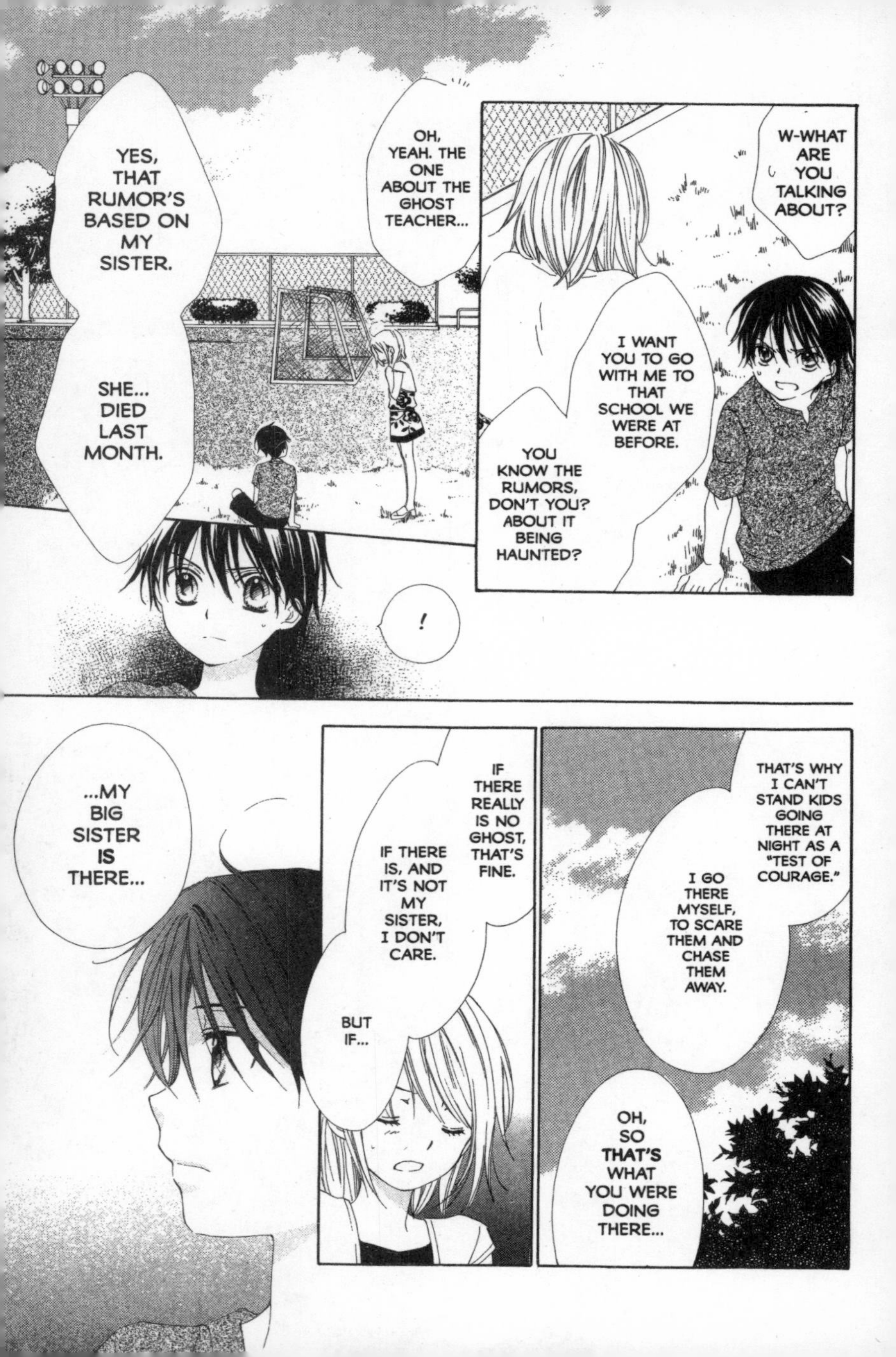
W-WHAT ARE YOU TALKING ABOUT?
I WANT YOU TO GO WITH ME TO THAT SCHOOL WE WERE AT BEFORE.
YOU KNOW THE RUMORS, DON'T YOU? ABOUT IT BEING HAUNTED?
OH, YEAH. THE ONE ABOUT THE GHOST TEACHER...
YES, THAT RUMOR'S BASED ON MY SISTER.
SHE... DIED LAST MONTH.
!
THAT'S WHY I CAN'T STAND KIDS GOING THERE AT NIGHT AS A "TEST OF COURAGE."
I GO THERE MYSELF, TO SCARE THEM AND CHASE THEM AWAY.
OH, SO **THAT'S** WHAT YOU WERE DOING THERE...
IF THERE REALLY IS NO GHOST, THAT'S FINE.
IF THERE IS, AND IT'S NOT MY SISTER, I DON'T CARE.
BUT IF...
...MY BIG SISTER **IS** THERE...

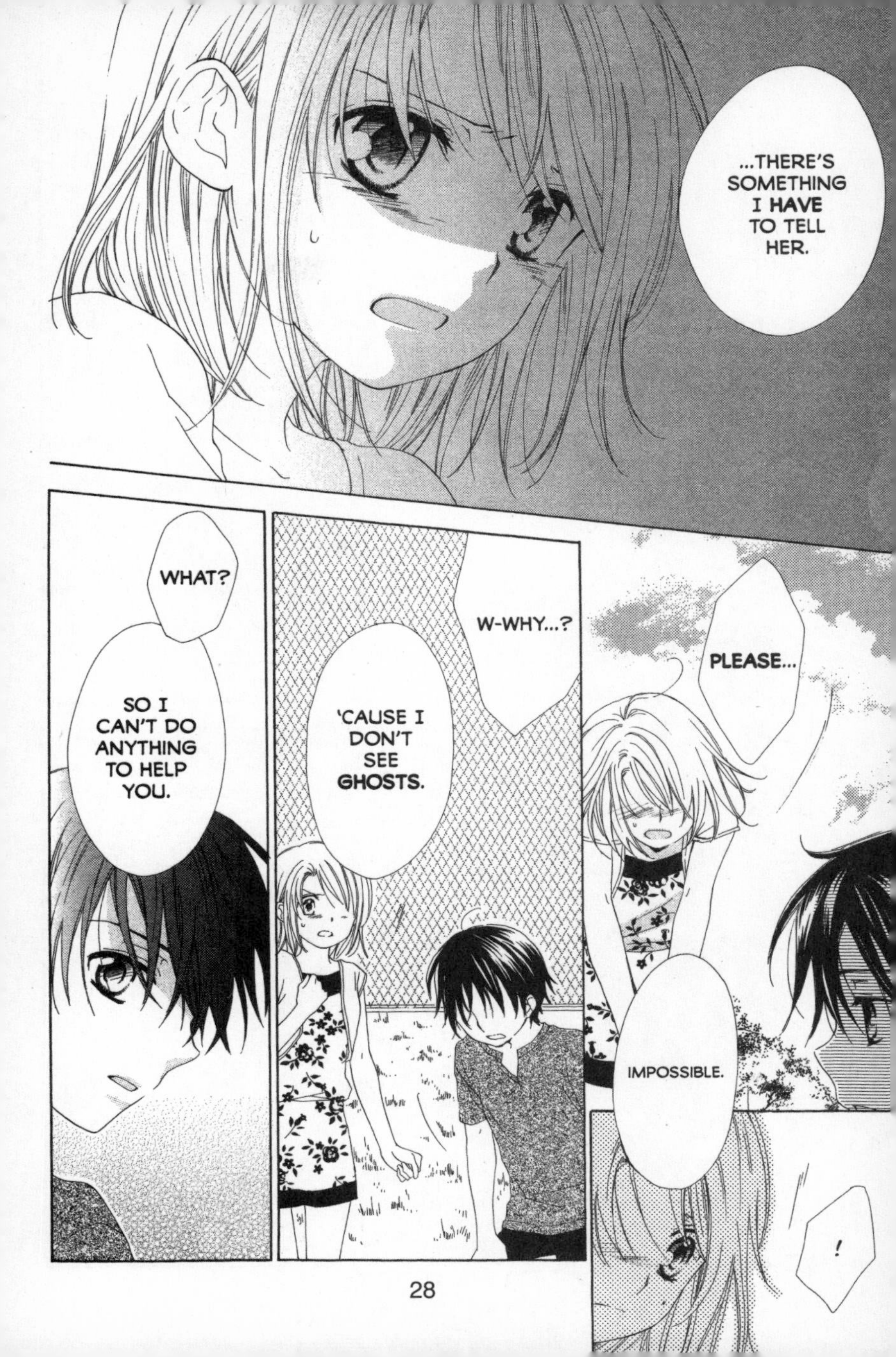
...THERE'S SOMETHING I HAVE TO TELL HER.
PLEASE...
IMPOSSIBLE.
!
W-WHY...?
'CAUSE I DON'T SEE GHOSTS.
WHAT?
SO I CAN'T DO ANYTHING TO HELP YOU.

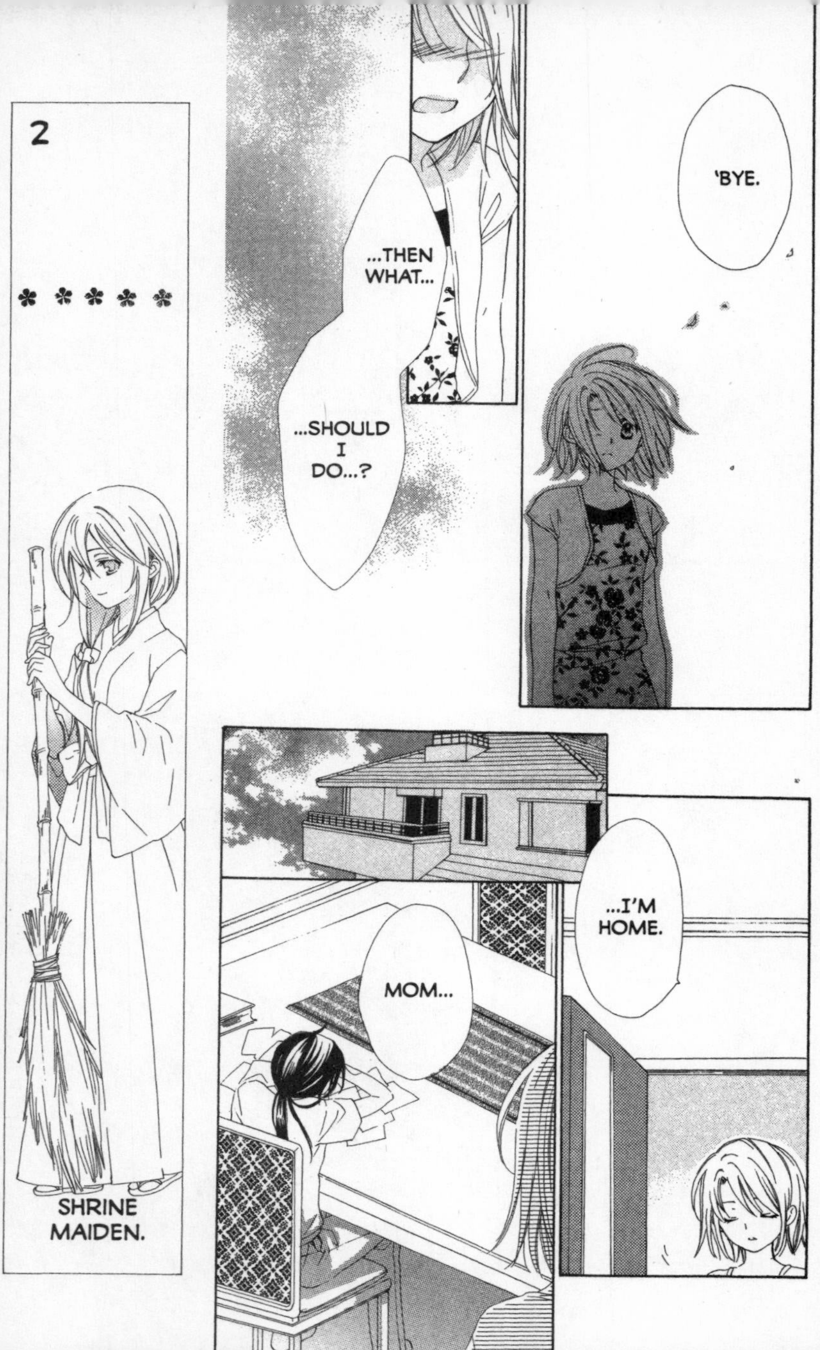
'BYE.
...THEN WHAT...
...SHOULD I DO...?
...I'M HOME.
MOM...
2
SHRINE MAIDEN.

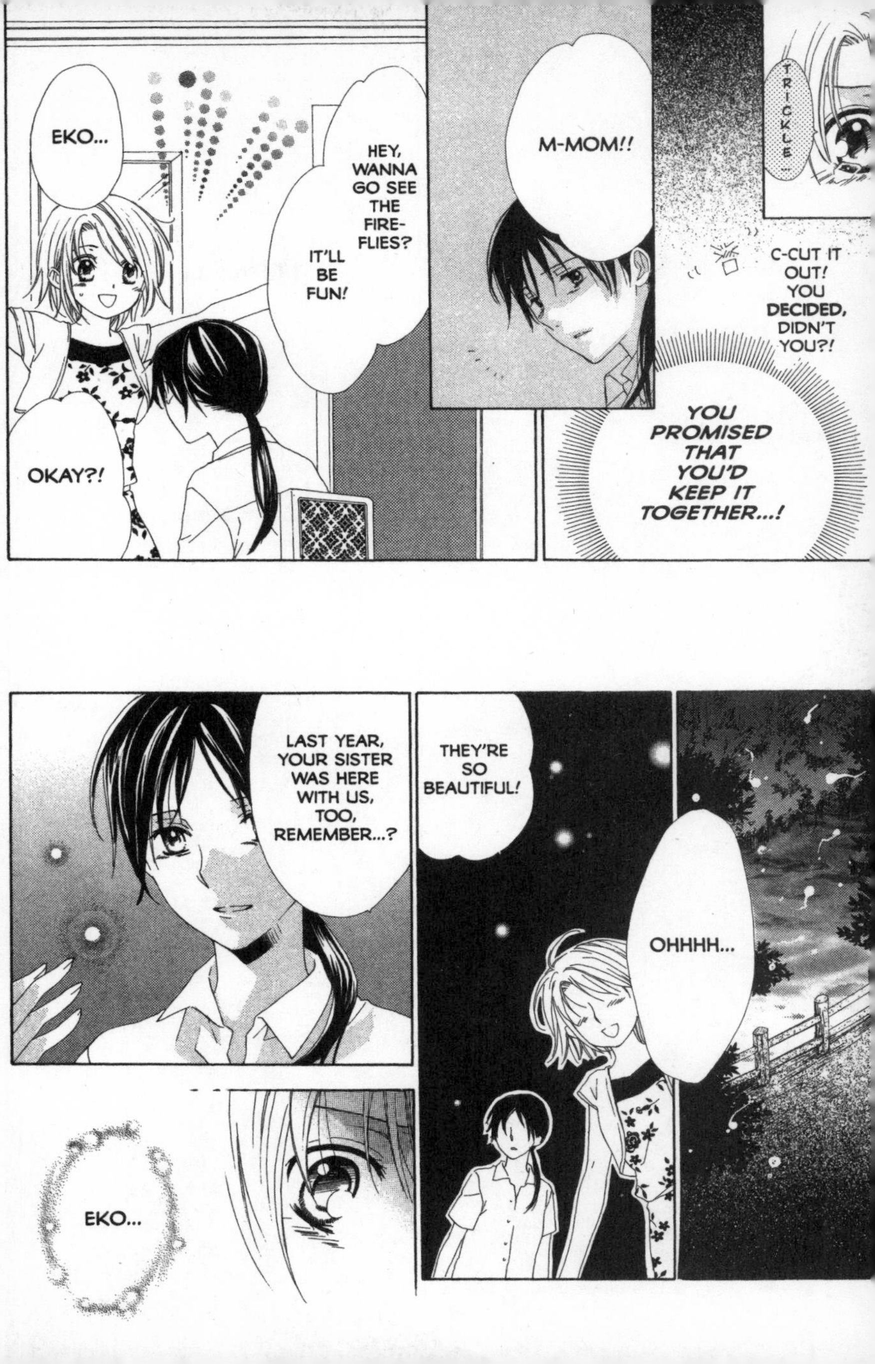
TRICKLE...
C-CUT IT OUT! YOU DECIDED, DIDN'T YOU?!
YOU PROMISED THAT YOU'D KEEP IT TOGETHER...!
M-MOM!!
EKO...
HEY, WANNA GO SEE THE FIRE-FLIES?
IT'LL BE FUN!
OKAY?!
OHHHH...
THEY'RE SO BEAUTIFUL!
LAST YEAR, YOUR SISTER WAS HERE WITH US, TOO, REMEMBER...?
EKO...

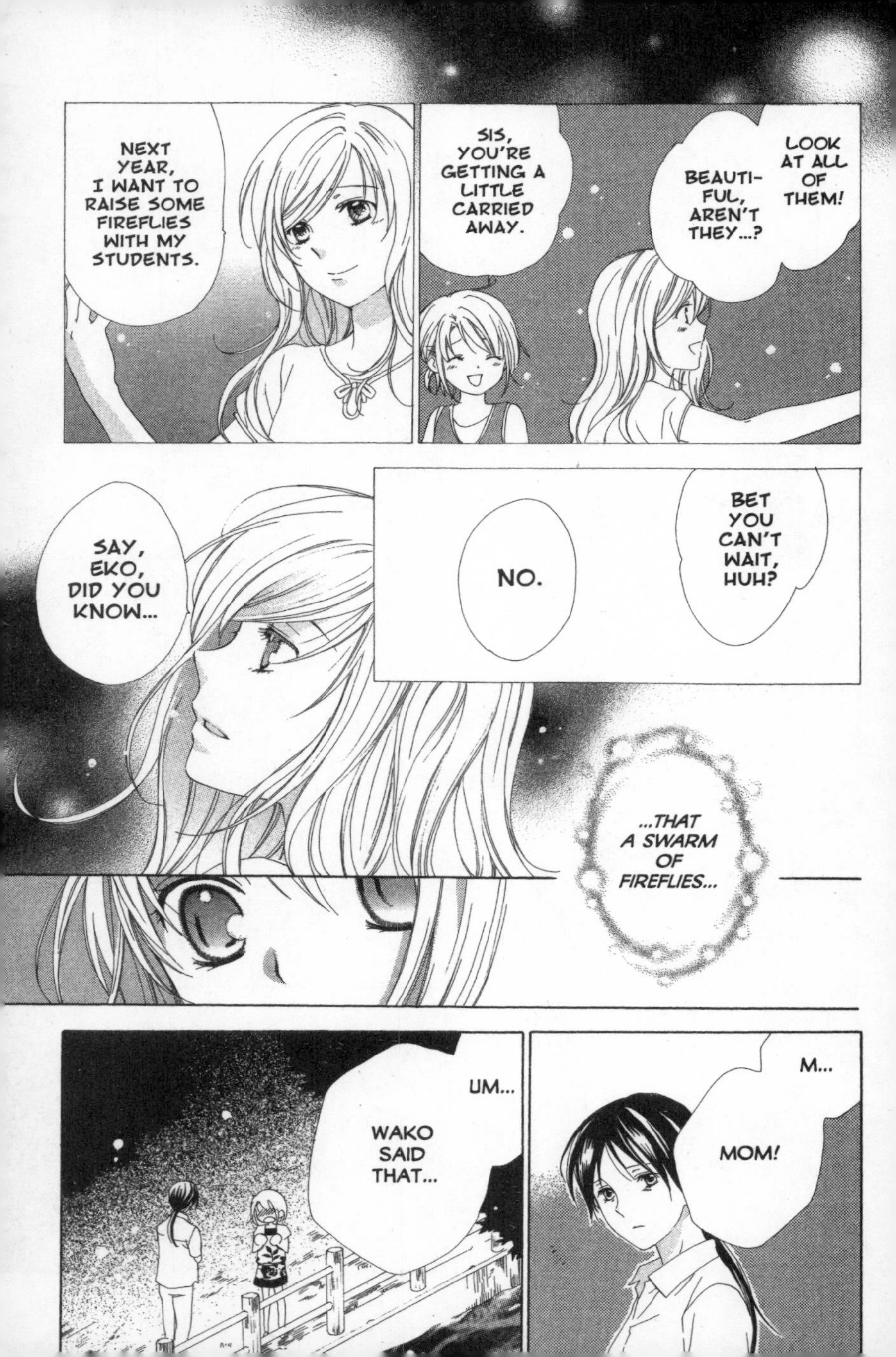
LOOK AT ALL OF THEM!
BEAUTIFUL, AREN'T THEY...?
SIS, YOU'RE GETTING A LITTLE CARRIED AWAY.
NEXT YEAR, I WANT TO RAISE SOME FIREFLIES WITH MY STUDENTS.
BET YOU CAN'T WAIT, HUH?
NO.
SAY, EKO, DID YOU KNOW...
...THAT A SWARM OF FIREFLIES...
M...
MOM!
UM...
WAKO SAID THAT...

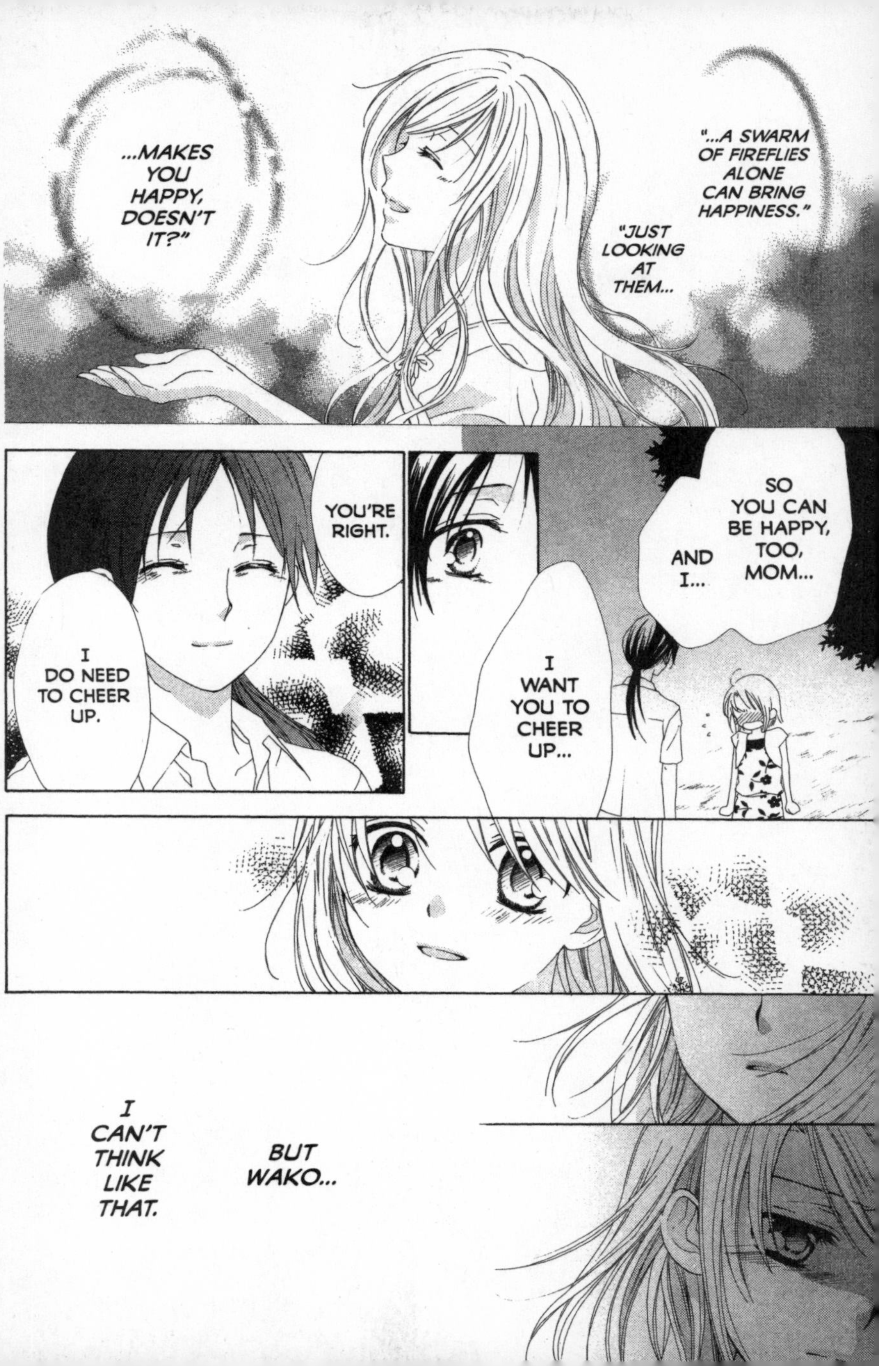
"...A SWARM OF FIREFLIES ALONE CAN BRING HAPPINESS."
"JUST LOOKING AT THEM...
...MAKES YOU HAPPY, DOESN'T IT?"
SO YOU CAN BE HAPPY, TOO, MOM...
AND I...
I WANT YOU TO CHEER UP...
YOU'RE RIGHT.
I DO NEED TO CHEER UP.
BUT WAKO...
I CAN'T THINK LIKE THAT.

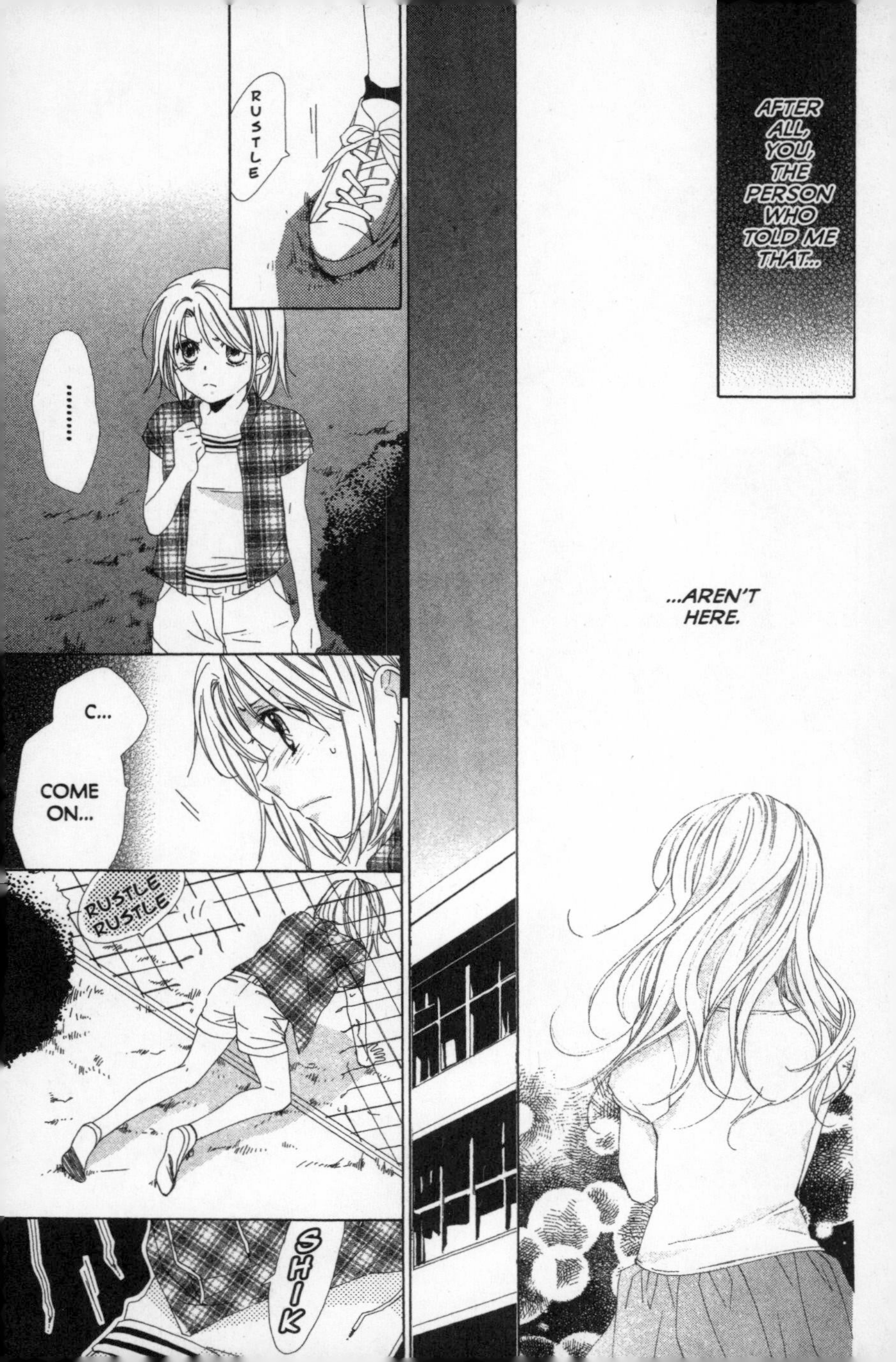
AFTER ALL, YOU, THE PERSON WHO TOLD ME THAT...
...AREN'T HERE.
RUSTLE
......
C...
COME ON...
RUSTLE RUSTLE
SHIK

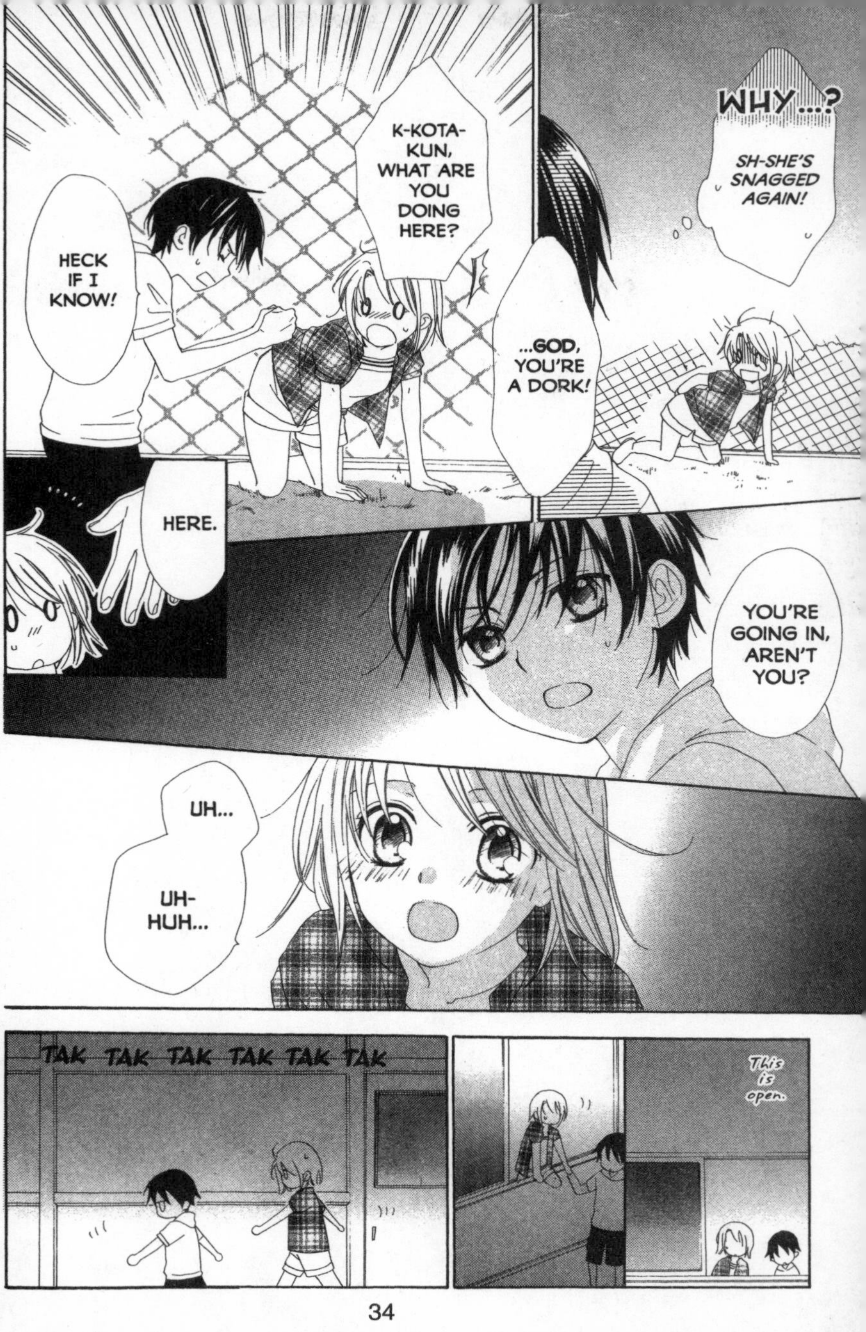
WHY...?
SH-SHE'S SNAGGED AGAIN!
...GOD, YOU'RE A DORK!
K-KOTA-KUN, WHAT ARE YOU DOING HERE?
HECK IF I KNOW!
HERE.
YOU'RE GOING IN, AREN'T YOU?
UH... UH-HUH...
This is open.
TAK TAK TAK TAK TAK TAK

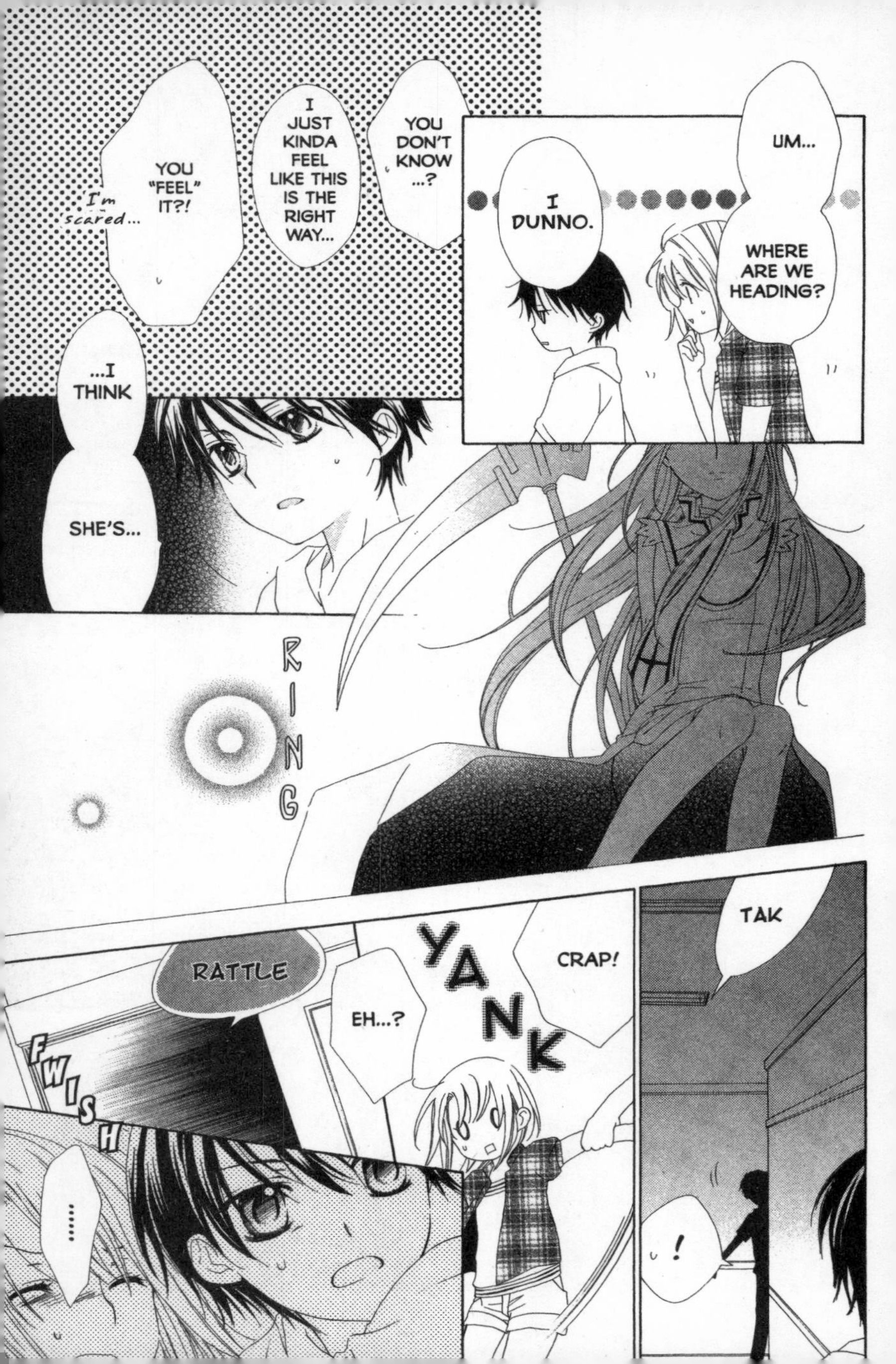
UM...
WHERE ARE WE HEADING?
I DUNNO.
YOU DON'T KNOW ...?
I JUST KINDA FEEL LIKE THIS IS THE RIGHT WAY...
YOU "FEEL" IT?!
I'm scared...
...I THINK
SHE'S...
RING
TAK
!
CRAP!
YANK
EH...?
RATTLE
FWISH
......

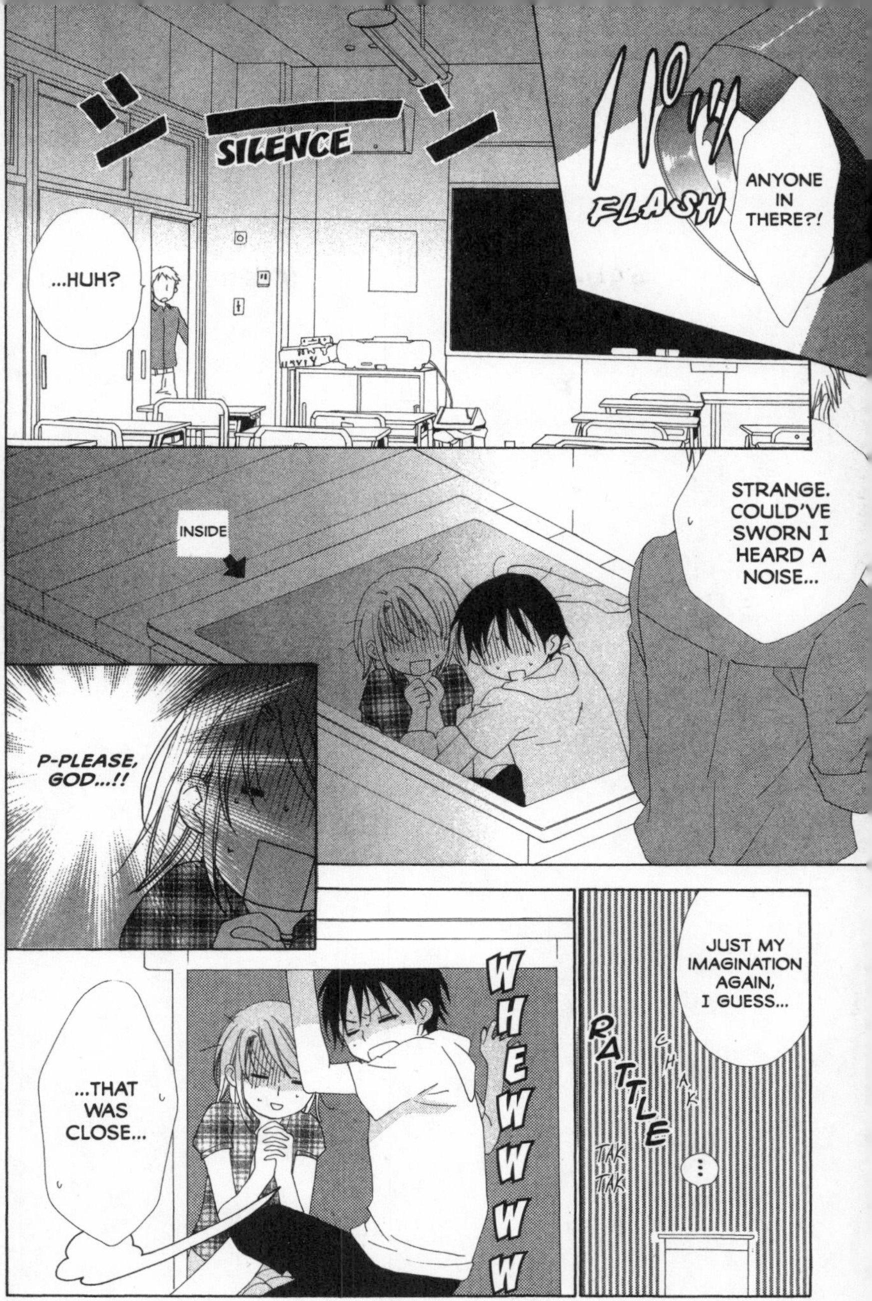

FLASH
ANYONE IN THERE?!
SILENCE
...HUH?
STRANGE. COULD'VE SWORN I HEARD A NOISE...
INSIDE
P-PLEASE, GOD...!!
JUST MY IMAGINATION AGAIN, I GUESS...
RATTLE
CHAK
TIAK TIAK
...
WHEWWWWW
...THAT WAS CLOSE...

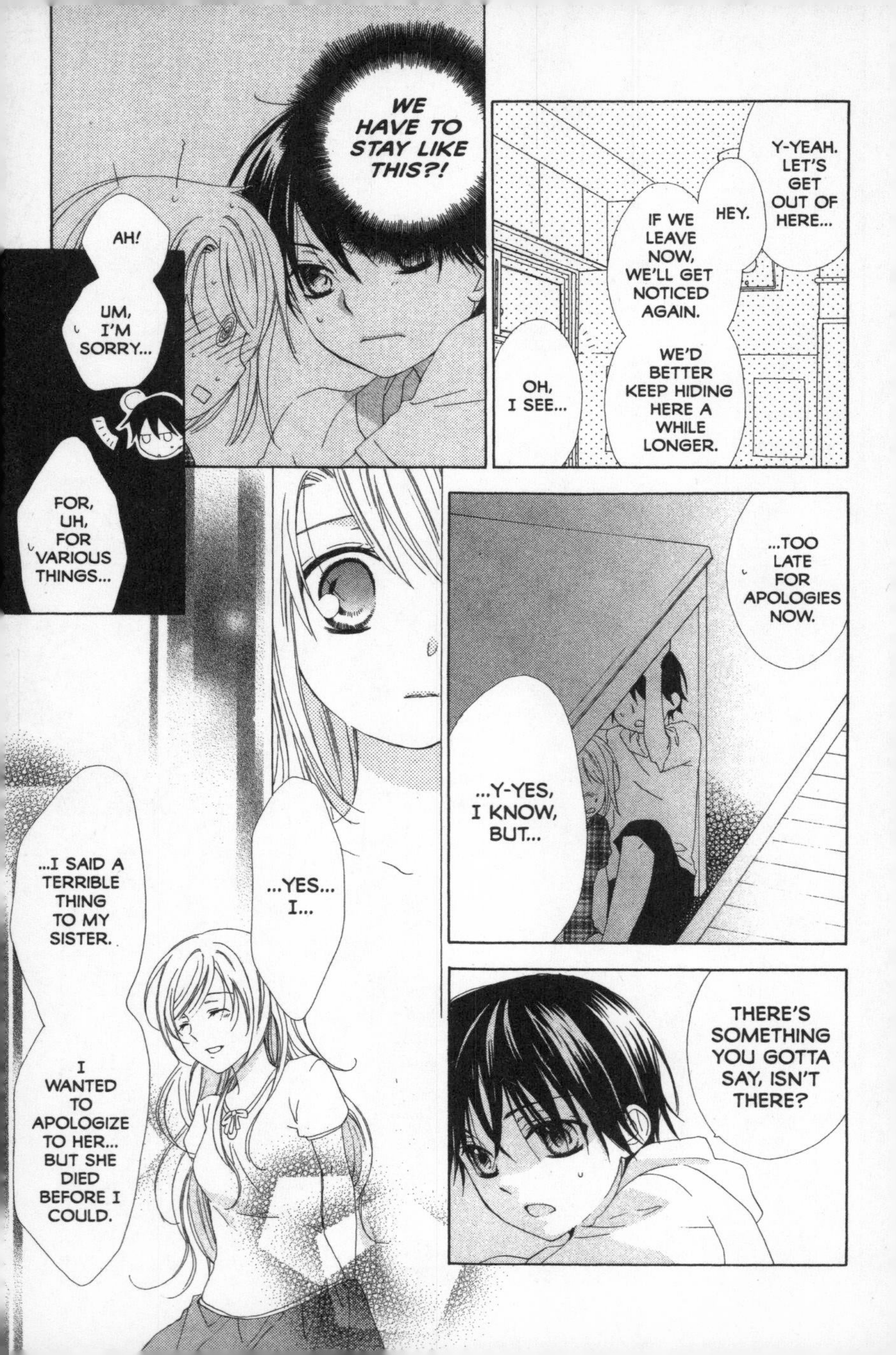
Y-YEAH. LET'S GET OUT OF HERE...
HEY.
IF WE LEAVE NOW, WE'LL GET NOTICED AGAIN.
WE'D BETTER KEEP HIDING HERE A WHILE LONGER.
OH, I SEE...
WE HAVE TO STAY LIKE THIS?!
AH!
UM, I'M SORRY...
FOR, UH, FOR VARIOUS THINGS...
...TOO LATE FOR APOLOGIES NOW.
...Y-YES, I KNOW, BUT...
THERE'S SOMETHING YOU GOTTA SAY, ISN'T THERE?
...YES... I...
...I SAID A TERRIBLE THING TO MY SISTER.
I WANTED TO APOLOGIZE TO HER... BUT SHE DIED BEFORE I COULD.

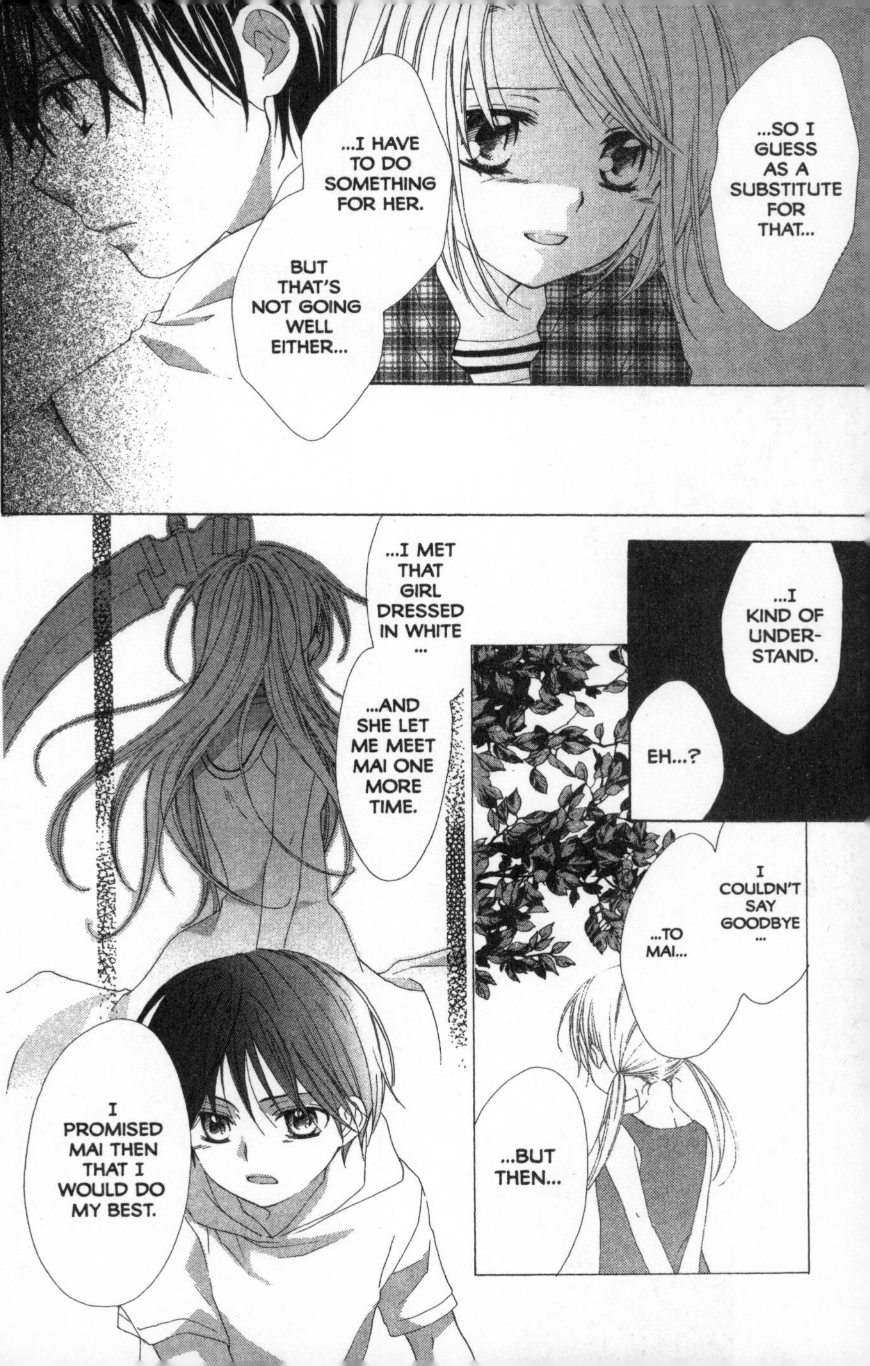
...SO I GUESS AS A SUBSTITUTE FOR THAT...
...I HAVE TO DO SOMETHING FOR HER.
BUT THAT'S NOT GOING WELL EITHER...
...I KIND OF UNDER-STAND.
EH...?
I COULDN'T SAY GOODBYE ...
...TO MAI...
...BUT THEN...
...I MET THAT GIRL DRESSED IN WHITE ...
...AND SHE LET ME MEET MAI ONE MORE TIME.
I PROMISED MAI THEN THAT I WOULD DO MY BEST.

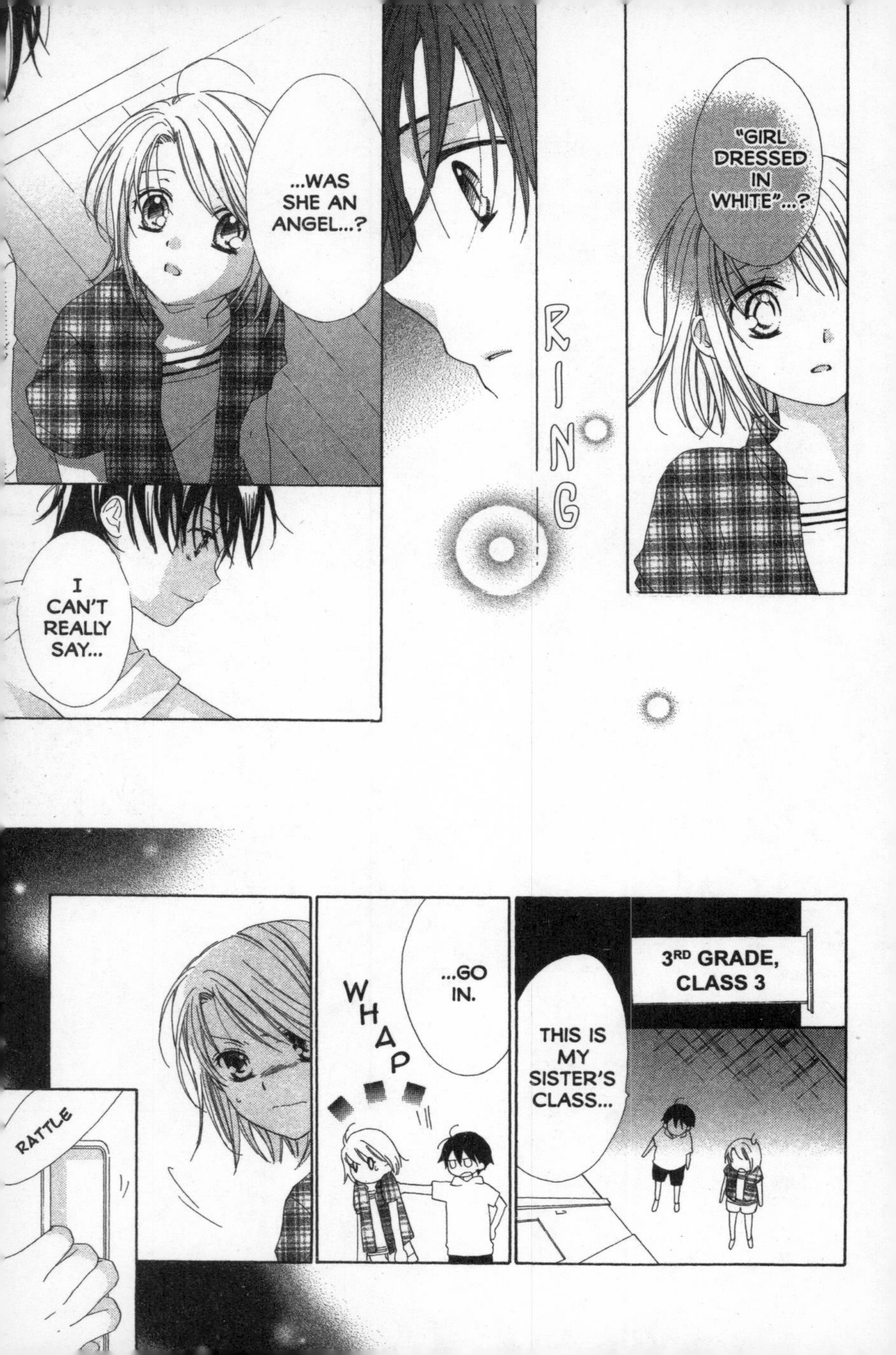
"GIRL DRESSED IN WHITE"...?
RING
...WAS SHE AN ANGEL...?
I CAN'T REALLY SAY...
3RD GRADE, CLASS 3
THIS IS MY SISTER'S CLASS...
...GO IN.
WHAP
RATTLE

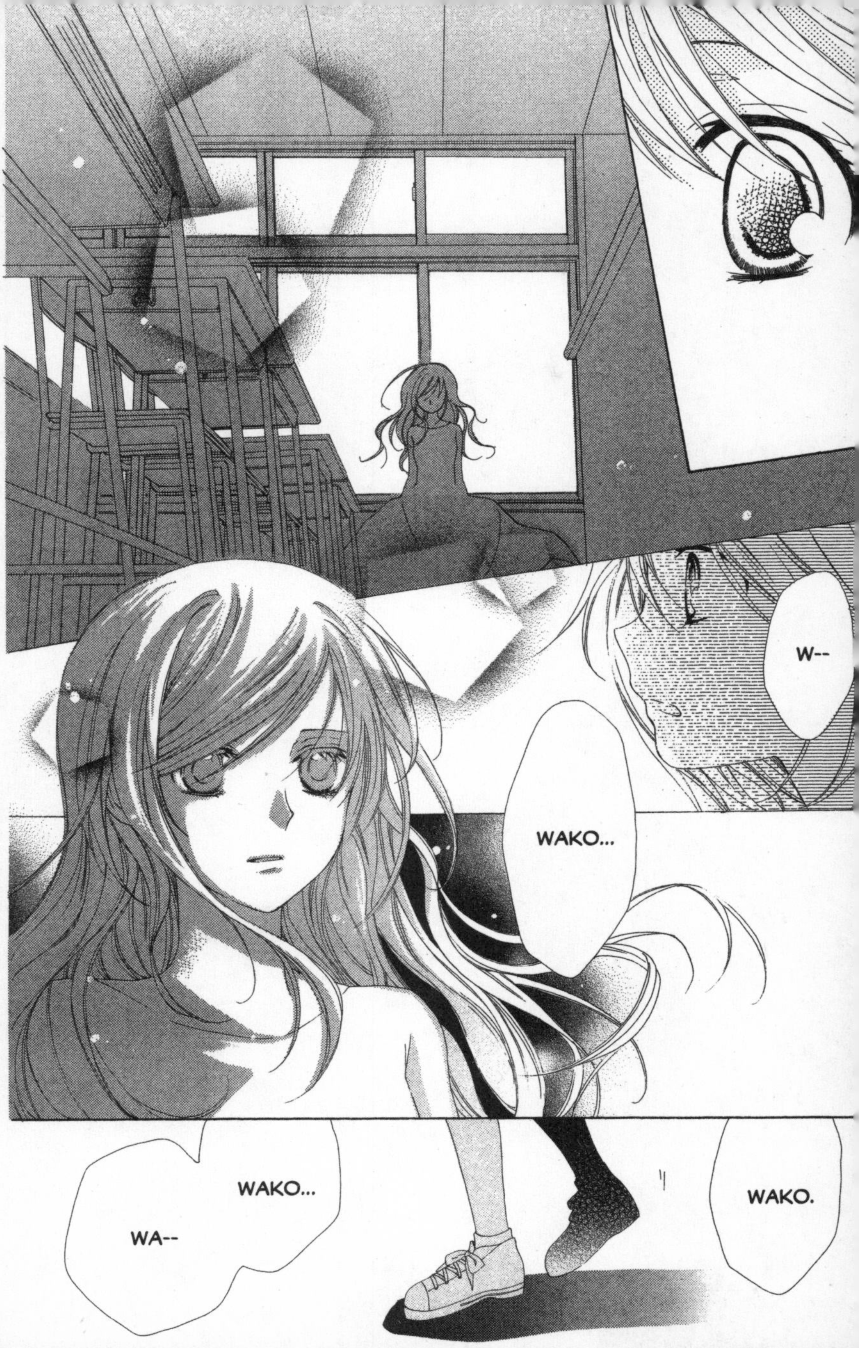
W--
WAKO...
WAKO.
WAKO...
WA--

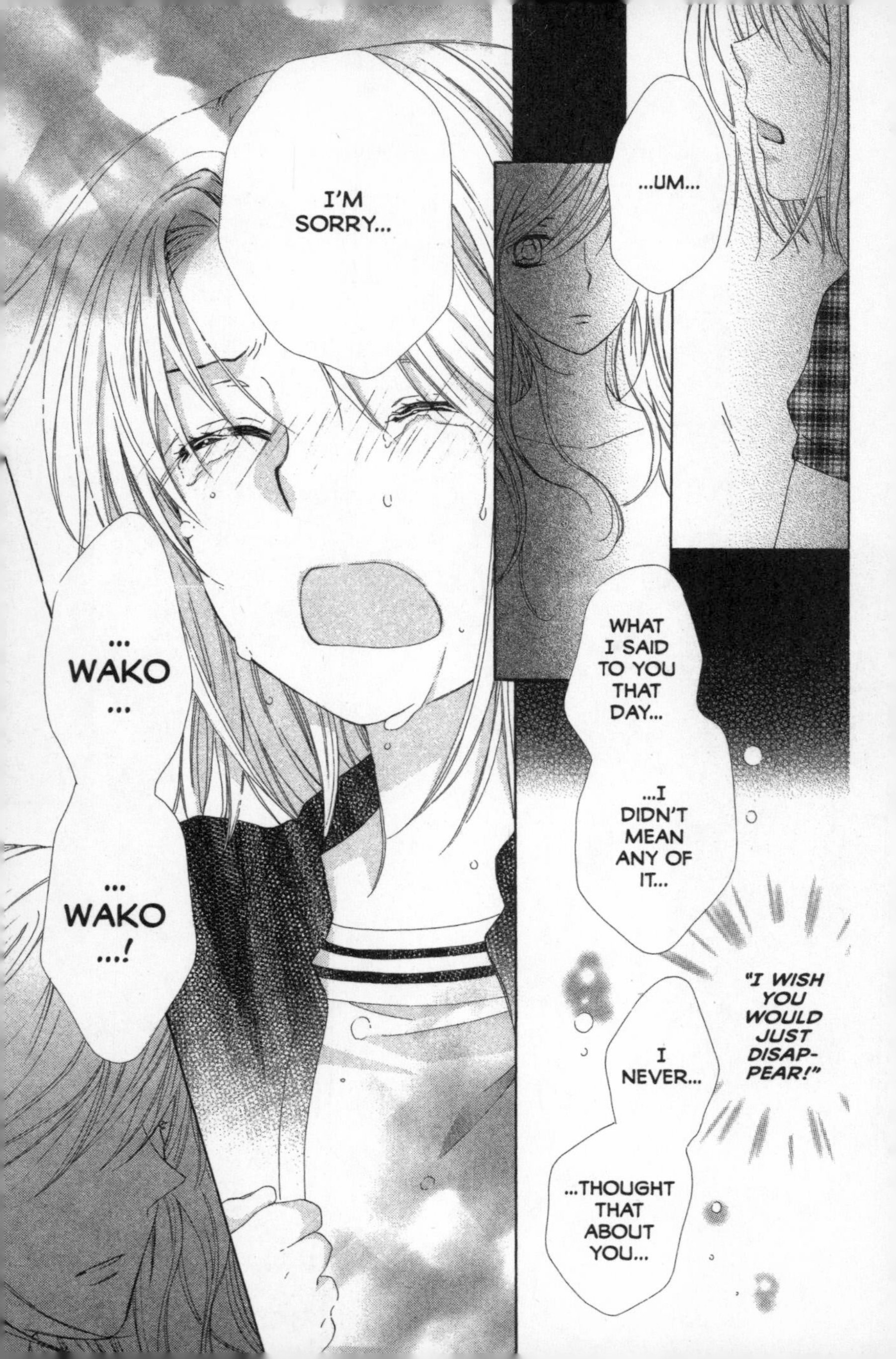
...UM...
WHAT I SAID TO YOU THAT DAY...
...I DIDN'T MEAN ANY OF IT...
"I WISH YOU WOULD JUST DISAP-PEAR!"
I NEVER...
...THOUGHT THAT ABOUT YOU...
I'M SORRY...
...WAKO...
...WAKO...!

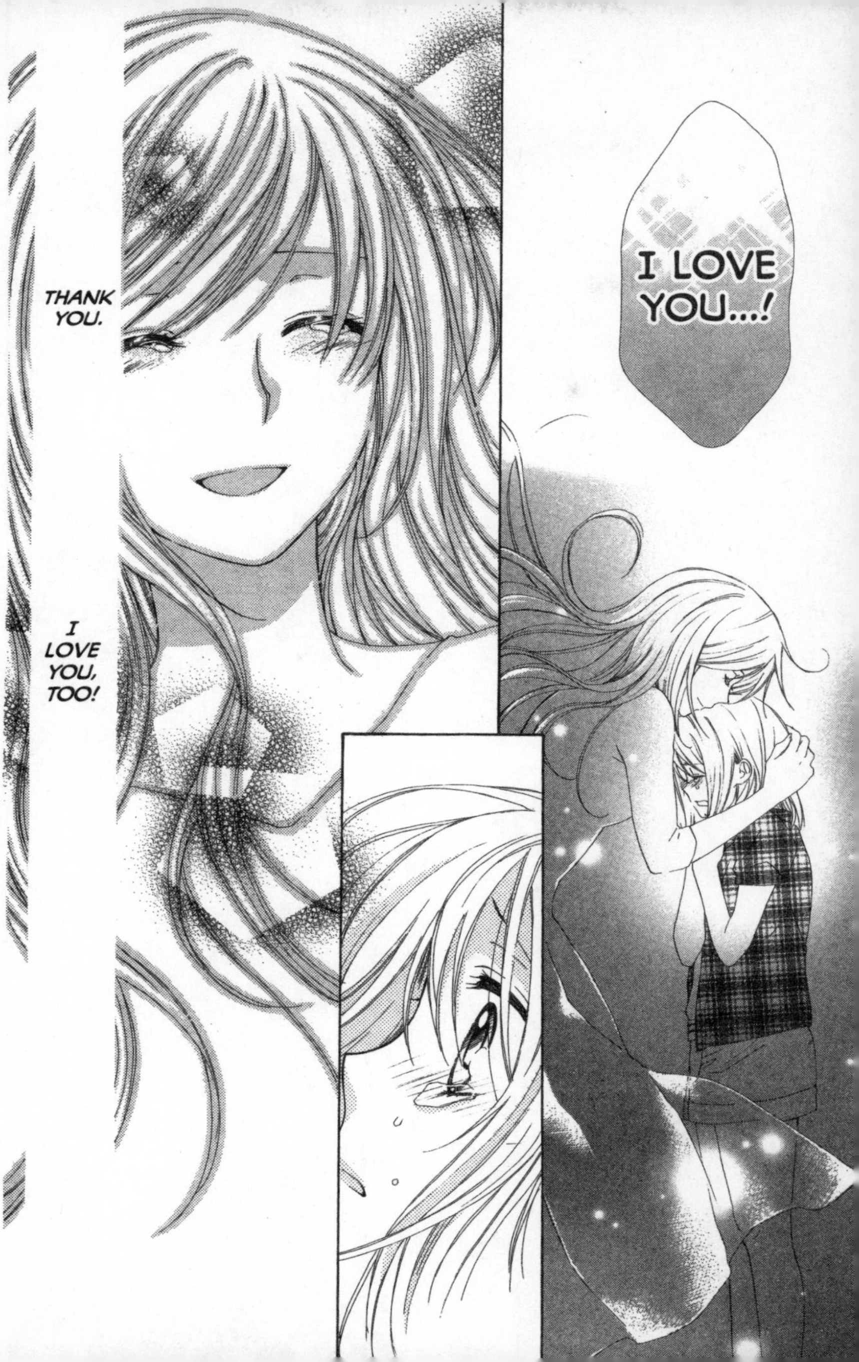
I LOVE YOU...!
THANK YOU.
I LOVE YOU, TOO!

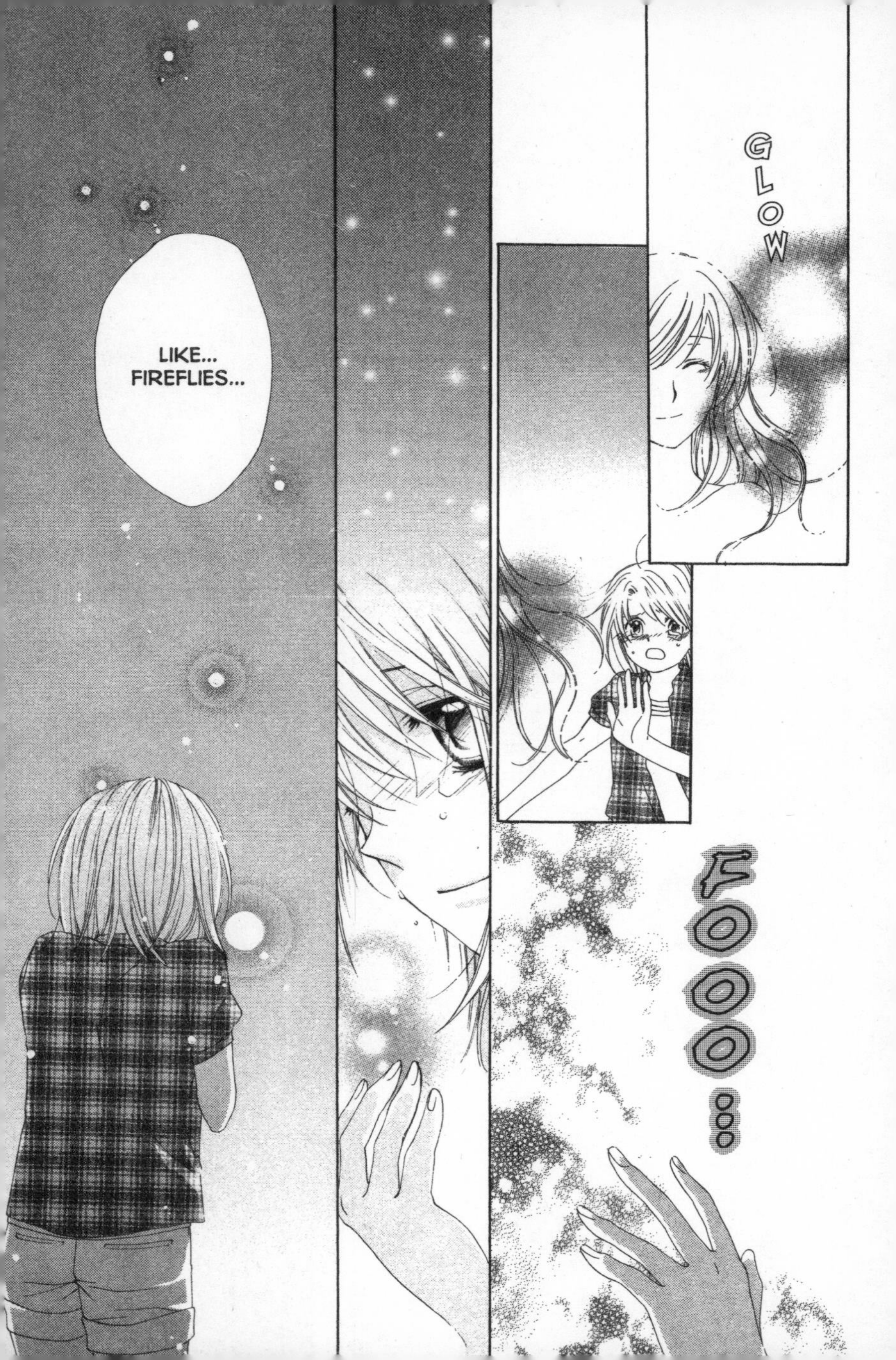
GLOW
FOOO...
LIKE... FIREFLIES...

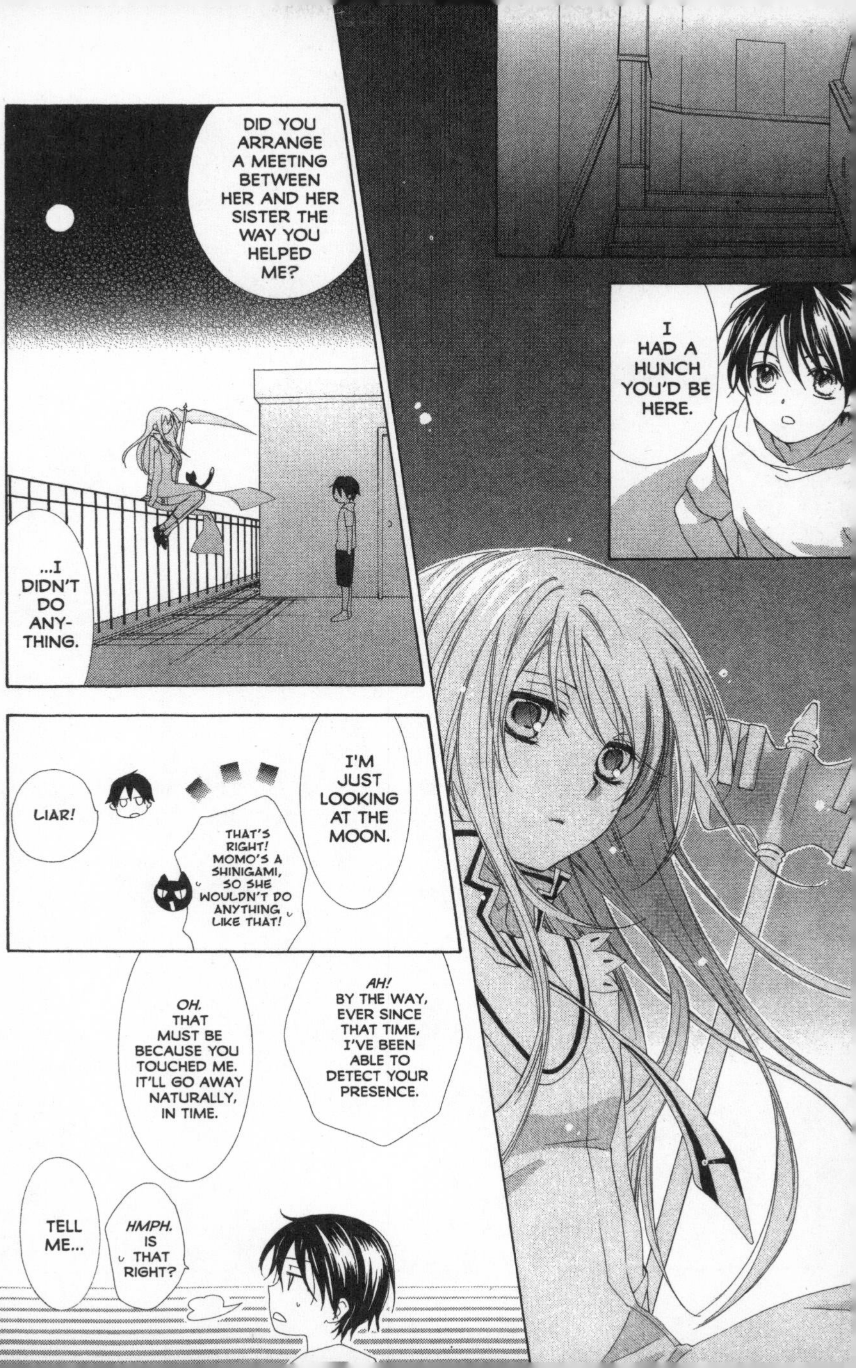
I HAD A HUNCH YOU'D BE HERE.
DID YOU ARRANGE A MEETING BETWEEN HER AND HER SISTER THE WAY YOU HELPED ME?
...I DIDN'T DO ANYTHING.
I'M JUST LOOKING AT THE MOON.
LIAR!
THAT'S RIGHT! MOMO'S A SHINIGAMI, SO SHE WOULDN'T DO ANYTHING LIKE THAT!
AH! BY THE WAY, EVER SINCE THAT TIME, I'VE BEEN ABLE TO DETECT YOUR PRESENCE.
OH. THAT MUST BE BECAUSE YOU TOUCHED ME. IT'LL GO AWAY NATURALLY, IN TIME.
HMPH. IS THAT RIGHT?
TELL ME...

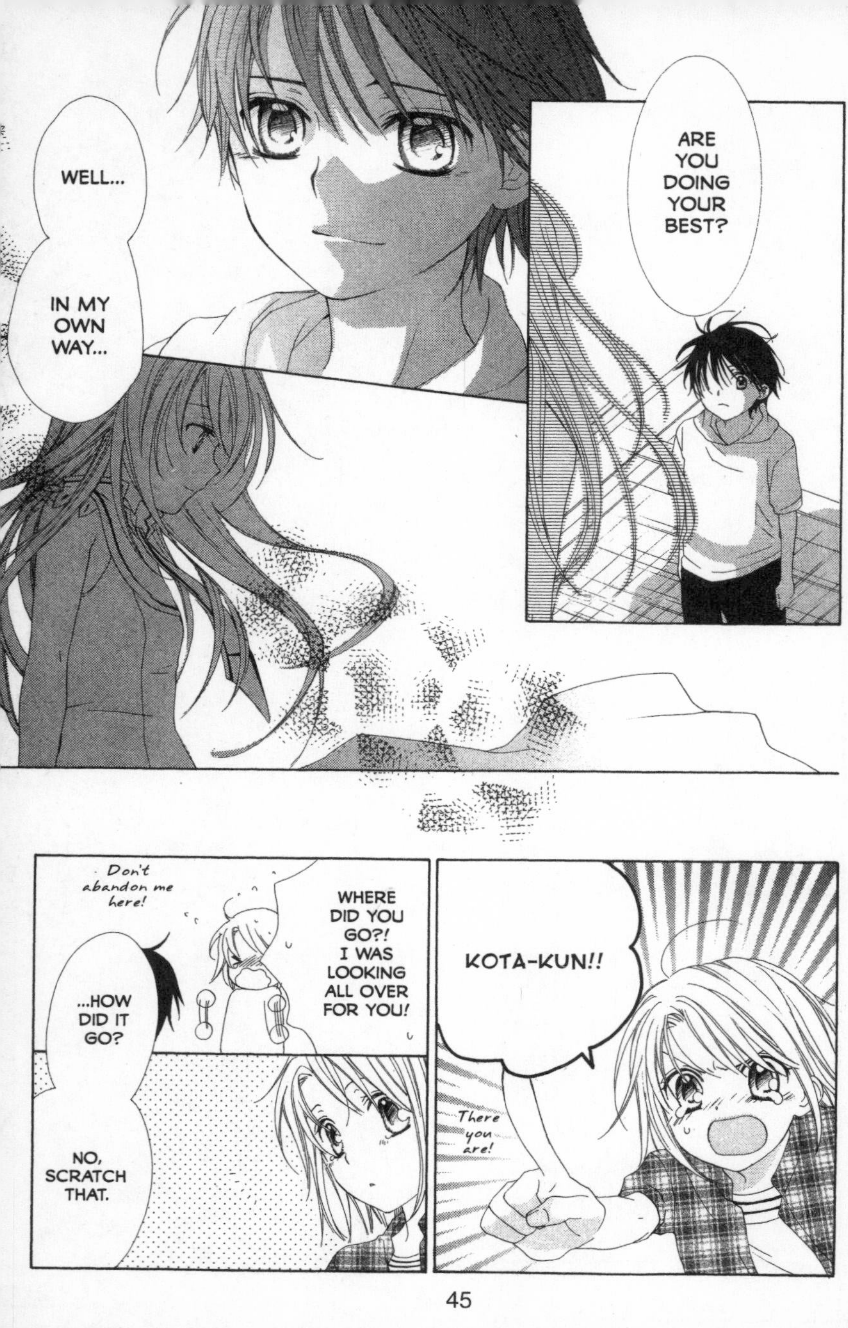
ARE YOU DOING YOUR BEST?
WELL...
IN MY OWN WAY...
KOTA-KUN!!
There you are!
WHERE DID YOU GO?! I WAS LOOKING ALL OVER FOR YOU!
Don't abandon me here!
...HOW DID IT GO?
NO, SCRATCH THAT.

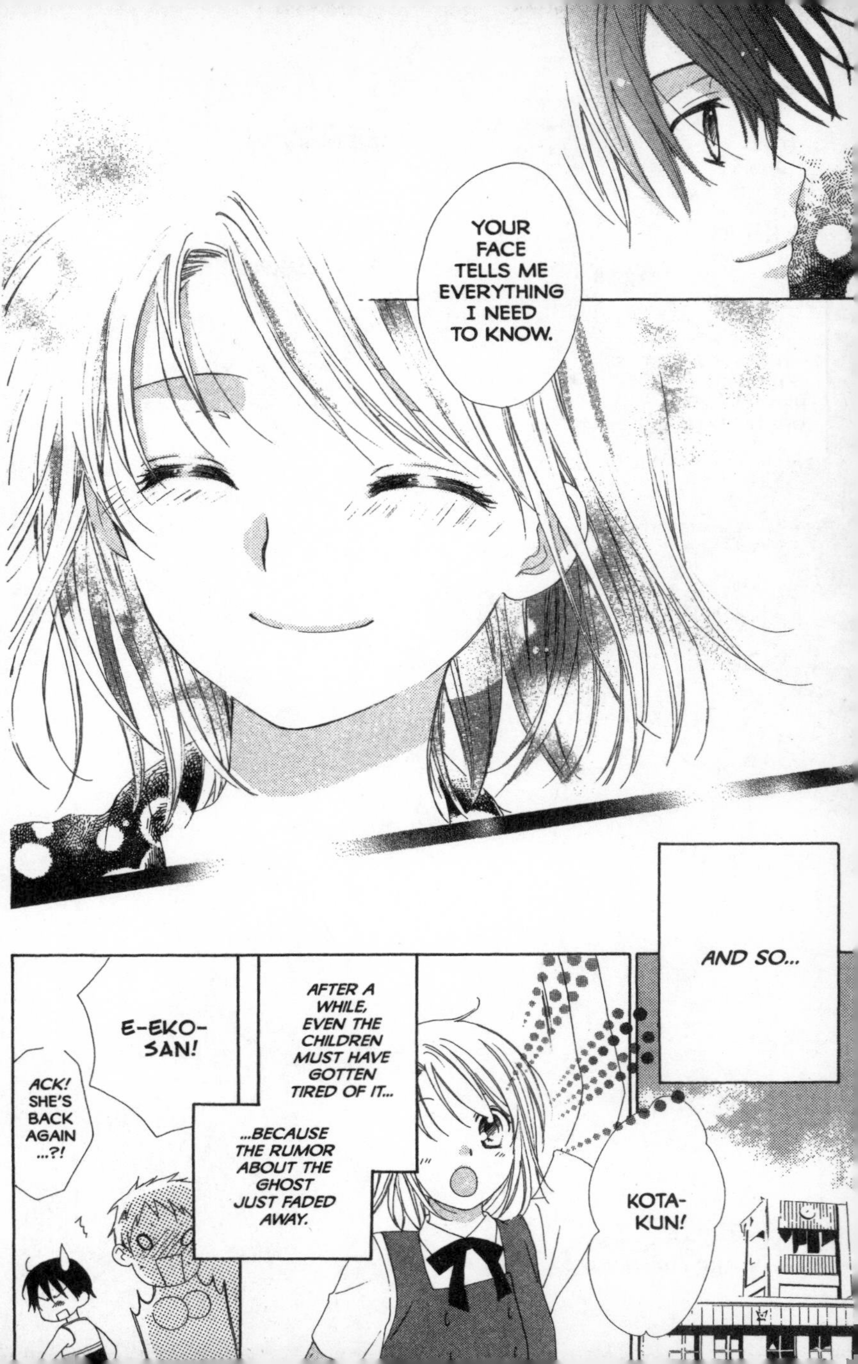
YOUR FACE TELLS ME EVERYTHING I NEED TO KNOW.
AND SO...
KOTA-KUN!
AFTER A WHILE, EVEN THE CHILDREN MUST HAVE GOTTEN TIRED OF IT...
...BECAUSE THE RUMOR ABOUT THE GHOST JUST FADED AWAY.
E-EKO-SAN!
ACK! SHE'S BACK AGAIN ...?!

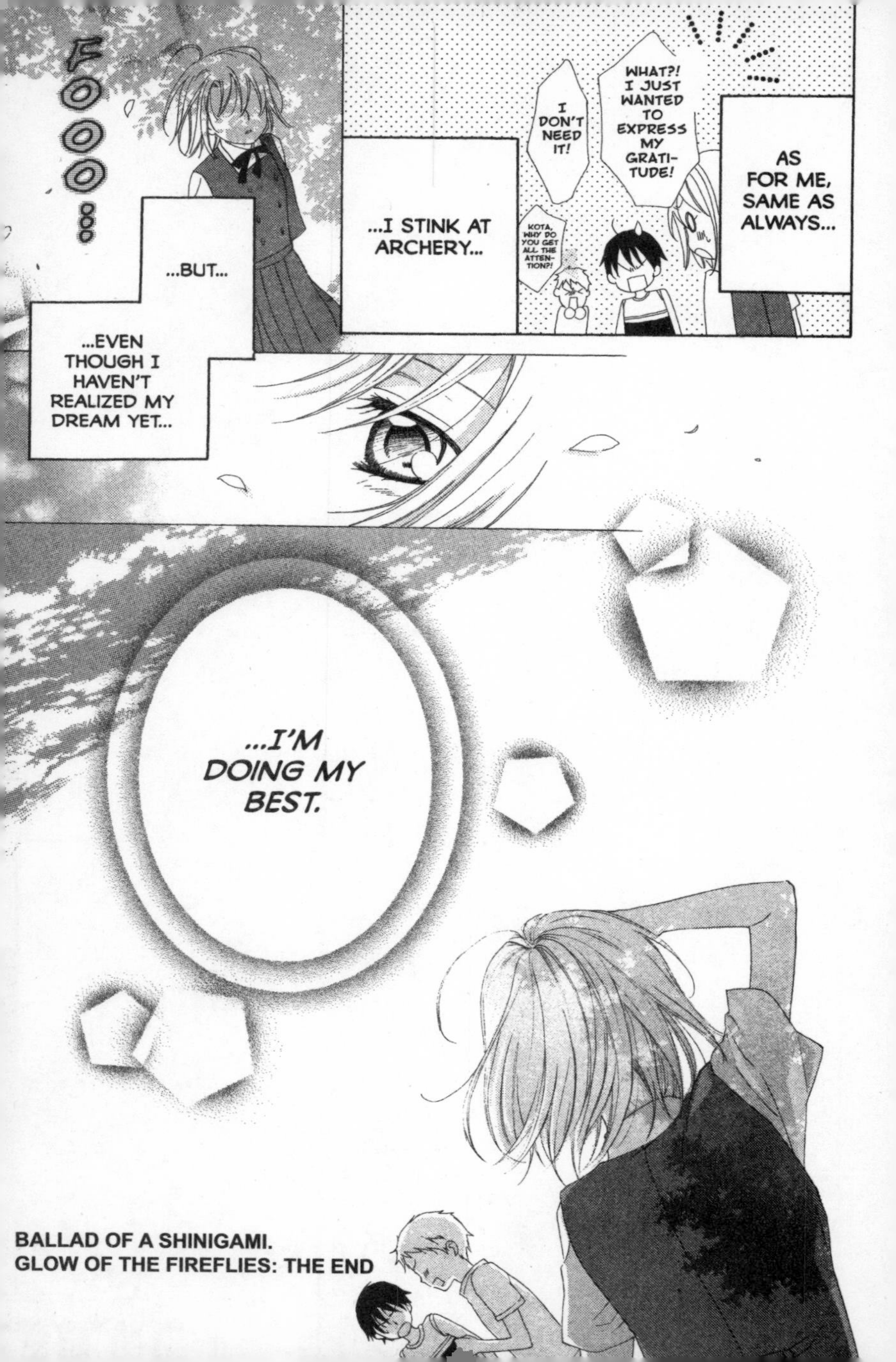
AS FOR ME, SAME AS ALWAYS...
WHAT?! I JUST WANTED TO EXPRESS MY GRATITUDE!
I DON'T NEED IT!
KOTA, WHY DO YOU GET ALL THE ATTENTION?!
...I STINK AT ARCHERY...
FOOOO...
...BUT...
...EVEN THOUGH I HAVEN'T REALIZED MY DREAM YET...
...I'M DOING MY BEST.
BALLAD OF A SHINIGAMI.
GLOW OF THE FIREFLIES: THE END

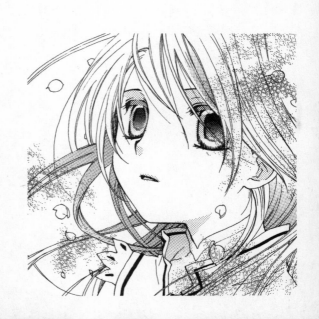

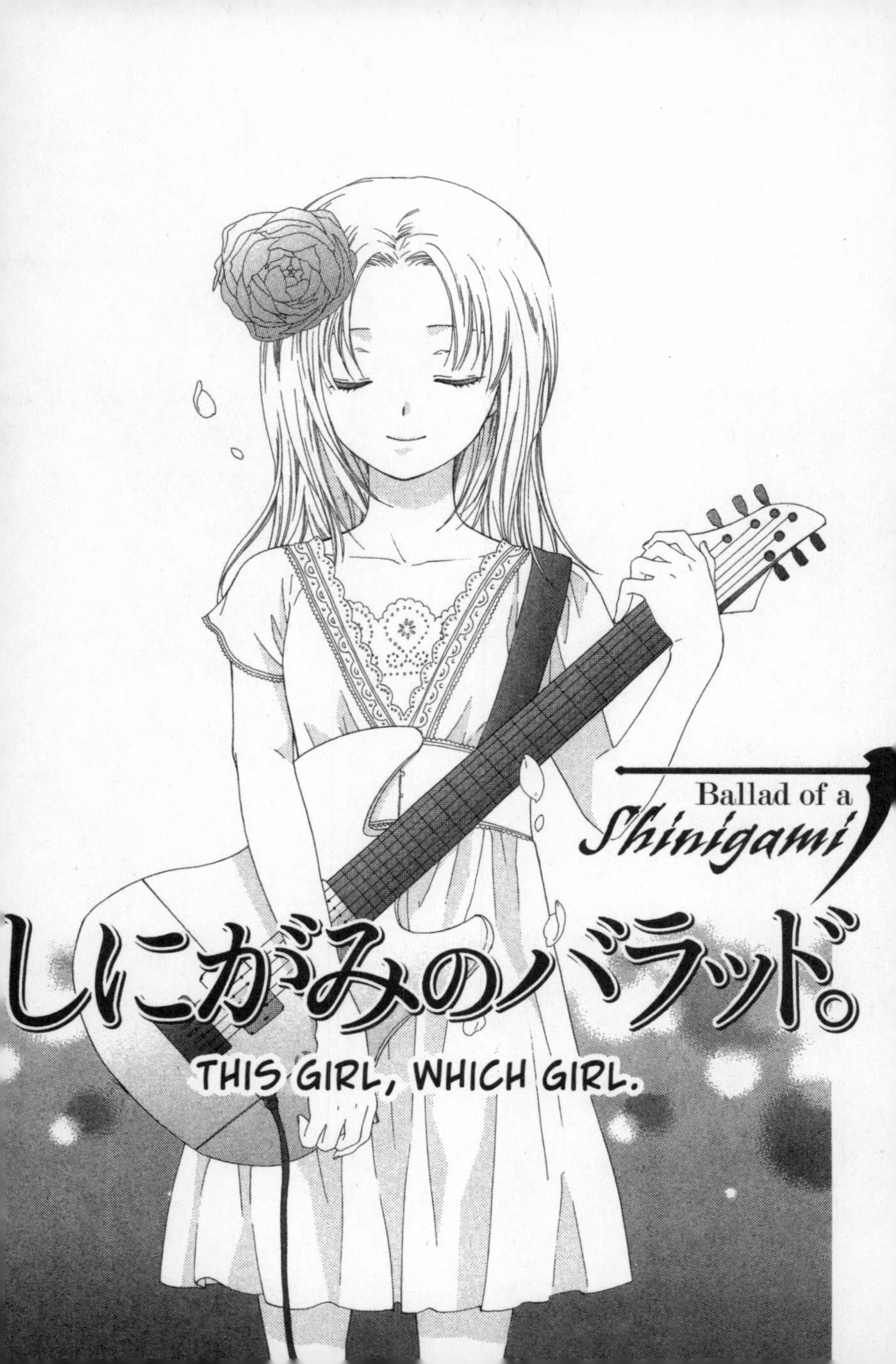
Ballad of a Shinigami
しにがみのバラッド。
THIS GIRL, WHICH GIRL.

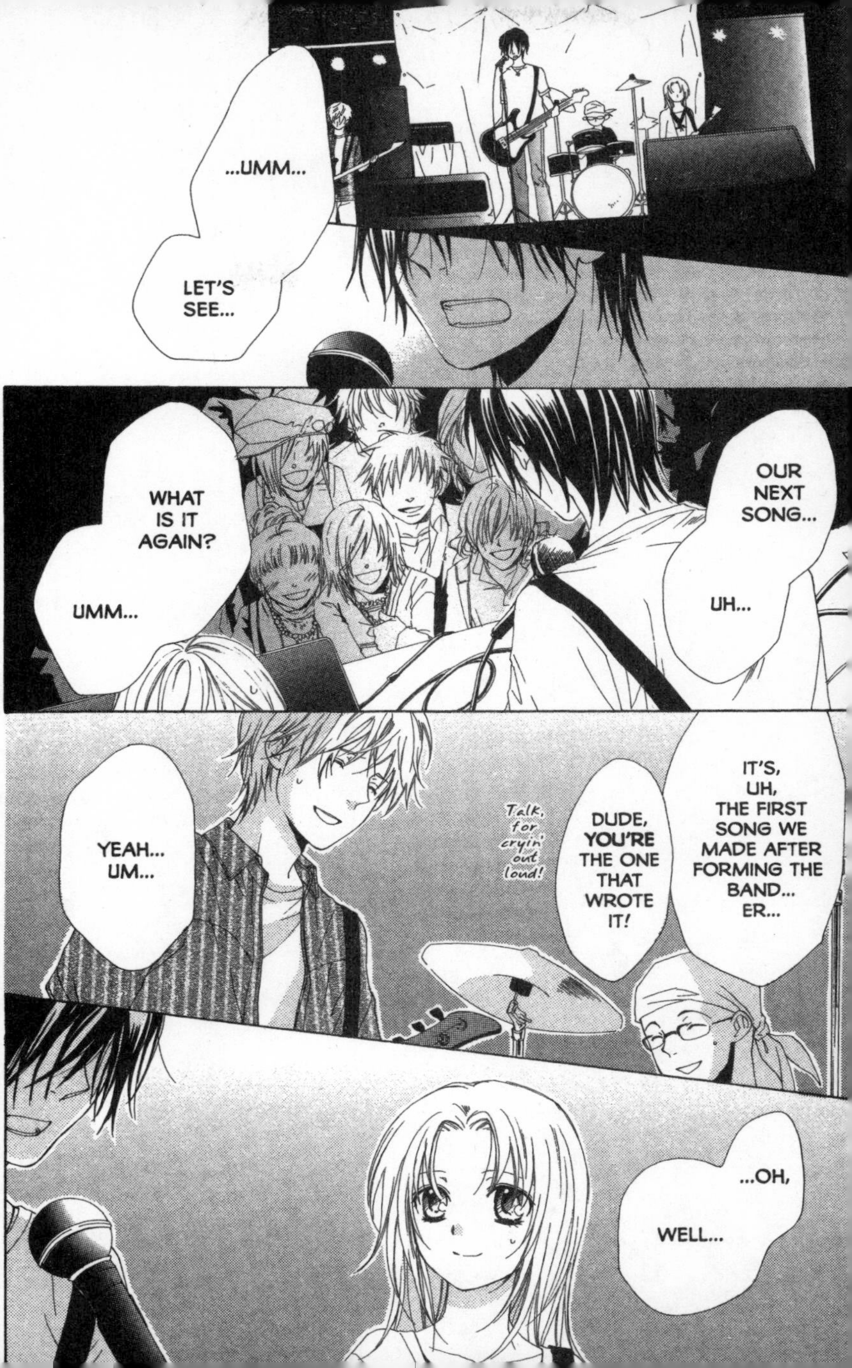
...UMM...
LET'S SEE...
OUR NEXT SONG...
UH...
WHAT IS IT AGAIN?
UMM...
IT'S, UH, THE FIRST SONG WE MADE AFTER FORMING THE BAND... ER...
DUDE, **YOU'RE** THE ONE THAT WROTE IT!
Talk, for cryin' out loud!
YEAH... UM...
...OH,
WELL...

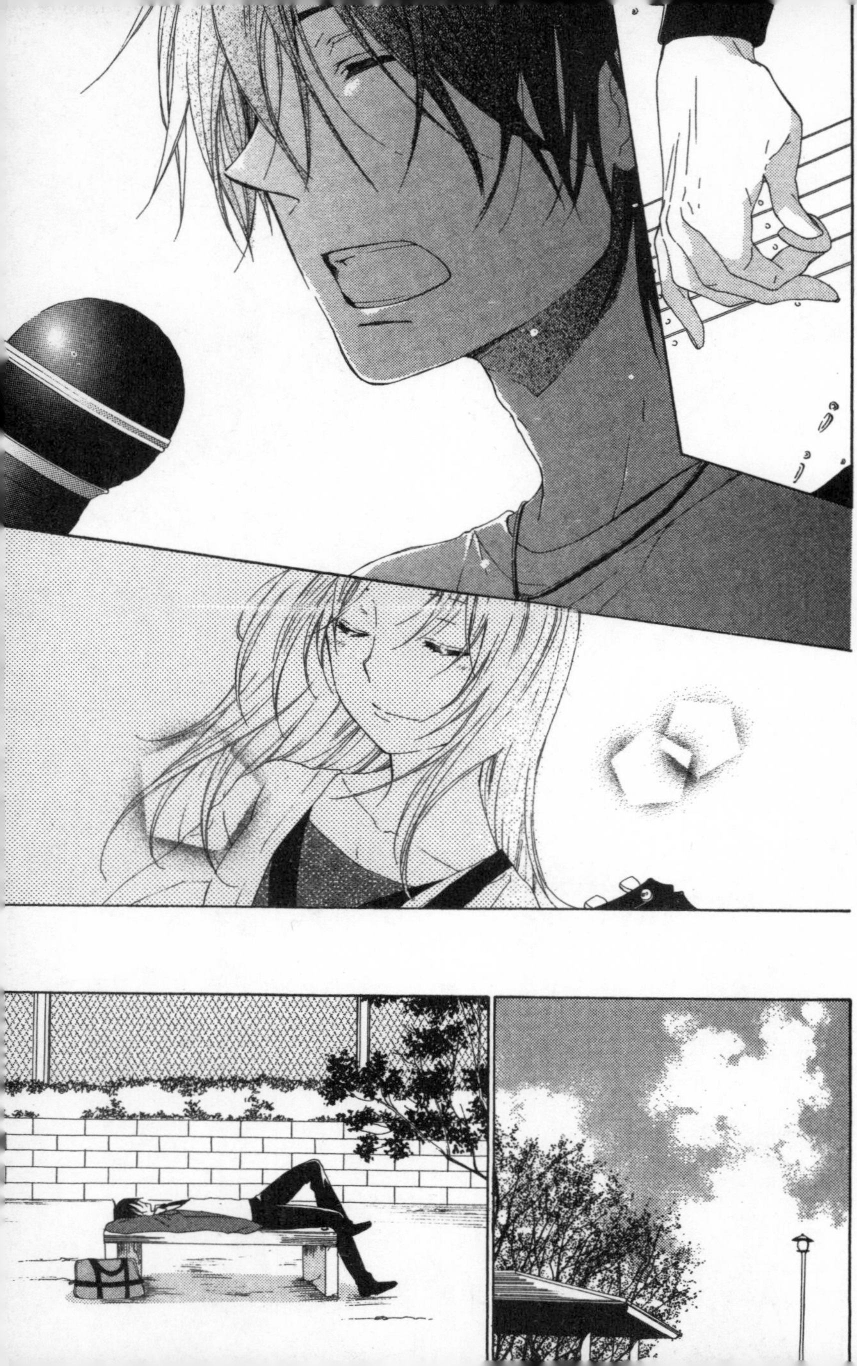

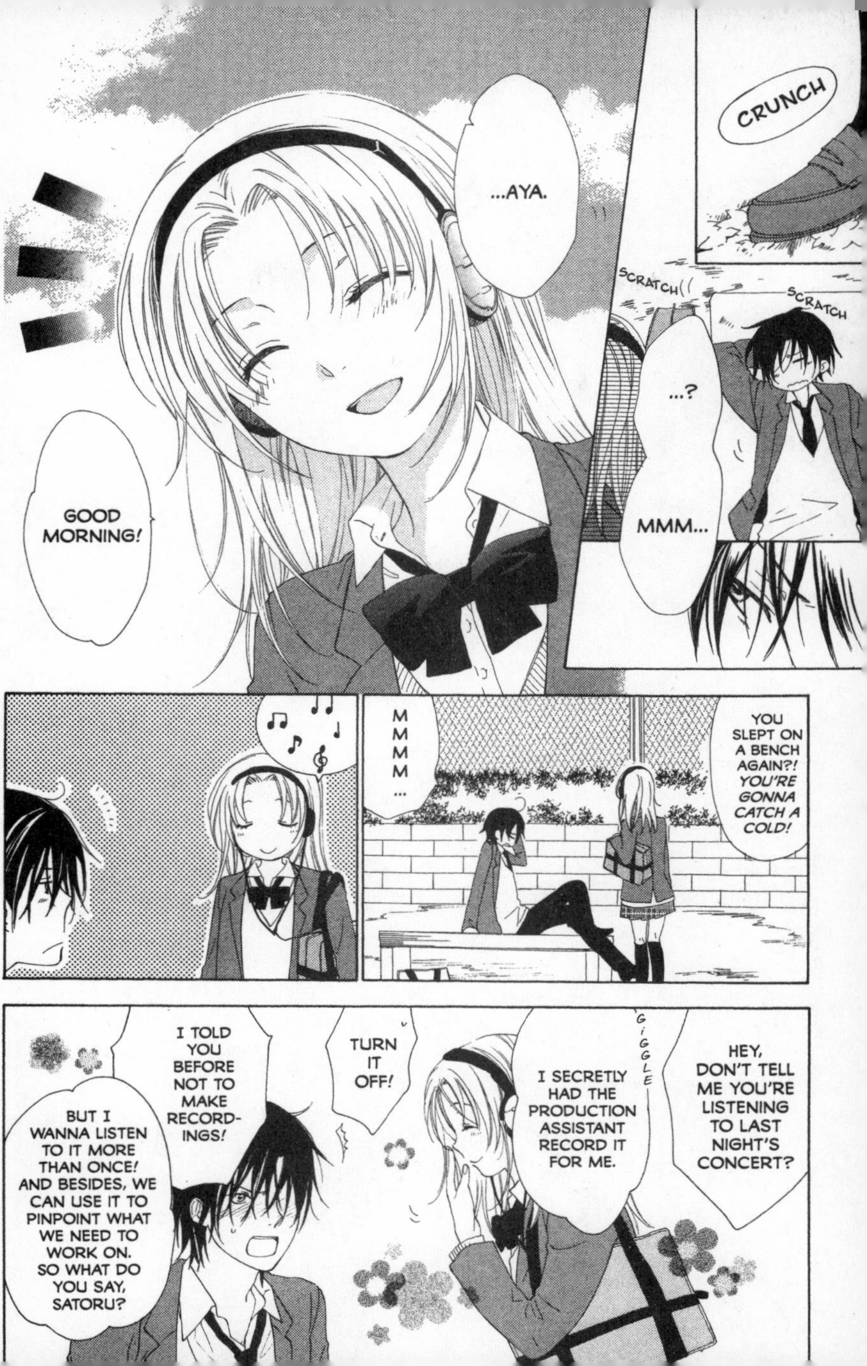
CRUNCH
SCRATCH
SCRATCH
...?
MMM...
...AYA.
GOOD MORNING!
YOU SLEPT ON A BENCH AGAIN?! *YOU'RE GONNA CATCH A COLD!*
MMMM...
HEY, DON'T TELL ME YOU'RE LISTENING TO LAST NIGHT'S CONCERT?
GIGGLE
I SECRETLY HAD THE PRODUCTION ASSISTANT RECORD IT FOR ME.
TURN IT OFF!
I TOLD YOU BEFORE NOT TO MAKE RECORD-INGS!
BUT I WANNA LISTEN TO IT MORE THAN ONCE! AND BESIDES, WE CAN USE IT TO PINPOINT WHAT WE NEED TO WORK ON. SO WHAT DO YOU SAY, SATORU?

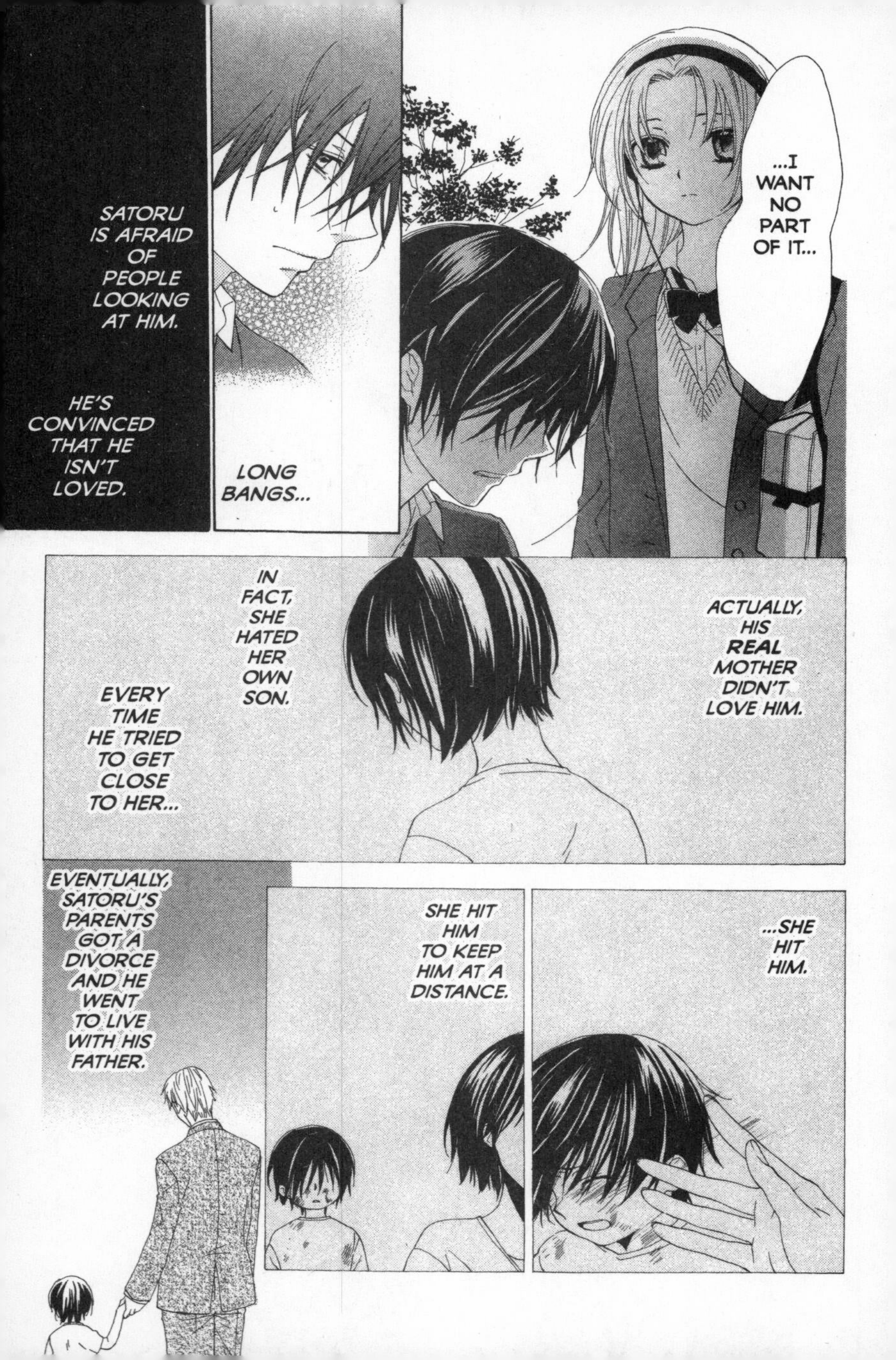
...I WANT NO PART OF IT...
LONG BANGS...
SATORU IS AFRAID OF PEOPLE LOOKING AT HIM.
HE'S CONVINCED THAT HE ISN'T LOVED.
ACTUALLY, HIS **REAL** MOTHER DIDN'T LOVE HIM.
IN FACT, SHE HATED HER OWN SON.
EVERY TIME HE TRIED TO GET CLOSE TO HER...
...SHE HIT HIM.
SHE HIT HIM TO KEEP HIM AT A DISTANCE.
EVENTUALLY, SATORU'S PARENTS GOT A DIVORCE AND HE WENT TO LIVE WITH HIS FATHER.

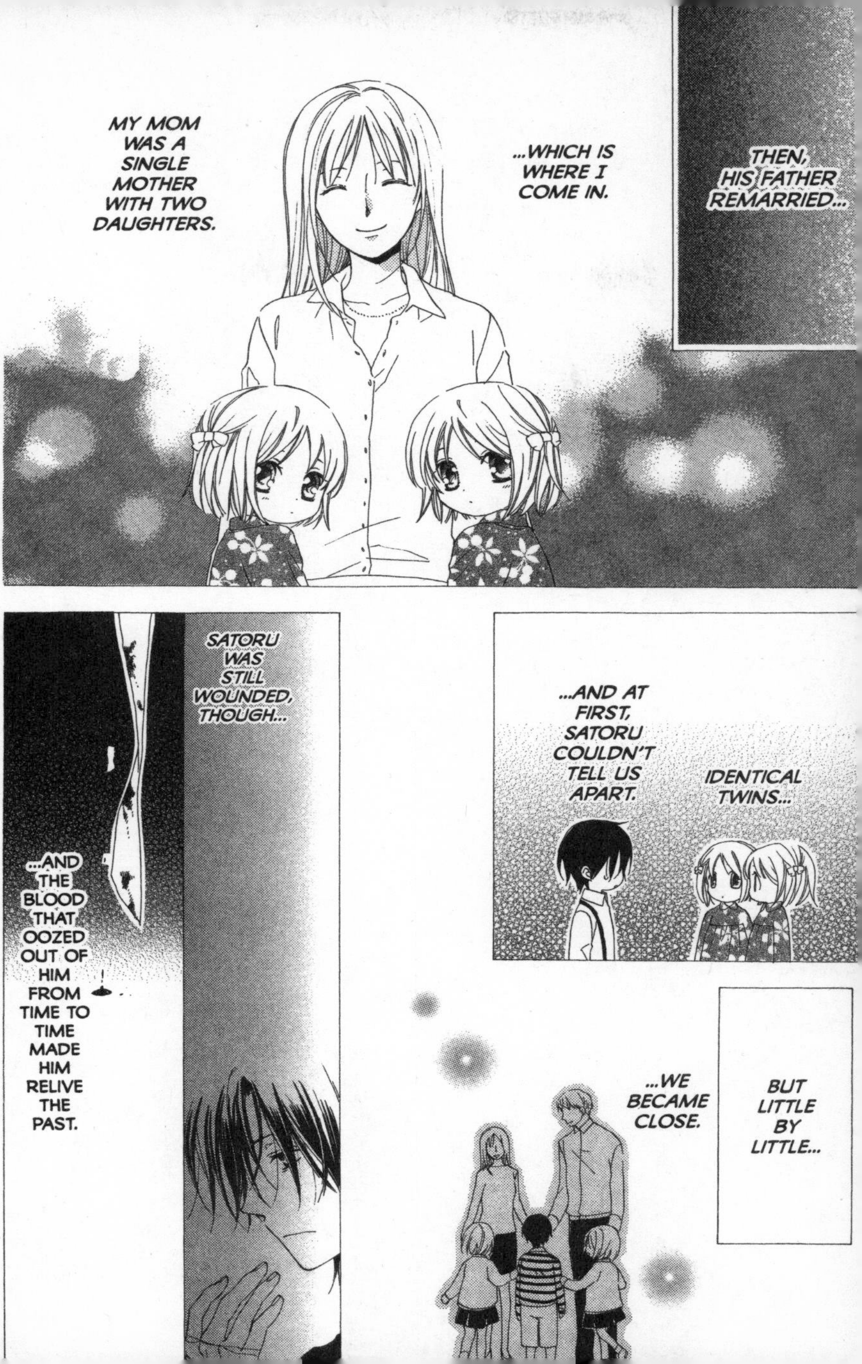
THEN, HIS FATHER REMARRIED...
MY MOM WAS A SINGLE MOTHER WITH TWO DAUGHTERS.
...WHICH IS WHERE I COME IN.
IDENTICAL TWINS...
...AND AT FIRST, SATORU COULDN'T TELL US APART.
BUT LITTLE BY LITTLE...
...WE BECAME CLOSE.
SATORU WAS STILL WOUNDED, THOUGH...
...AND THE BLOOD THAT OOZED OUT OF HIM FROM TIME TO TIME MADE HIM RELIVE THE PAST.

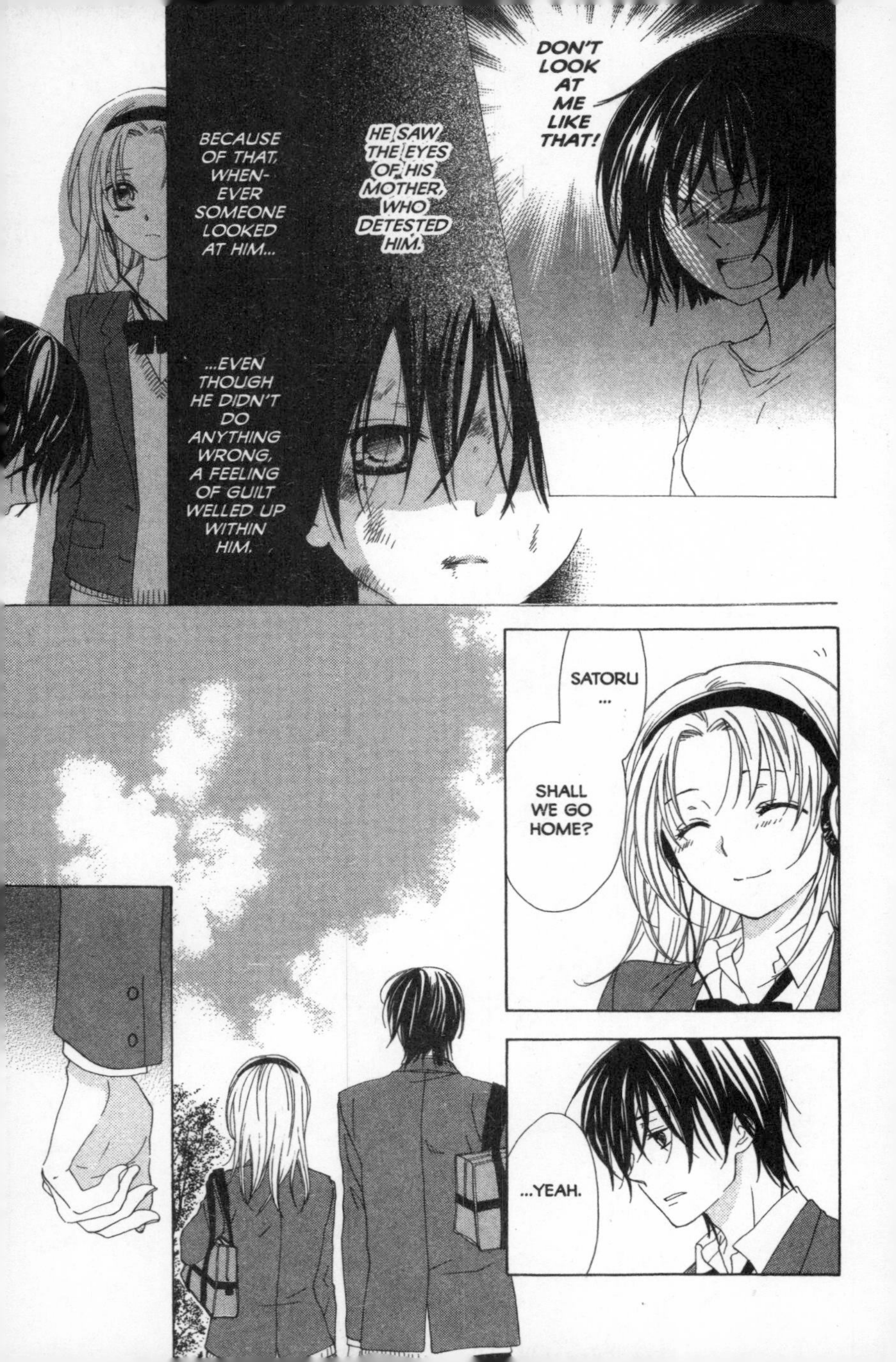
DON'T LOOK AT ME LIKE THAT!
HE SAW THE EYES OF HIS MOTHER, WHO DETESTED HIM.
BECAUSE OF THAT, WHEN-EVER SOMEONE LOOKED AT HIM...
...EVEN THOUGH HE DIDN'T DO ANYTHING WRONG, A FEELING OF GUILT WELLED UP WITHIN HIM.
SATORU...
SHALL WE GO HOME?
...YEAH.

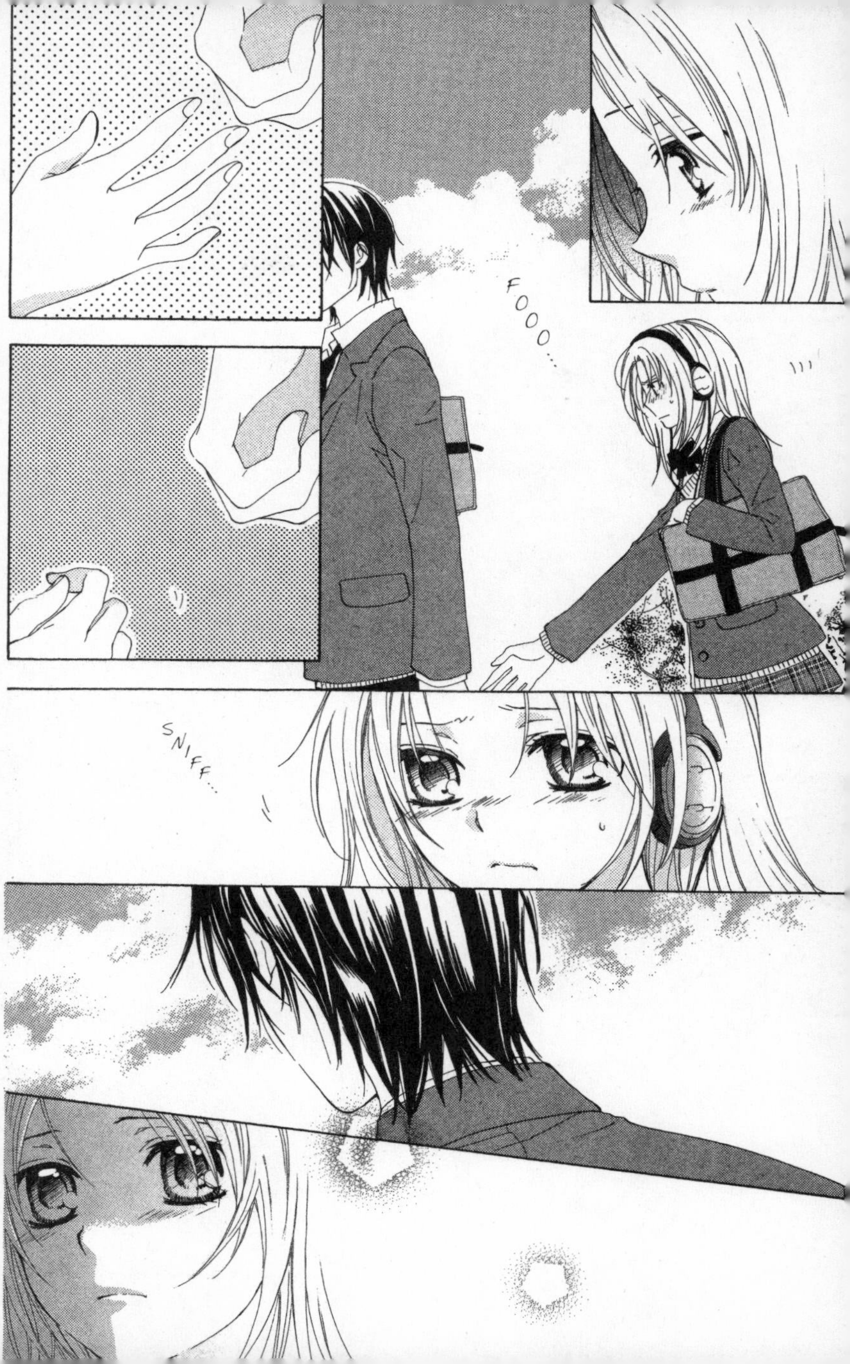
FOOO...
SNIFF...

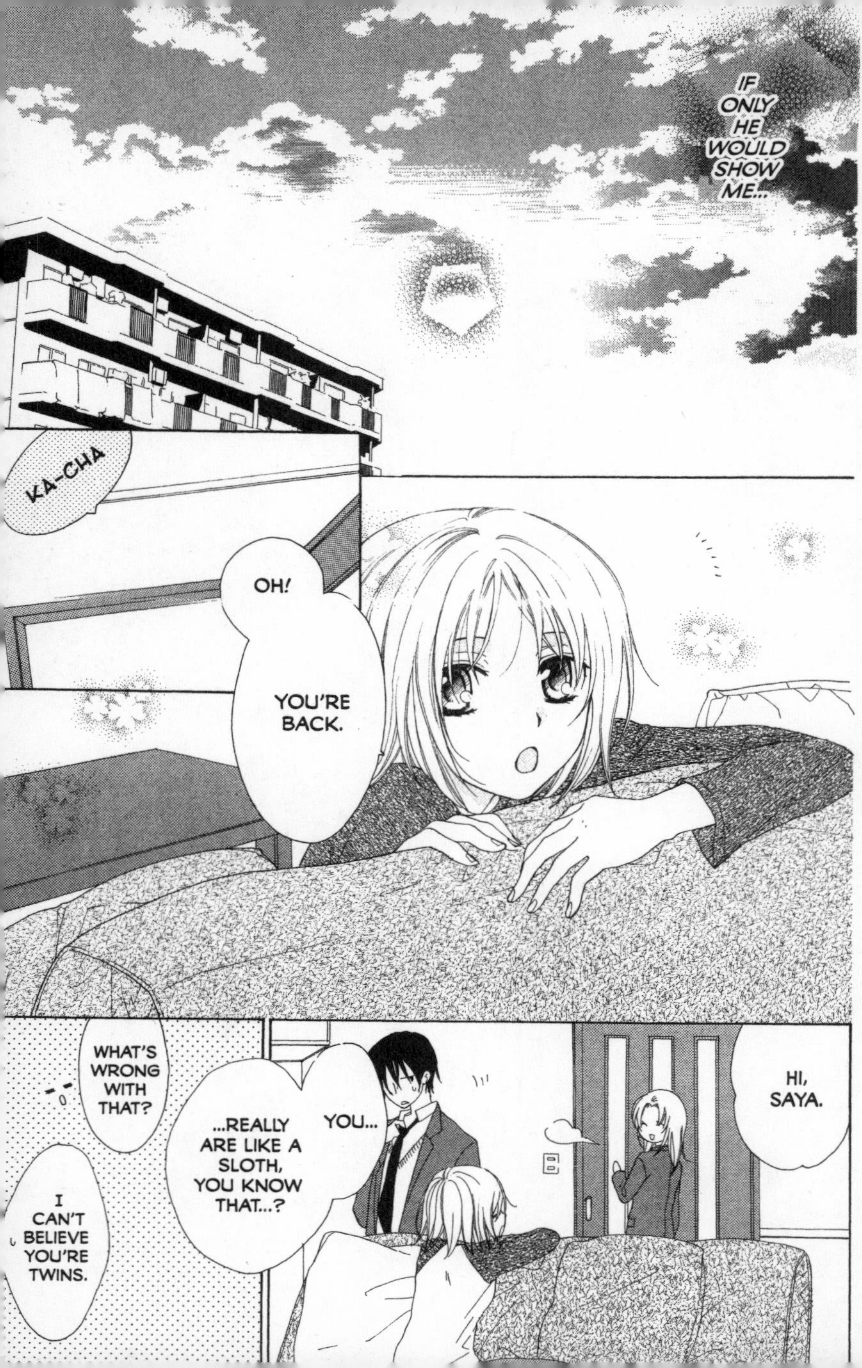
IF ONLY HE WOULD SHOW ME...
KA-CHA
OH!
YOU'RE BACK.
HI, SAYA.
YOU...
...REALLY ARE LIKE A SLOTH, YOU KNOW THAT...?
WHAT'S WRONG WITH THAT?
I CAN'T BELIEVE YOU'RE TWINS.

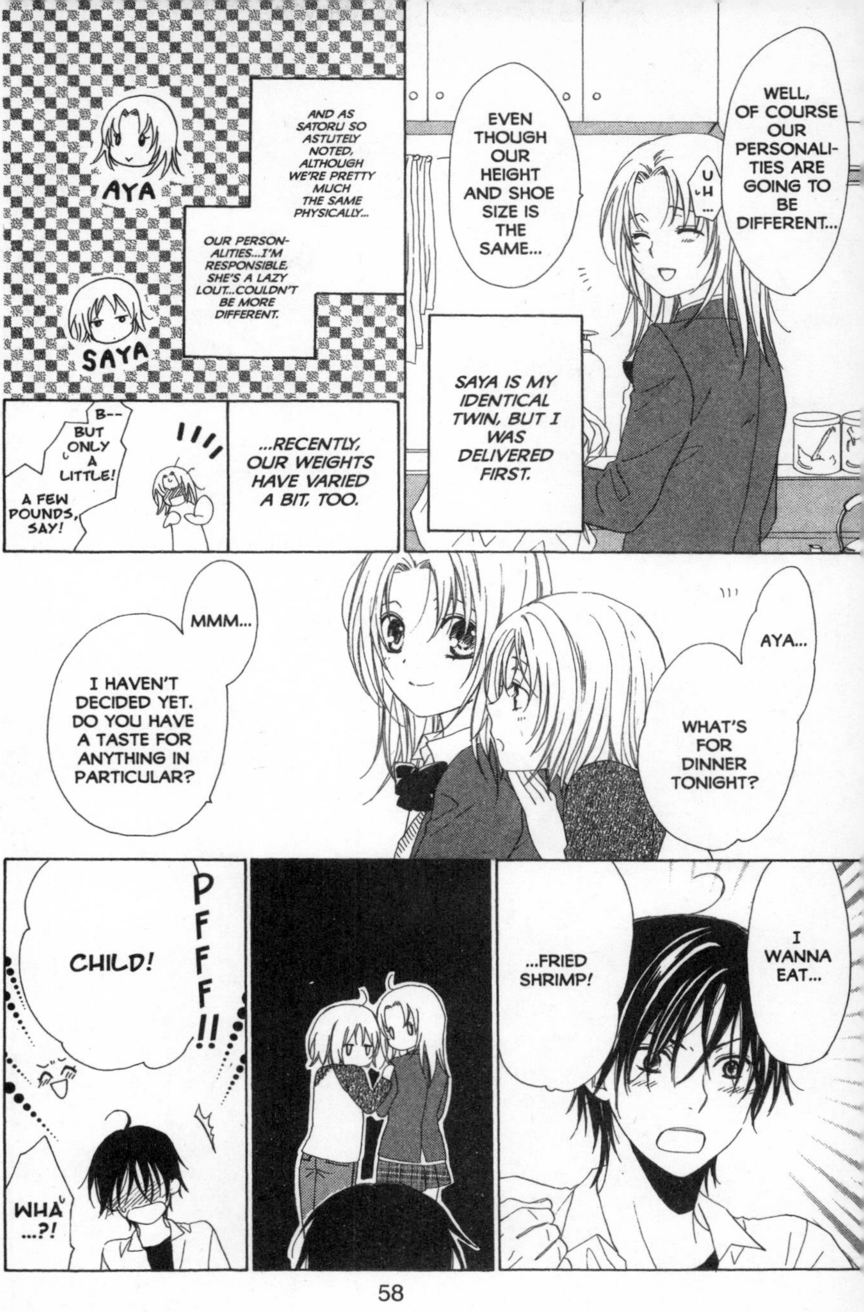
WELL, OF COURSE OUR PERSONALITIES ARE GOING TO BE DIFFERENT...
UH...
EVEN THOUGH OUR HEIGHT AND SHOE SIZE IS THE SAME...
SAYA IS MY IDENTICAL TWIN, BUT I WAS DELIVERED FIRST.
AND AS SATORU SO ASTUTELY NOTED, ALTHOUGH WE'RE PRETTY MUCH THE SAME PHYSICALLY...
OUR PERSONALITIES...I'M RESPONSIBLE, SHE'S A LAZY LOUT...COULDN'T BE MORE DIFFERENT.
AYA
SAYA
...RECENTLY, OUR WEIGHTS HAVE VARIED A BIT, TOO.
B-- BUT ONLY A LITTLE!
A FEW POUNDS, SAY!
AYA...
WHAT'S FOR DINNER TONIGHT?
MMM...
I HAVEN'T DECIDED YET. DO YOU HAVE A TASTE FOR ANYTHING IN PARTICULAR?
I WANNA EAT...
...FRIED SHRIMP!
CHILD!
PFFF!!
WHA ...?!

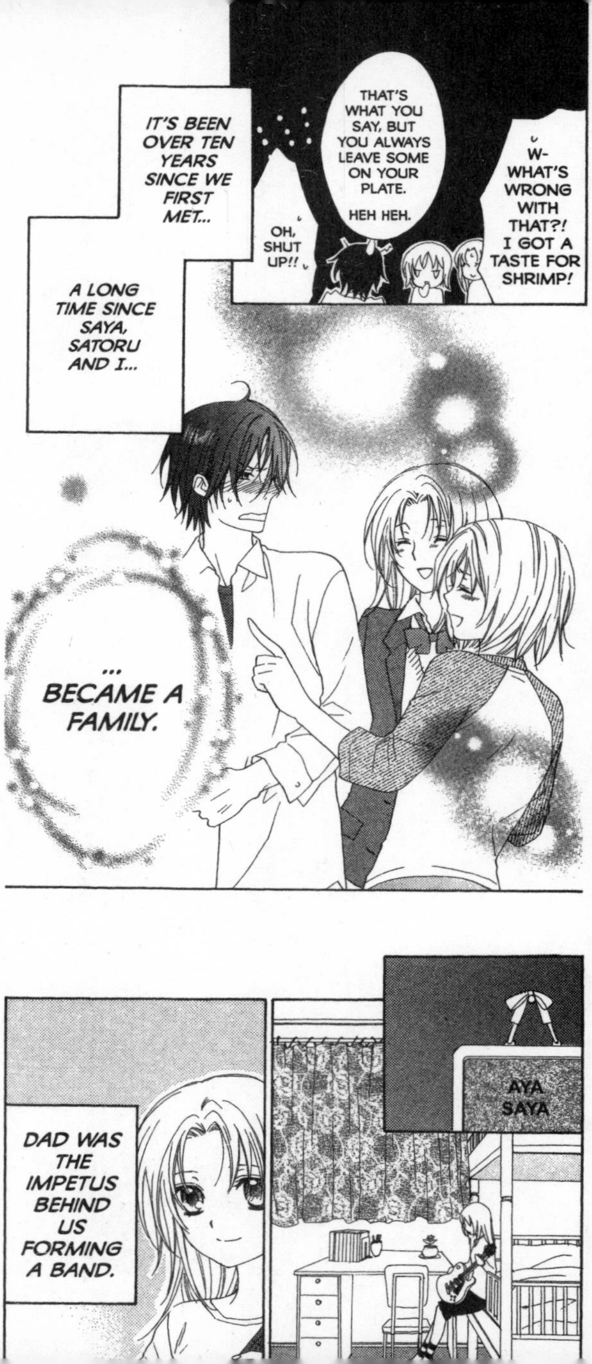
THAT'S WHAT YOU SAY, BUT YOU ALWAYS LEAVE SOME ON YOUR PLATE.
HEH HEH.
W- WHAT'S WRONG WITH THAT?! I GOT A TASTE FOR SHRIMP!
OH, SHUT UP!!
IT'S BEEN OVER TEN YEARS SINCE WE FIRST MET...
A LONG TIME SINCE SAYA, SATORU AND I...
... BECAME A FAMILY.
AYA
SAYA
DAD WAS THE IMPETUS BEHIND US FORMING A BAND.

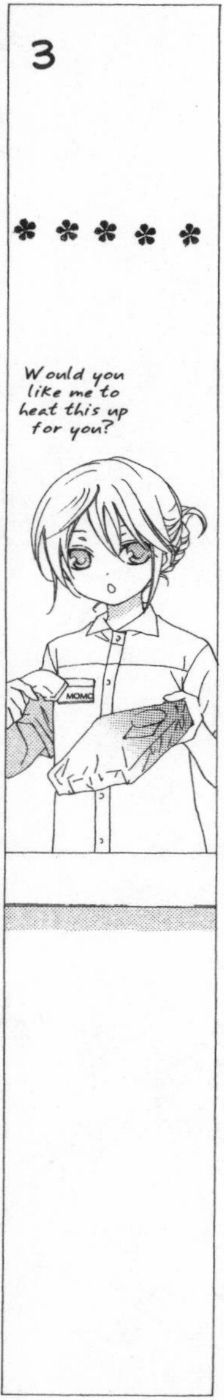
3
Would you like me to heat this up for you?
MOMO

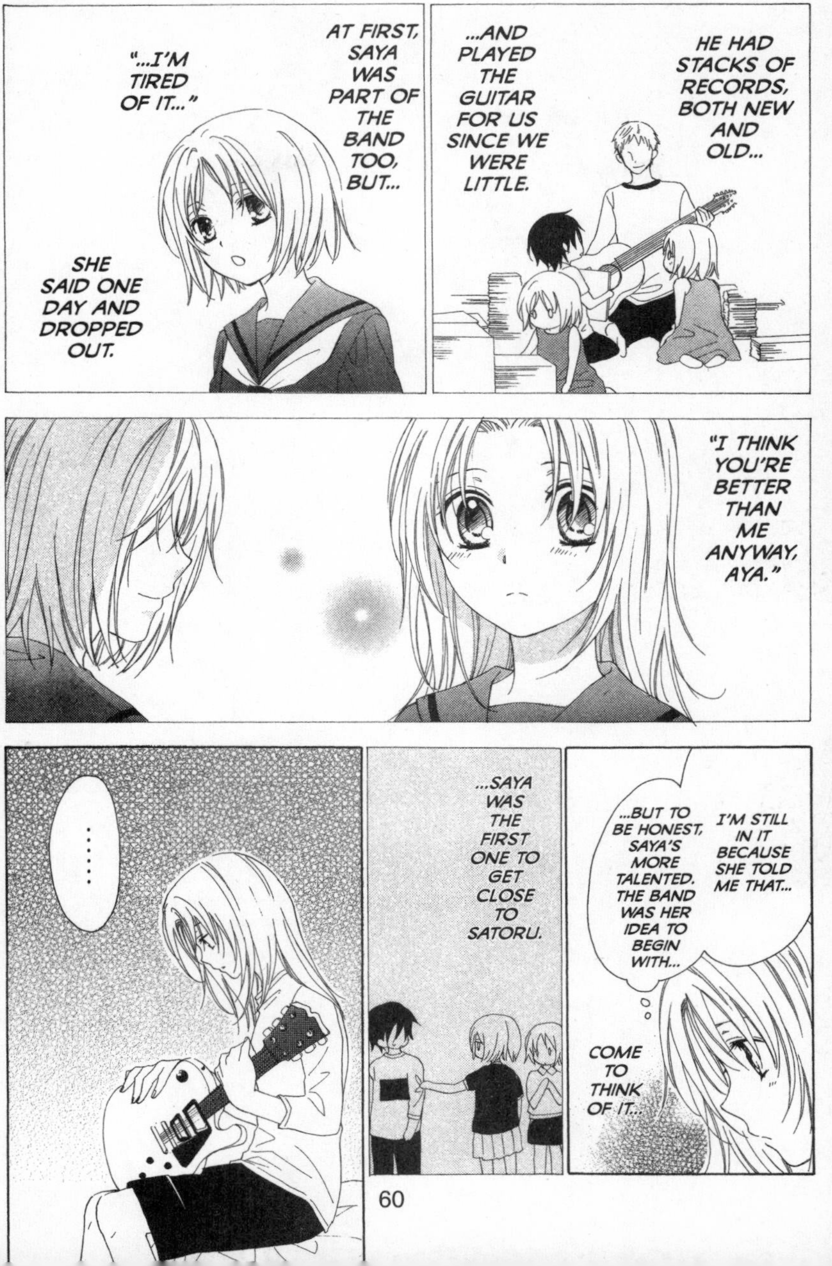
HE HAD STACKS OF RECORDS, BOTH NEW AND OLD...
...AND PLAYED THE GUITAR FOR US SINCE WE WERE LITTLE.
AT FIRST, SAYA WAS PART OF THE BAND TOO, BUT...
"...I'M TIRED OF IT..."
SHE SAID ONE DAY AND DROPPED OUT.
"I THINK YOU'RE BETTER THAN ME ANYWAY, AYA."
I'M STILL IN IT BECAUSE SHE TOLD ME THAT...
...BUT TO BE HONEST, SAYA'S MORE TALENTED. THE BAND WAS HER IDEA TO BEGIN WITH...
COME TO THINK OF IT...
...SAYA WAS THE FIRST ONE TO GET CLOSE TO SATORU.
......

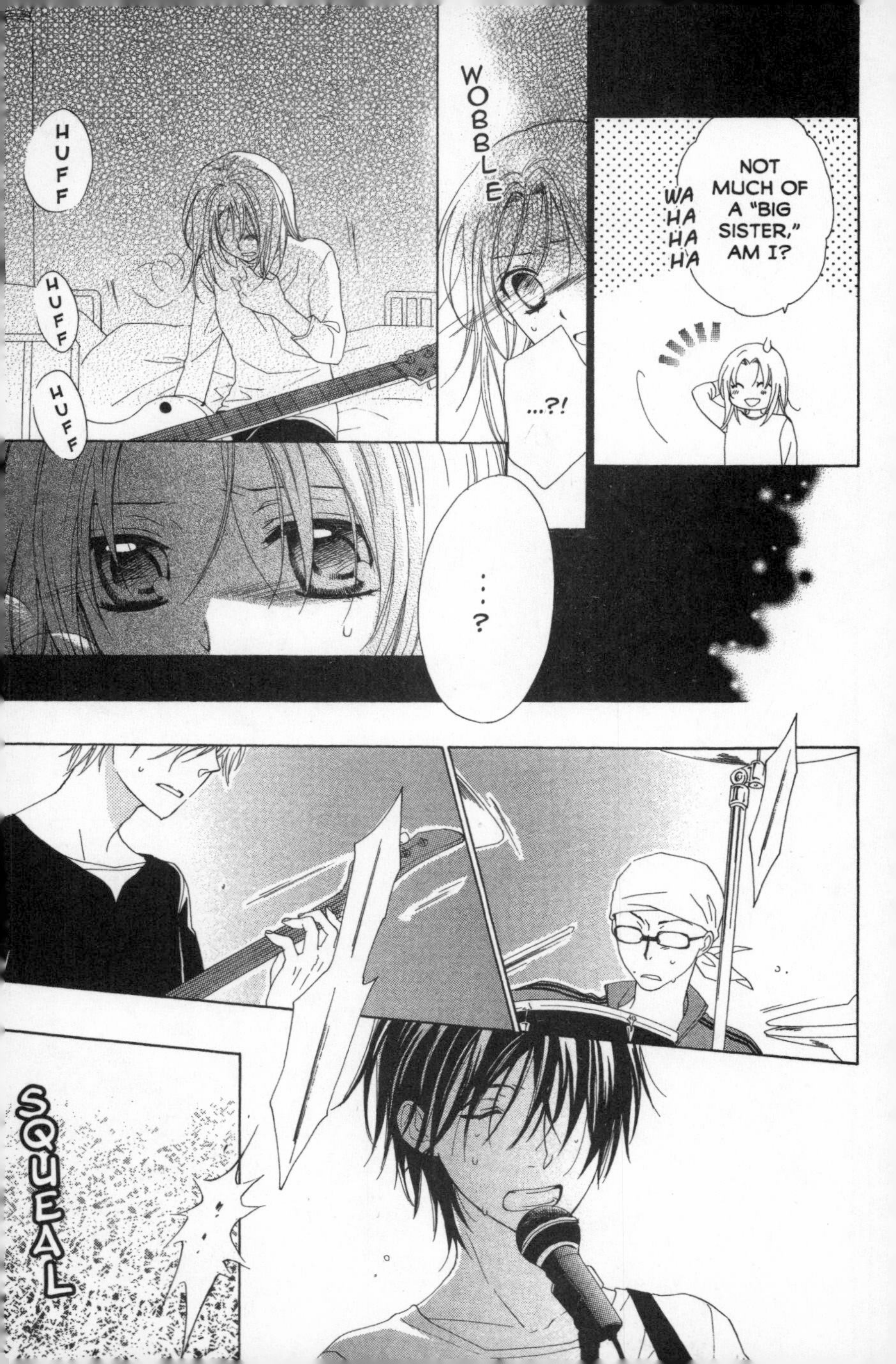
NOT MUCH OF A "BIG SISTER," AM I?
WA HA HA HA
WOBBLE
...?!
HUFF
HUFF
HUFF
...?
SQUEAL

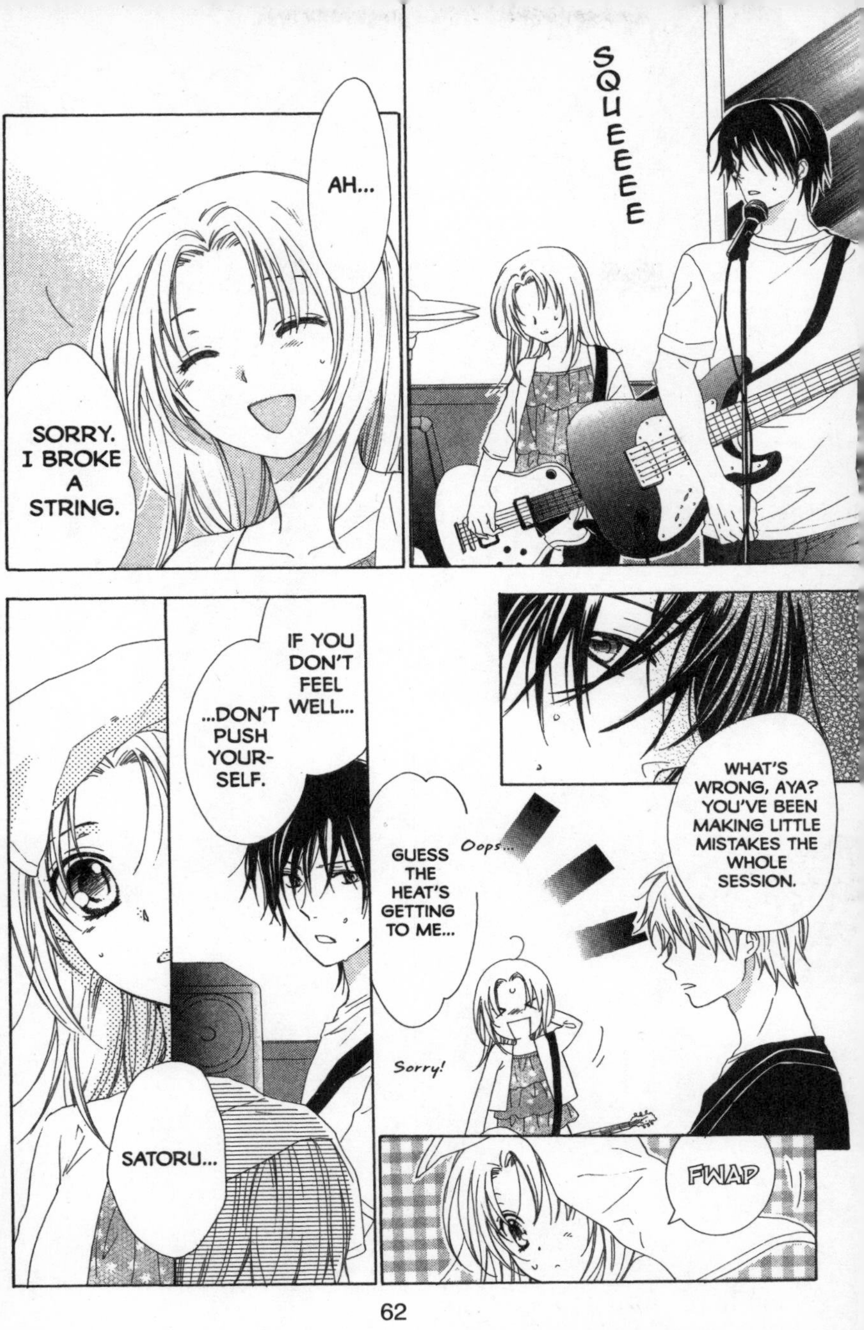
SQUEEEE
AH...
SORRY. I BROKE A STRING.
WHAT'S WRONG, AYA? YOU'VE BEEN MAKING LITTLE MISTAKES THE WHOLE SESSION.
Oops...
GUESS THE HEAT'S GETTING TO ME...
Sorry!
FWAP
IF YOU DON'T FEEL WELL...
...DON'T PUSH YOURSELF.
SATORU...

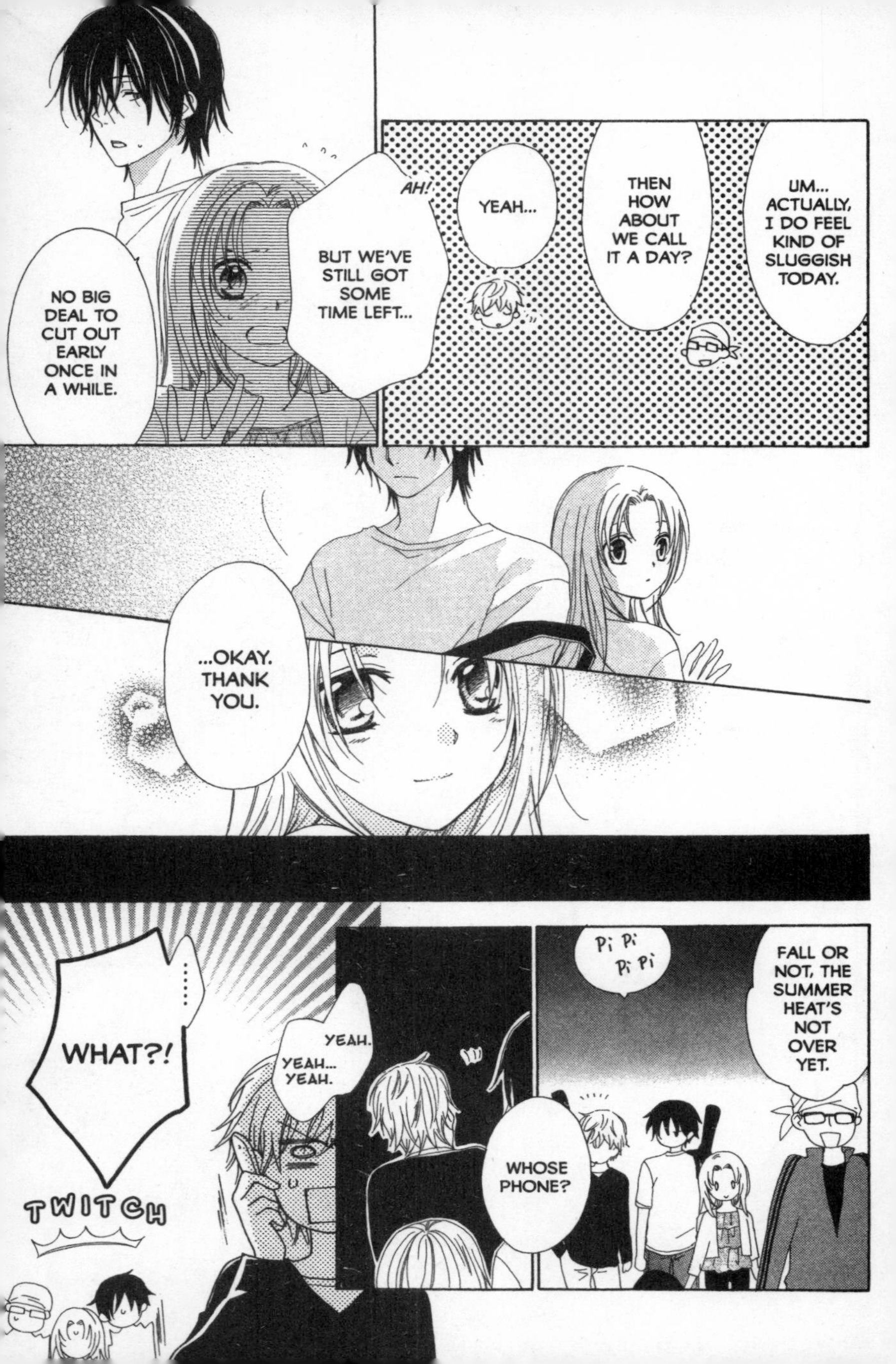
UM... ACTUALLY, I DO FEEL KIND OF SLUGGISH TODAY.
THEN HOW ABOUT WE CALL IT A DAY?
YEAH...
AH!
BUT WE'VE STILL GOT SOME TIME LEFT...
NO BIG DEAL TO CUT OUT EARLY ONCE IN A WHILE.
...OKAY. THANK YOU.
FALL OR NOT, THE SUMMER HEAT'S NOT OVER YET.
Pi Pi Pi Pi
WHOSE PHONE?
YEAH.
YEAH... YEAH.
......
WHAT?!
TWITCH

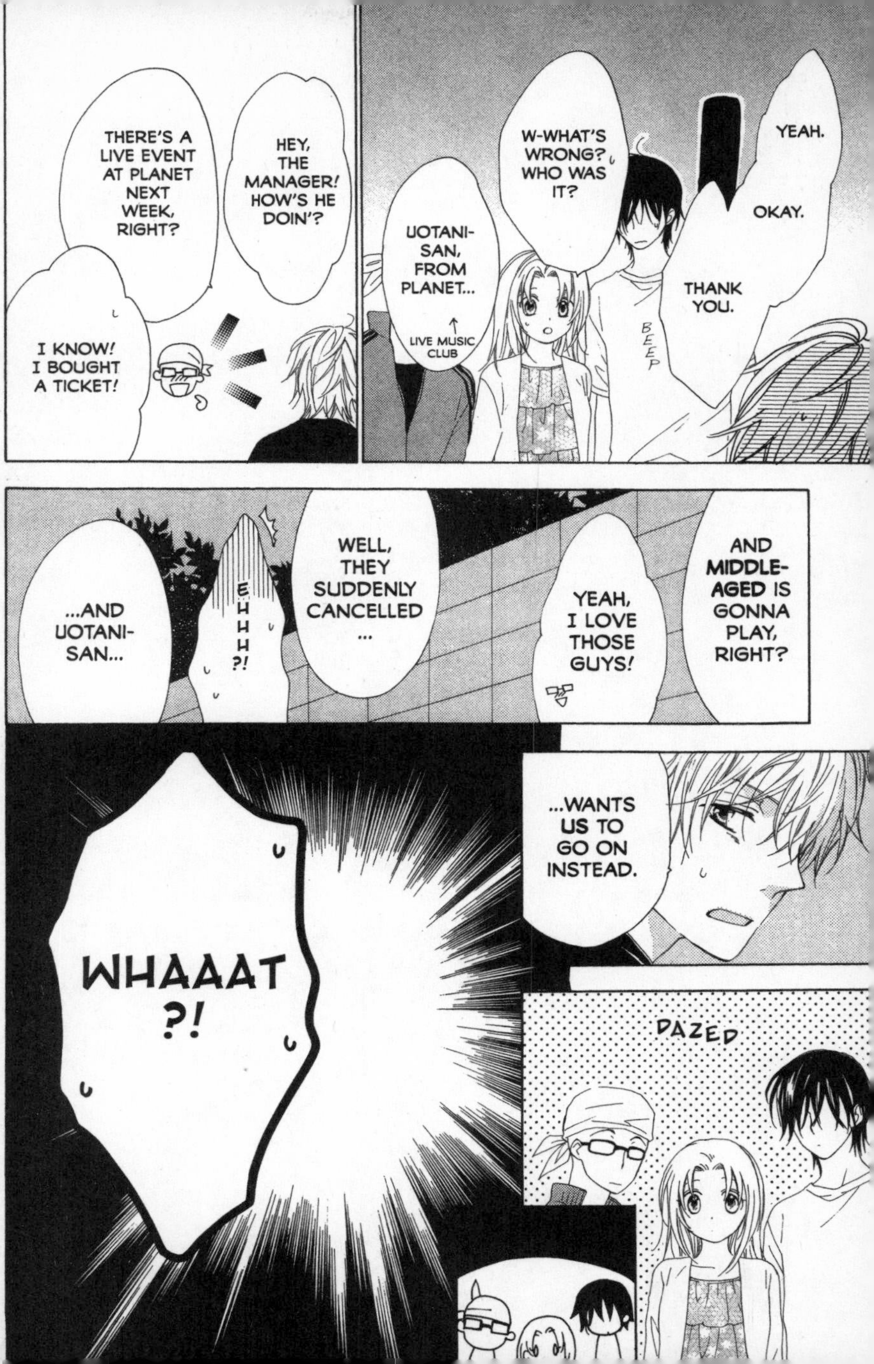
YEAH.
OKAY.
THANK YOU.
BEEP
W-WHAT'S WRONG? WHO WAS IT?
UOTANI-SAN, FROM PLANET...
LIVE MUSIC CLUB
HEY, THE MANAGER! HOW'S HE DOIN'?
THERE'S A LIVE EVENT AT PLANET NEXT WEEK, RIGHT?
I KNOW! I BOUGHT A TICKET!
AND MIDDLE-AGED IS GONNA PLAY, RIGHT?
YEAH, I LOVE THOSE GUYS!
WELL, THEY SUDDENLY CANCELLED ...
EHHHH?!
...AND UOTANI-SAN...
...WANTS US TO GO ON INSTEAD.
DAZED
WHAAAT ?!

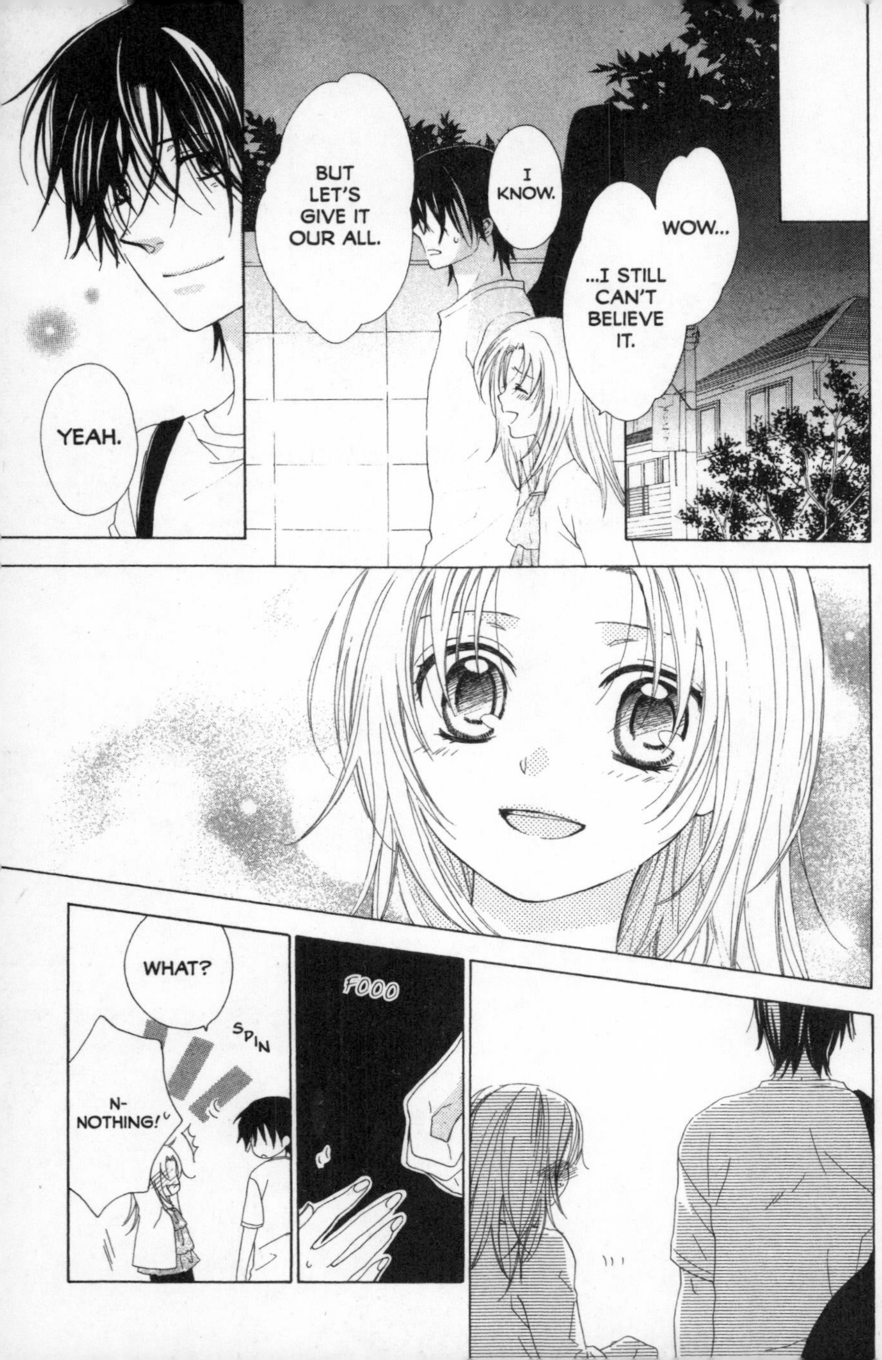
WOW...
...I STILL CAN'T BELIEVE IT.
I KNOW.
BUT LET'S GIVE IT OUR ALL.
YEAH.
FOOO
WHAT?
SPIN
N-NOTHING!

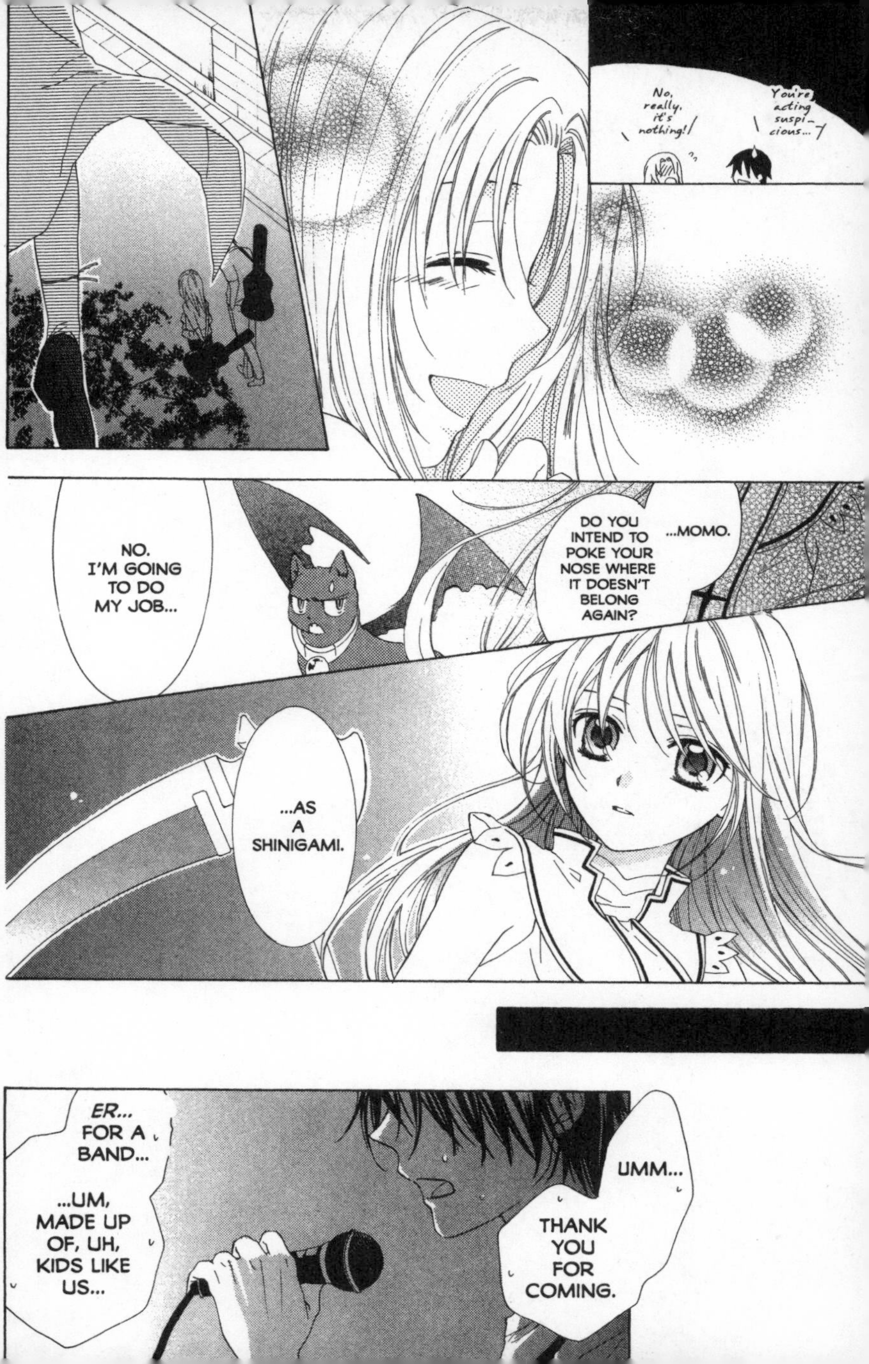

You're acting suspi-cious...
No, really, it's nothing!
...MOMO.
DO YOU INTEND TO POKE YOUR NOSE WHERE IT DOESN'T BELONG AGAIN?
NO. I'M GOING TO DO MY JOB...
...AS A SHINIGAMI.
UMM...
THANK YOU FOR COMING.
ER... FOR A BAND...
...UM, MADE UP OF, UH, KIDS LIKE US...

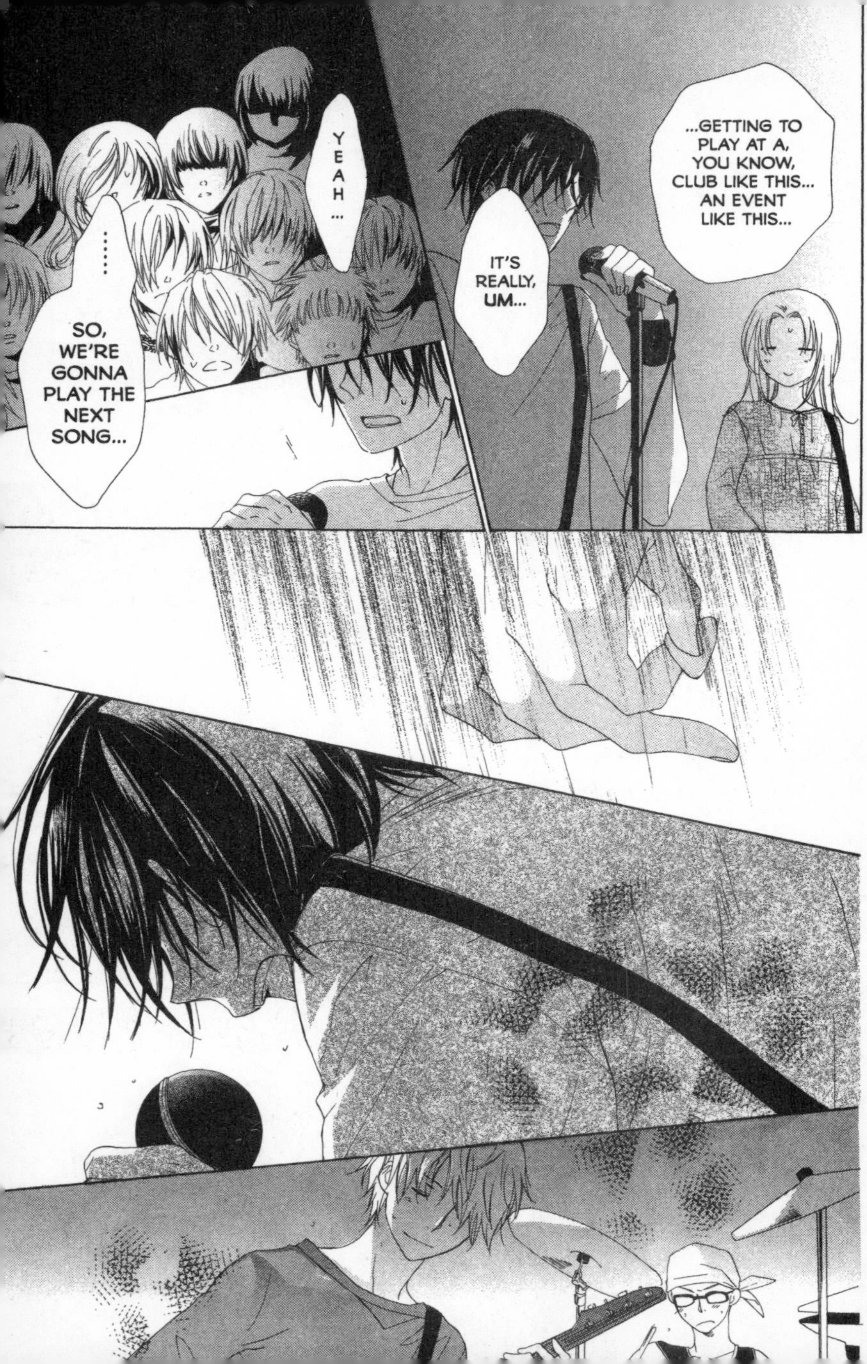
IT'S REALLY, UM...
...GETTING TO PLAY AT A, YOU KNOW, CLUB LIKE THIS... AN EVENT LIKE THIS...
YEAH...
......
SO, WE'RE GONNA PLAY THE NEXT SONG...

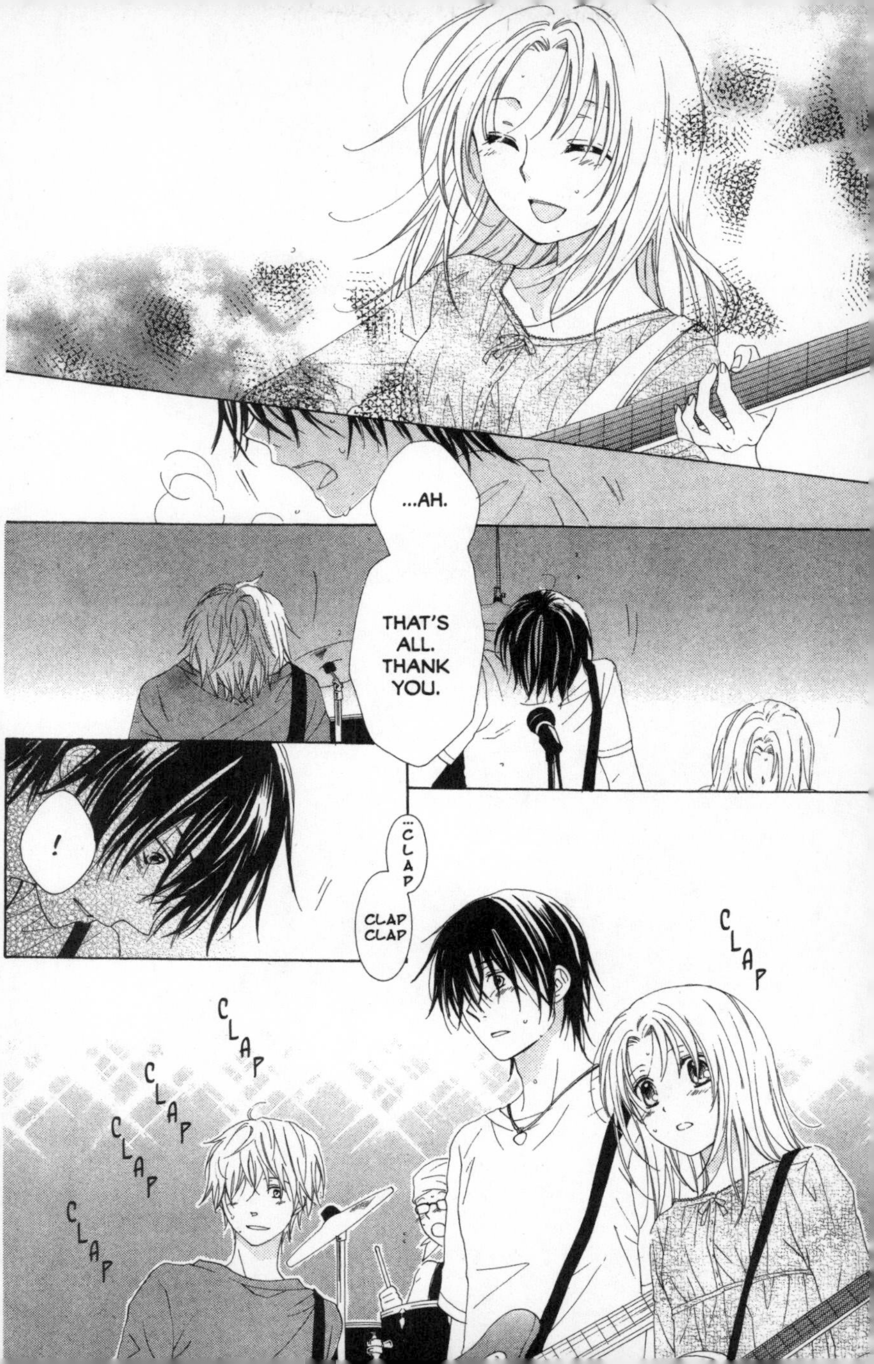
...AH.
THAT'S ALL. THANK YOU.
...CLAP
CLAP CLAP
!
CLAP
CLAP
CLAP
CLAP
CLAP

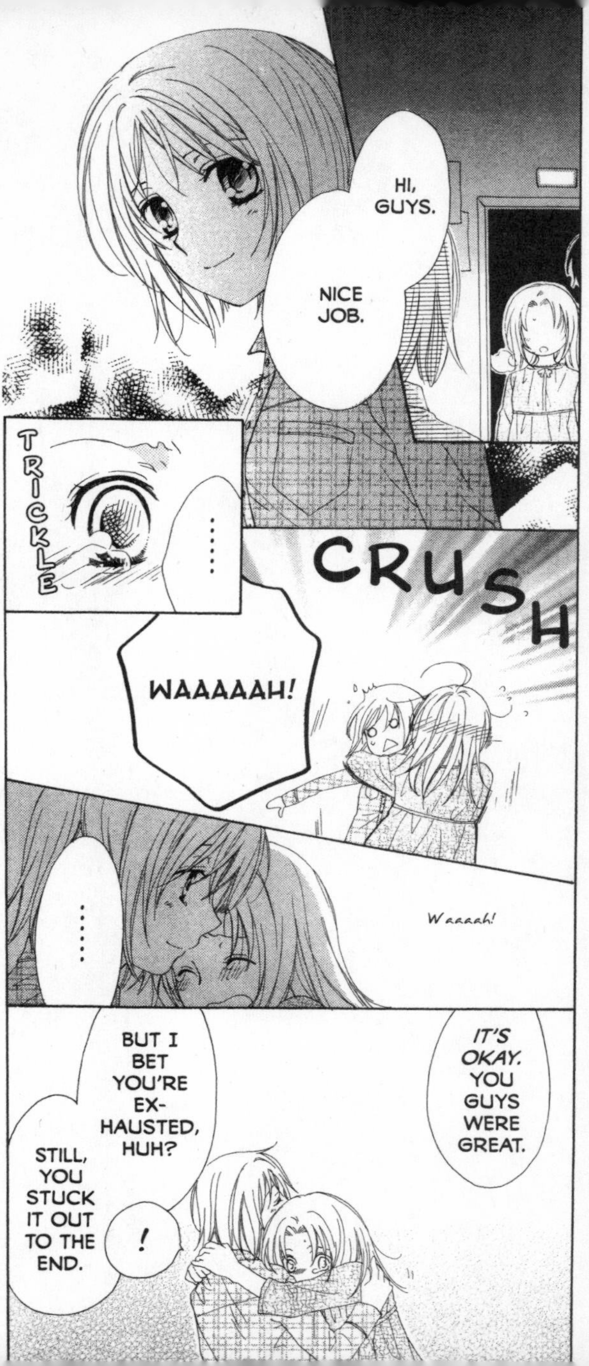
HI, GUYS.
NICE JOB.
TRICKLE
......
CRUSH
WAAAAAH!
Waaaah!
......
IT'S OKAY. YOU GUYS WERE GREAT.
BUT I BET YOU'RE EX-HAUSTED, HUH?
!
STILL, YOU STUCK IT OUT TO THE END.

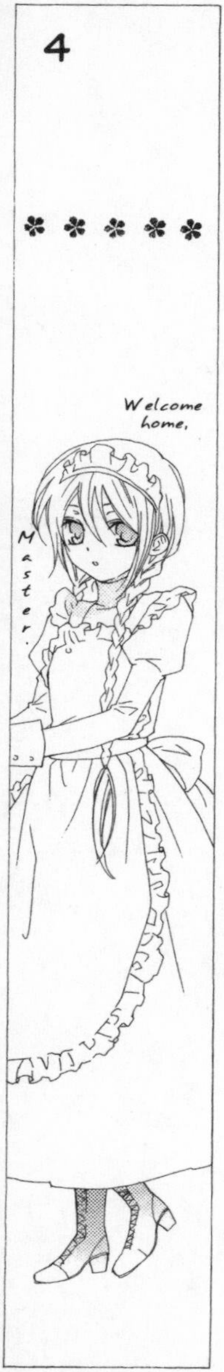
4
✽ ✽ ✽ ✽ ✽
Welcome home,
Master.

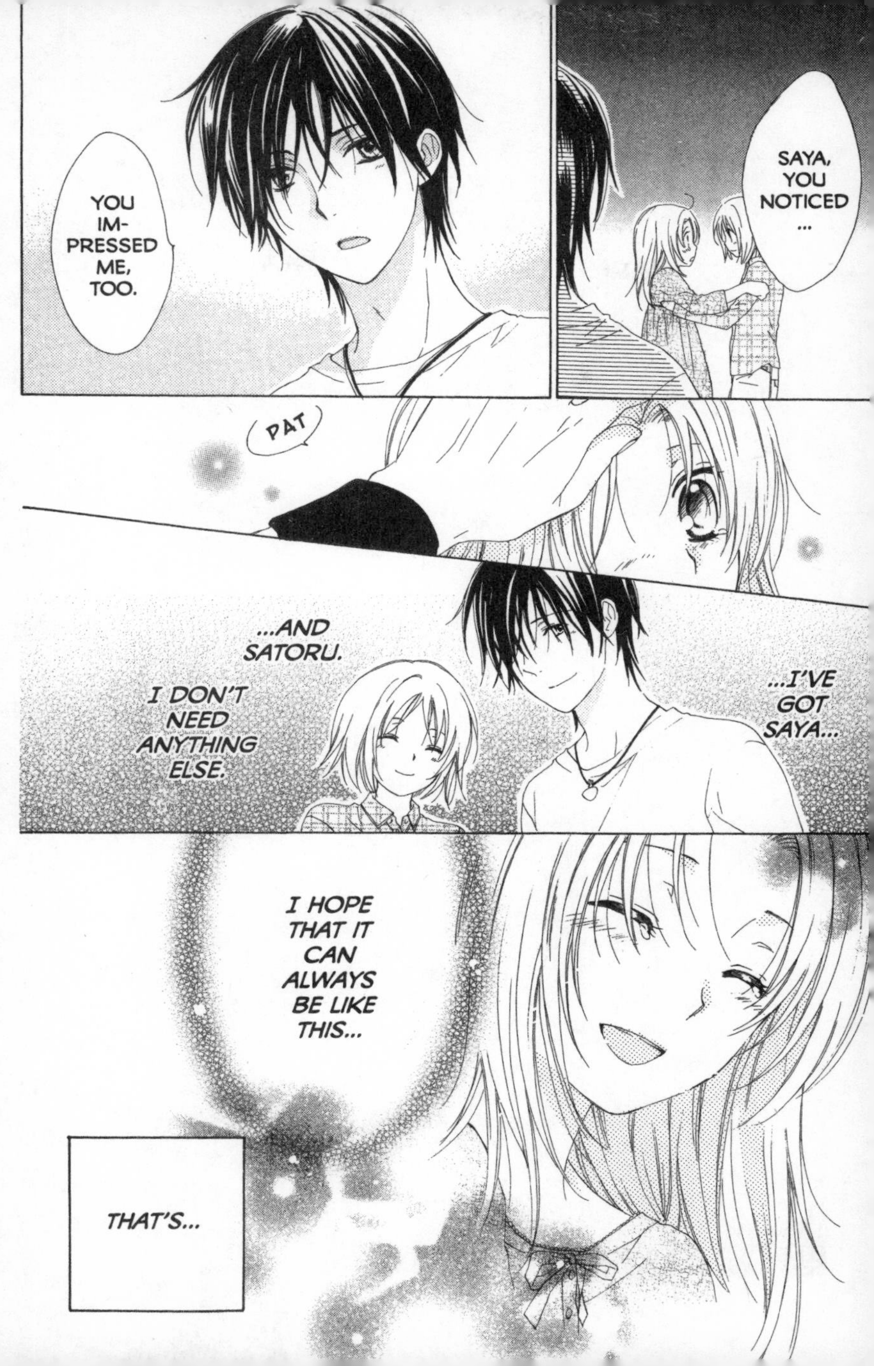
SAYA, YOU NOTICED ...
YOU IM-PRESSED ME, TOO.
PAT
...I'VE GOT SAYA...
...AND SATORU.
I DON'T NEED ANYTHING ELSE.
I HOPE THAT IT CAN ALWAYS BE LIKE THIS...
THAT'S...

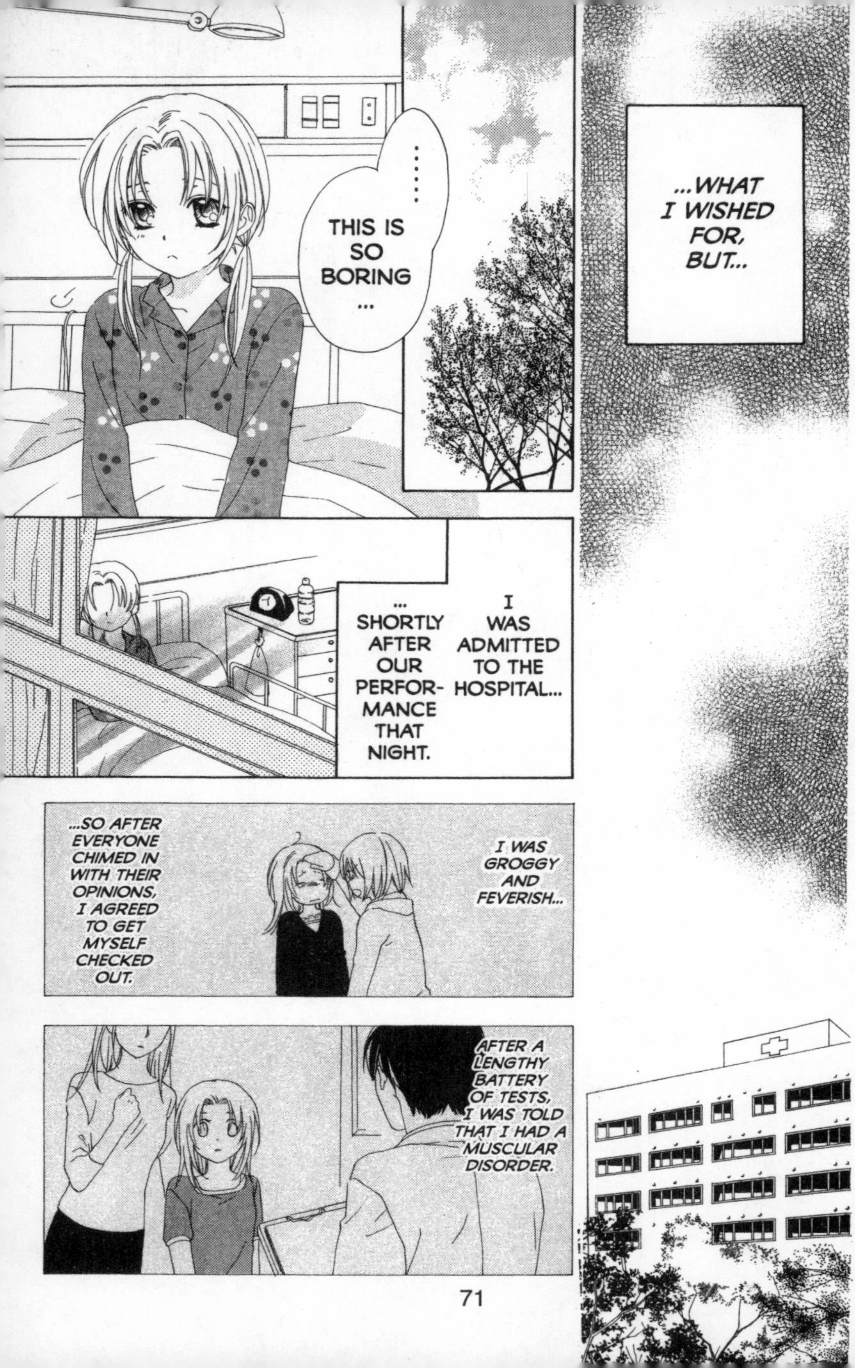
...WHAT I WISHED FOR, BUT...
......
THIS IS SO BORING ...
I WAS ADMITTED TO THE HOSPITAL...
... SHORTLY AFTER OUR PERFORMANCE THAT NIGHT.
I WAS GROGGY AND FEVERISH...
...SO AFTER EVERYONE CHIMED IN WITH THEIR OPINIONS, I AGREED TO GET MYSELF CHECKED OUT.
AFTER A LENGTHY BATTERY OF TESTS, I WAS TOLD THAT I HAD A MUSCULAR DISORDER.

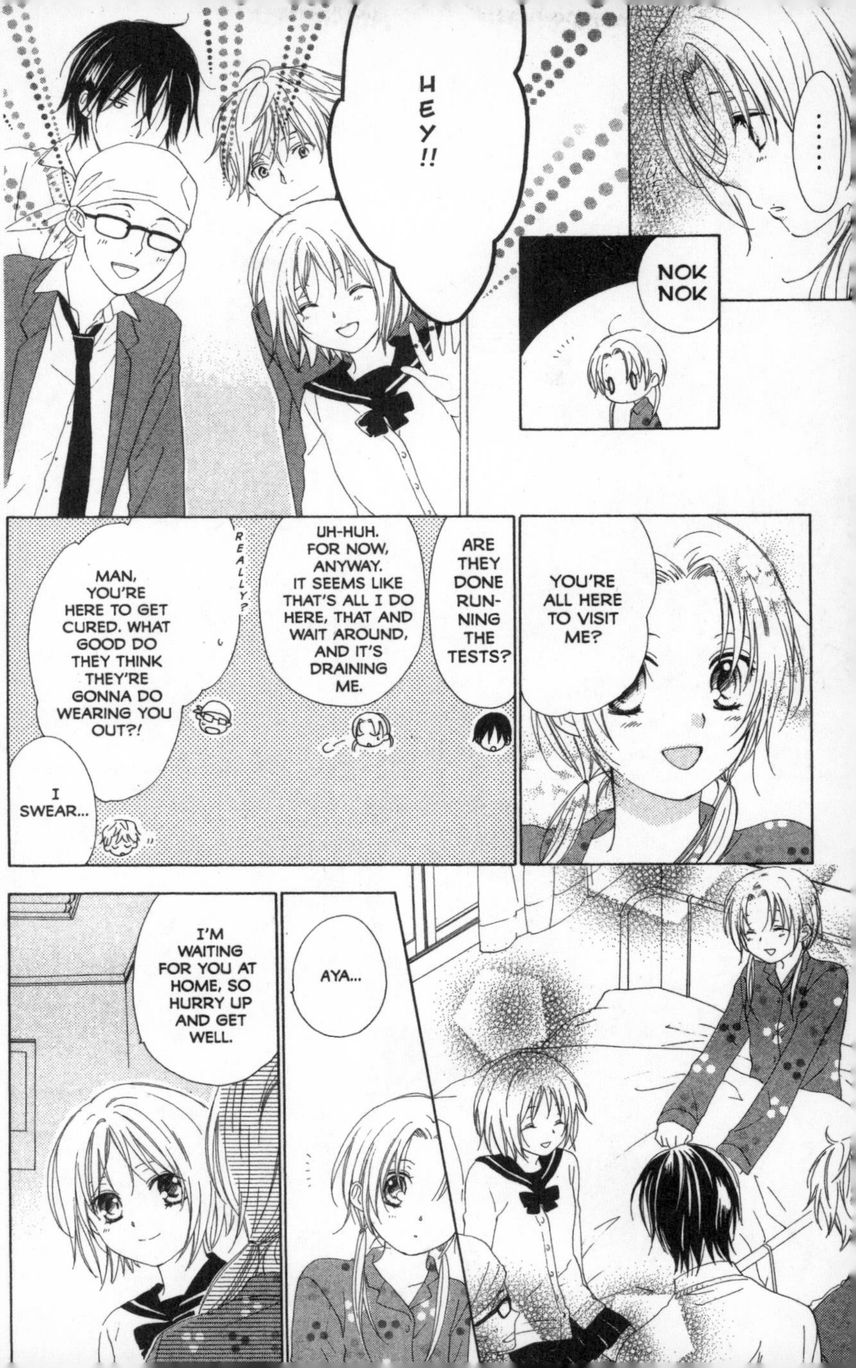
......
NOK NOK
HEY!!
YOU'RE ALL HERE TO VISIT ME?
ARE THEY DONE RUN-NING THE TESTS?
UH-HUH. FOR NOW, ANYWAY. IT SEEMS LIKE THAT'S ALL I DO HERE, THAT AND WAIT AROUND, AND IT'S DRAINING ME.
REALLY?
MAN, YOU'RE HERE TO GET CURED. WHAT GOOD DO THEY THINK THEY'RE GONNA DO WEARING YOU OUT?!
I SWEAR...
AYA...
I'M WAITING FOR YOU AT HOME, SO HURRY UP AND GET WELL.

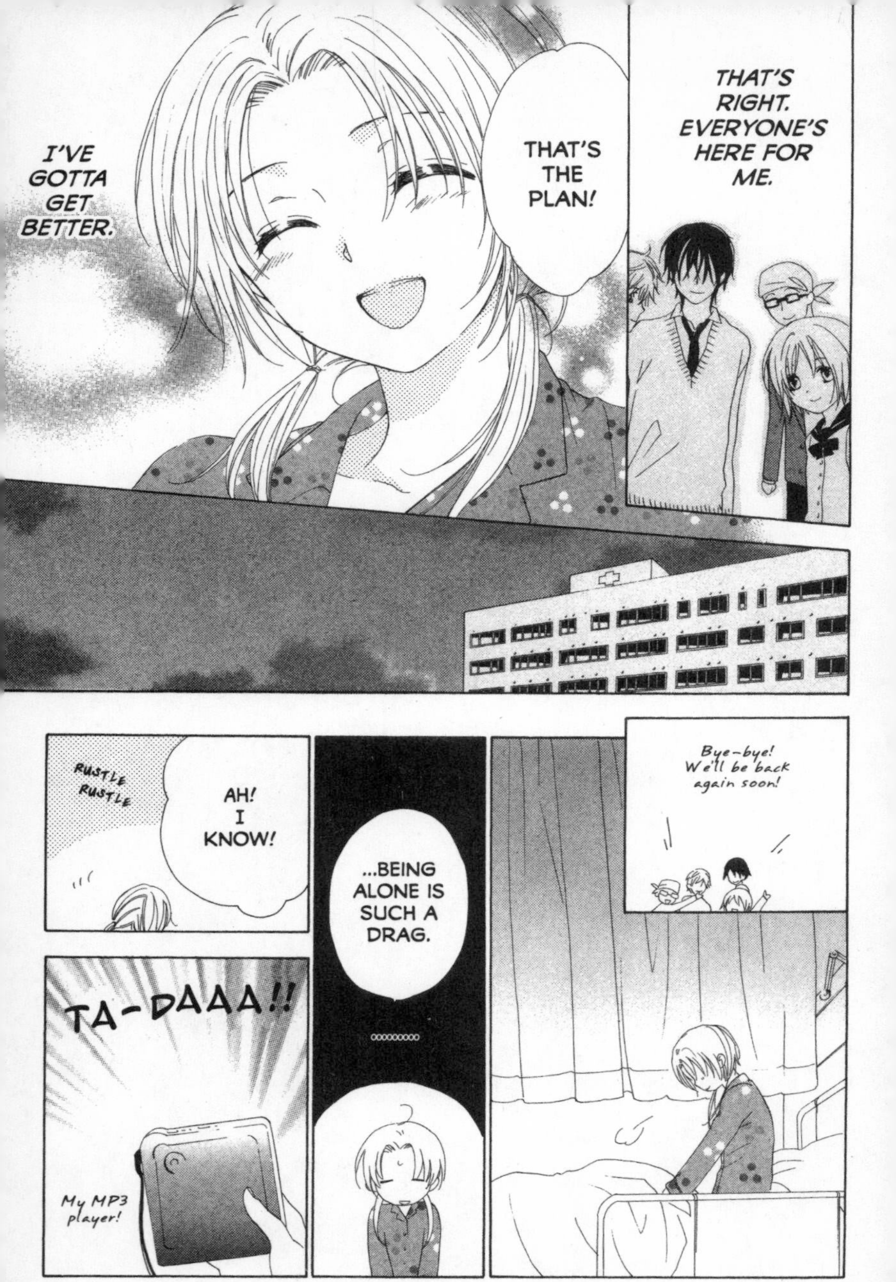
THAT'S RIGHT. EVERYONE'S HERE FOR ME.
THAT'S THE PLAN!
I'VE GOTTA GET BETTER.
Bye-bye! We'll be back again soon!
...BEING ALONE IS SUCH A DRAG.
RUSTLE RUSTLE
AH! I KNOW!
TA-DAAA!!
My MP3 player!

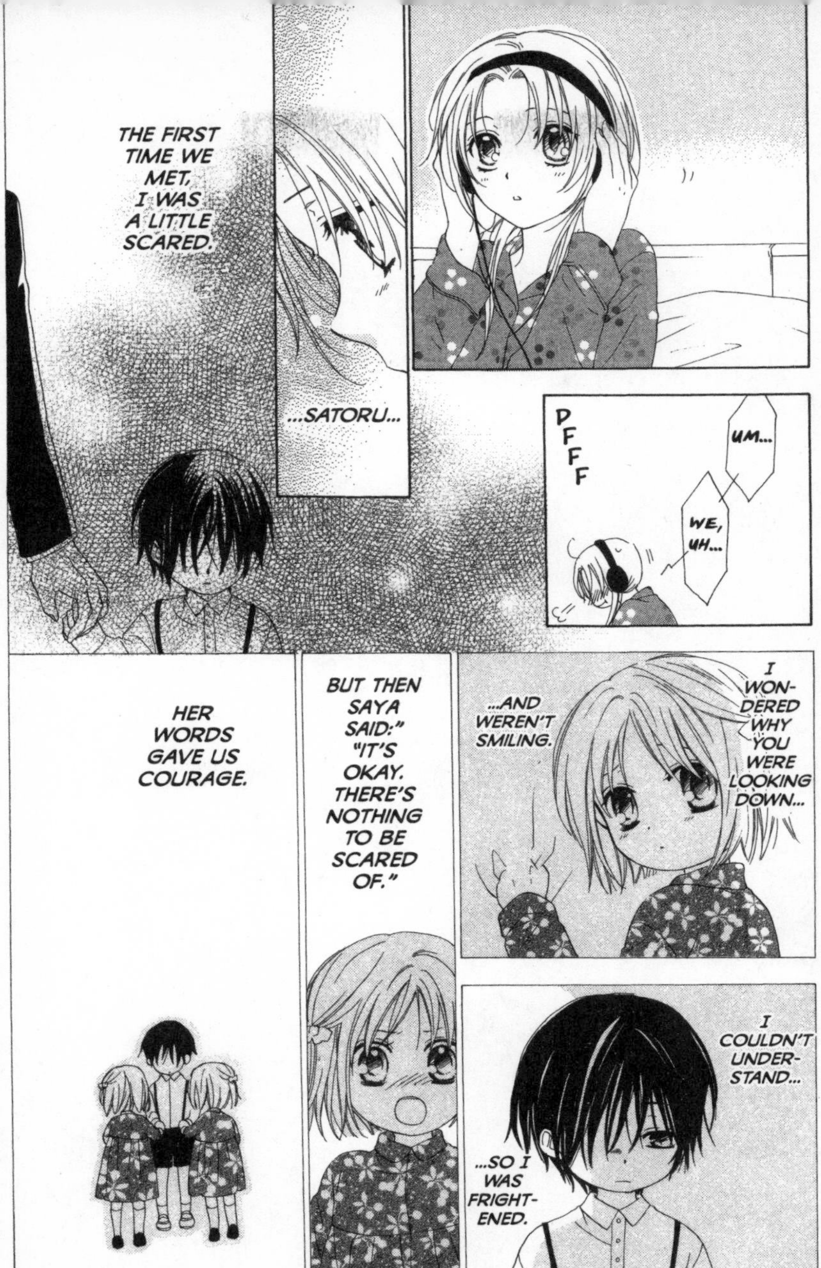
...SATORU...
PFFF
UM...
WE, UH...
THE FIRST TIME WE MET, I WAS A LITTLE SCARED.
I WONDERED WHY YOU WERE LOOKING DOWN...
...AND WEREN'T SMILING.
I COULDN'T UNDERSTAND...
...SO I WAS FRIGHTENED.
BUT THEN SAYA SAID:" "IT'S OKAY. THERE'S NOTHING TO BE SCARED OF."
HER WORDS GAVE US COURAGE.

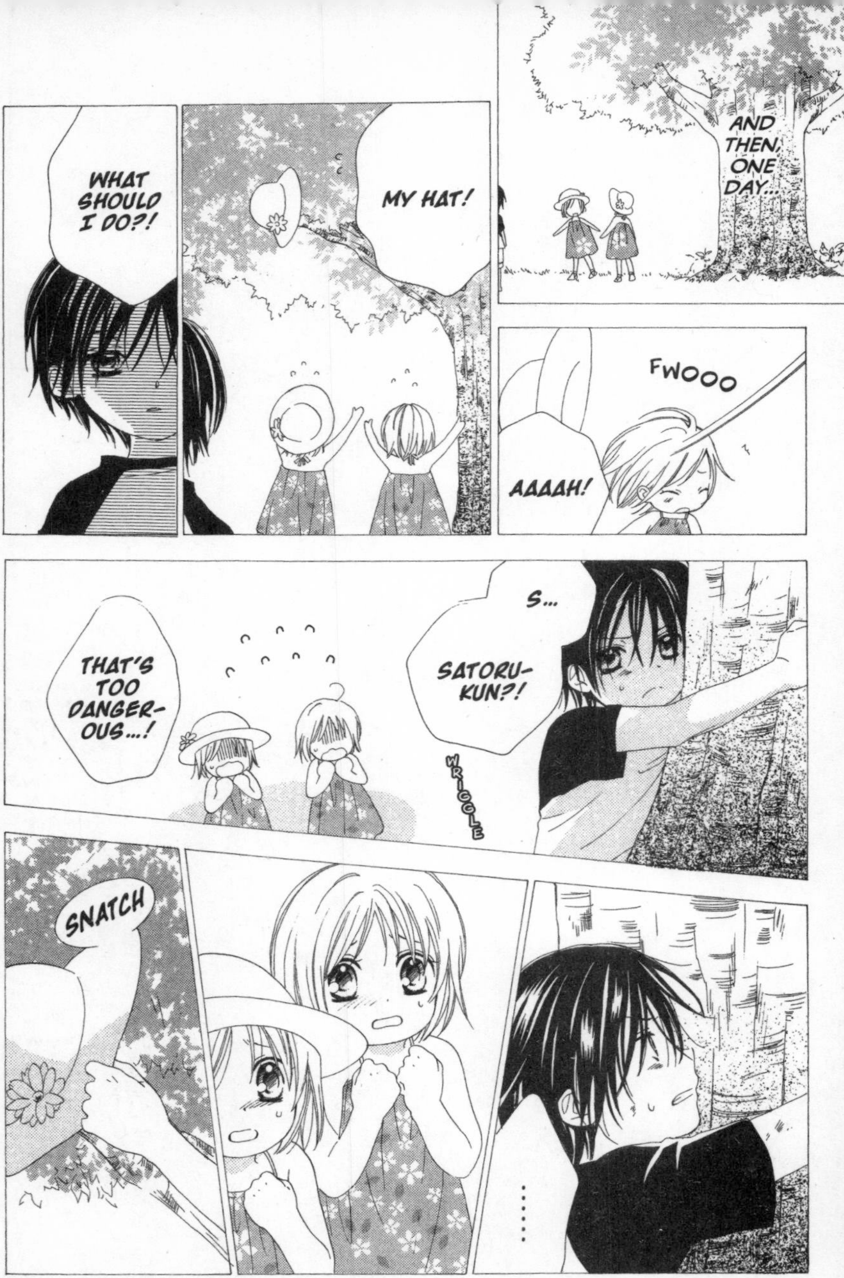
AND THEN, ONE DAY...
FWOOO
AAAAH!
MY HAT!
WHAT SHOULD I DO?!
S...
SATORU-KUN?!
WRIGGLE
THAT'S TOO DANGER-OUS...!
......
SNATCH

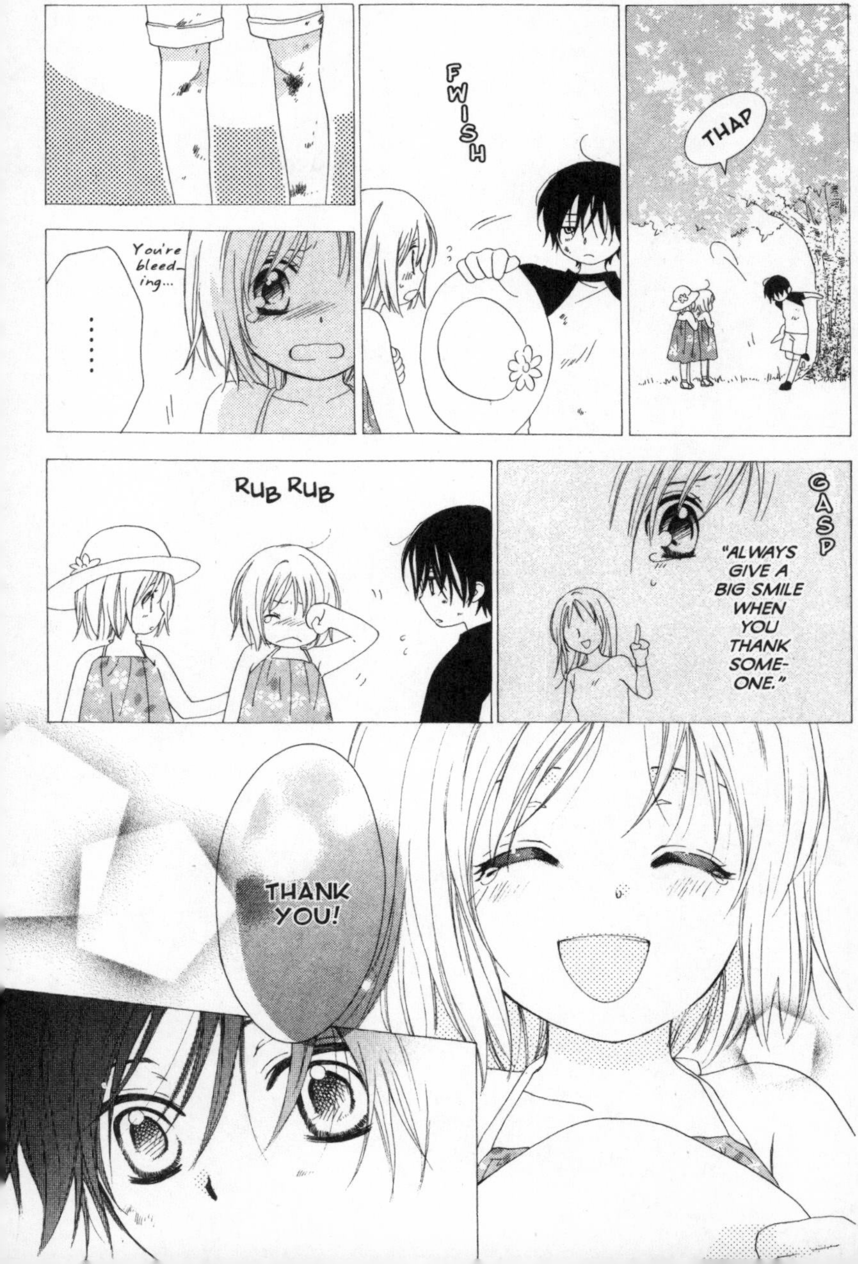
THAP
FWISH
You're bleed-ing...
......
GASP
"ALWAYS GIVE A BIG SMILE WHEN YOU THANK SOME-ONE."
RUB RUB
THANK YOU!

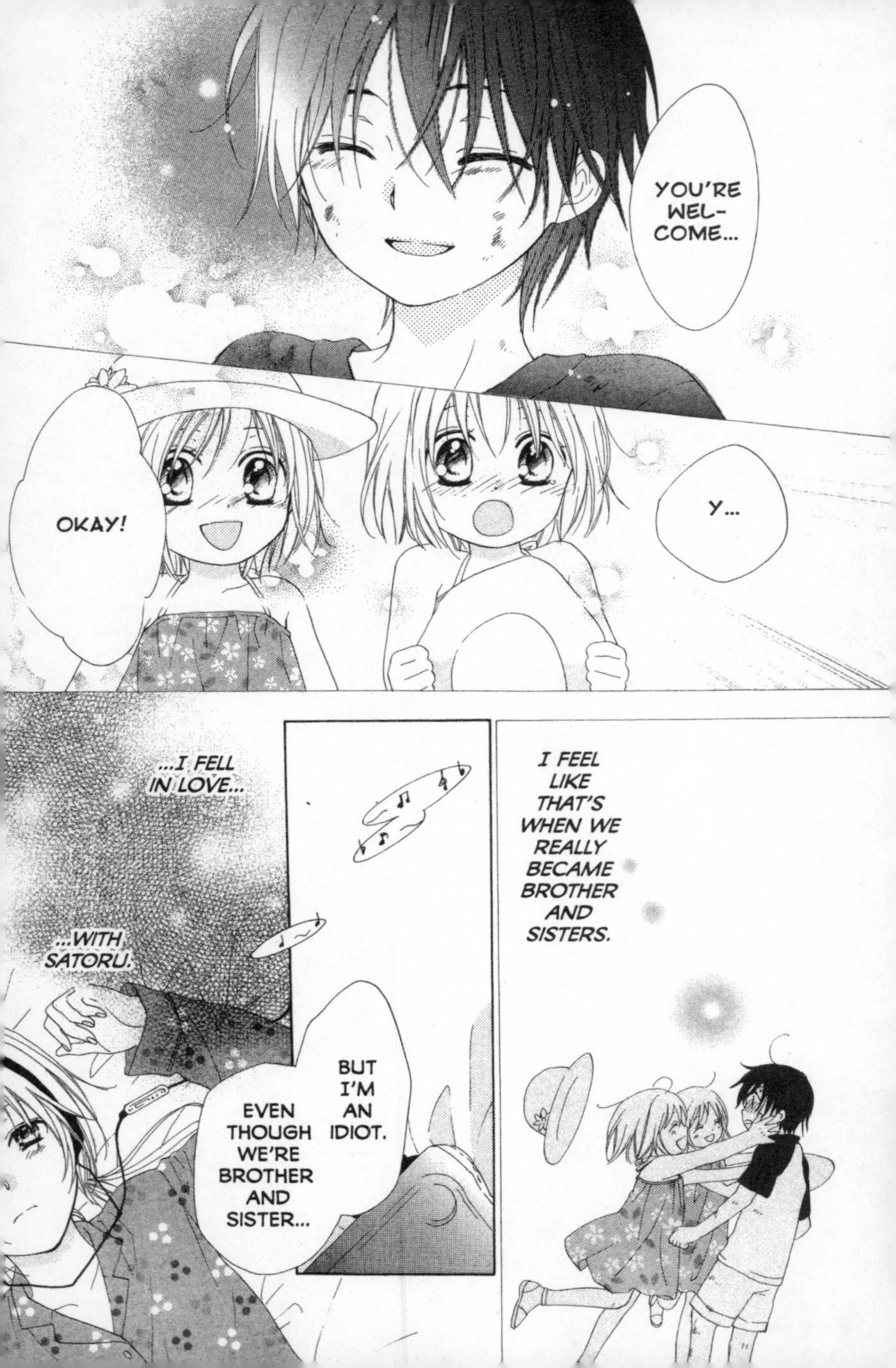
YOU'RE WEL- COME...
Y...
OKAY!
I FEEL LIKE THAT'S WHEN WE REALLY BECAME BROTHER AND SISTERS.
BUT I'M AN IDIOT.
EVEN THOUGH WE'RE BROTHER AND SISTER...
...I FELL IN LOVE...
...WITH SATORU.

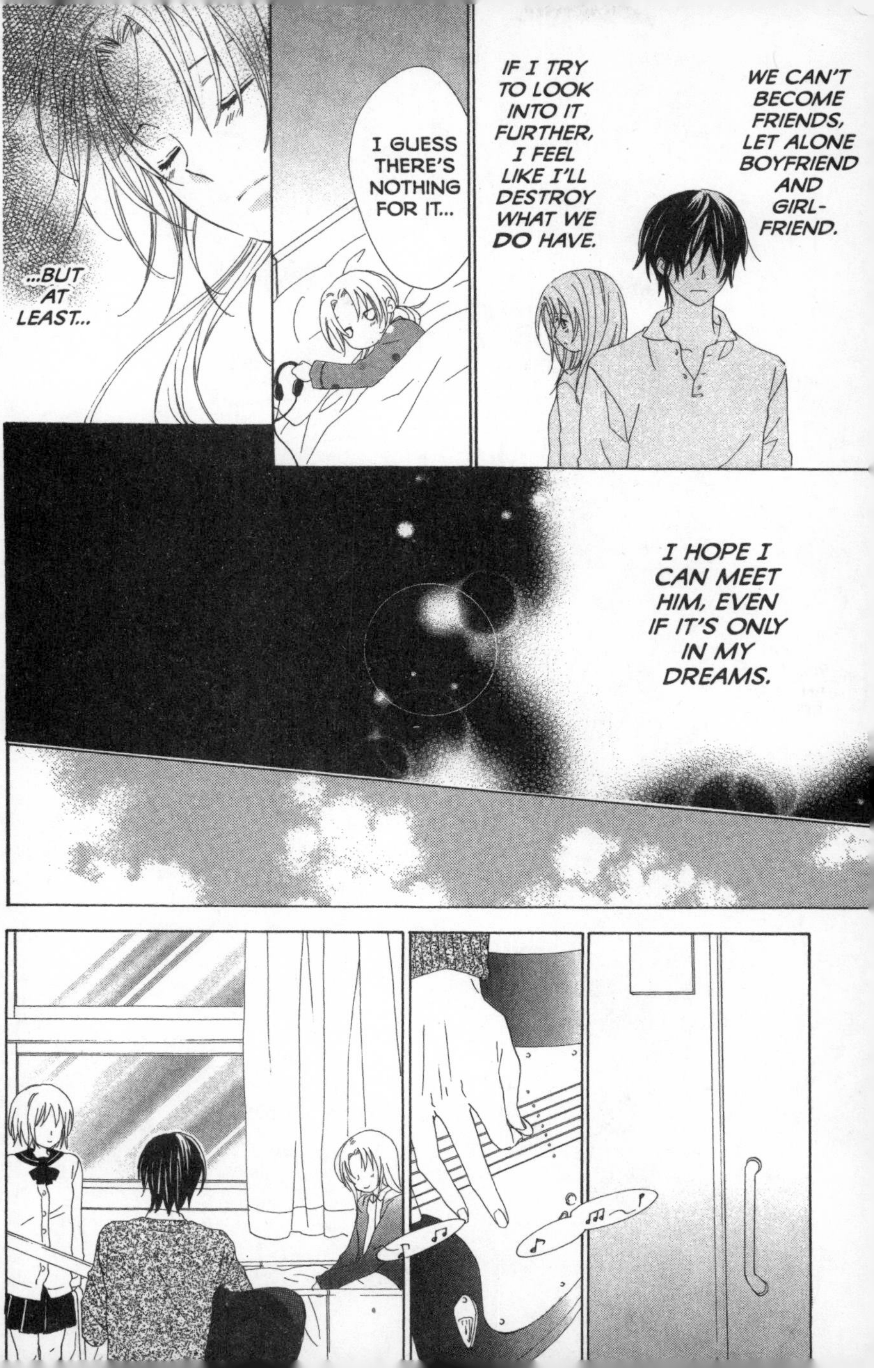
WE CAN'T BECOME FRIENDS, LET ALONE BOYFRIEND AND GIRL-FRIEND.
IF I TRY TO LOOK INTO IT FURTHER, I FEEL LIKE I'LL DESTROY WHAT WE DO HAVE.
I GUESS THERE'S NOTHING FOR IT...
...BUT AT LEAST...
I HOPE I CAN MEET HIM, EVEN IF IT'S ONLY IN MY DREAMS.

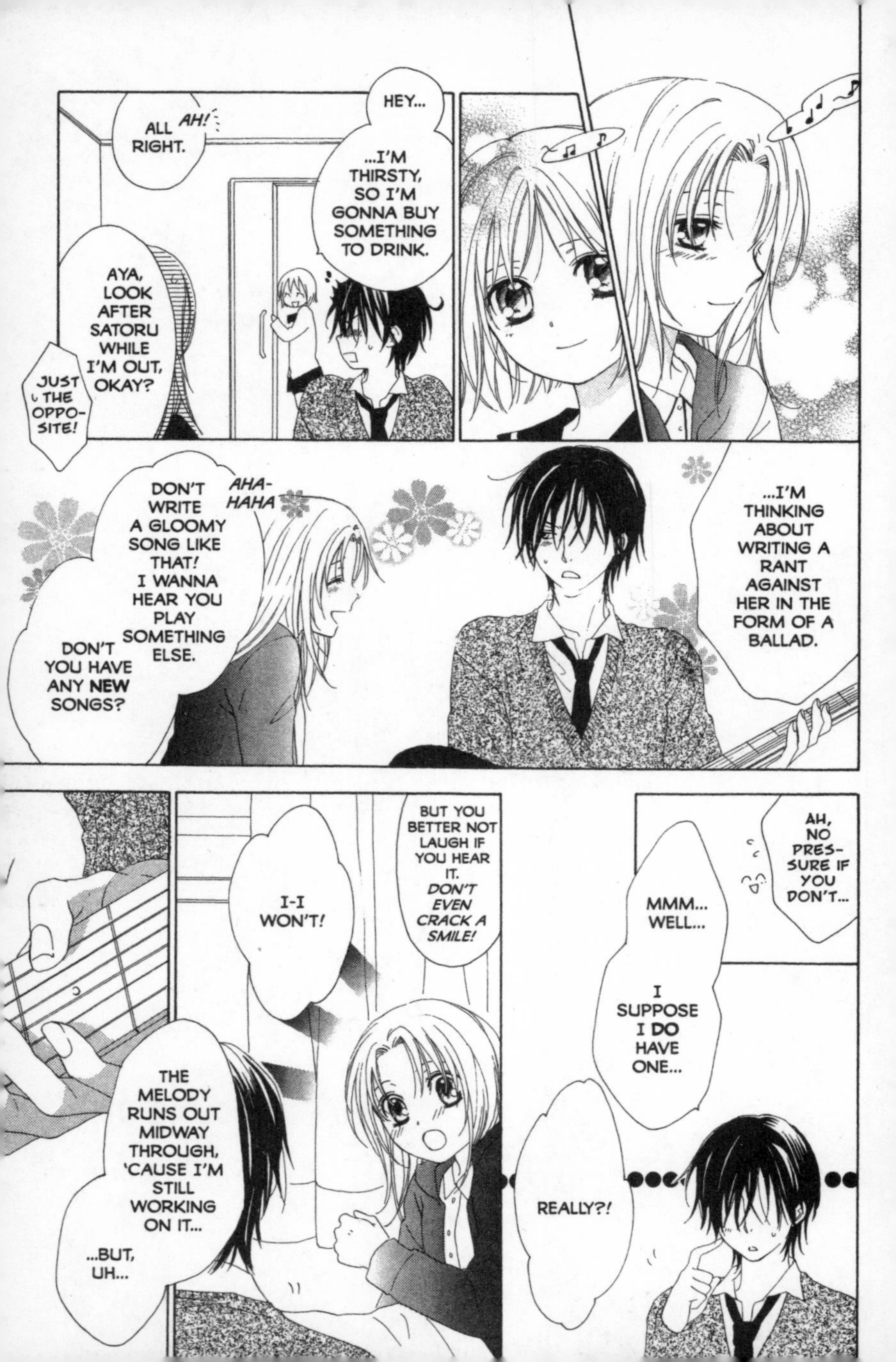
HEY...
...I'M THIRSTY, SO I'M GONNA BUY SOMETHING TO DRINK.
AH! ALL RIGHT.
AYA, LOOK AFTER SATORU WHILE I'M OUT, OKAY?
JUST THE OPPOSITE!
...I'M THINKING ABOUT WRITING A RANT AGAINST HER IN THE FORM OF A BALLAD.
AHAHAHA
DON'T WRITE A GLOOMY SONG LIKE THAT! I WANNA HEAR YOU PLAY SOMETHING ELSE.
DON'T YOU HAVE ANY NEW SONGS?
AH, NO PRESSURE IF YOU DON'T...
MMM... WELL...
I SUPPOSE I DO HAVE ONE...
REALLY?!
BUT YOU BETTER NOT LAUGH IF YOU HEAR IT. DON'T EVEN CRACK A SMILE!
I-I WON'T!
THE MELODY RUNS OUT MIDWAY THROUGH, 'CAUSE I'M STILL WORKING ON IT...
...BUT, UH...

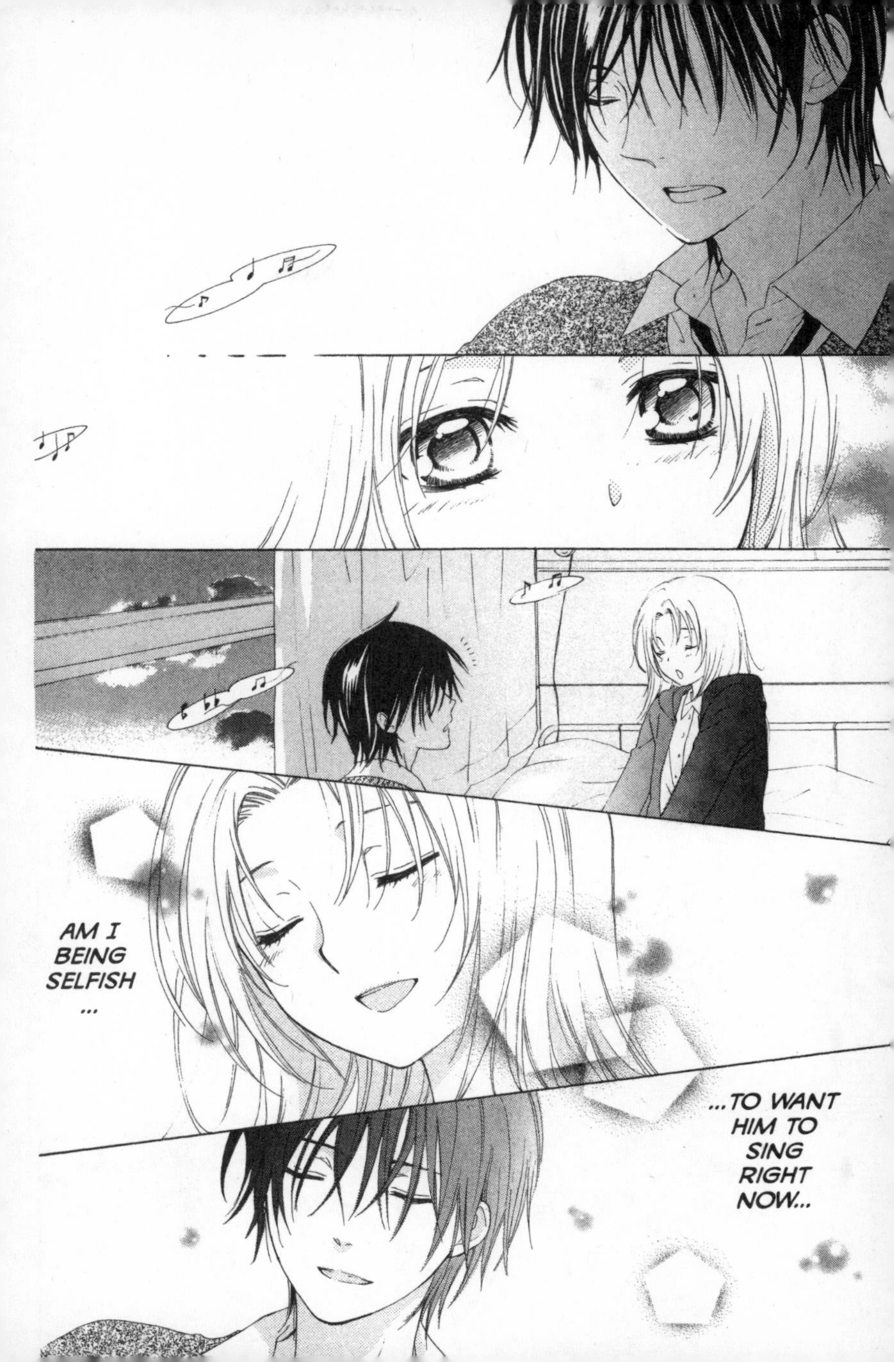
AM I BEING SELFISH ...
...TO WANT HIM TO SING RIGHT NOW...

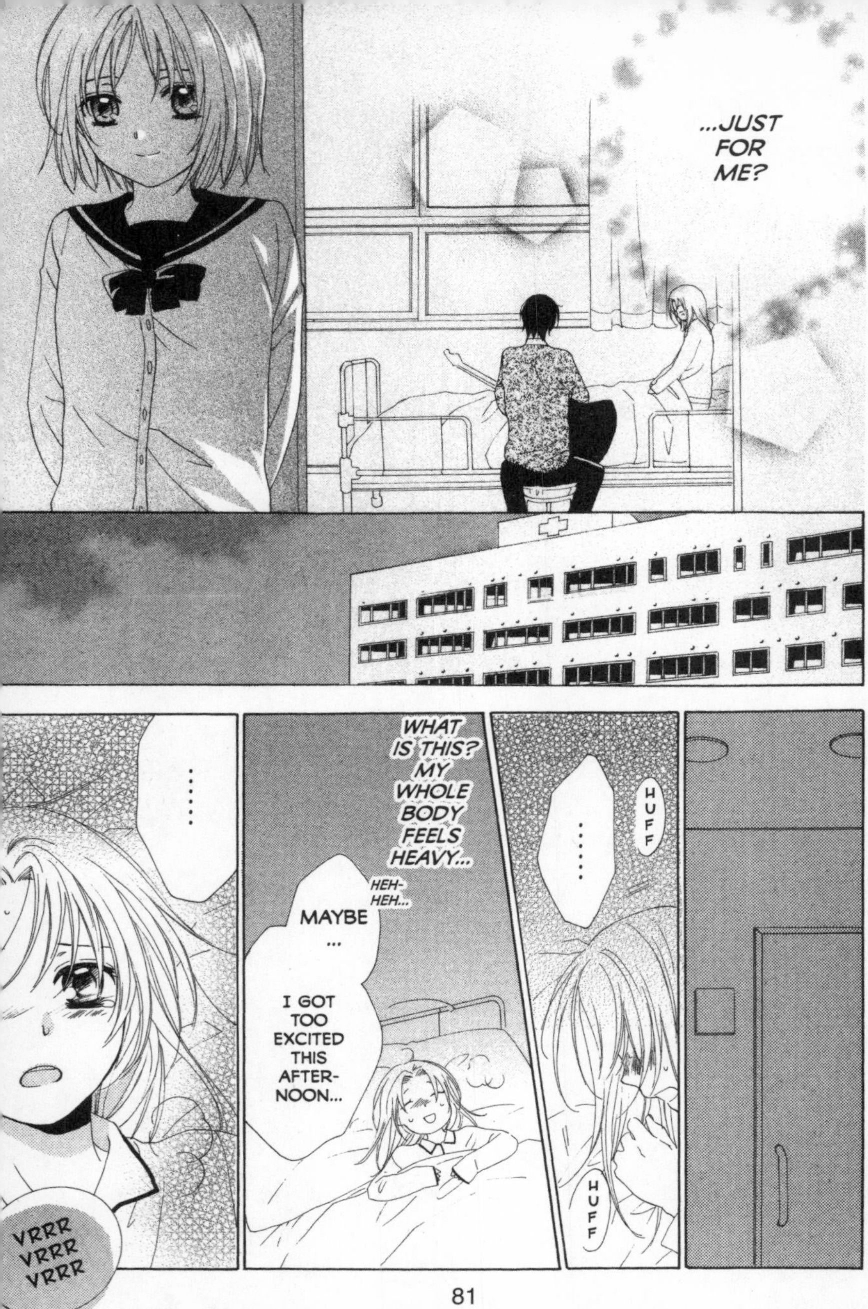
...JUST FOR ME?
HUFF
......
HUFF
WHAT IS THIS? MY WHOLE BODY FEELS HEAVY...
HEH-HEH...
MAYBE ...
I GOT TOO EXCITED THIS AFTERNOON...
......
VRRR VRRR VRRR

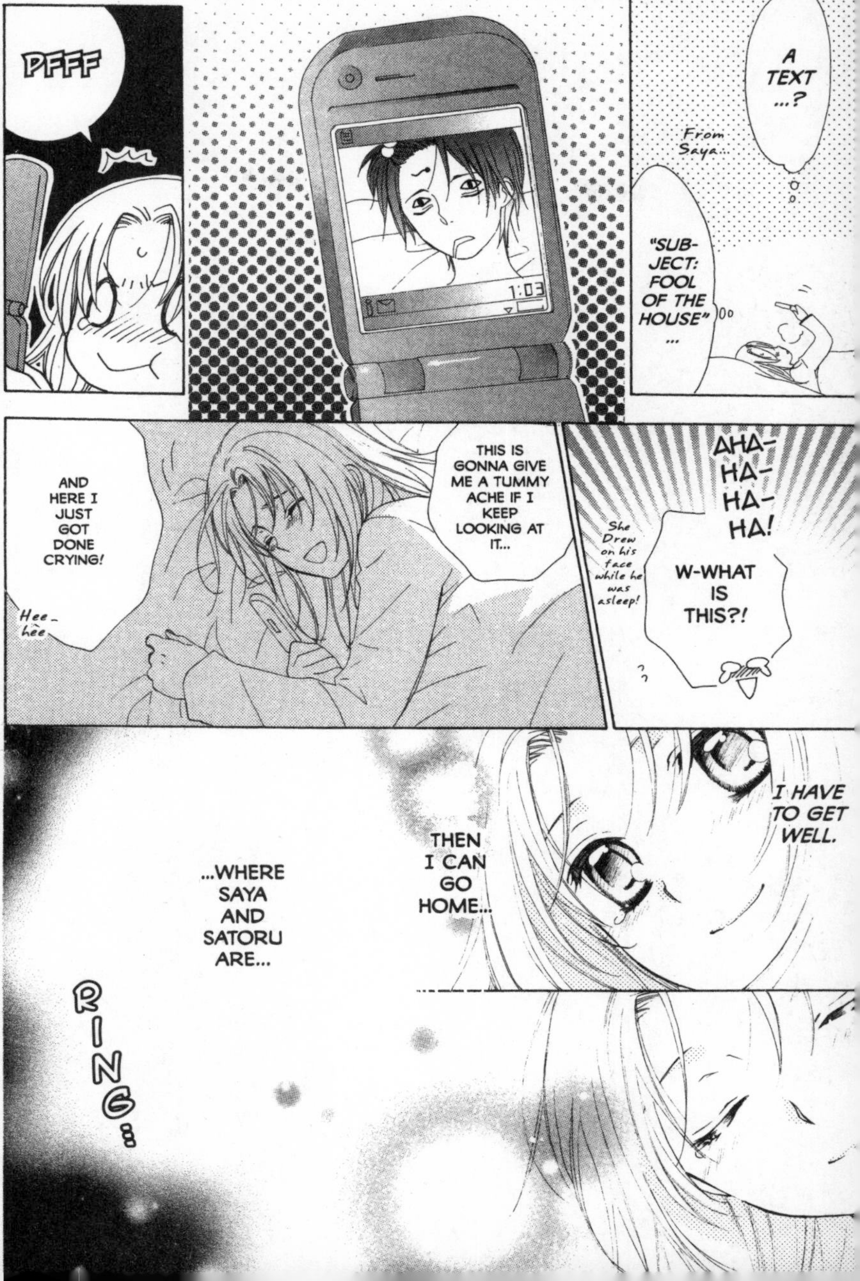
A TEXT ...?
From Saya...
"SUB-JECT: FOOL OF THE HOUSE" ...
1:03
PFFF
AHA-HA-HA-HA!
W-WHAT IS THIS?!
She Drew on his face while he was asleep!
THIS IS GONNA GIVE ME A TUMMY ACHE IF I KEEP LOOKING AT IT...
AND HERE I JUST GOT DONE CRYING!
Hee-hee
I HAVE TO GET WELL.
THEN I CAN GO HOME...
...WHERE SAYA AND SATORU ARE...
RING...

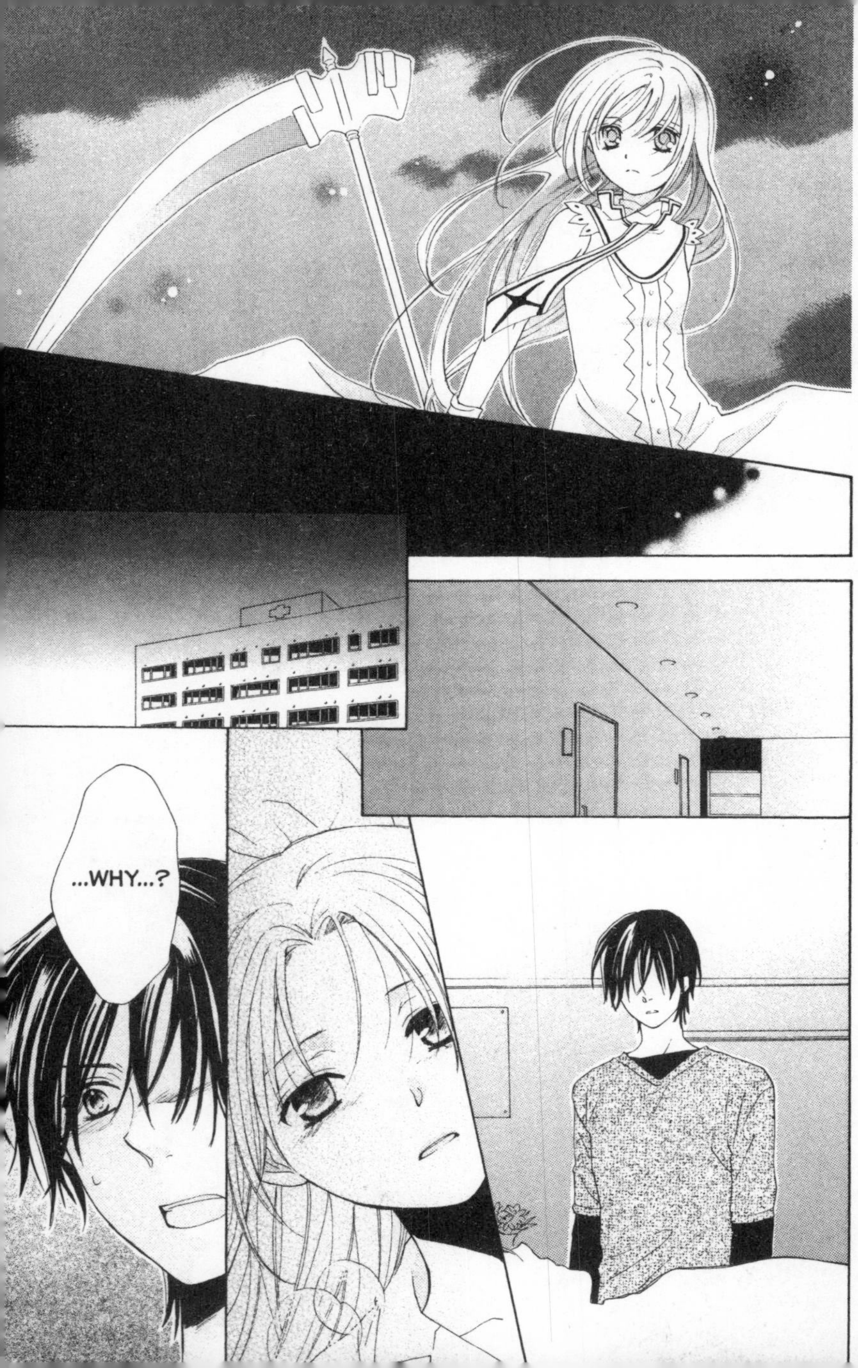
...WHY...?

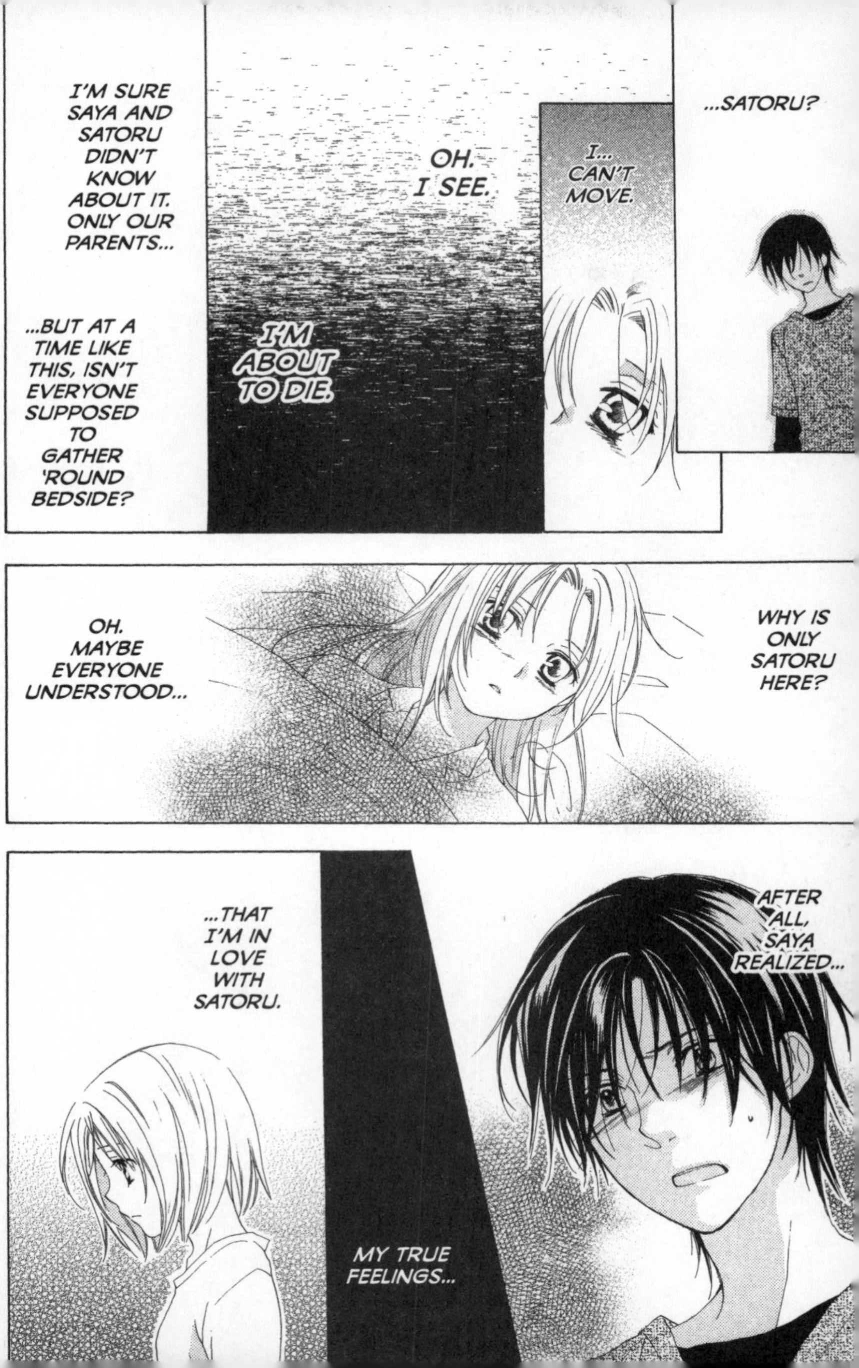
...SATORU?
I... CAN'T MOVE.
OH. I SEE.
I'M ABOUT TO DIE.
I'M SURE SAYA AND SATORU DIDN'T KNOW ABOUT IT. ONLY OUR PARENTS...
...BUT AT A TIME LIKE THIS, ISN'T EVERYONE SUPPOSED TO GATHER 'ROUND BEDSIDE?
WHY IS ONLY SATORU HERE?
OH. MAYBE EVERYONE UNDERSTOOD...
AFTER ALL, SAYA REALIZED...
MY TRUE FEELINGS...
...THAT I'M IN LOVE WITH SATORU.

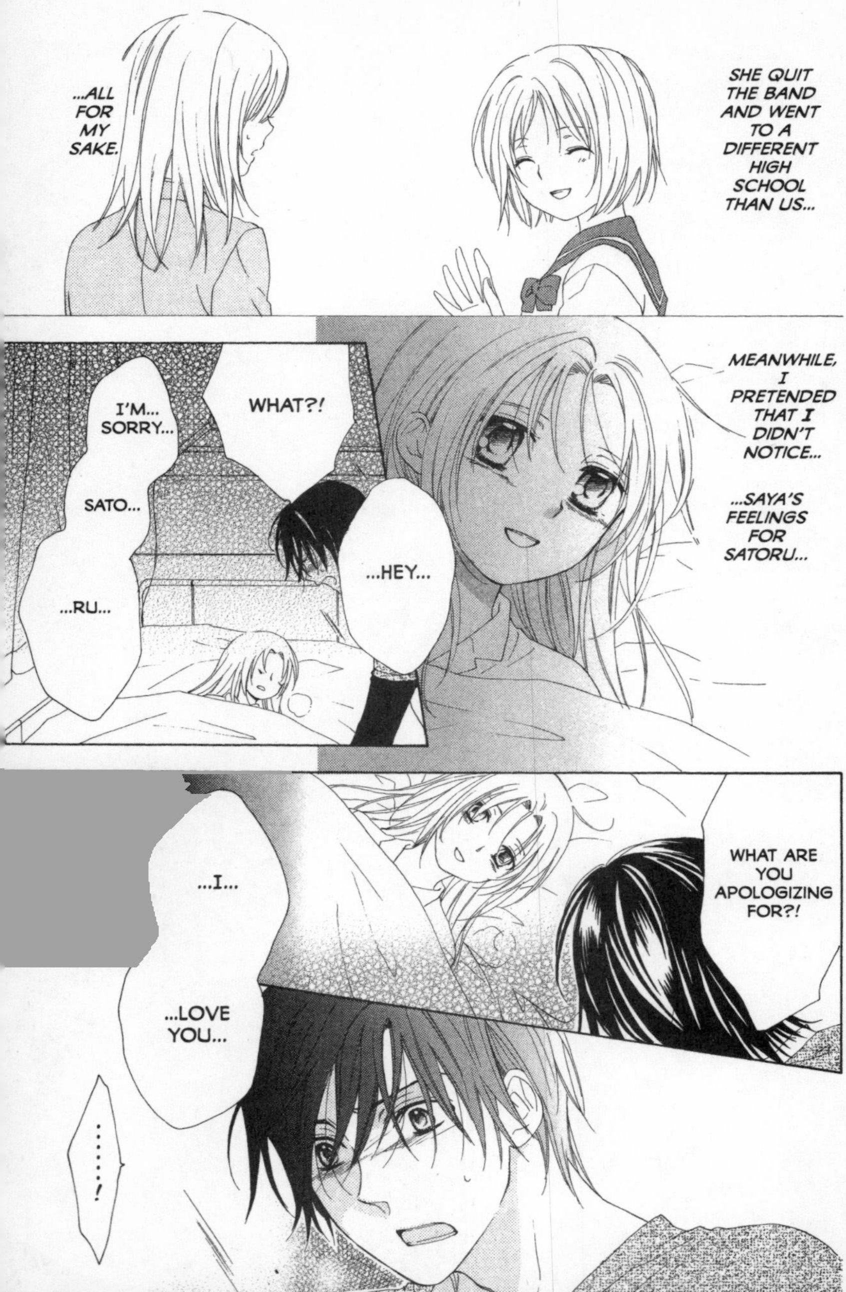
SHE QUIT THE BAND AND WENT TO A DIFFERENT HIGH SCHOOL THAN US...
...ALL FOR MY SAKE.
MEANWHILE, I PRETENDED THAT I DIDN'T NOTICE...
...SAYA'S FEELINGS FOR SATORU...
...HEY...
I'M... SORRY...
SATO...
...RU...
WHAT?!
WHAT ARE YOU APOLOGIZING FOR?!
...I...
...LOVE YOU...
......!

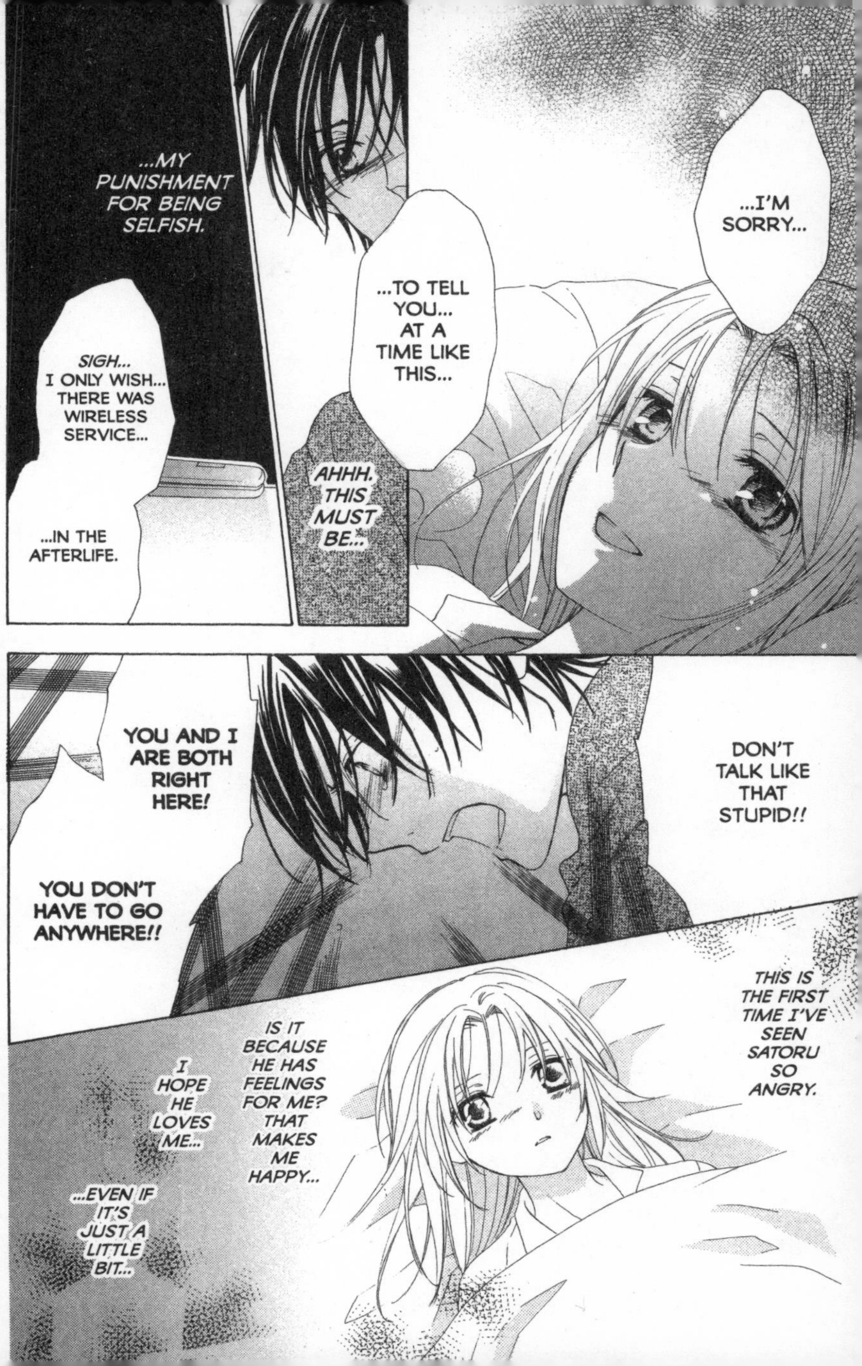
...I'M SORRY...
...TO TELL YOU... AT A TIME LIKE THIS...
AHHH. THIS MUST BE...
...MY PUNISHMENT FOR BEING SELFISH.
SIGH... I ONLY WISH... THERE WAS WIRELESS SERVICE...
...IN THE AFTERLIFE.
DON'T TALK LIKE THAT STUPID!!
YOU AND I ARE BOTH RIGHT HERE!
YOU DON'T HAVE TO GO ANYWHERE!!
THIS IS THE FIRST TIME I'VE SEEN SATORU SO ANGRY.
IS IT BECAUSE HE HAS FEELINGS FOR ME? THAT MAKES ME HAPPY...
I HOPE HE LOVES ME...
...EVEN IF IT'S JUST A LITTLE BIT...

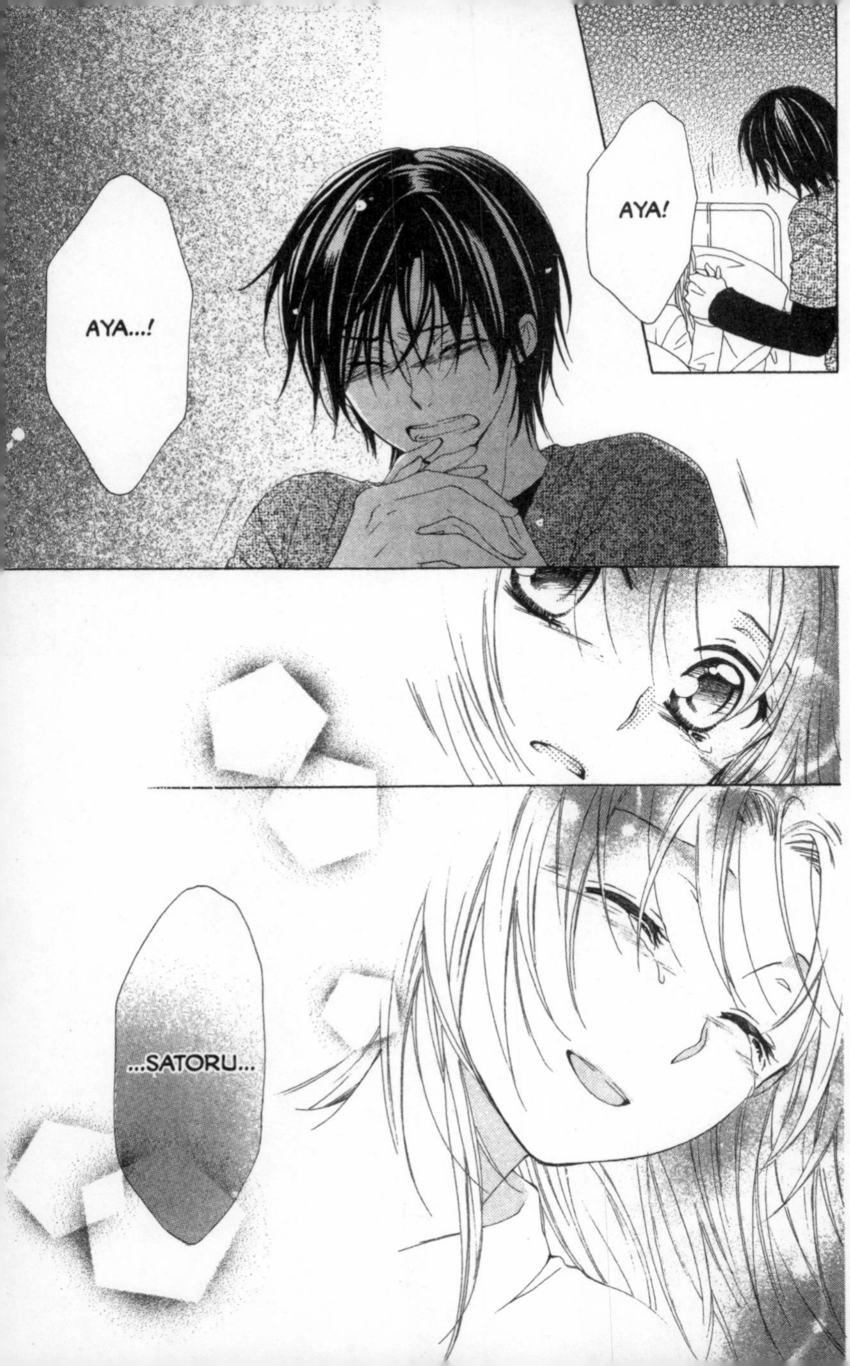
AYA!
AYA...!
...SATORU...

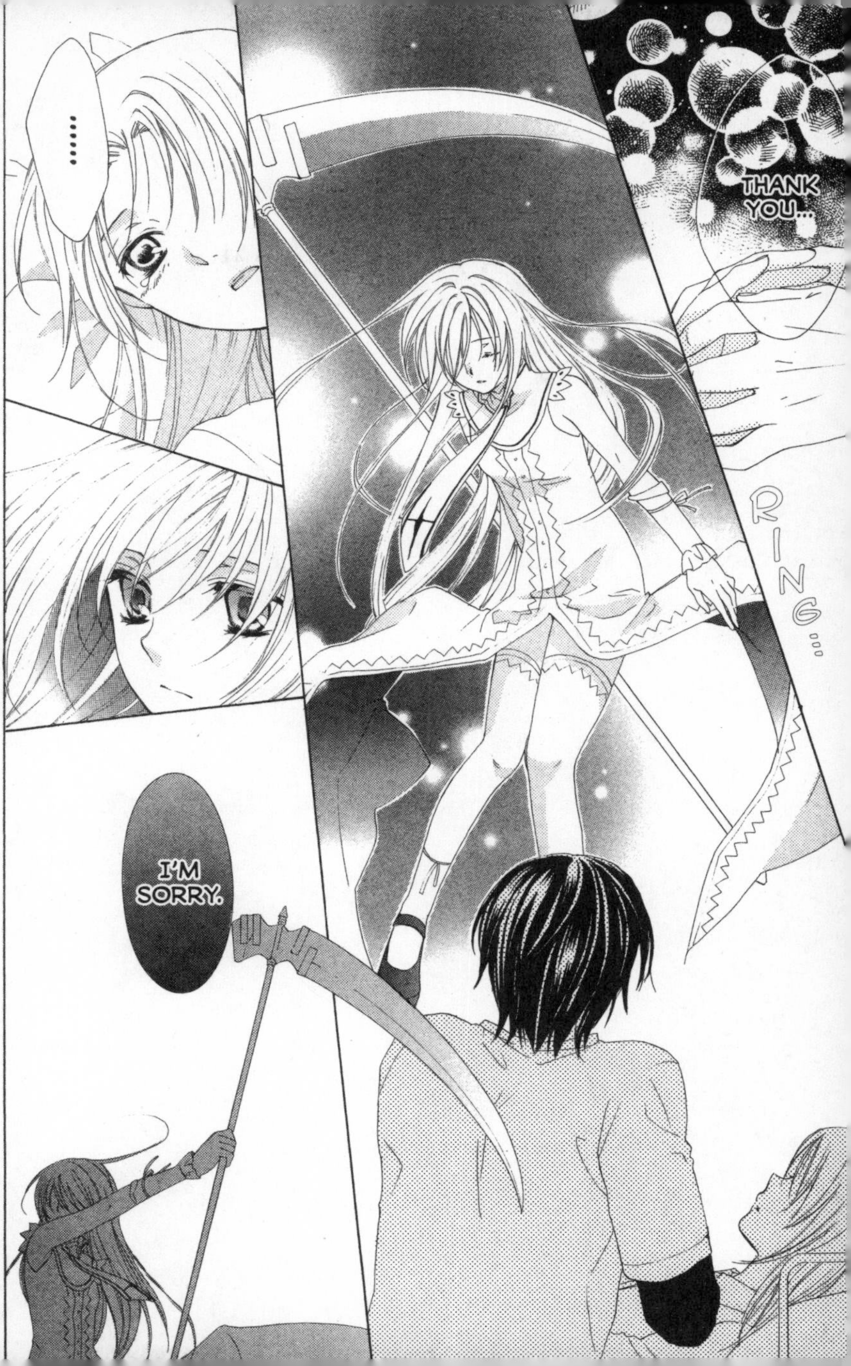
THANK YOU...
RING...
......
I'M SORRY.

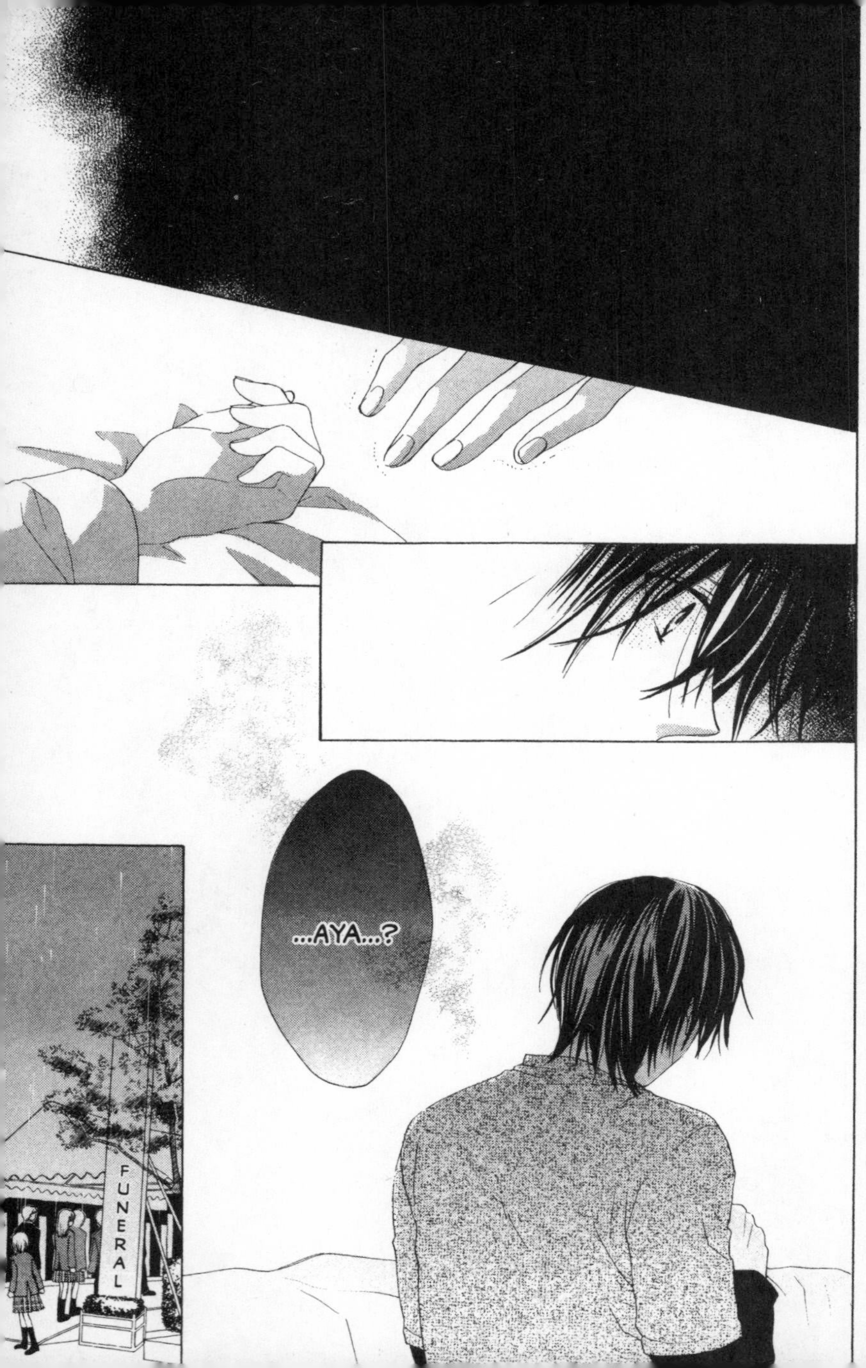
...AYA...?
FUNERAL

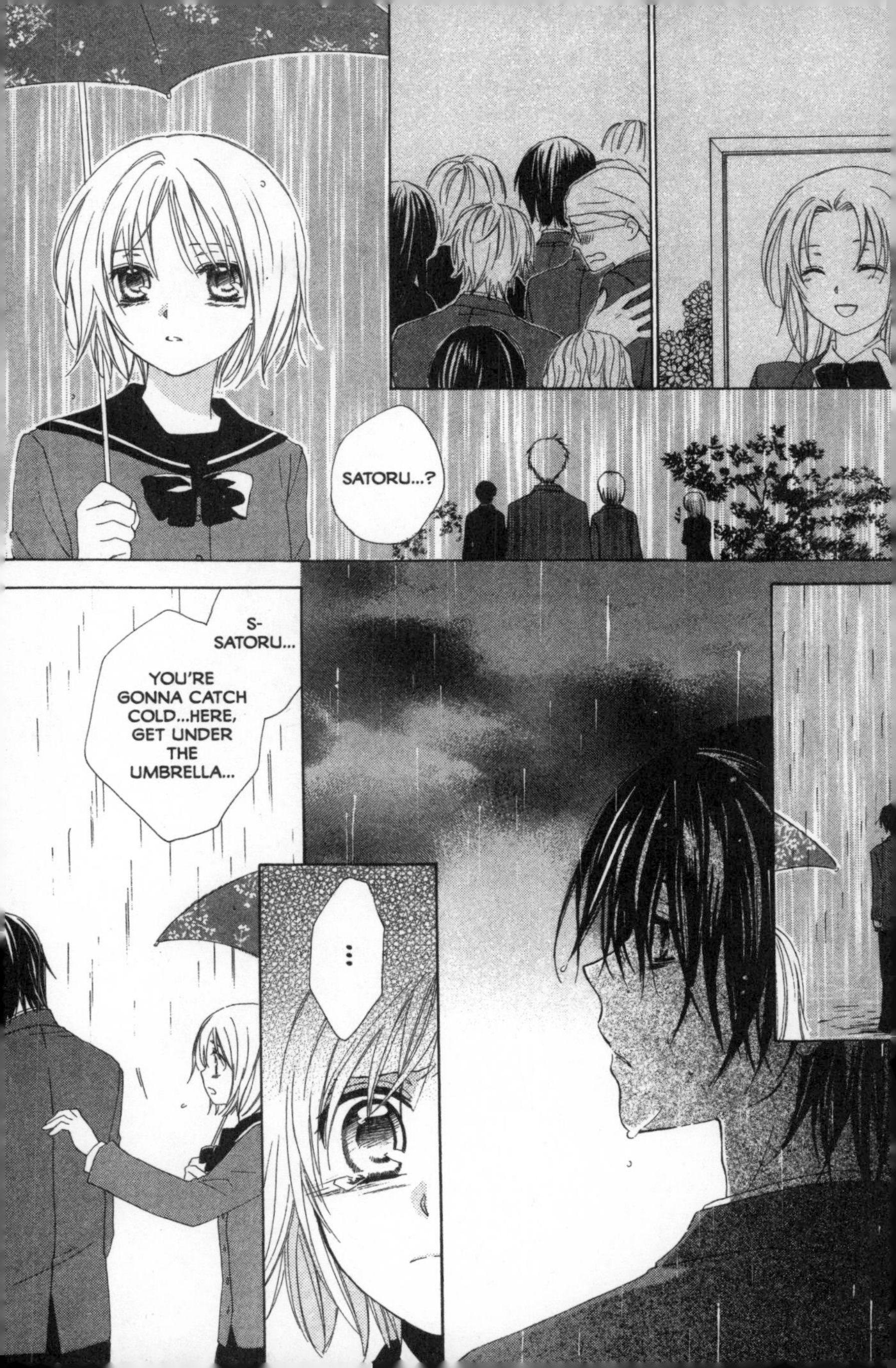
SATORU...?
S-SATORU...
YOU'RE GONNA CATCH COLD...HERE, GET UNDER THE UMBRELLA...
...

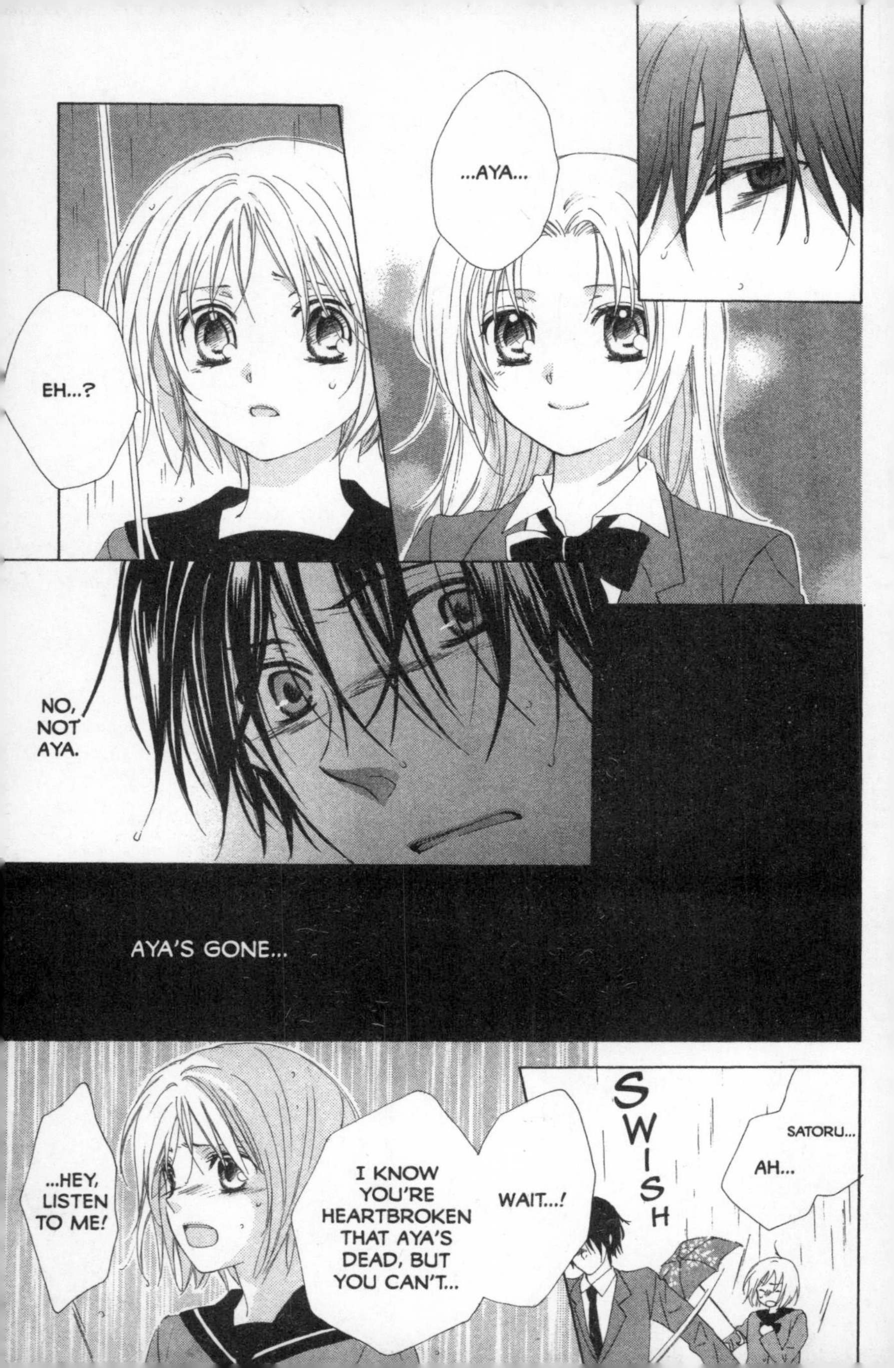
...AYA...
EH...?
NO, NOT AYA.
AYA'S GONE...
SATORU...
AH...
SWISH
WAIT...!
I KNOW YOU'RE HEARTBROKEN THAT AYA'S DEAD, BUT YOU CAN'T...
...HEY, LISTEN TO ME!

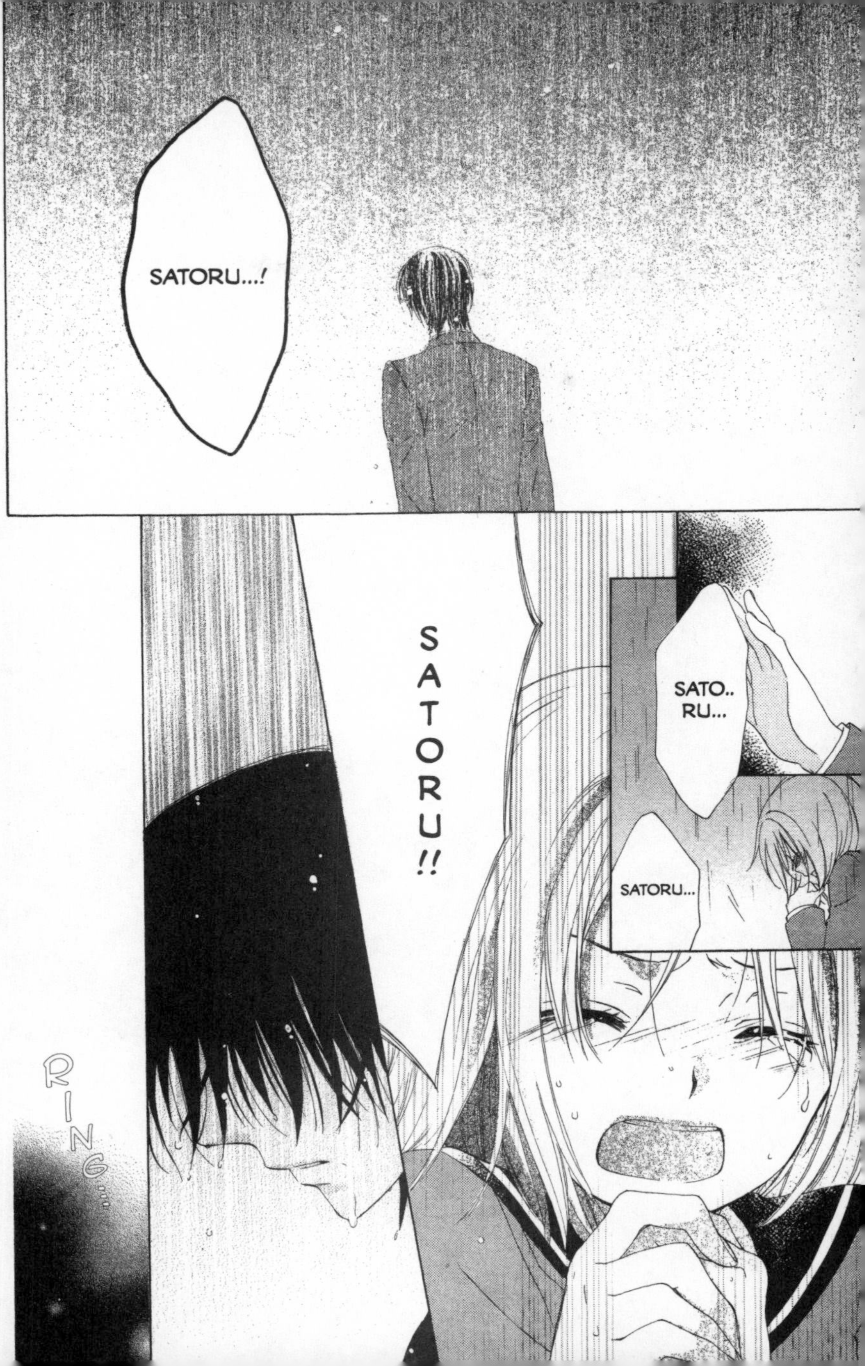
SATORU...!
SATO.. RU...
SATORU...
SATORU!!
RING...

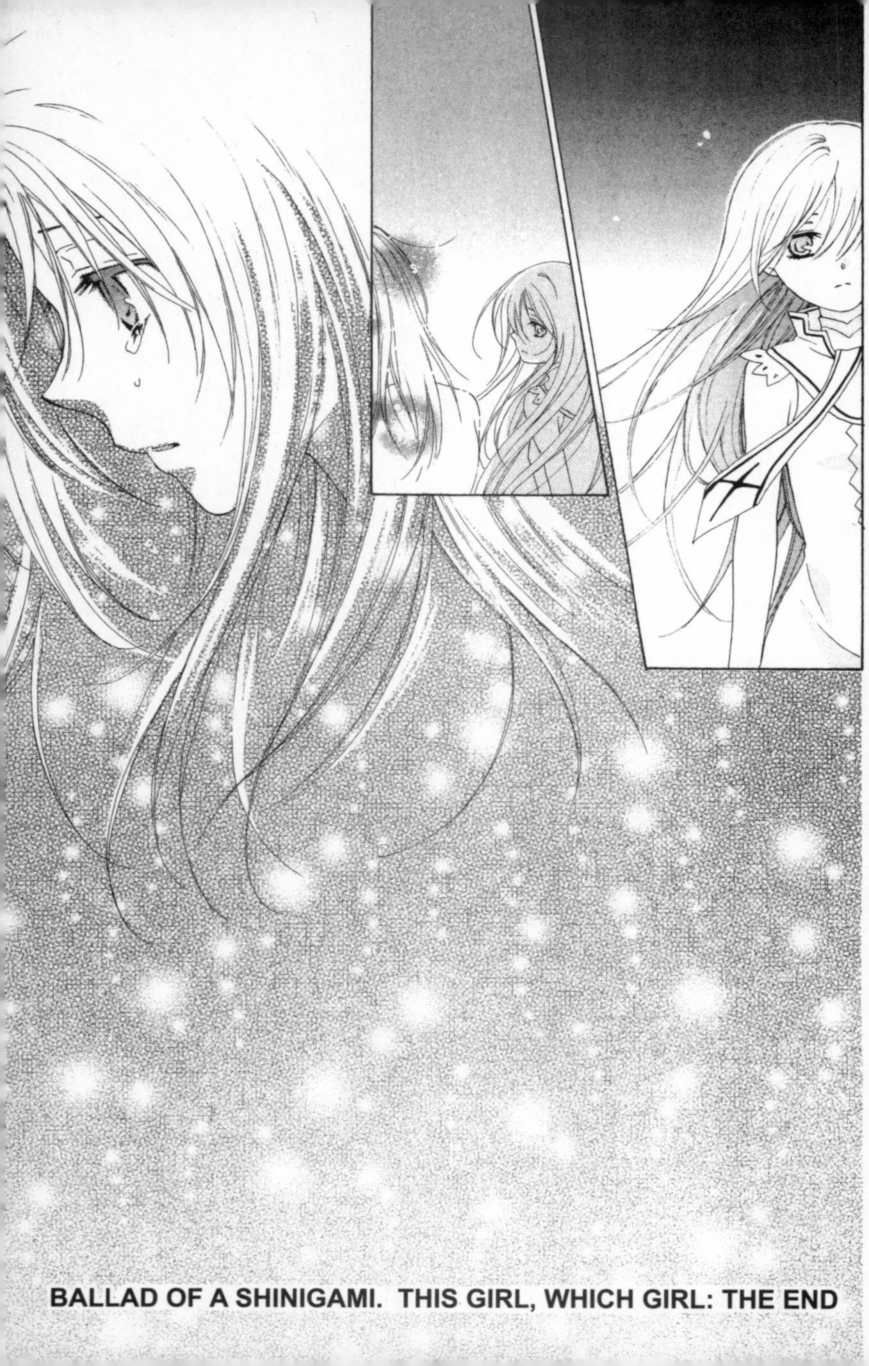
BALLAD OF A SHINIGAMI. THIS GIRL, WHICH GIRL: THE END

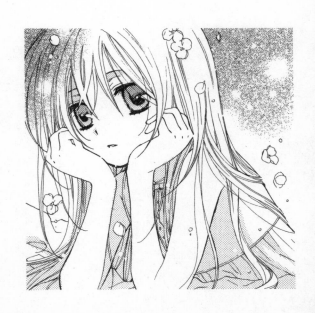

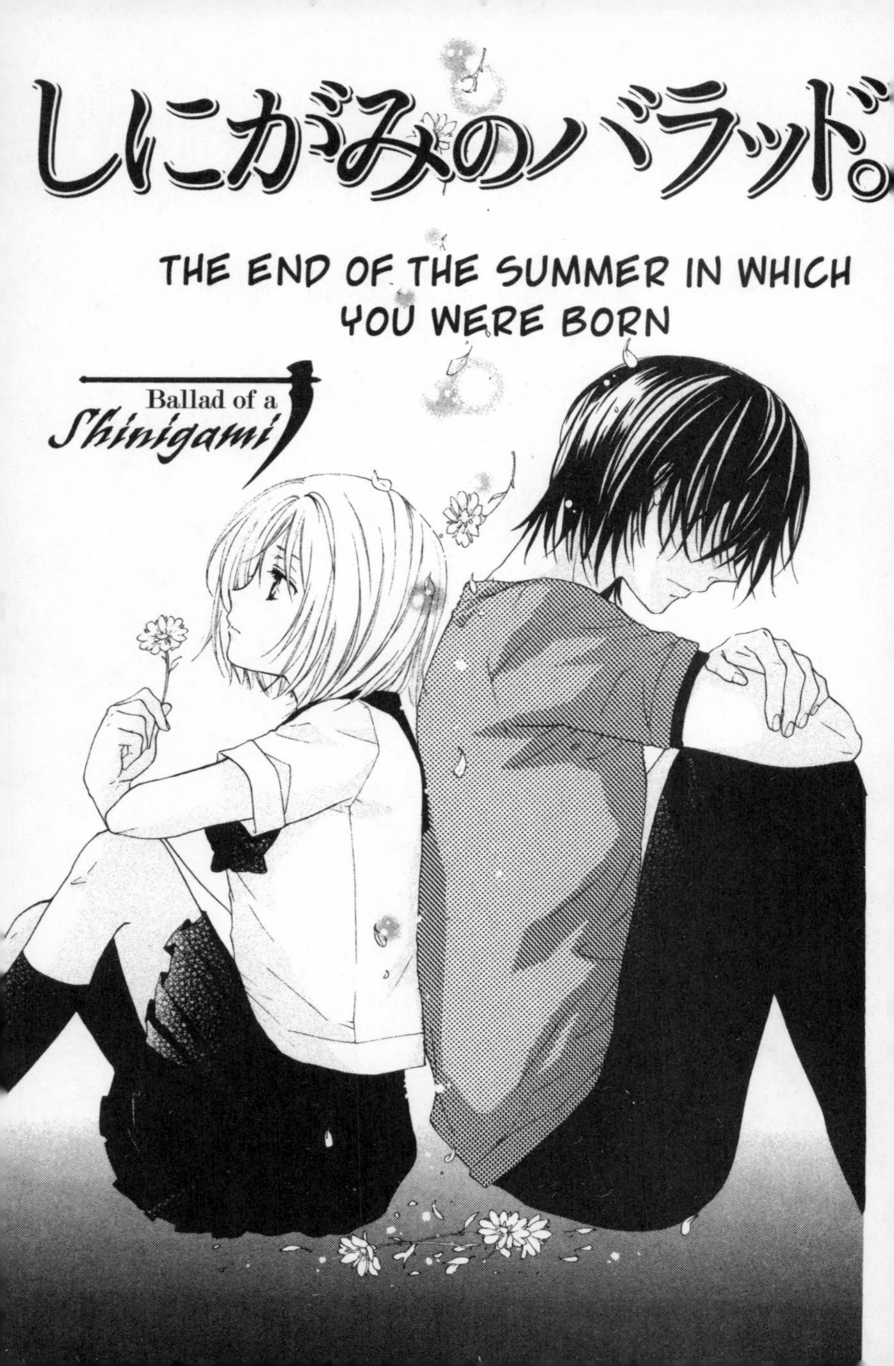
しにがみのバラッド。
THE END OF THE SUMMER IN WHICH YOU WERE BORN
Ballad of a Shinigami

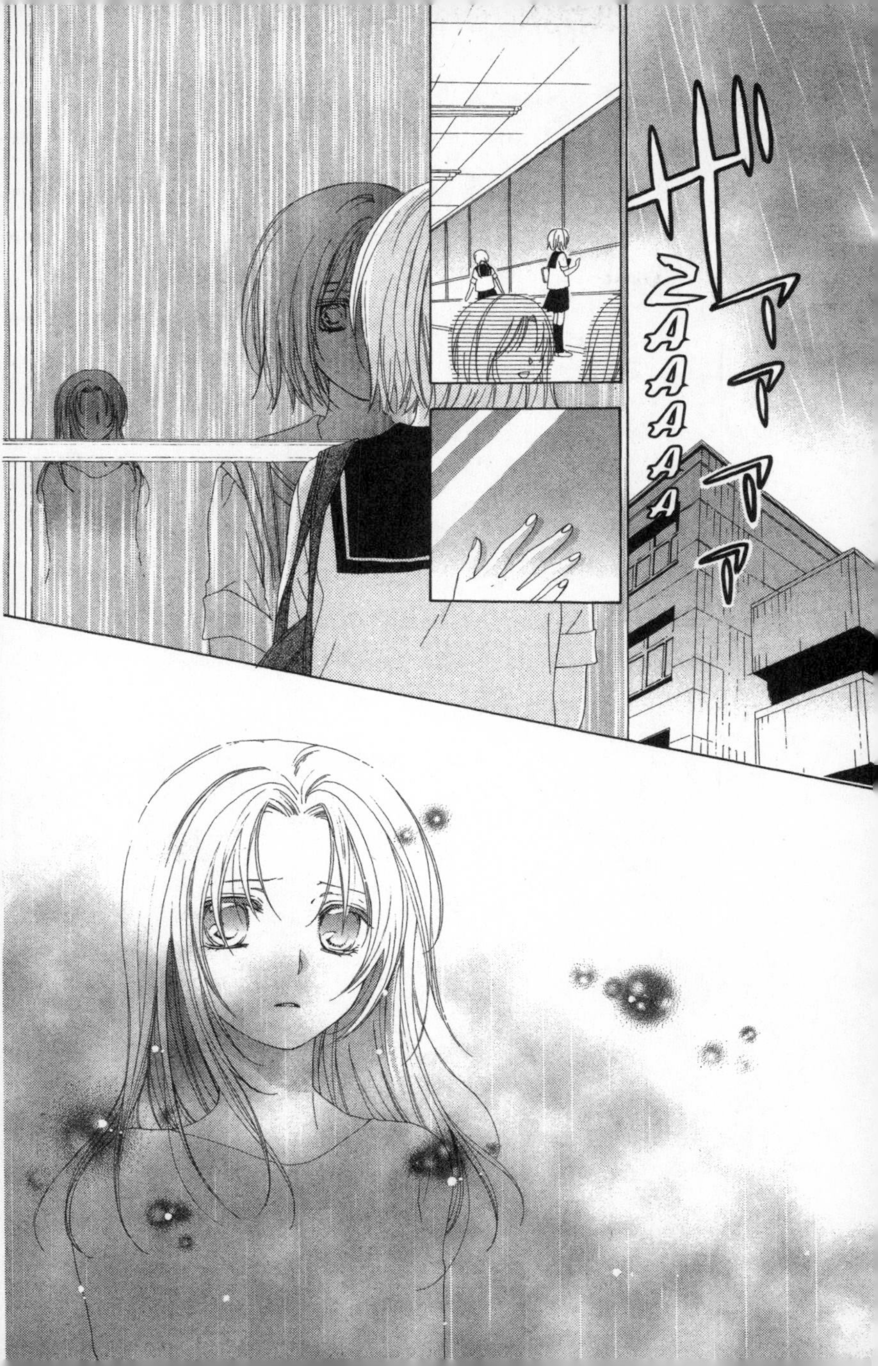
ザアアアア
ZAAAAA

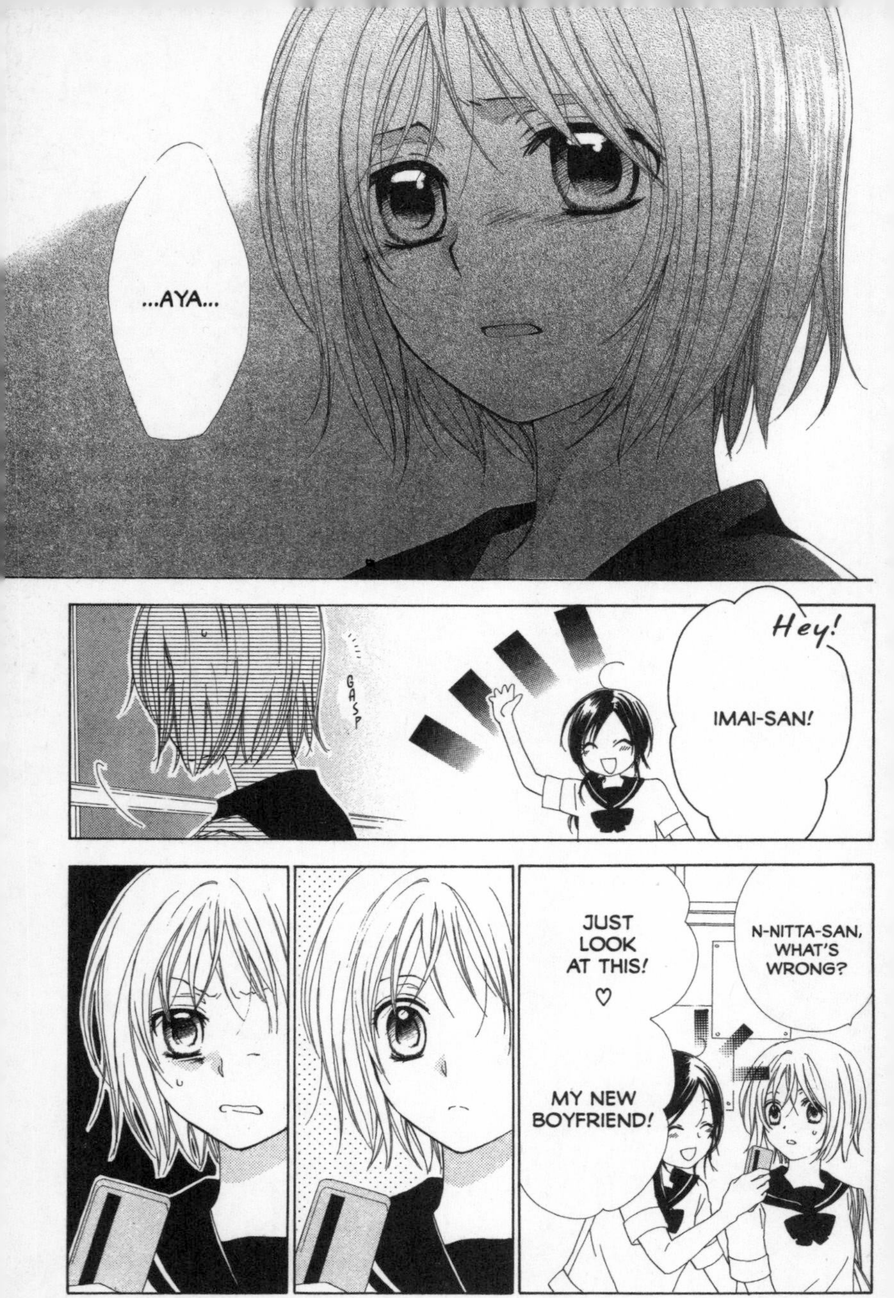
...AYA...
Hey!
IMAI-SAN!
GASP
N-NITTA-SAN, WHAT'S WRONG?
JUST LOOK AT THIS! ♡
MY NEW BOYFRIEND!

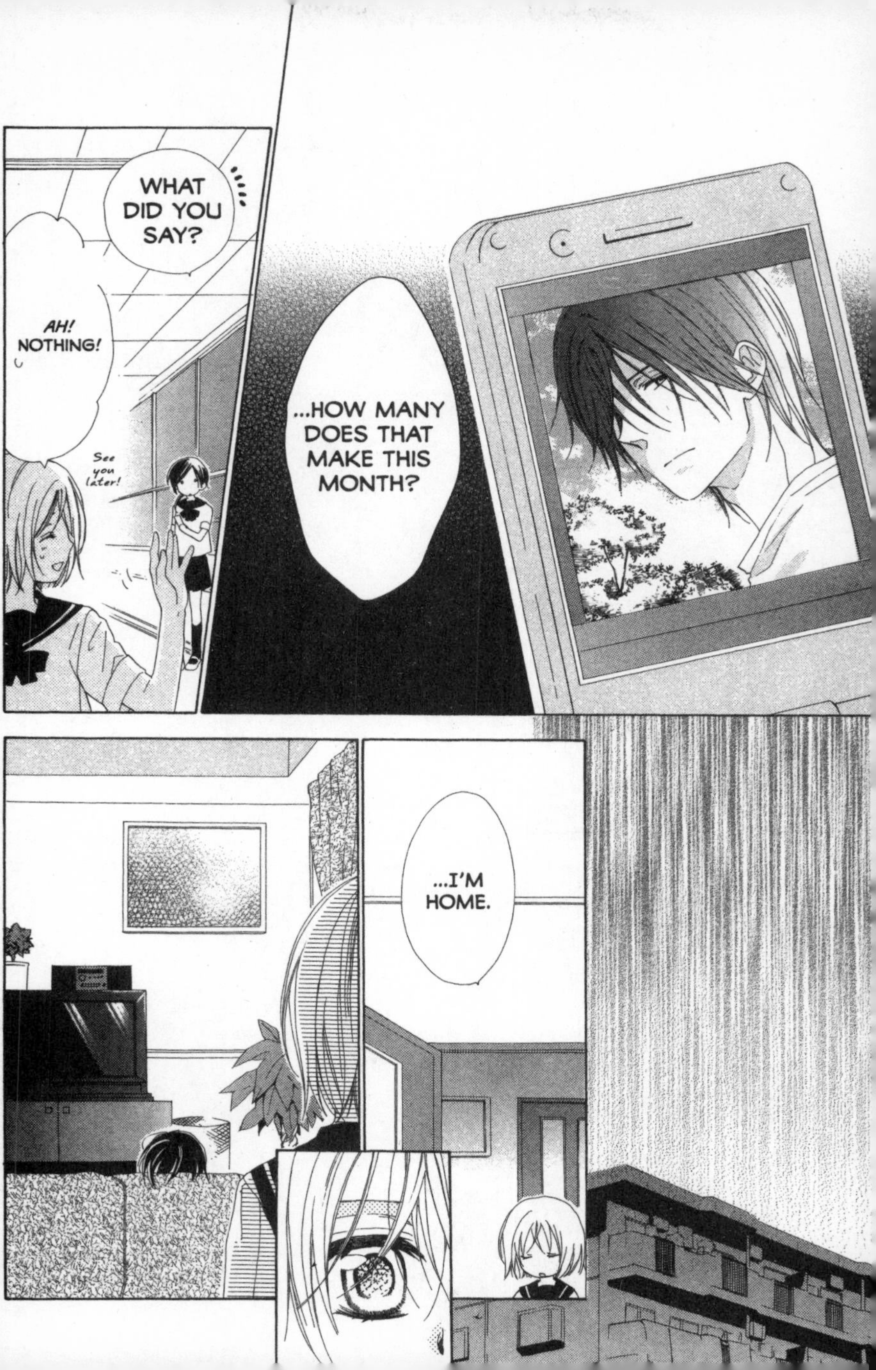
...HOW MANY DOES THAT MAKE THIS MONTH?
WHAT DID YOU SAY?
AH! NOTHING!
See you later!
...I'M HOME.

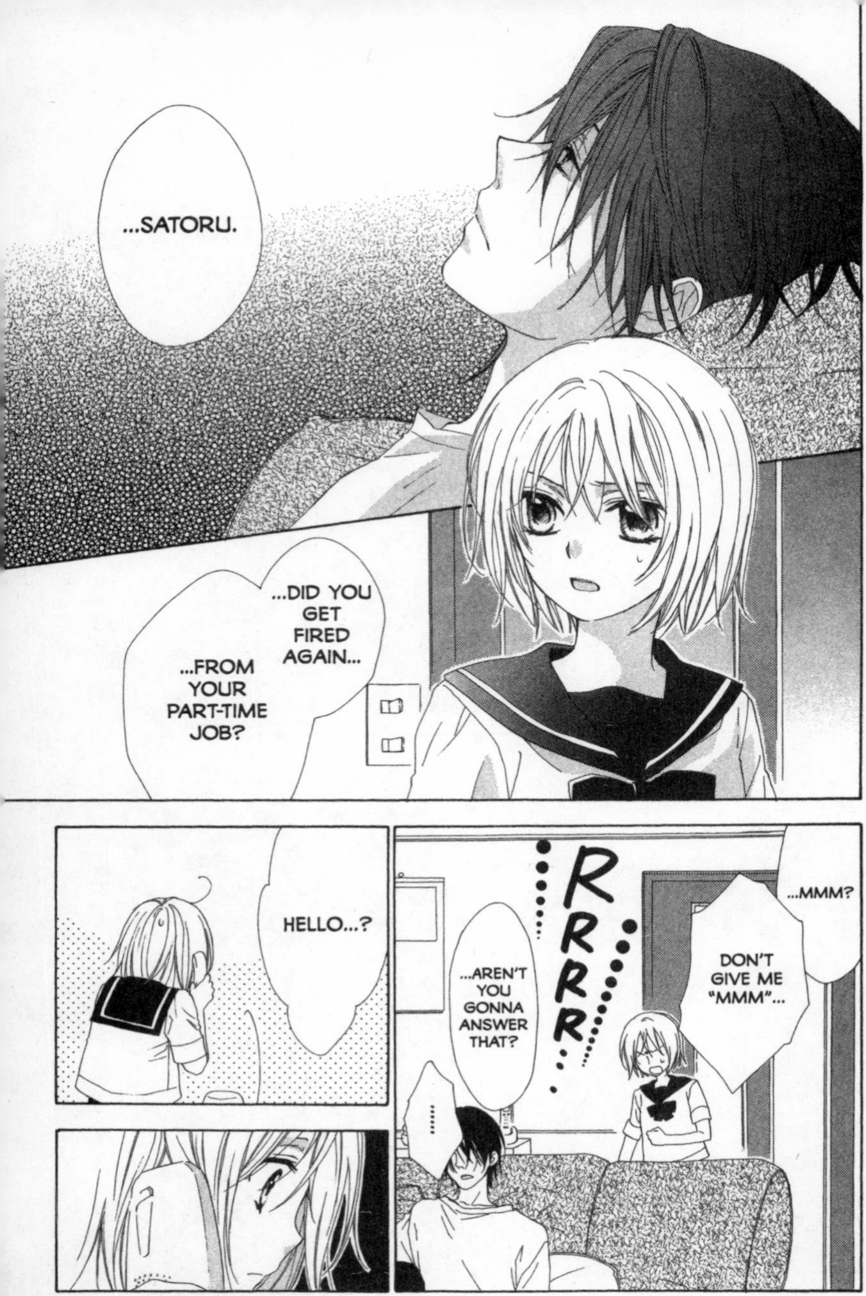
...SATORU.
...DID YOU GET FIRED AGAIN...
...FROM YOUR PART-TIME JOB?
...MMM?
DON'T GIVE ME "MMM"...
RRRR
...AREN'T YOU GONNA ANSWER THAT?
......
HELLO...?

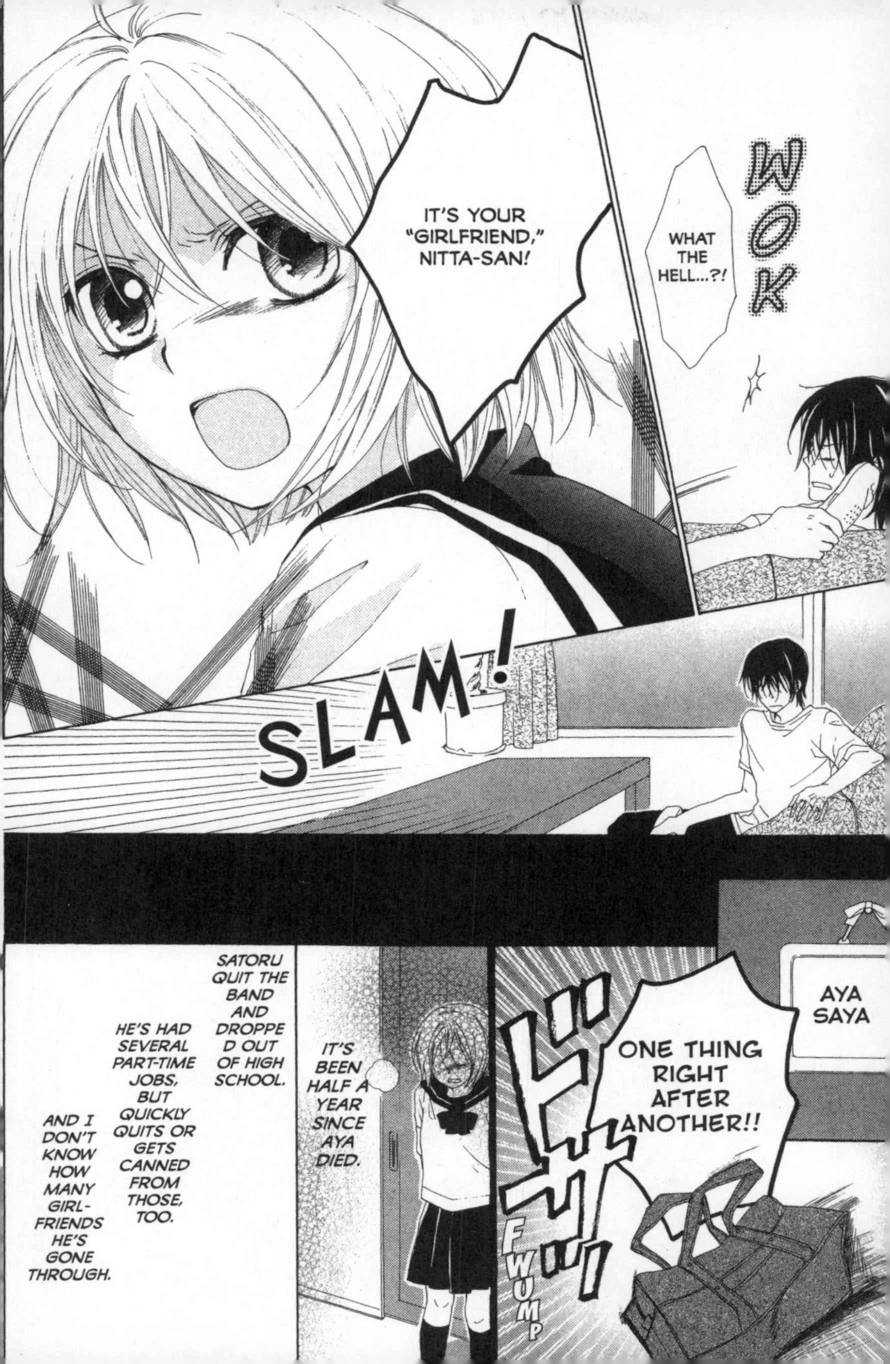
WOK
WHAT THE HELL...?!
IT'S YOUR "GIRLFRIEND," NITTA-SAN!
SLAM!
AYA SAYA
ONE THING RIGHT AFTER ANOTHER!!
FWUMP
IT'S BEEN HALF A YEAR SINCE AYA DIED.
SATORU QUIT THE BAND AND DROPPED OUT OF HIGH SCHOOL.
HE'S HAD SEVERAL PART-TIME JOBS, BUT QUICKLY QUITS OR GETS CANNED FROM THOSE, TOO.
AND I DON'T KNOW HOW MANY GIRL-FRIENDS HE'S GONE THROUGH.

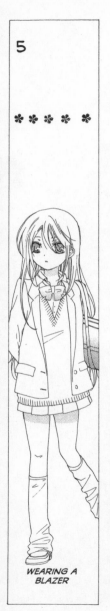

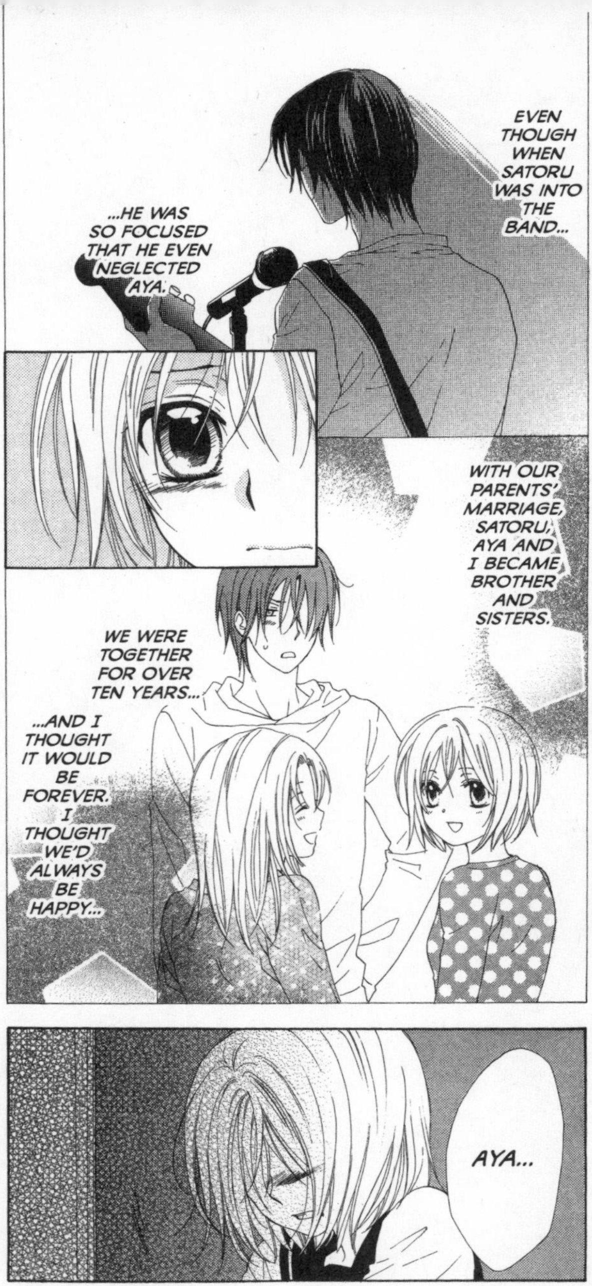
EVEN THOUGH WHEN SATORU WAS INTO THE BAND...
...HE WAS SO FOCUSED THAT HE EVEN NEGLECTED AYA.
WITH OUR PARENTS' MARRIAGE, SATORU, AYA AND I BECAME BROTHER AND SISTERS.
WE WERE TOGETHER FOR OVER TEN YEARS...
...AND I THOUGHT IT WOULD BE FOREVER. I THOUGHT WE'D ALWAYS BE HAPPY...
AYA...

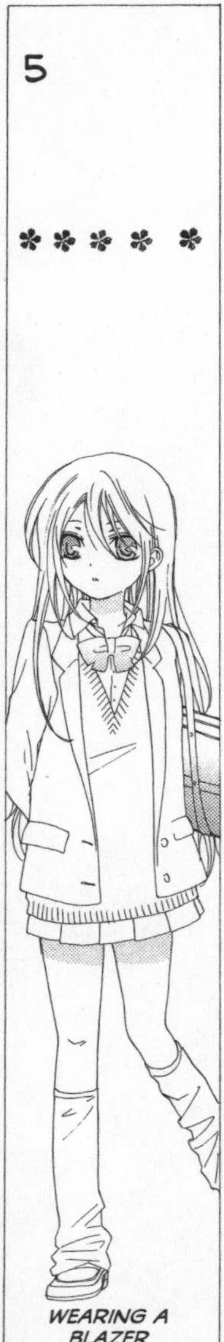
5
✽✽✽✽ ✽
WEARING A BLAZER

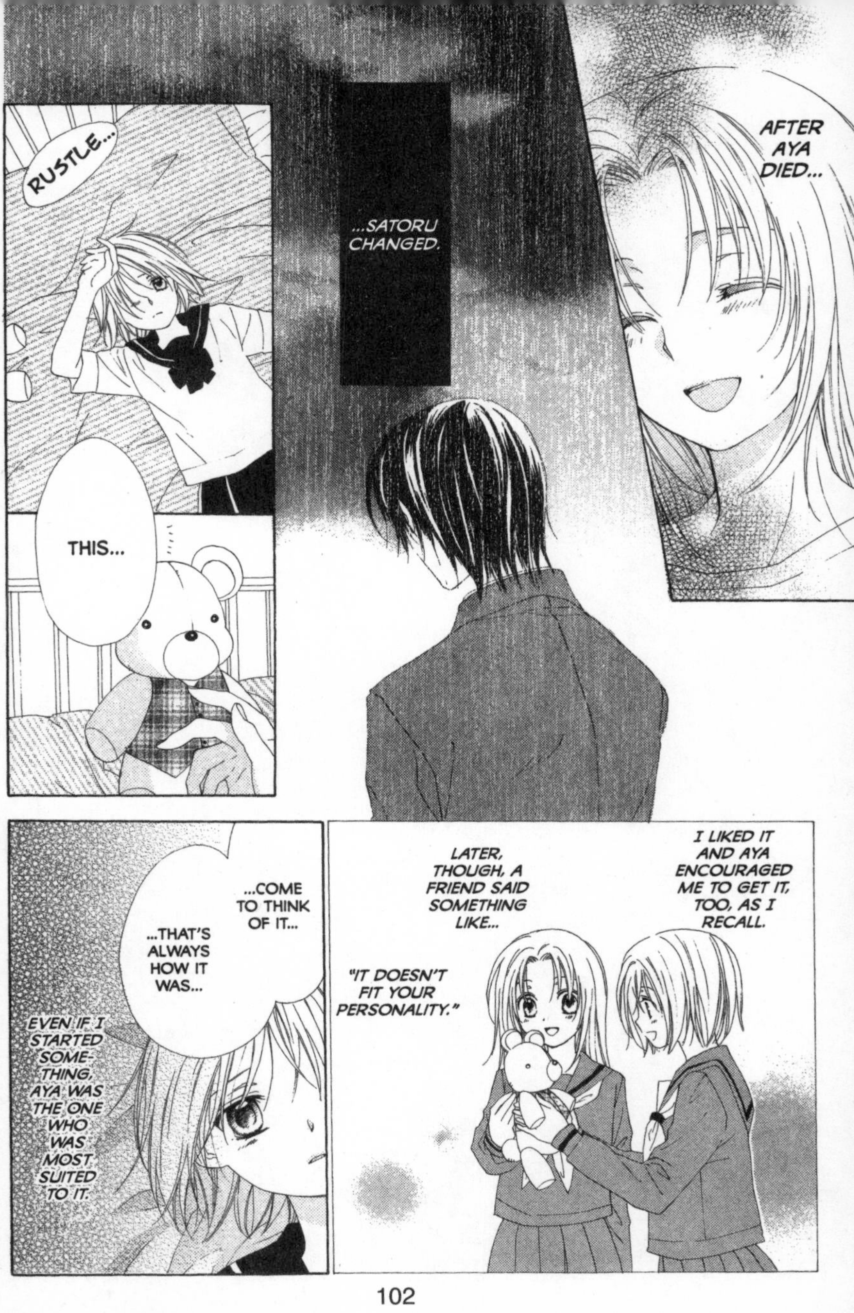
AFTER AYA DIED...
...SATORU CHANGED.
RUSTLE...
THIS...
I LIKED IT AND AYA ENCOURAGED ME TO GET IT, TOO, AS I RECALL.
LATER, THOUGH, A FRIEND SAID SOMETHING LIKE...
"IT DOESN'T FIT YOUR PERSONALITY."
...COME TO THINK OF IT...
...THAT'S ALWAYS HOW IT WAS...
EVEN IF I STARTED SOME-THING, AYA WAS THE ONE WHO WAS MOST SUITED TO IT.

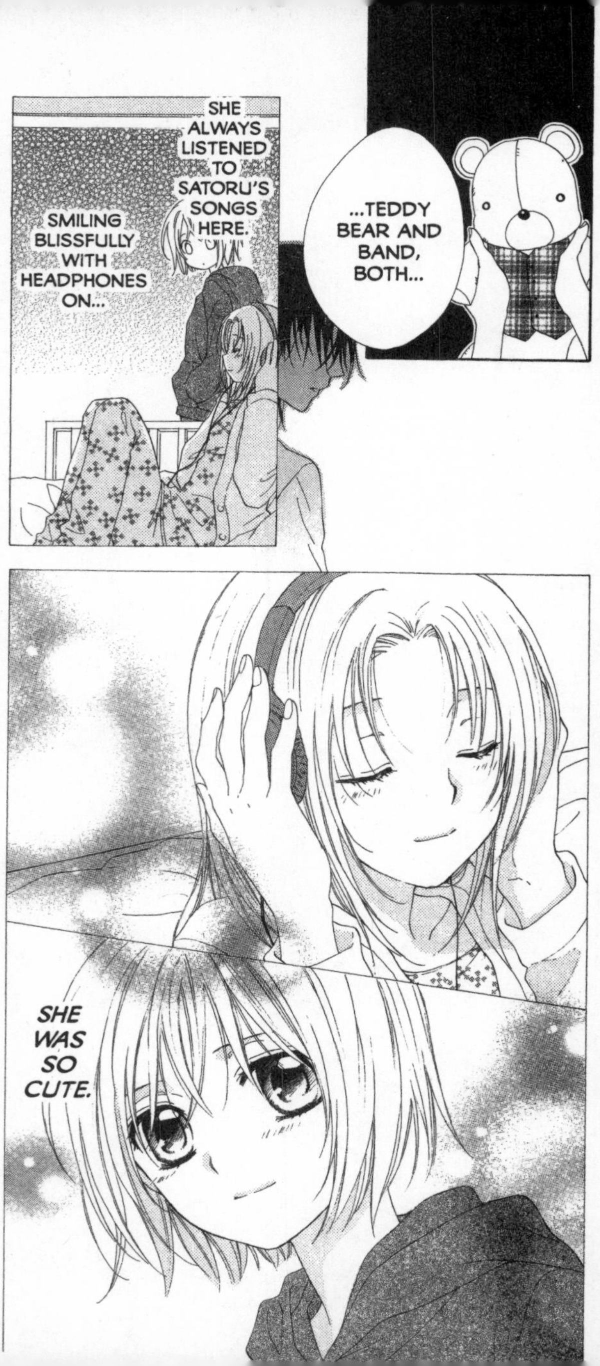

...TEDDY BEAR AND BAND, BOTH...
SHE ALWAYS LISTENED TO SATORU'S SONGS HERE.
SMILING BLISSFULLY WITH HEADPHONES ON...
SHE WAS SO CUTE.

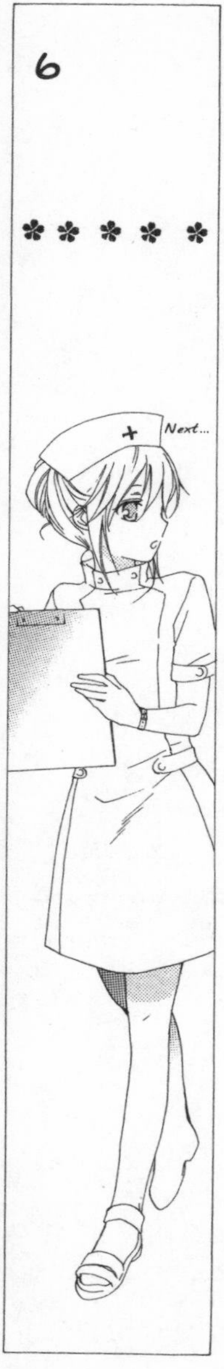

6
✿ ✿ ✿ ✿ ✿
Next...

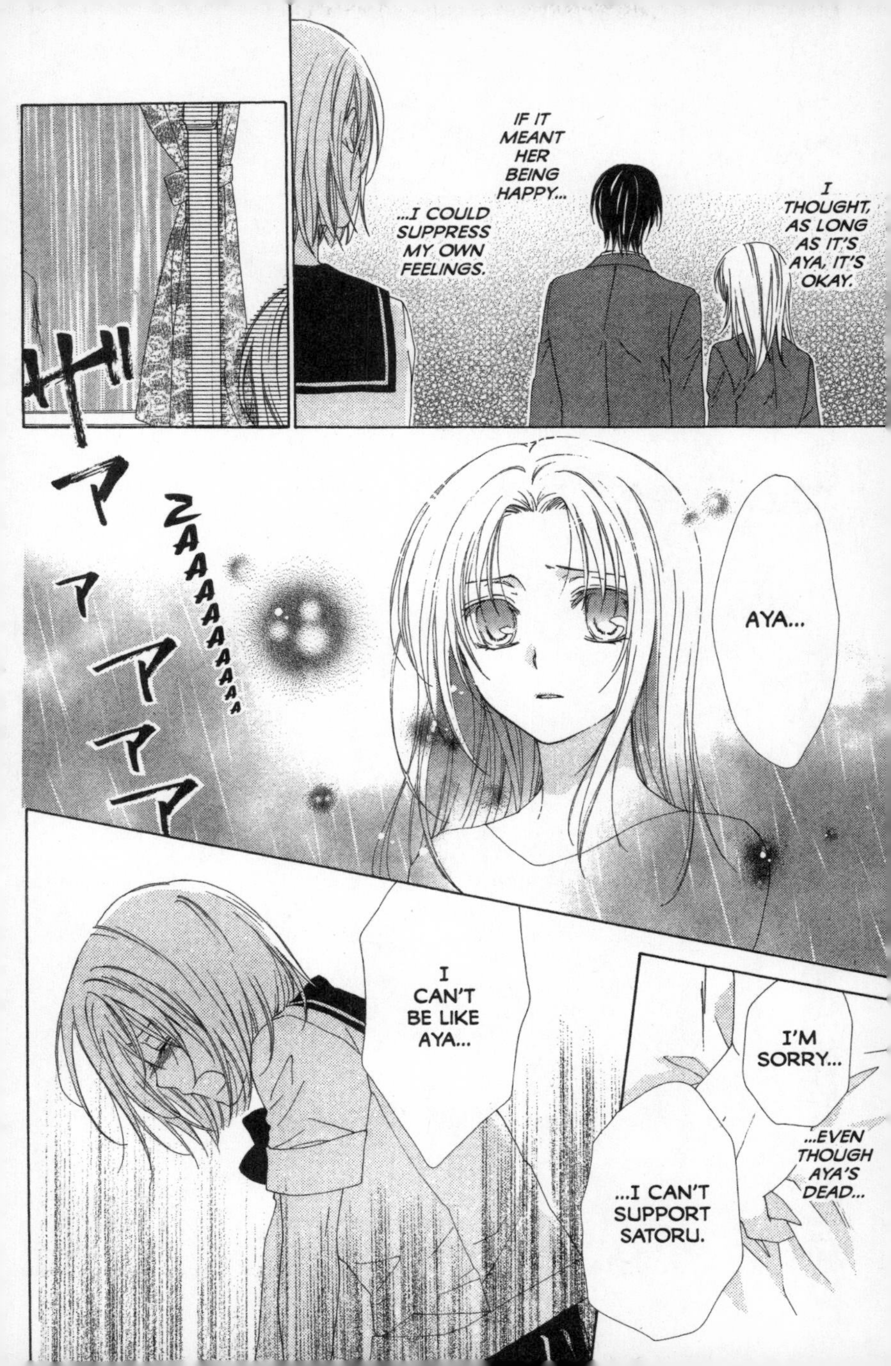
I THOUGHT, AS LONG AS IT'S AYA, IT'S OKAY.
IF IT MEANT HER BEING HAPPY...
...I COULD SUPPRESS MY OWN FEELINGS.
ザアアアアア
ZAAAAAAAAAAA
AYA...
I'M SORRY...
...EVEN THOUGH AYA'S DEAD...
...I CAN'T SUPPORT SATORU.
I CAN'T BE LIKE AYA...

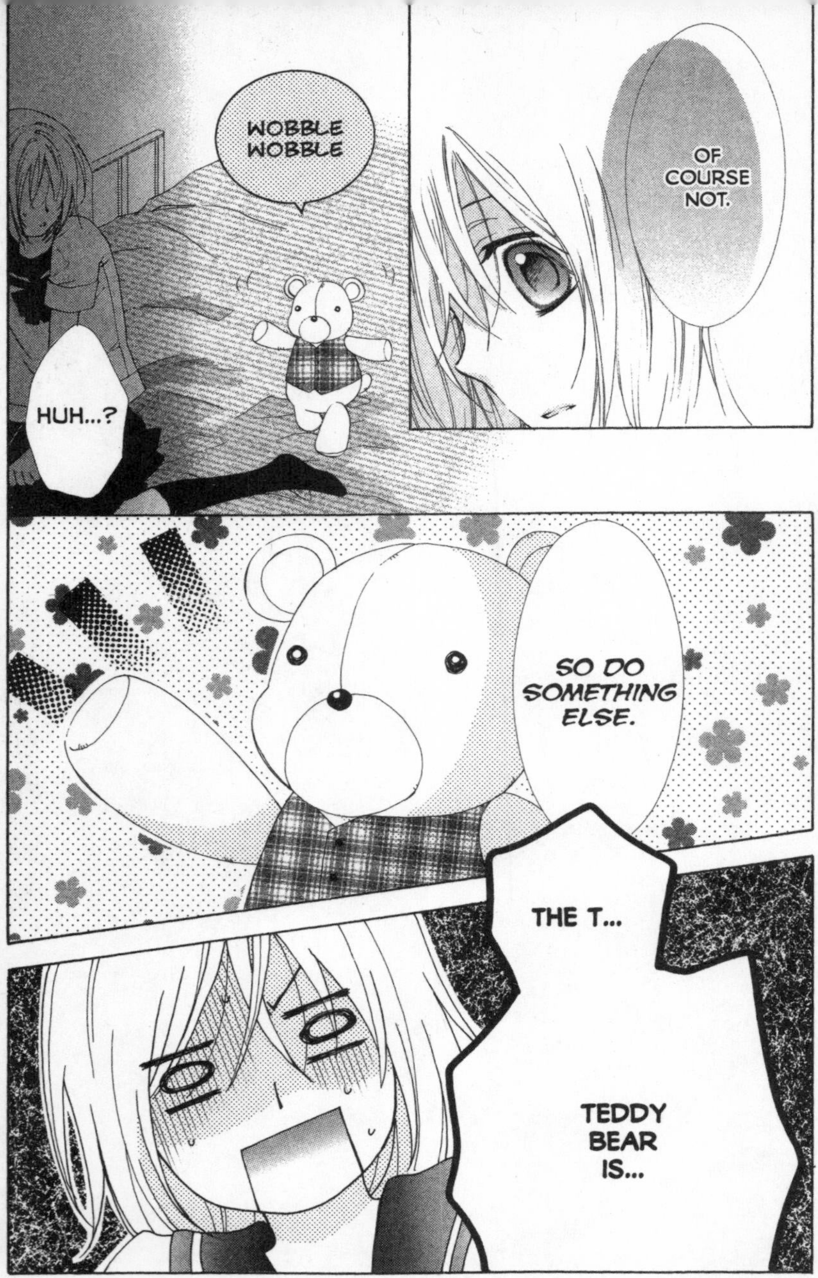
OF COURSE NOT.
WOBBLE WOBBLE
HUH...?
SO DO SOMETHING ELSE.
THE T...
TEDDY BEAR IS...

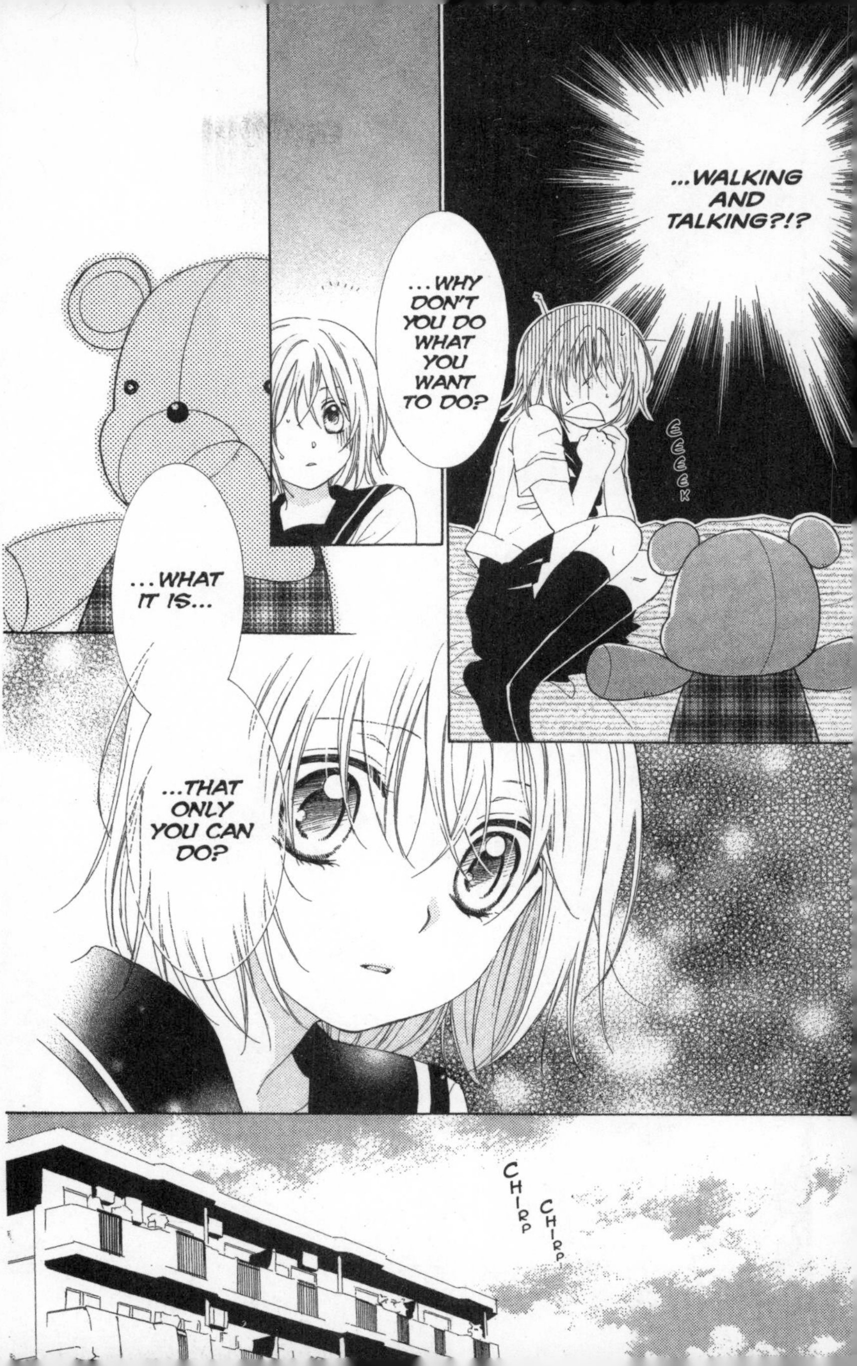
...WALKING AND TALKING?!?
EEEEK
...WHY DON'T YOU DO WHAT YOU WANT TO DO?
...WHAT IT IS...
...THAT ONLY YOU CAN DO?
CHIRP CHIRP

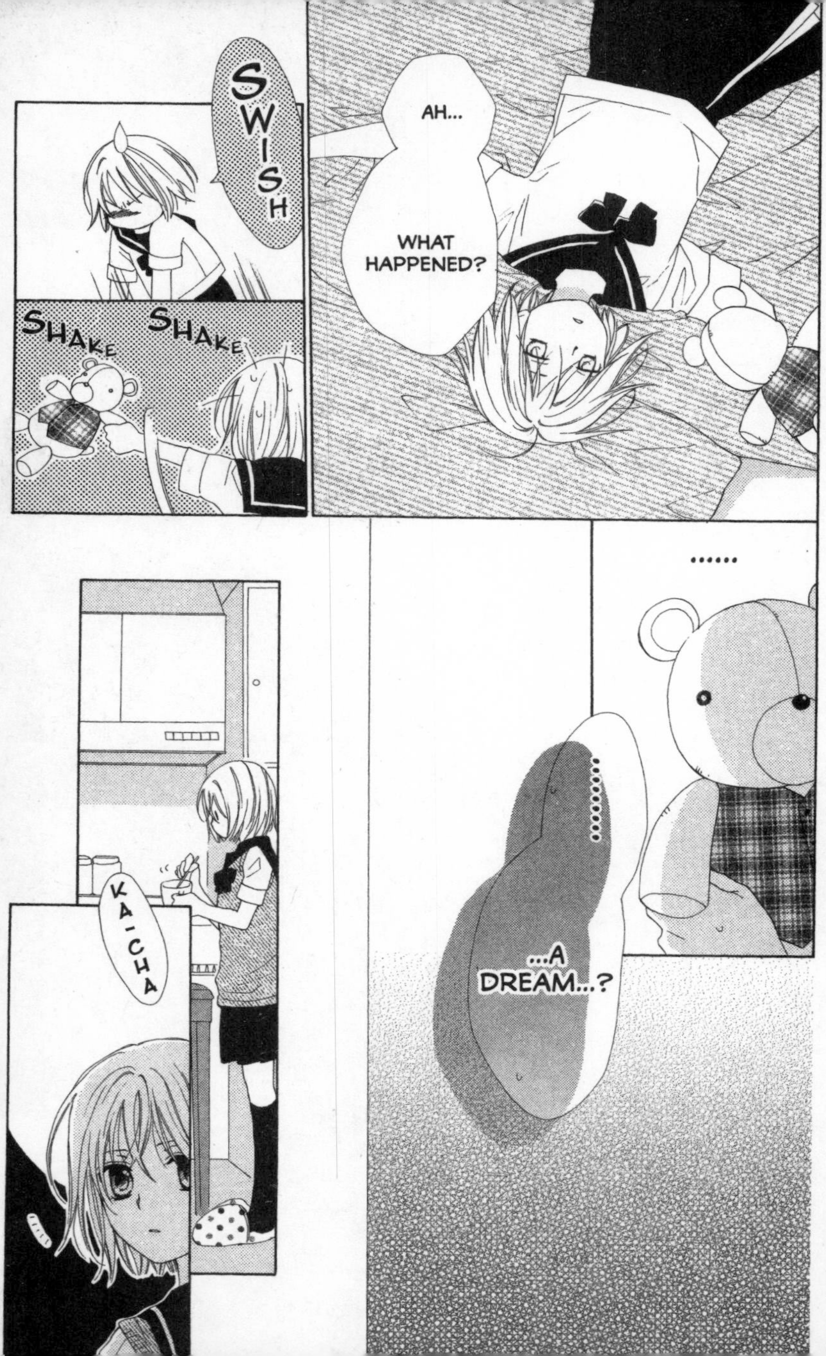
AH...
WHAT HAPPENED?
SWISH
SHAKE
SHAKE
......
....
...A DREAM...?
KA-CHA

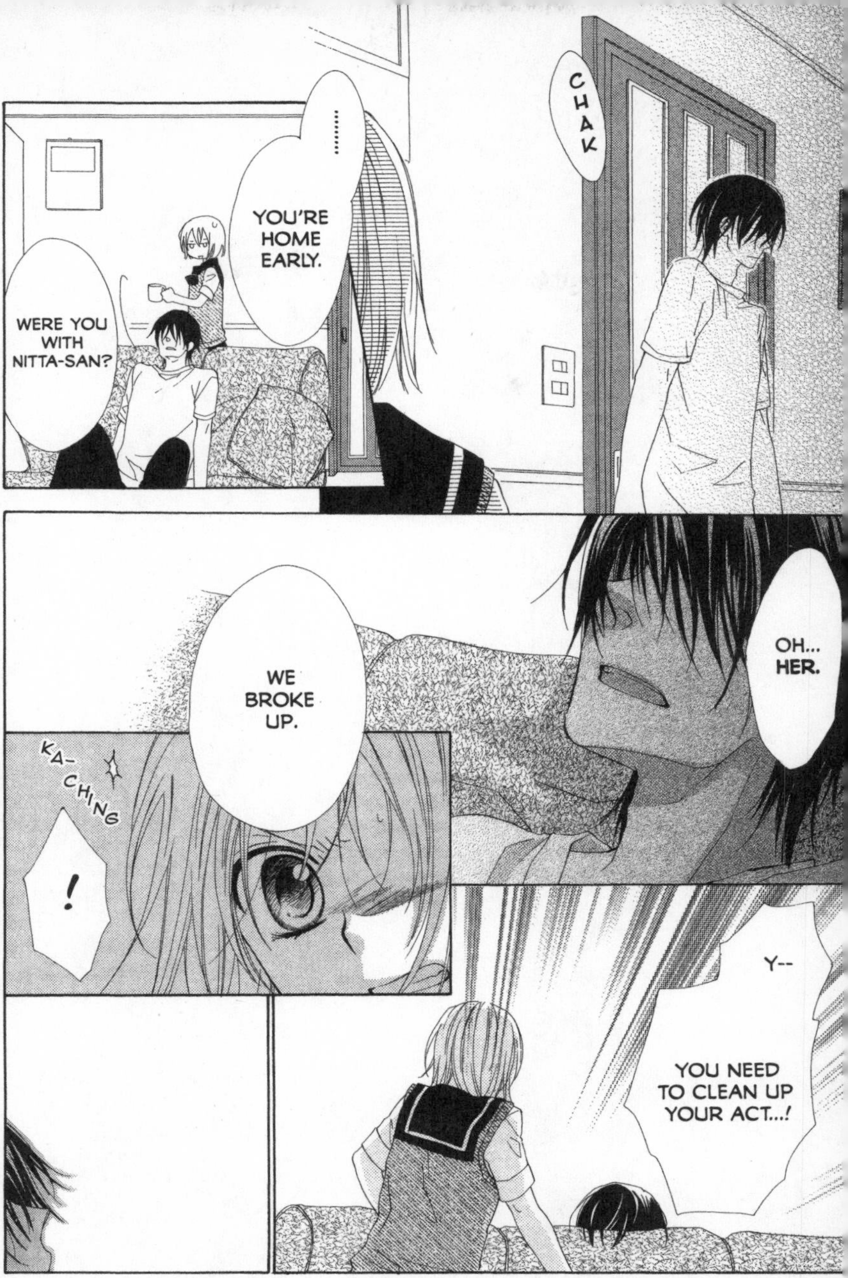
CHAK
......
YOU'RE HOME EARLY.
WERE YOU WITH NITTA-SAN?
OH... HER.
WE BROKE UP.
KA-CHING
!
Y--
YOU NEED TO CLEAN UP YOUR ACT...!

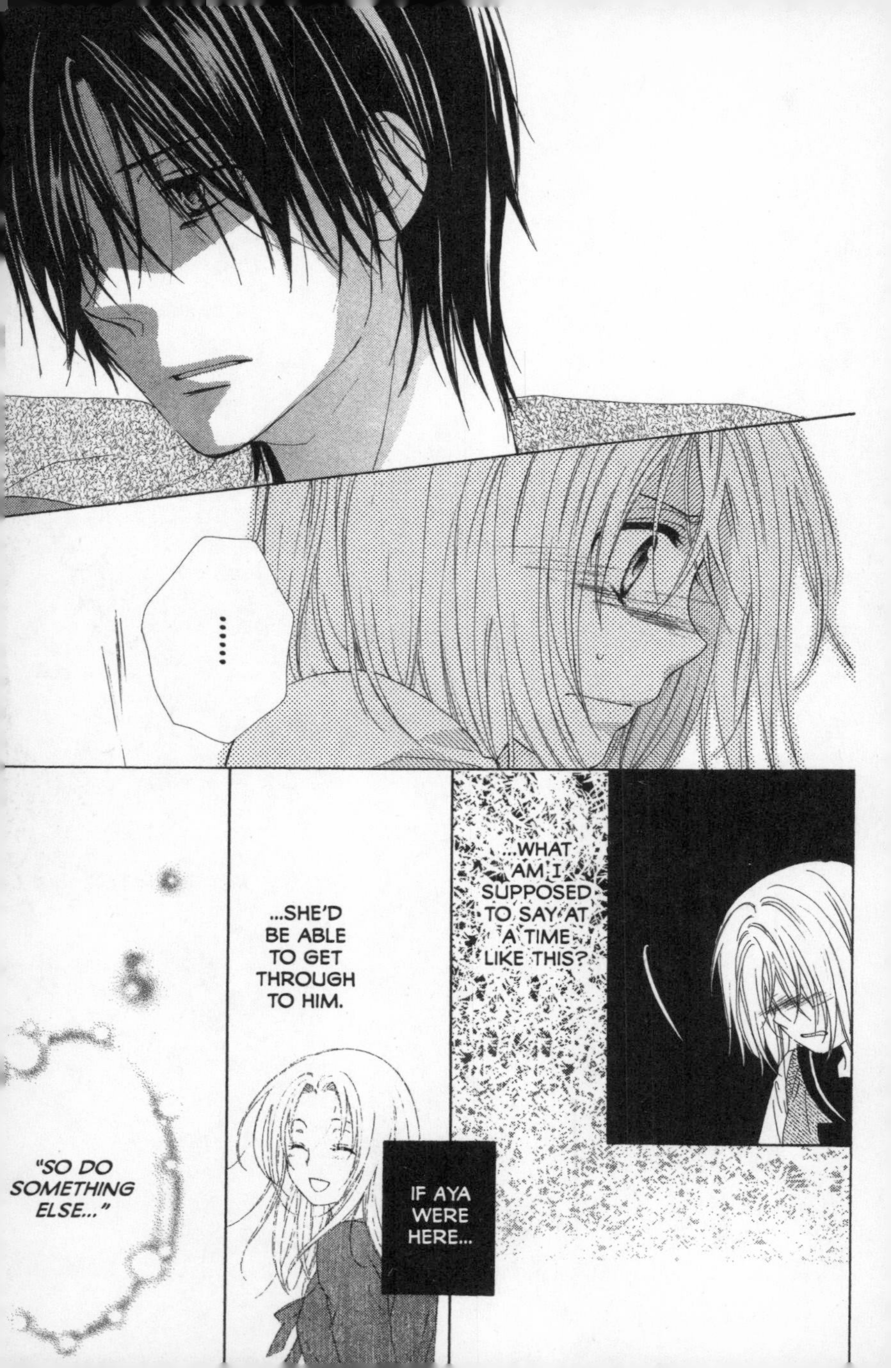
......
...WHAT AM I SUPPOSED TO SAY AT A TIME LIKE THIS?
IF AYA WERE HERE...
...SHE'D BE ABLE TO GET THROUGH TO HIM.
"SO DO SOMETHING ELSE..."

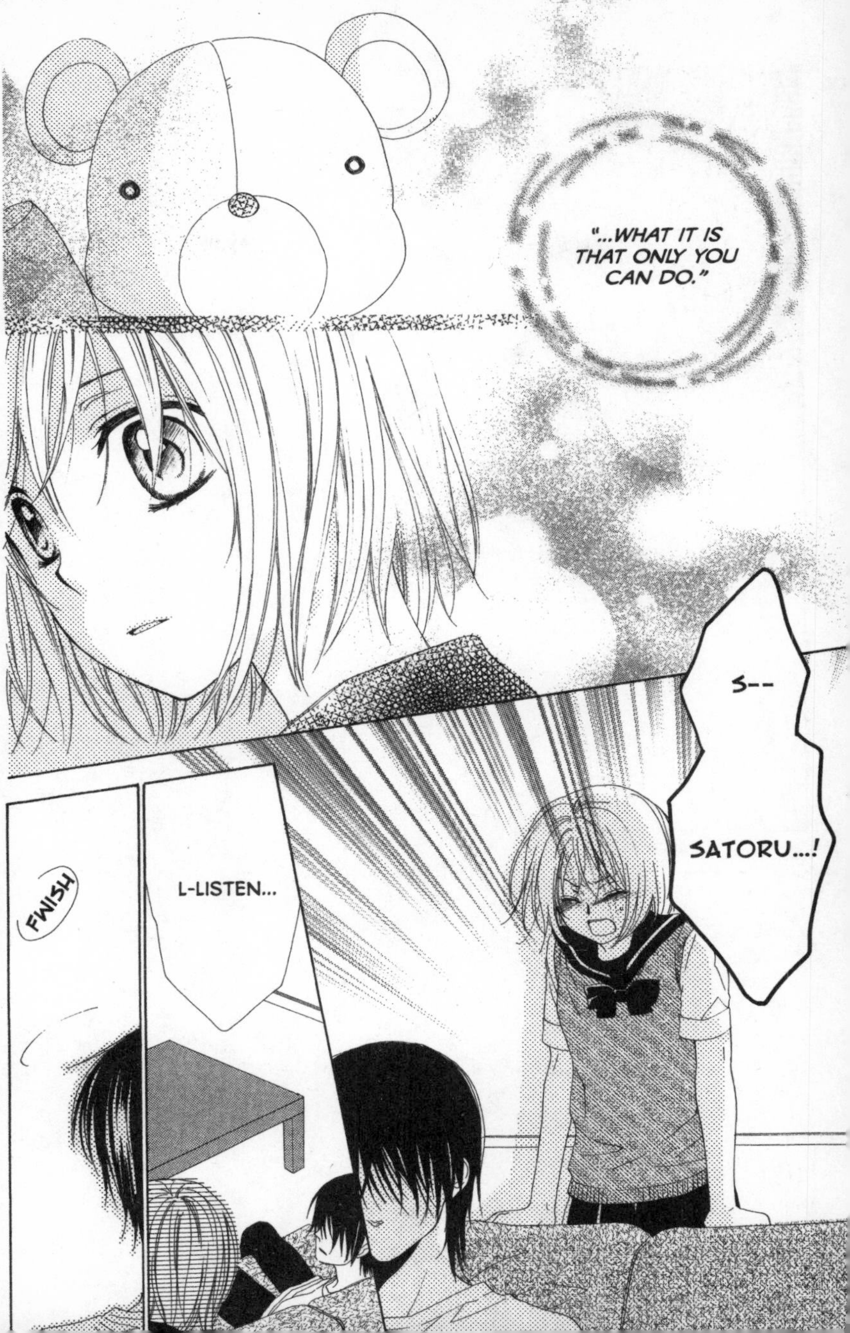
"...WHAT IT IS THAT ONLY YOU CAN DO."
S--
SATORU...!
L-LISTEN...
FWISH

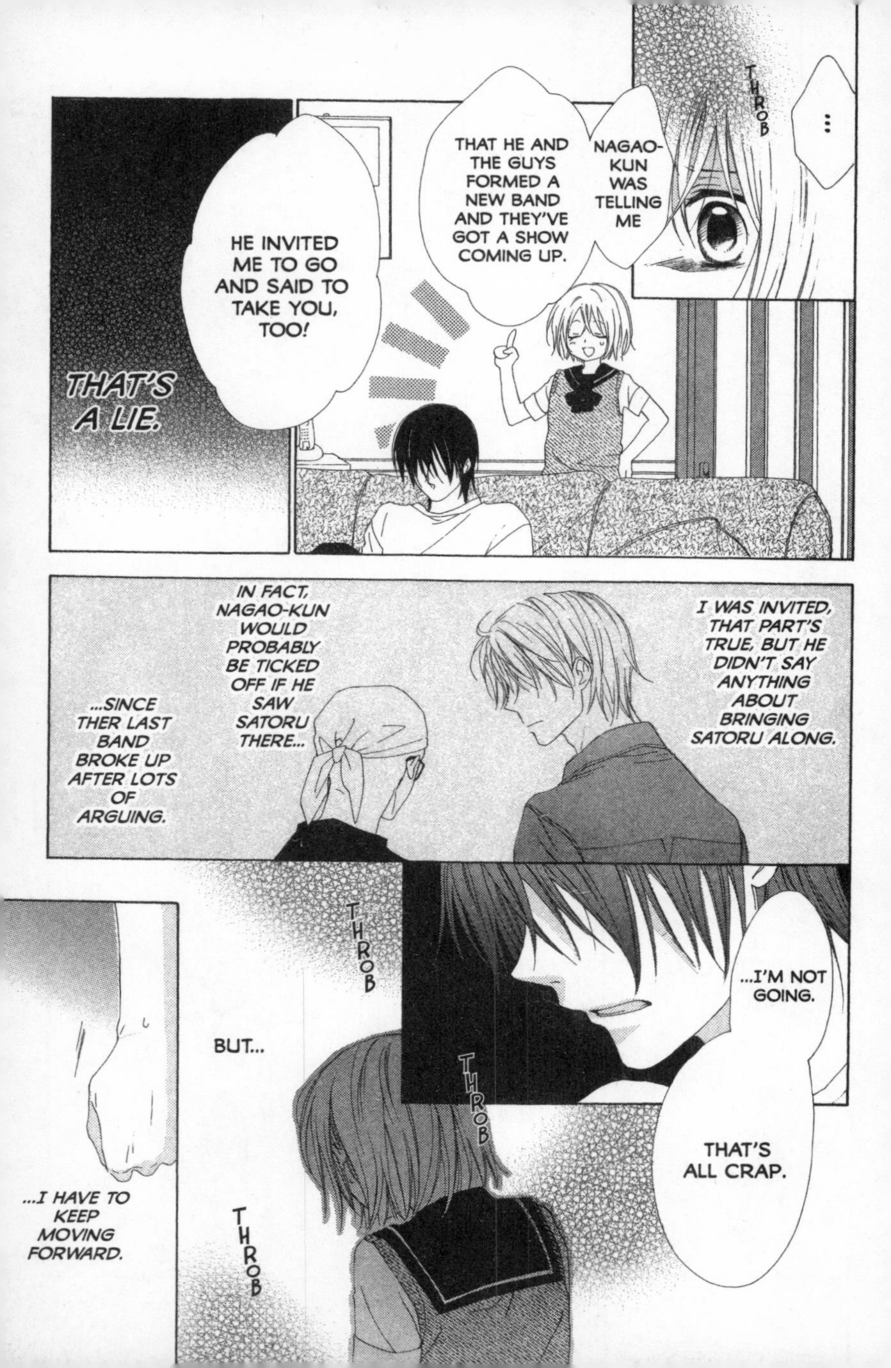
...
THROB
NAGAO-KUN WAS TELLING ME
THAT HE AND THE GUYS FORMED A NEW BAND AND THEY'VE GOT A SHOW COMING UP.
HE INVITED ME TO GO AND SAID TO TAKE YOU, TOO!
THAT'S A LIE.
I WAS INVITED, THAT PART'S TRUE, BUT HE DIDN'T SAY ANYTHING ABOUT BRINGING SATORU ALONG.
IN FACT, NAGAO-KUN WOULD PROBABLY BE TICKED OFF IF HE SAW SATORU THERE...
...SINCE THER LAST BAND BROKE UP AFTER LOTS OF ARGUING.
...I'M NOT GOING.
THAT'S ALL CRAP.
THROB
THROB
THROB
BUT...
...I HAVE TO KEEP MOVING FORWARD.

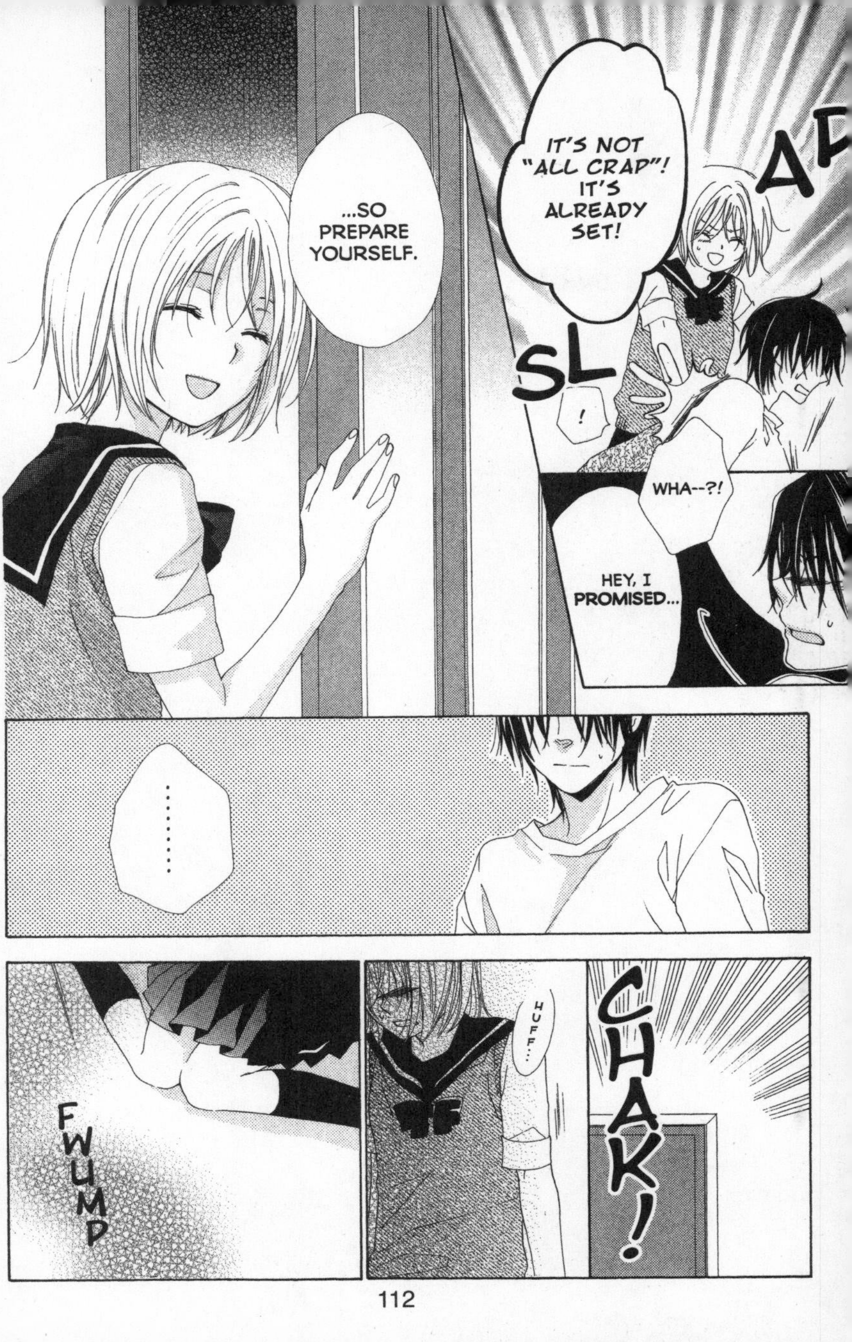
IT'S NOT "ALL CRAP"! IT'S ALREADY SET!
AP
SL
!
WHA--?!
HEY, I PROMISED...
...SO PREPARE YOURSELF.
......
CHAK!
HUFF...
FWUMP

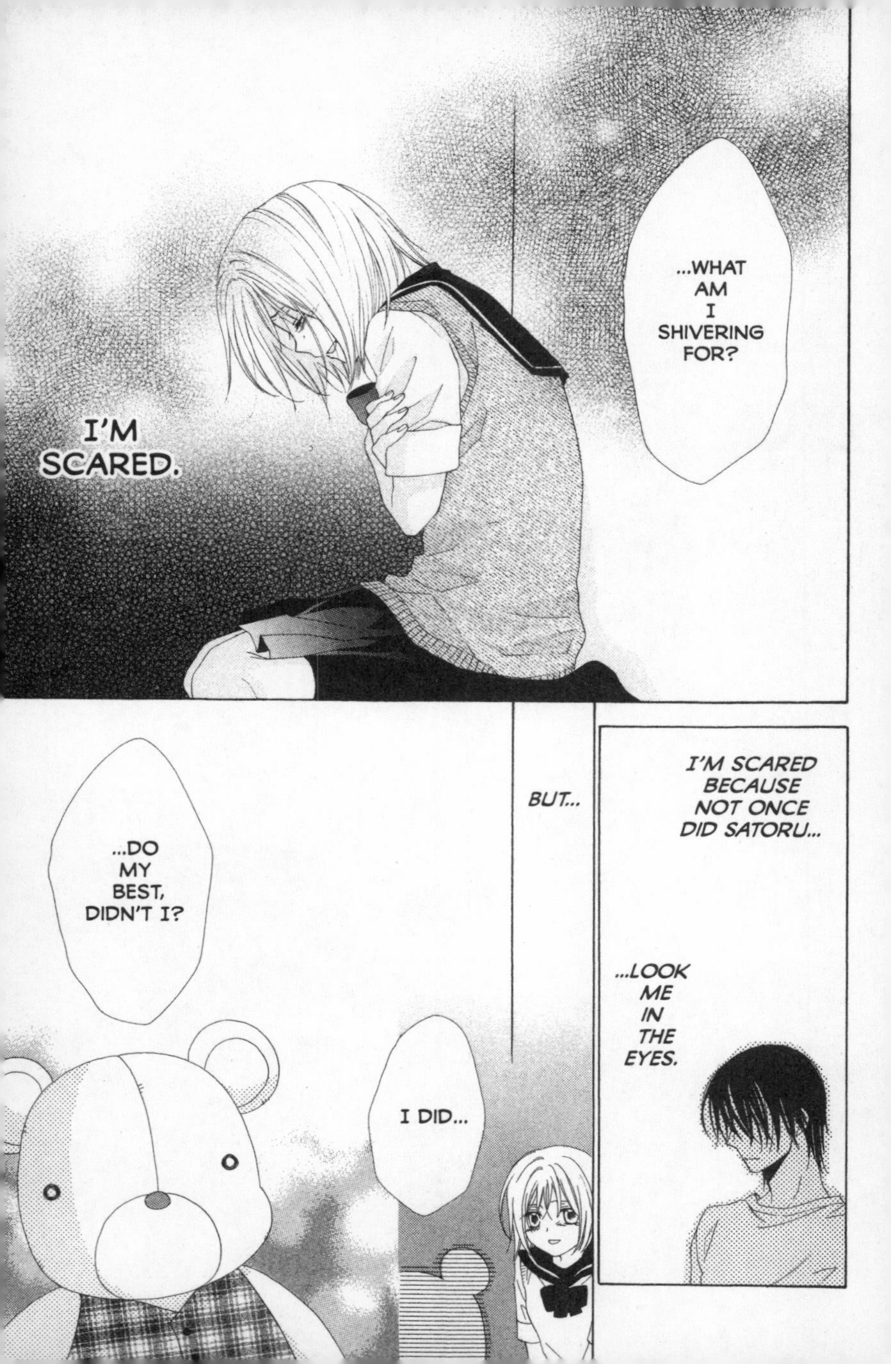
...WHAT AM I SHIVERING FOR?
I'M SCARED.
I'M SCARED BECAUSE NOT ONCE DID SATORU...
...LOOK ME IN THE EYES.
BUT...
I DID...
...DO MY BEST, DIDN'T I?

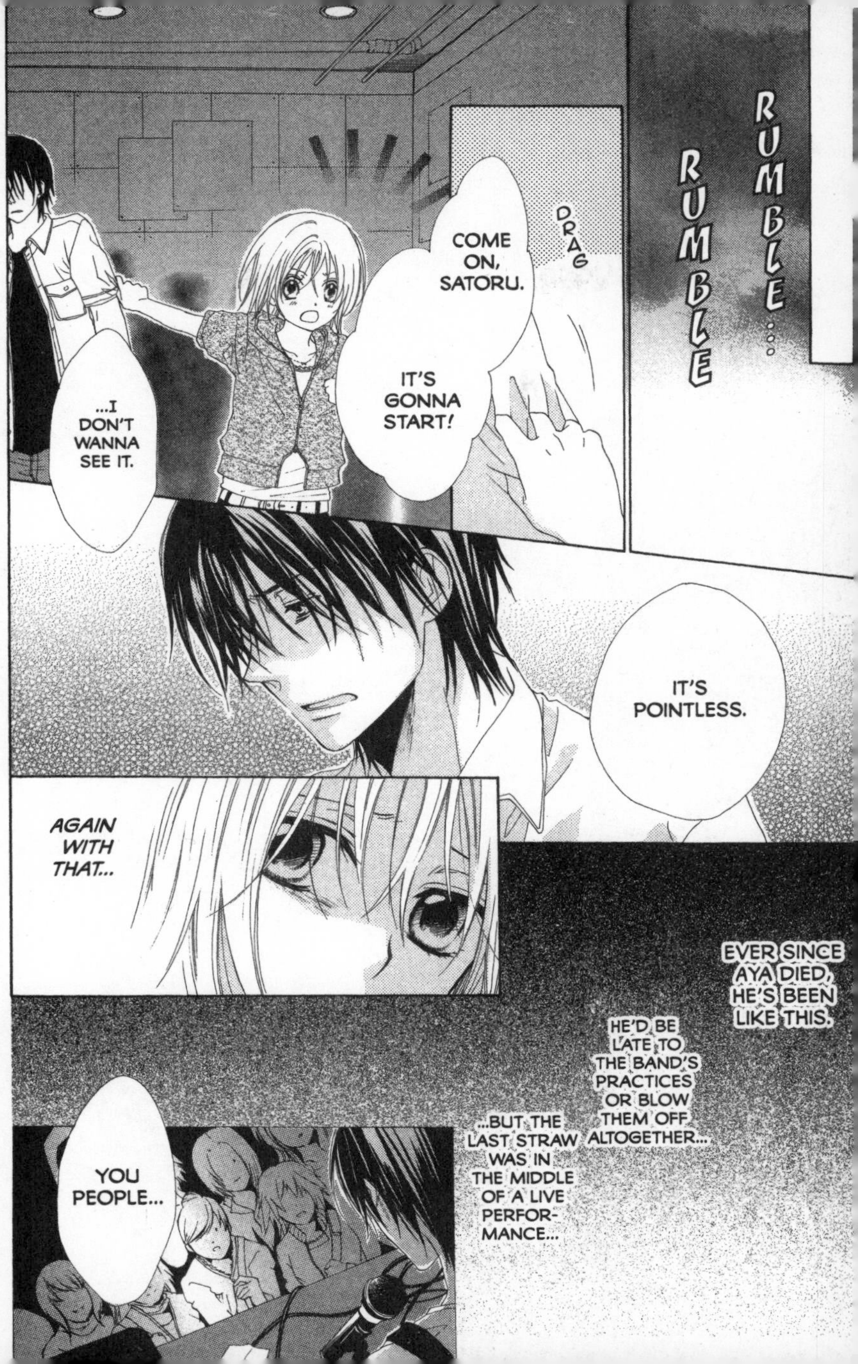
RUMBLE...
RUMBLE
DRAG
COME ON, SATORU.
IT'S GONNA START!
...I DON'T WANNA SEE IT.
IT'S POINTLESS.
AGAIN WITH THAT...
EVER SINCE AYA DIED, HE'S BEEN LIKE THIS.
HE'D BE LATE TO THE BAND'S PRACTICES OR BLOW THEM OFF ALTOGETHER...
...BUT THE LAST STRAW WAS IN THE MIDDLE OF A LIVE PERFORMANCE...
YOU PEOPLE...

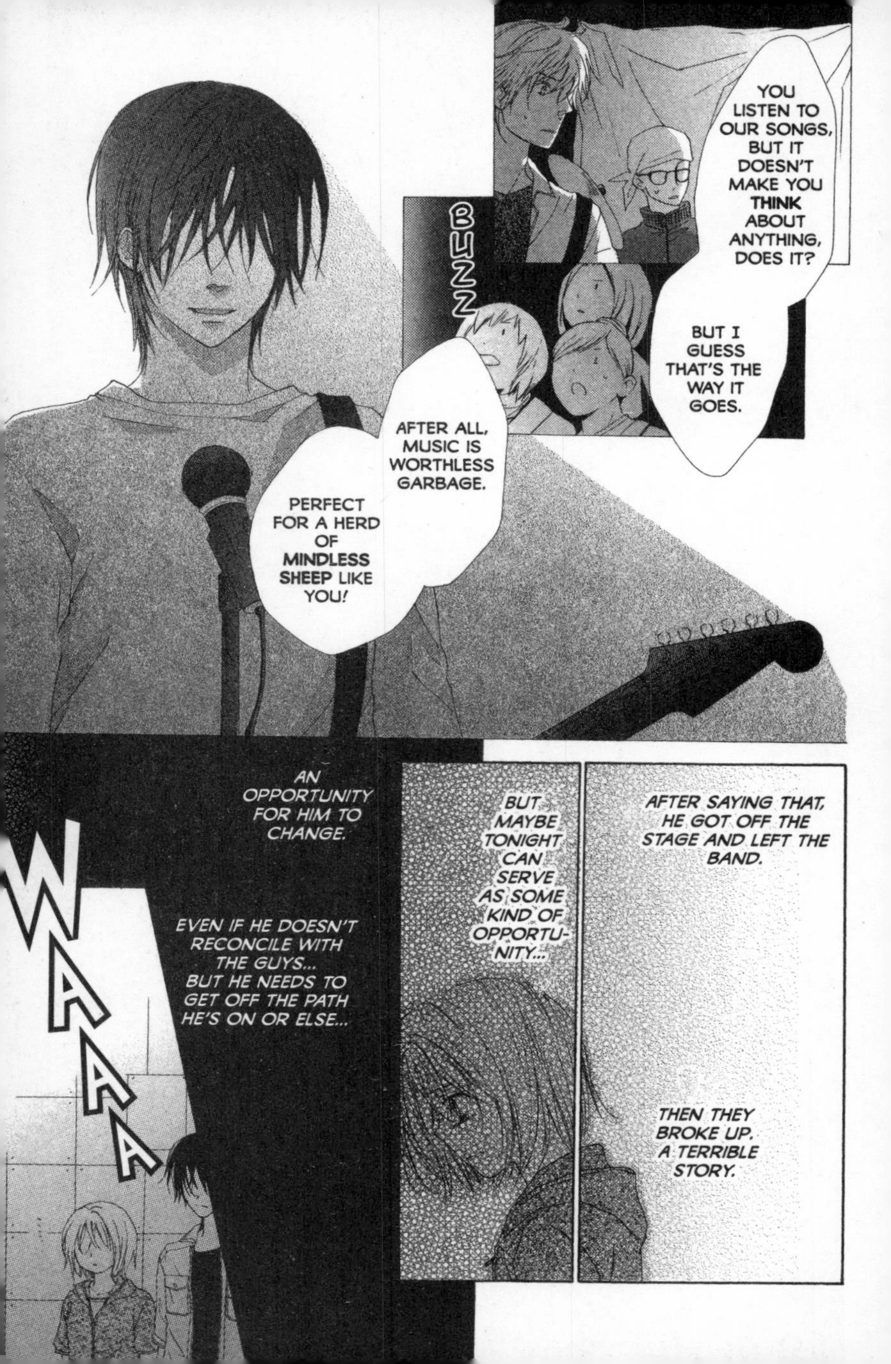
YOU LISTEN TO OUR SONGS, BUT IT DOESN'T MAKE YOU THINK ABOUT ANYTHING, DOES IT?
BUT I GUESS THAT'S THE WAY IT GOES.
BUZZ
AFTER ALL, MUSIC IS WORTHLESS GARBAGE.
PERFECT FOR A HERD OF MINDLESS SHEEP LIKE YOU!
AFTER SAYING THAT, HE GOT OFF THE STAGE AND LEFT THE BAND.
THEN THEY BROKE UP. A TERRIBLE STORY.
BUT MAYBE TONIGHT CAN SERVE AS SOME KIND OF OPPORTU-NITY...
AN OPPORTUNITY FOR HIM TO CHANGE.
EVEN IF HE DOESN'T RECONCILE WITH THE GUYS... BUT HE NEEDS TO GET OFF THE PATH HE'S ON OR ELSE...
WAAAA

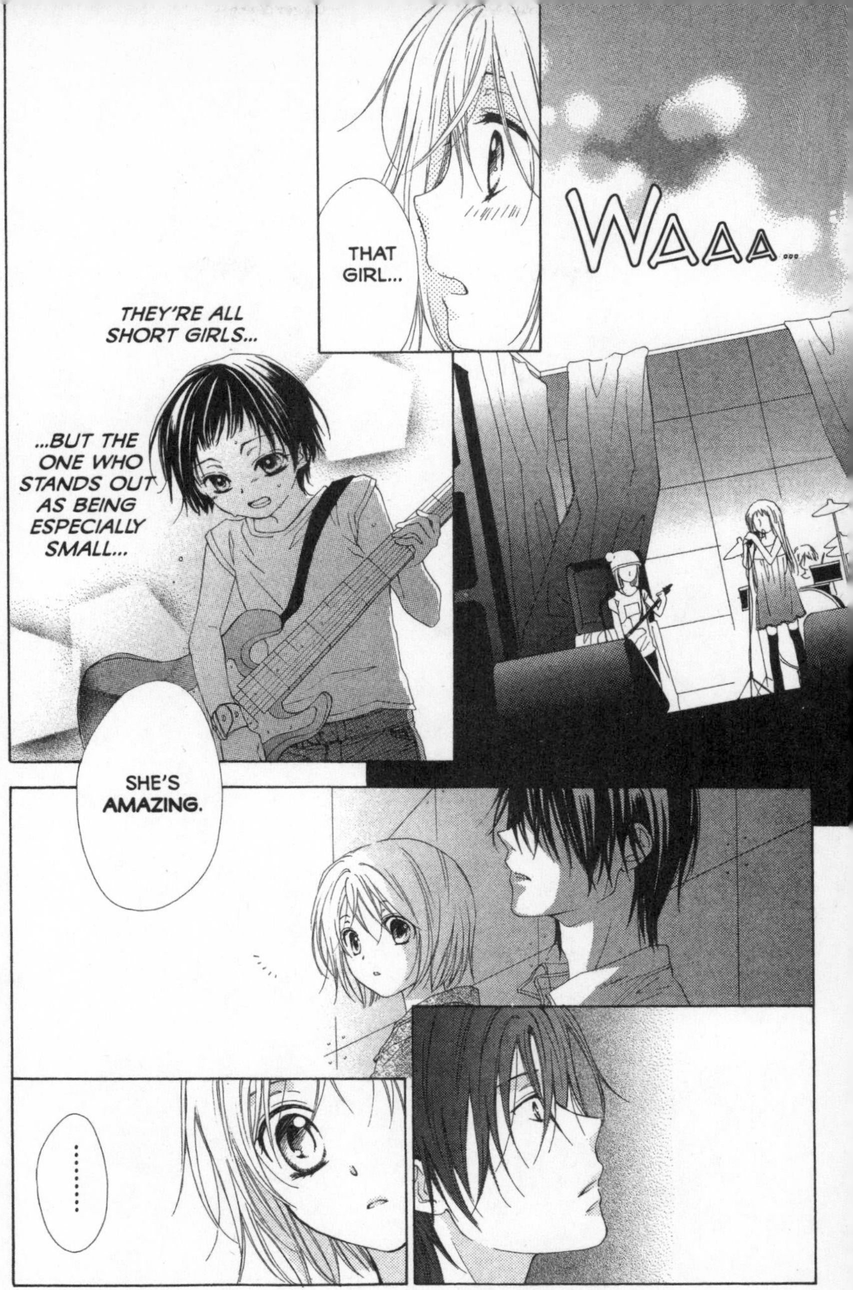
WAAA...
THAT GIRL...
THEY'RE ALL SHORT GIRLS...
...BUT THE ONE WHO STANDS OUT AS BEING ESPECIALLY SMALL...
SHE'S **AMAZING.**
....

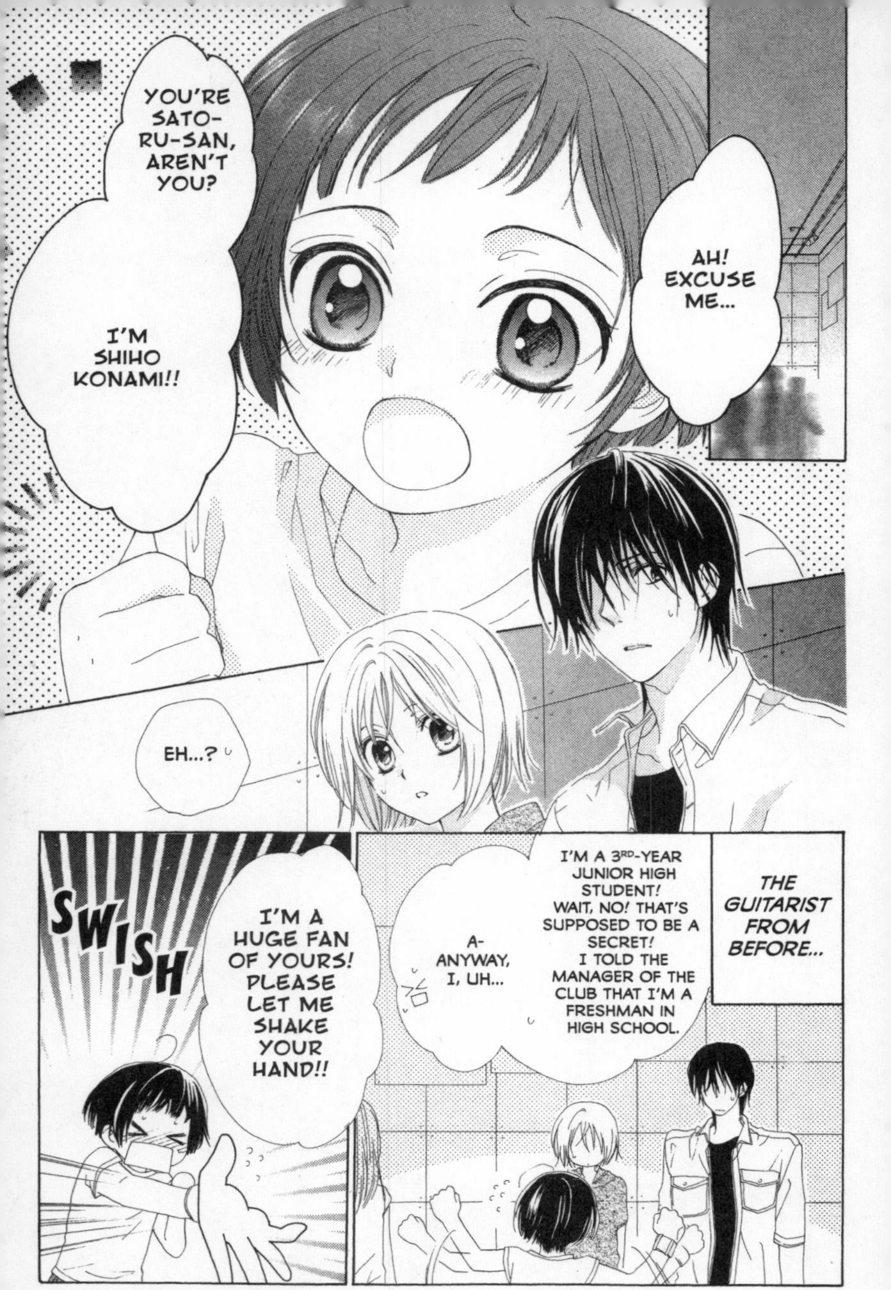
AH! EXCUSE ME...
YOU'RE SATO-RU-SAN, AREN'T YOU?
I'M SHIHO KONAMI!!
EH...?
THE GUITARIST FROM BEFORE...
I'M A 3RD-YEAR JUNIOR HIGH STUDENT! WAIT, NO! THAT'S SUPPOSED TO BE A SECRET! I TOLD THE MANAGER OF THE CLUB THAT I'M A FRESHMAN IN HIGH SCHOOL.
A- ANYWAY, I, UH...
SWISH
I'M A HUGE FAN OF YOURS! PLEASE LET ME SHAKE YOUR HAND!!

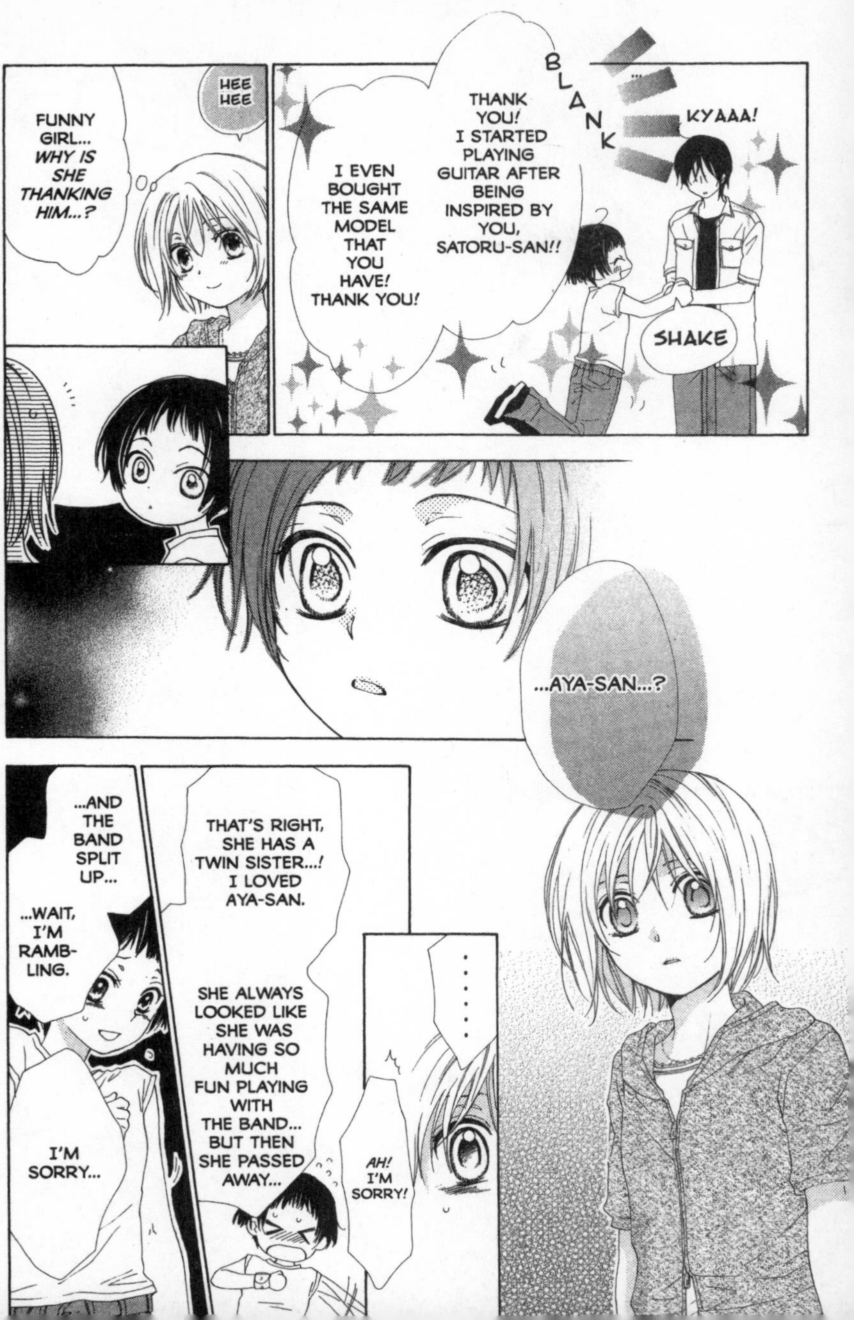
BLANK
...
KYAAA!
THANK YOU! I STARTED PLAYING GUITAR AFTER BEING INSPIRED BY YOU, SATORU-SAN!!
I EVEN BOUGHT THE SAME MODEL THAT YOU HAVE! THANK YOU!
SHAKE
HEE HEE
FUNNY GIRL... *WHY IS SHE THANKING HIM...?*
...AYA-SAN...?
THAT'S RIGHT, SHE HAS A TWIN SISTER...! I LOVED AYA-SAN.
SHE ALWAYS LOOKED LIKE SHE WAS HAVING SO MUCH FUN PLAYING WITH THE BAND... BUT THEN SHE PASSED AWAY...
......
AH! I'M SORRY!
...AND THE BAND SPLIT UP...
...WAIT, I'M RAMBLING.
I'M SORRY...

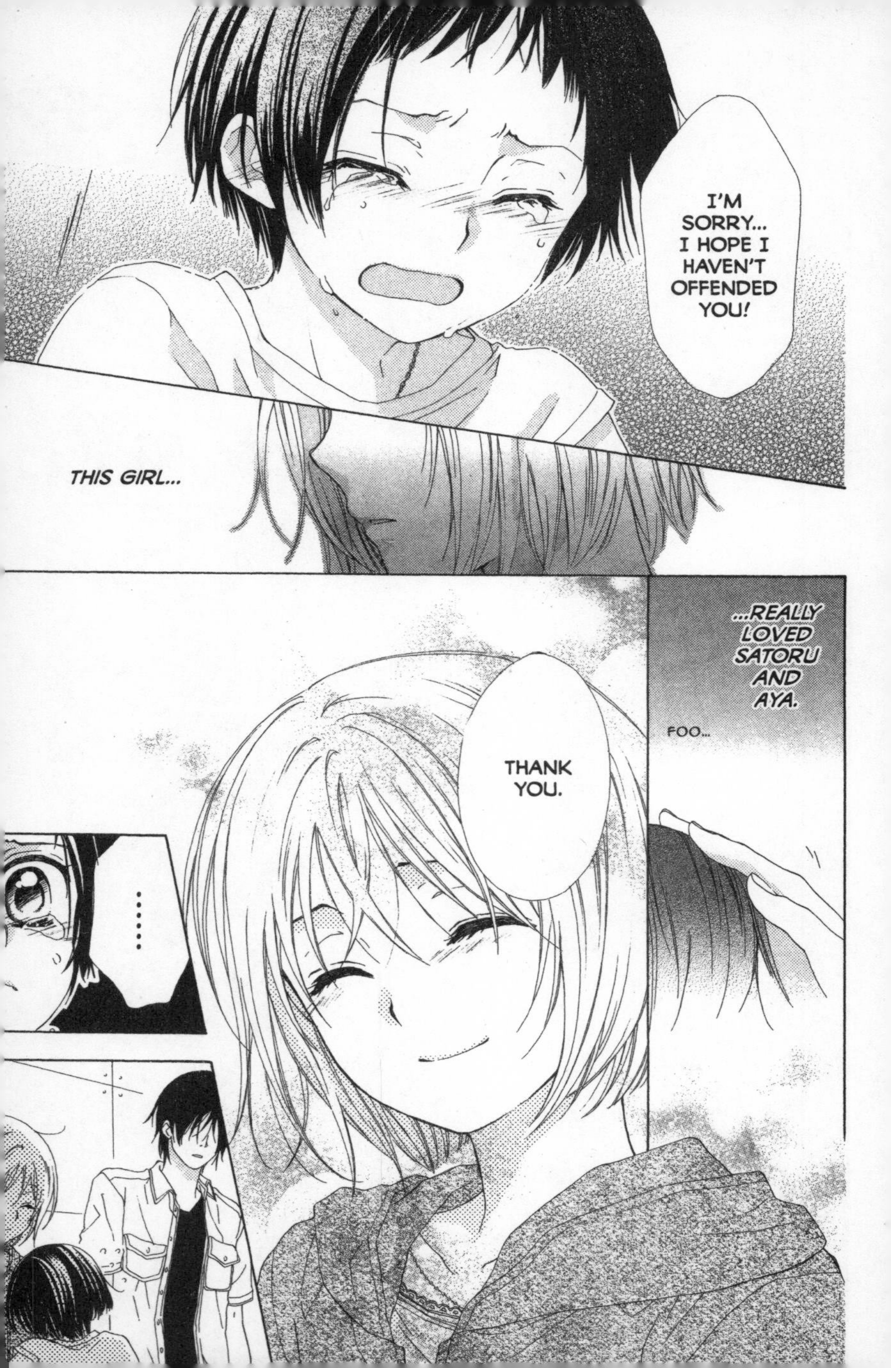
I'M SORRY... I HOPE I HAVEN'T OFFENDED YOU!
THIS GIRL...
...REALLY LOVED SATORU AND AYA.
FOO...
THANK YOU.
......

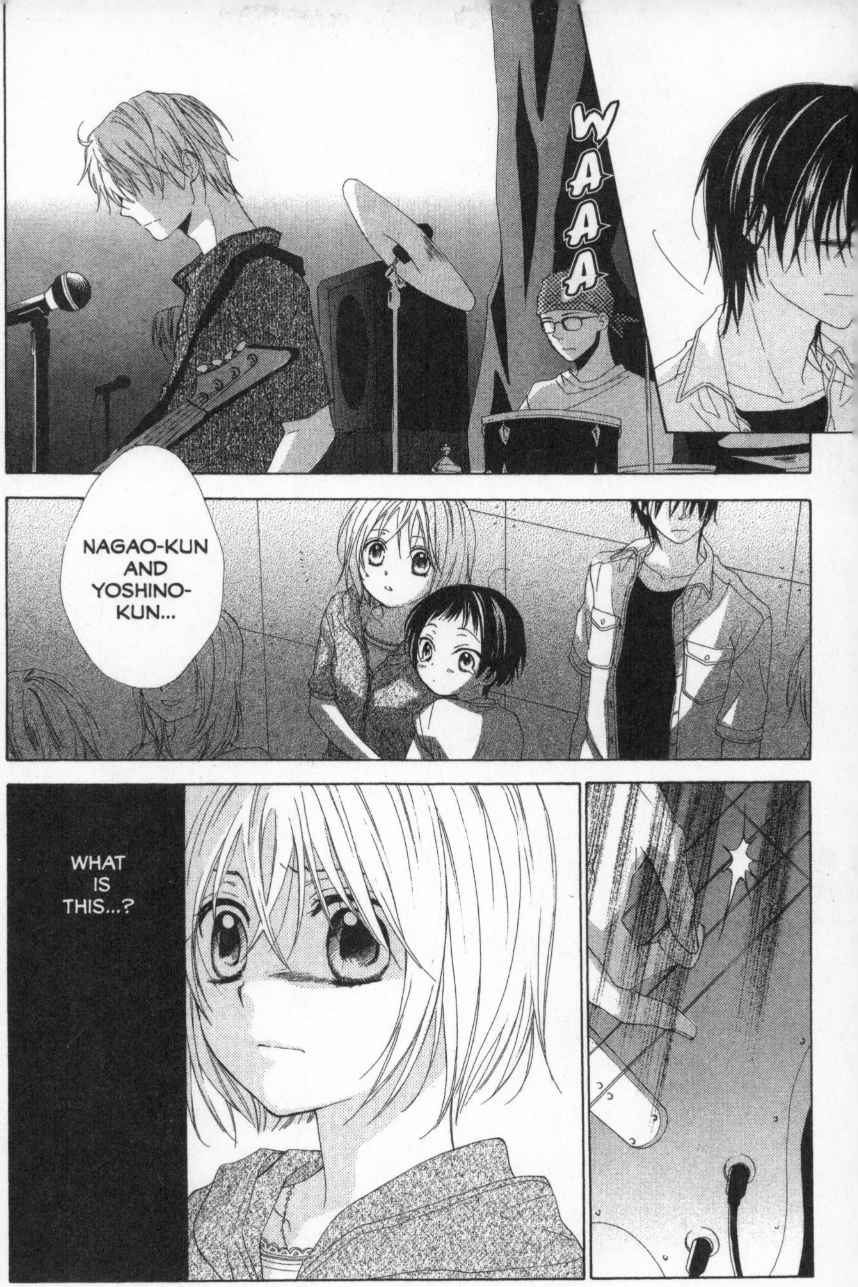
WAAAA
NAGAO-KUN AND YOSHINO-KUN...
WHAT IS THIS...?

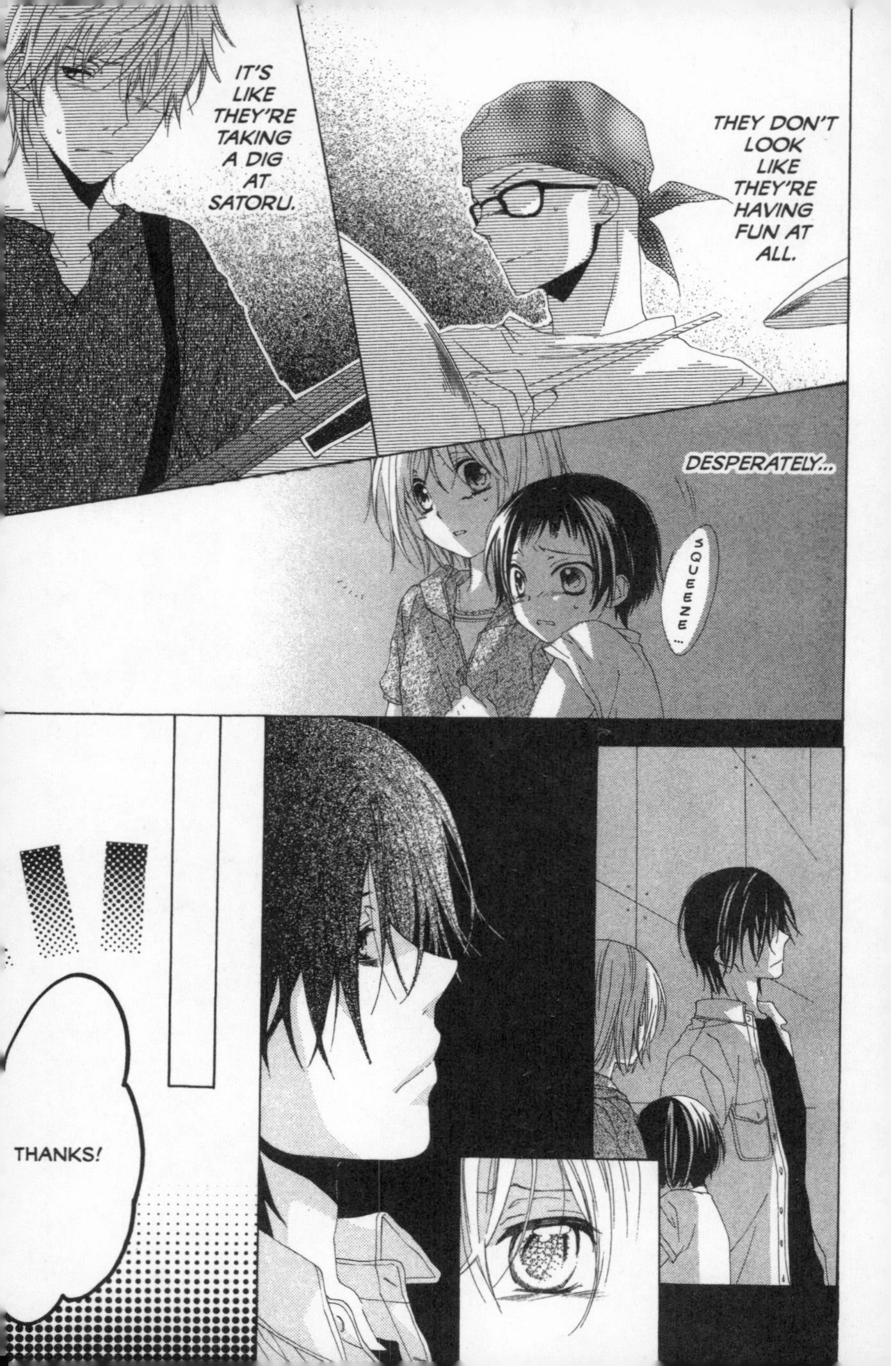
THEY DON'T LOOK LIKE THEY'RE HAVING FUN AT ALL.
IT'S LIKE THEY'RE TAKING A DIG AT SATORU.
DESPERATELY...
SQUEEZE...
THANKS!

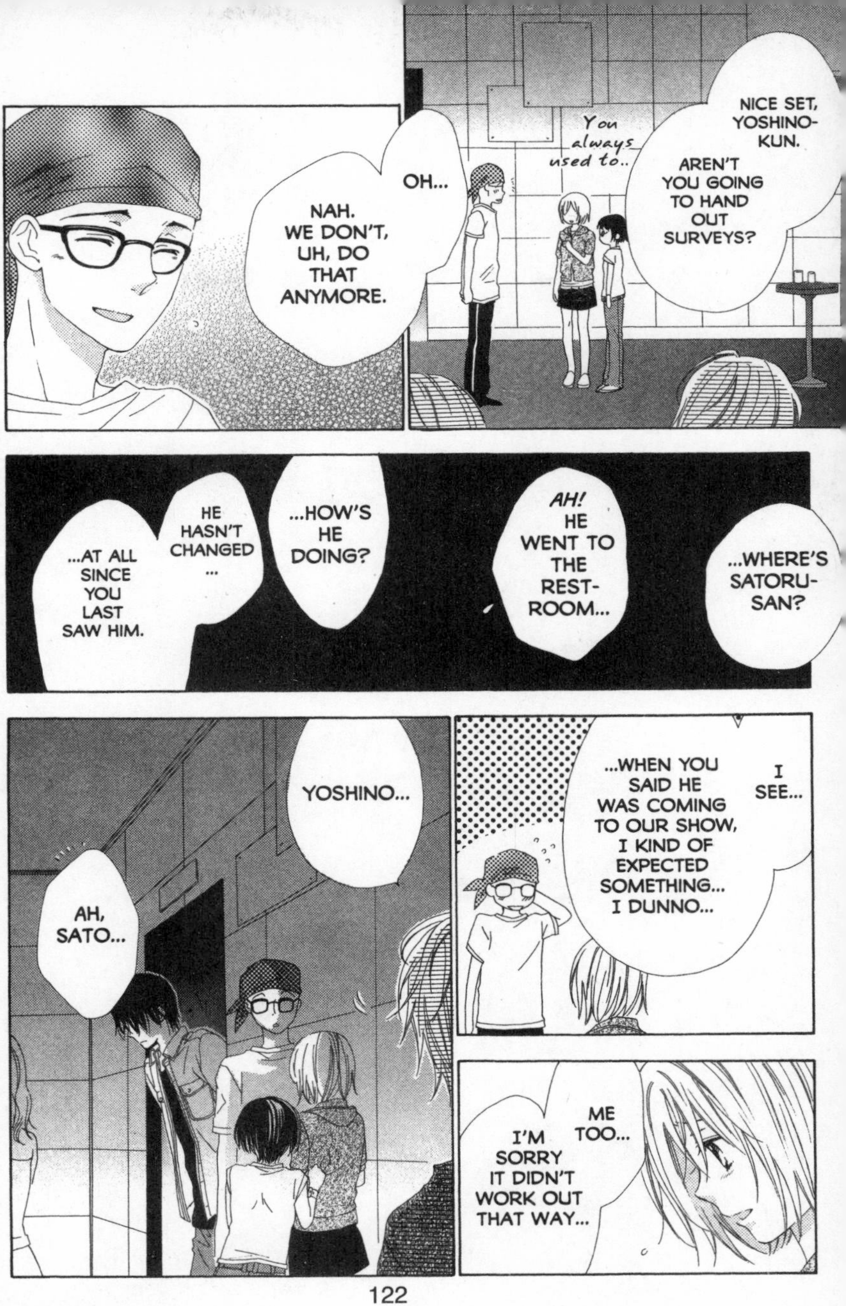
NICE SET, YOSHINO-KUN.
AREN'T YOU GOING TO HAND OUT SURVEYS?
You always used to..
OH...
NAH. WE DON'T, UH, DO THAT ANYMORE.
...WHERE'S SATORU-SAN?
AH! HE WENT TO THE REST-ROOM...
...HOW'S HE DOING?
HE HASN'T CHANGED...
...AT ALL SINCE YOU LAST SAW HIM.
I SEE...
...WHEN YOU SAID HE WAS COMING TO OUR SHOW, I KIND OF EXPECTED SOMETHING... I DUNNO...
ME TOO...
I'M SORRY IT DIDN'T WORK OUT THAT WAY...
YOSHINO...
AH, SATO...

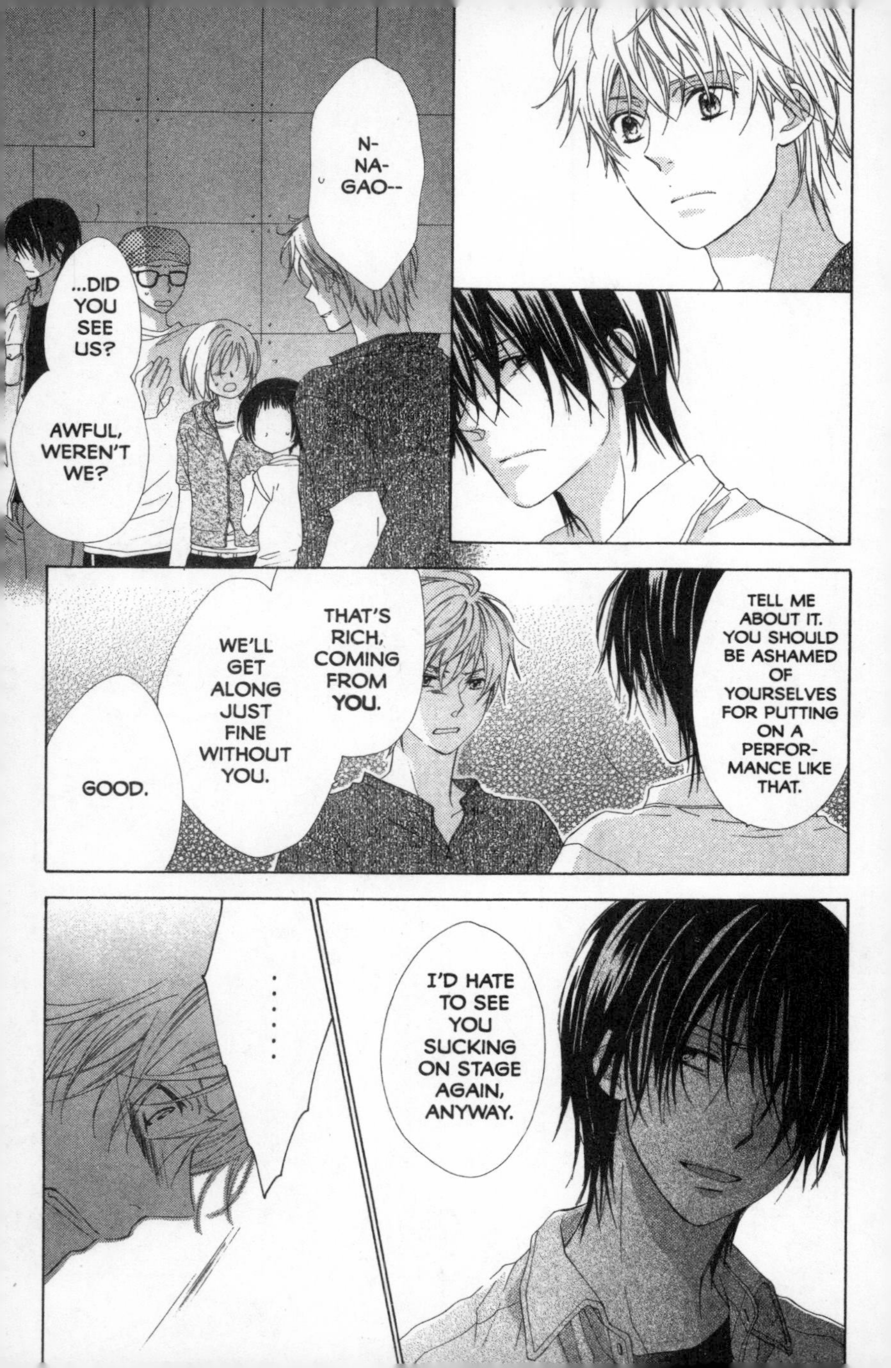
N-
NA-
GAO--
...DID YOU SEE US?
AWFUL, WEREN'T WE?
TELL ME ABOUT IT. YOU SHOULD BE ASHAMED OF YOURSELVES FOR PUTTING ON A PERFOR-MANCE LIKE THAT.
THAT'S RICH, COMING FROM **YOU**.
WE'LL GET ALONG JUST FINE WITHOUT YOU.
GOOD.
I'D HATE TO SEE YOU SUCKING ON STAGE AGAIN, ANYWAY.
......

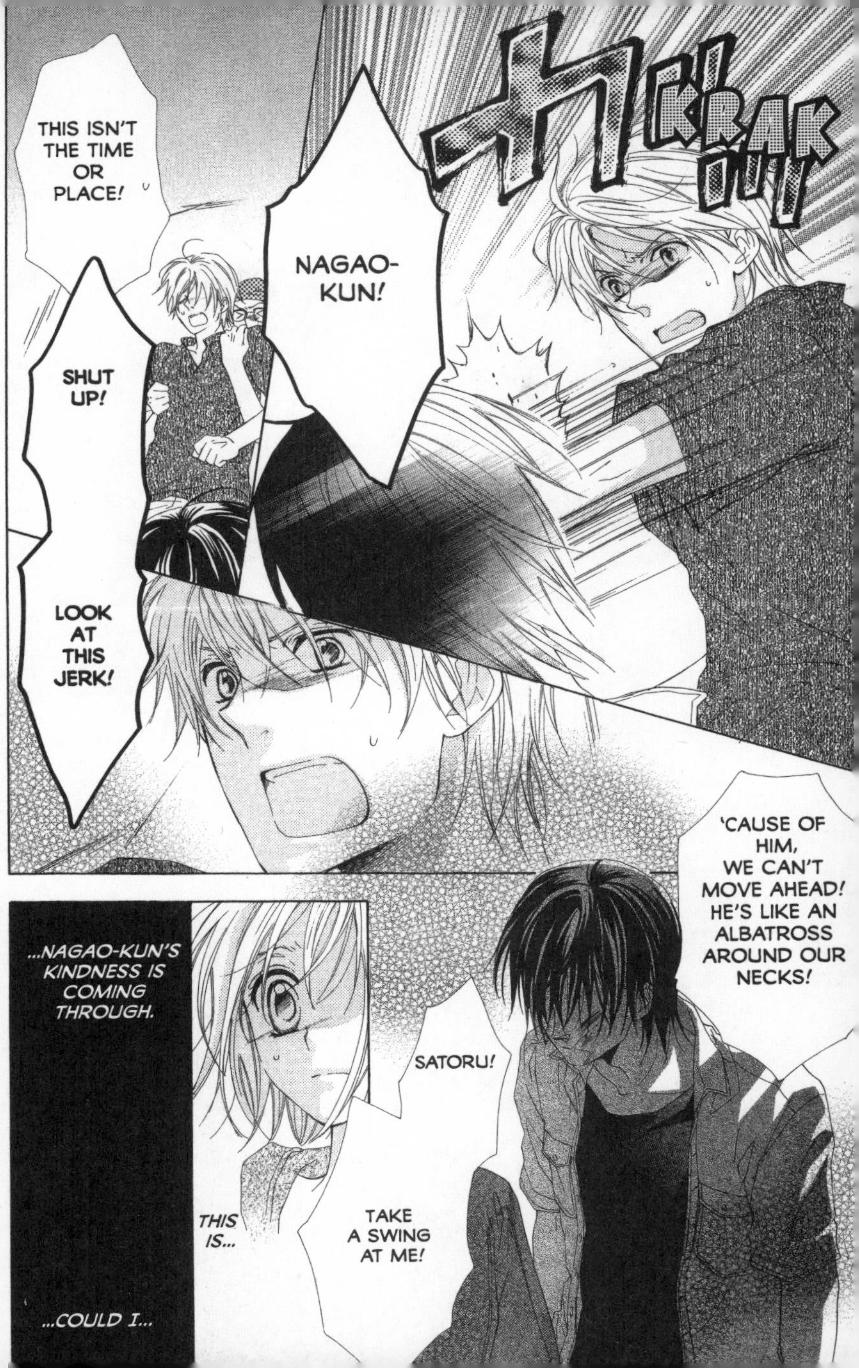
KRAK OUT
NAGAO-KUN!
THIS ISN'T THE TIME OR PLACE!
SHUT UP!
LOOK AT THIS JERK!
'CAUSE OF HIM, WE CAN'T MOVE AHEAD! HE'S LIKE AN ALBATROSS AROUND OUR NECKS!
SATORU!
TAKE A SWING AT ME!
THIS IS...
...NAGAO-KUN'S KINDNESS IS COMING THROUGH.
...COULD I...

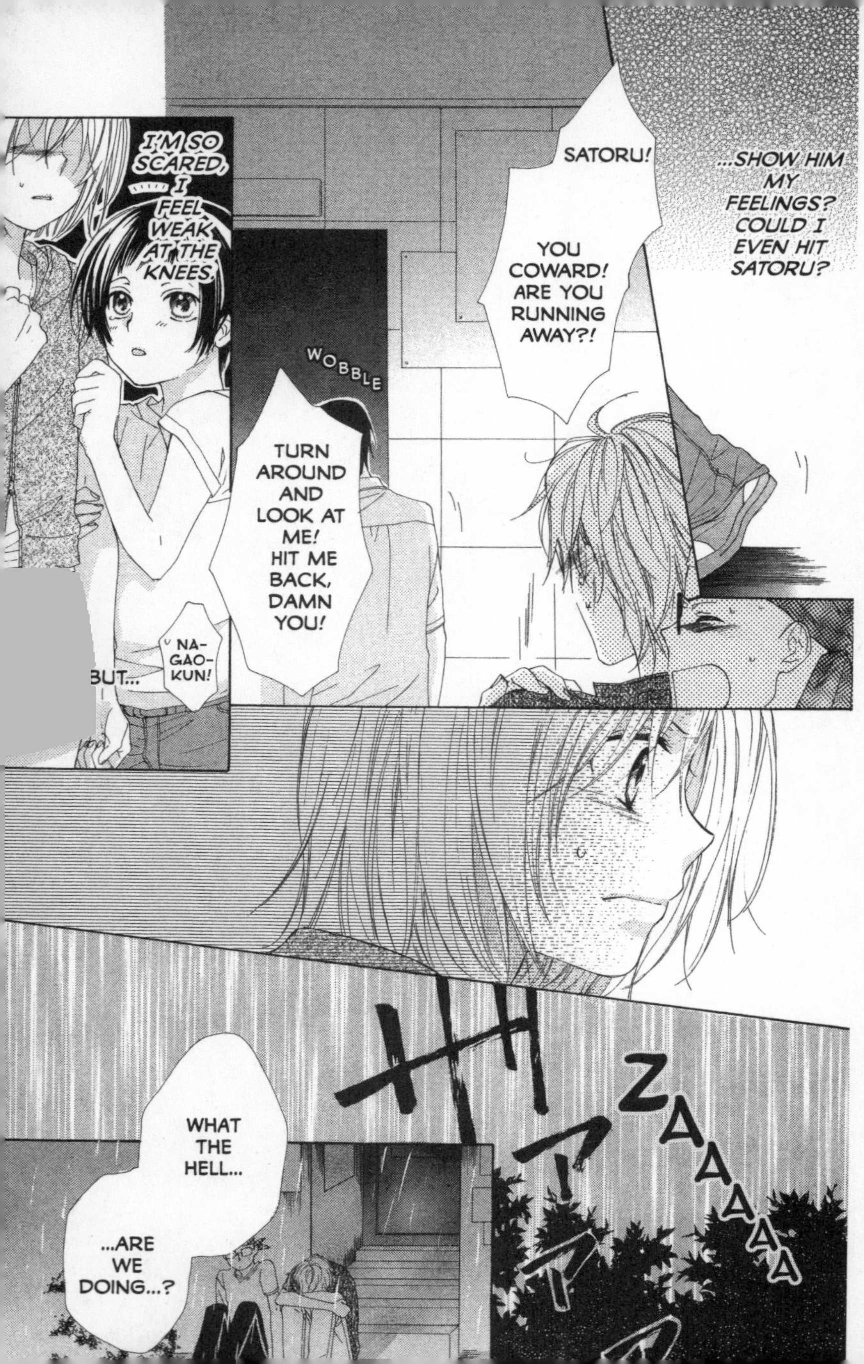
...SHOW HIM MY FEELINGS? COULD I EVEN HIT SATORU?
SATORU!
YOU COWARD! ARE YOU RUNNING AWAY?!
WOBBLE
TURN AROUND AND LOOK AT ME! HIT ME BACK, DAMN YOU!
I'M SO SCARED, I FEEL WEAK AT THE KNEES.
NAGAO-KUN!
BUT...
ZAAAAAA
WHAT THE HELL...
...ARE WE DOING...?

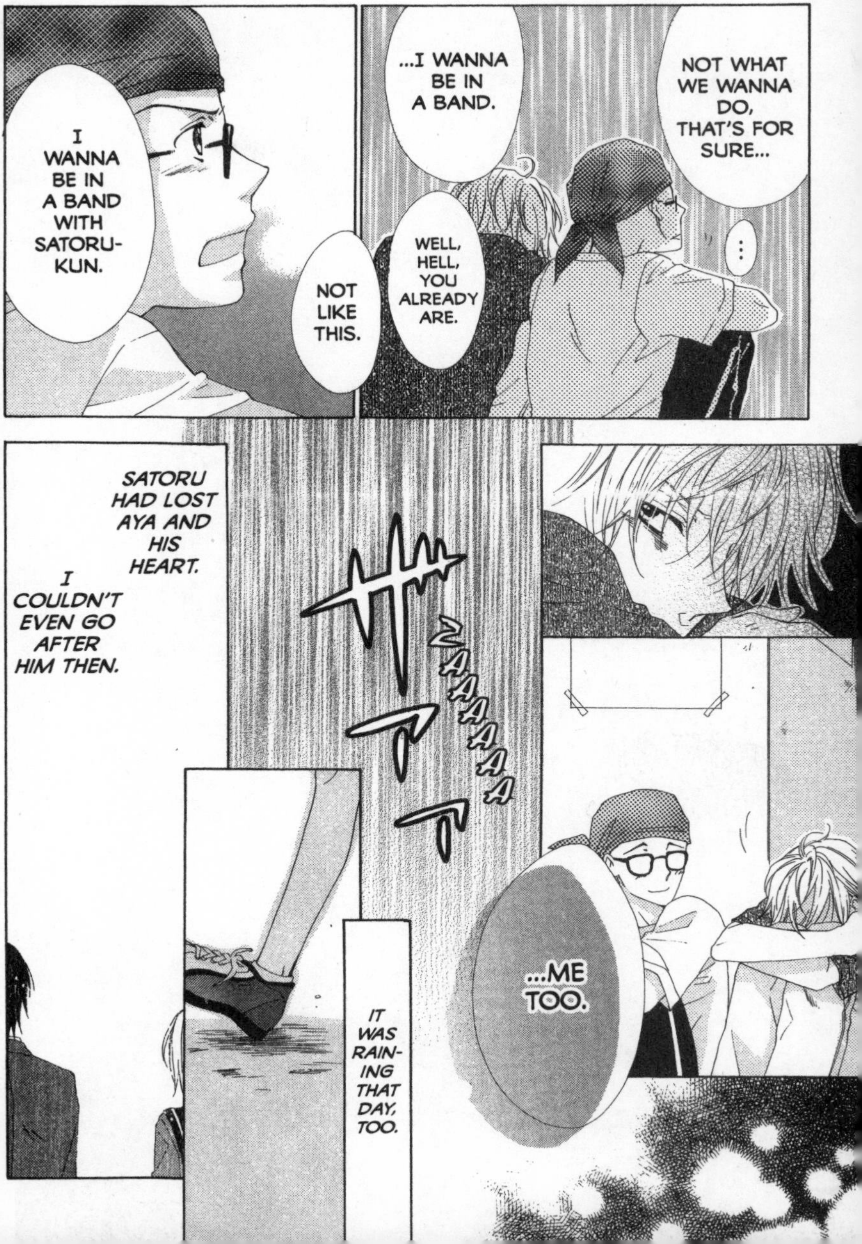
NOT WHAT WE WANNA DO, THAT'S FOR SURE...
...
...I WANNA BE IN A BAND.
WELL, HELL, YOU ALREADY ARE.
NOT LIKE THIS.
I WANNA BE IN A BAND WITH SATORU-KUN.
...ME TOO.
ZAAAAAAA
SATORU HAD LOST AYA AND HIS HEART.
I COULDN'T EVEN GO AFTER HIM THEN.
IT WAS RAINING THAT DAY, TOO.

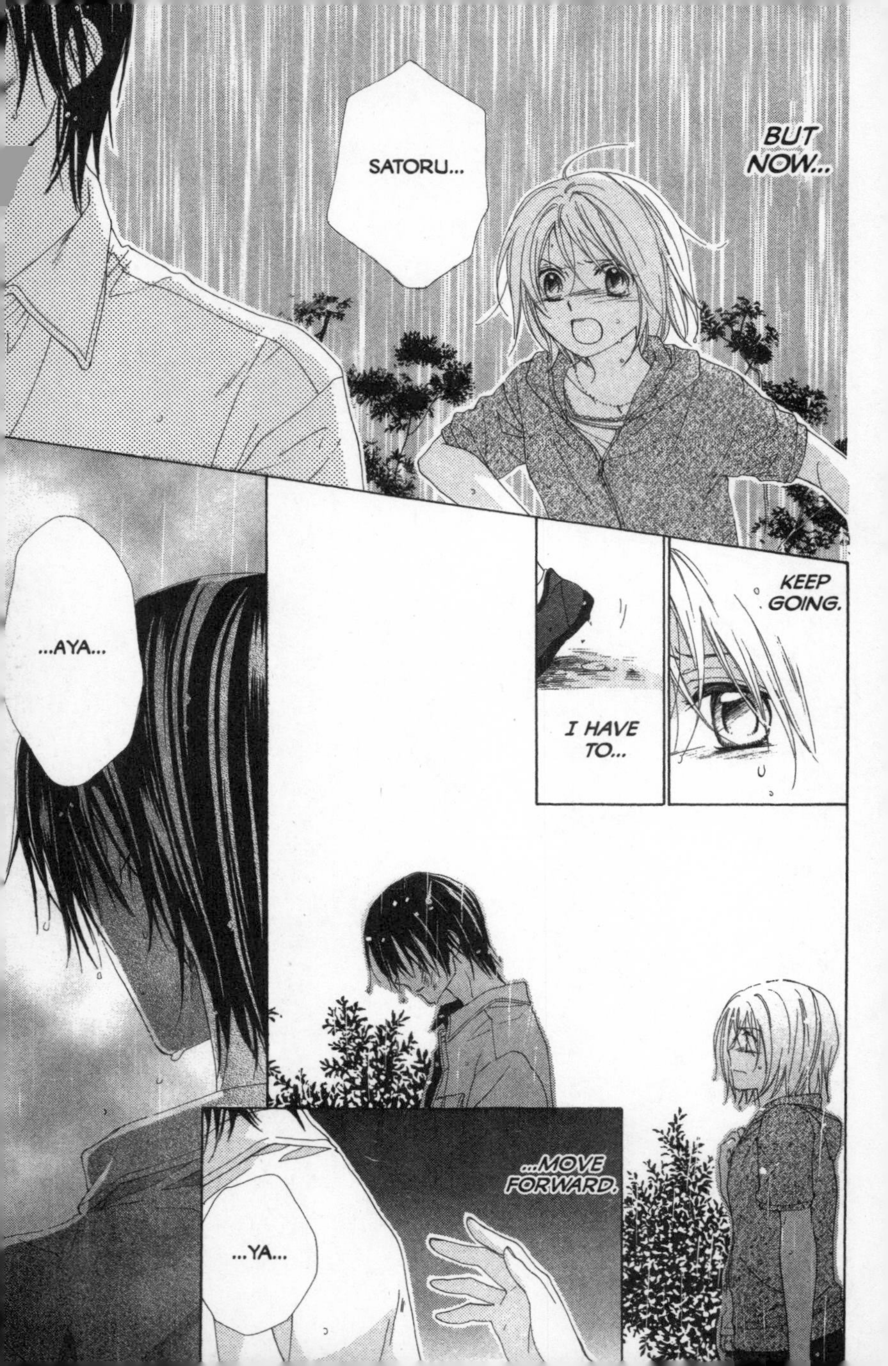

BUT NOW...
SATORU...
KEEP GOING.
I HAVE TO...
...AYA...
...MOVE FORWARD.
...YA...

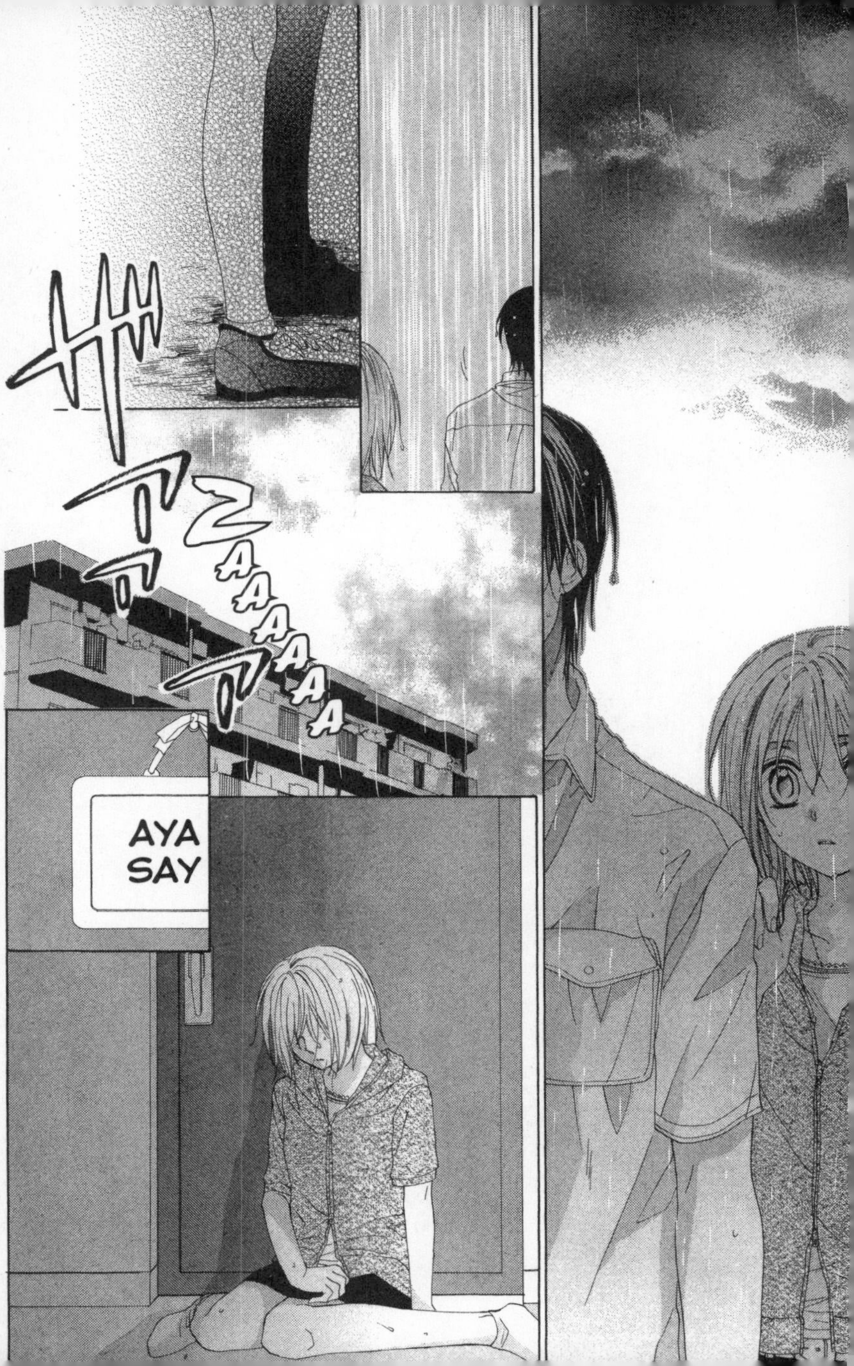
ZAAAAAA
AYA SAY

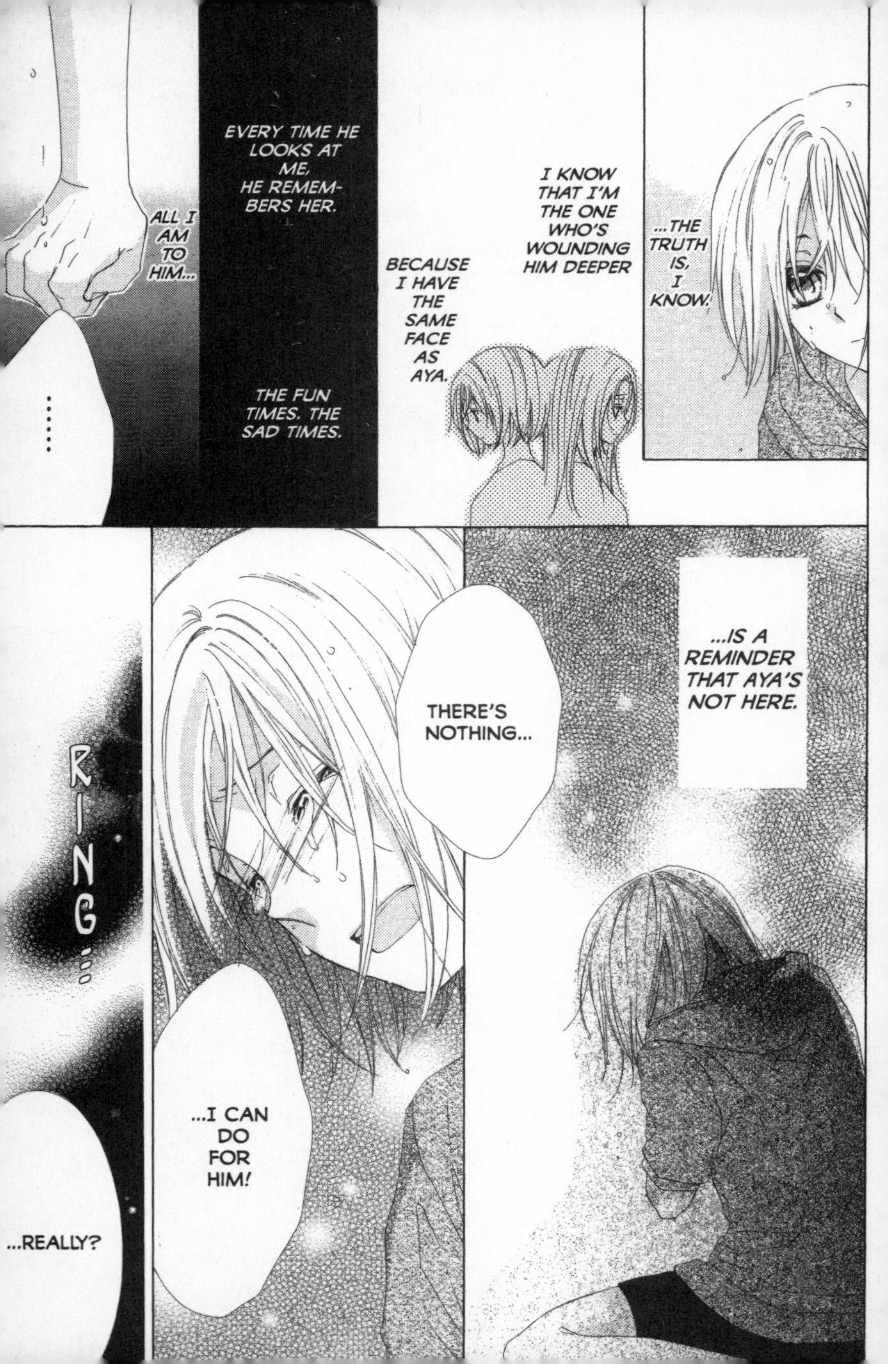
...THE TRUTH IS, I KNOW.
I KNOW THAT I'M THE ONE WHO'S WOUNDING HIM DEEPER
BECAUSE I HAVE THE SAME FACE AS AYA.
EVERY TIME HE LOOKS AT ME, HE REMEMBERS HER.
THE FUN TIMES. THE SAD TIMES.
ALL I AM TO HIM...
......
...IS A REMINDER THAT AYA'S NOT HERE.
THERE'S NOTHING...
...I CAN DO FOR HIM!
RING...
...REALLY?

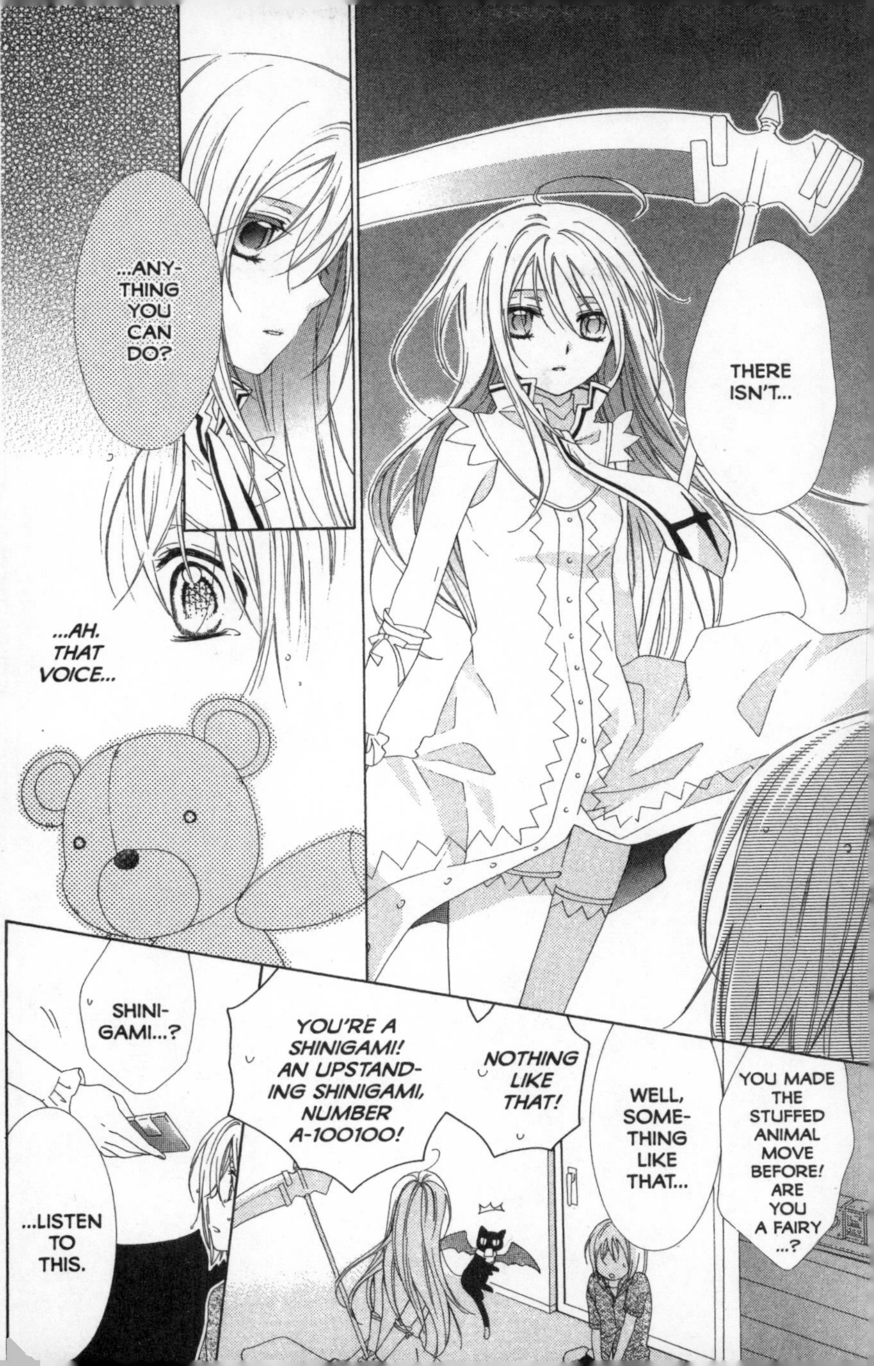
THERE ISN'T...
...ANY-THING YOU CAN DO?
...AH. THAT VOICE...
YOU MADE THE STUFFED ANIMAL MOVE BEFORE! ARE YOU A FAIRY ...?
WELL, SOME-THING LIKE THAT...
NOTHING LIKE THAT!
YOU'RE A SHINIGAMI! AN UPSTAND-ING SHINIGAMI, NUMBER A-100100!
SHINI-GAMI...?
...LISTEN TO THIS.

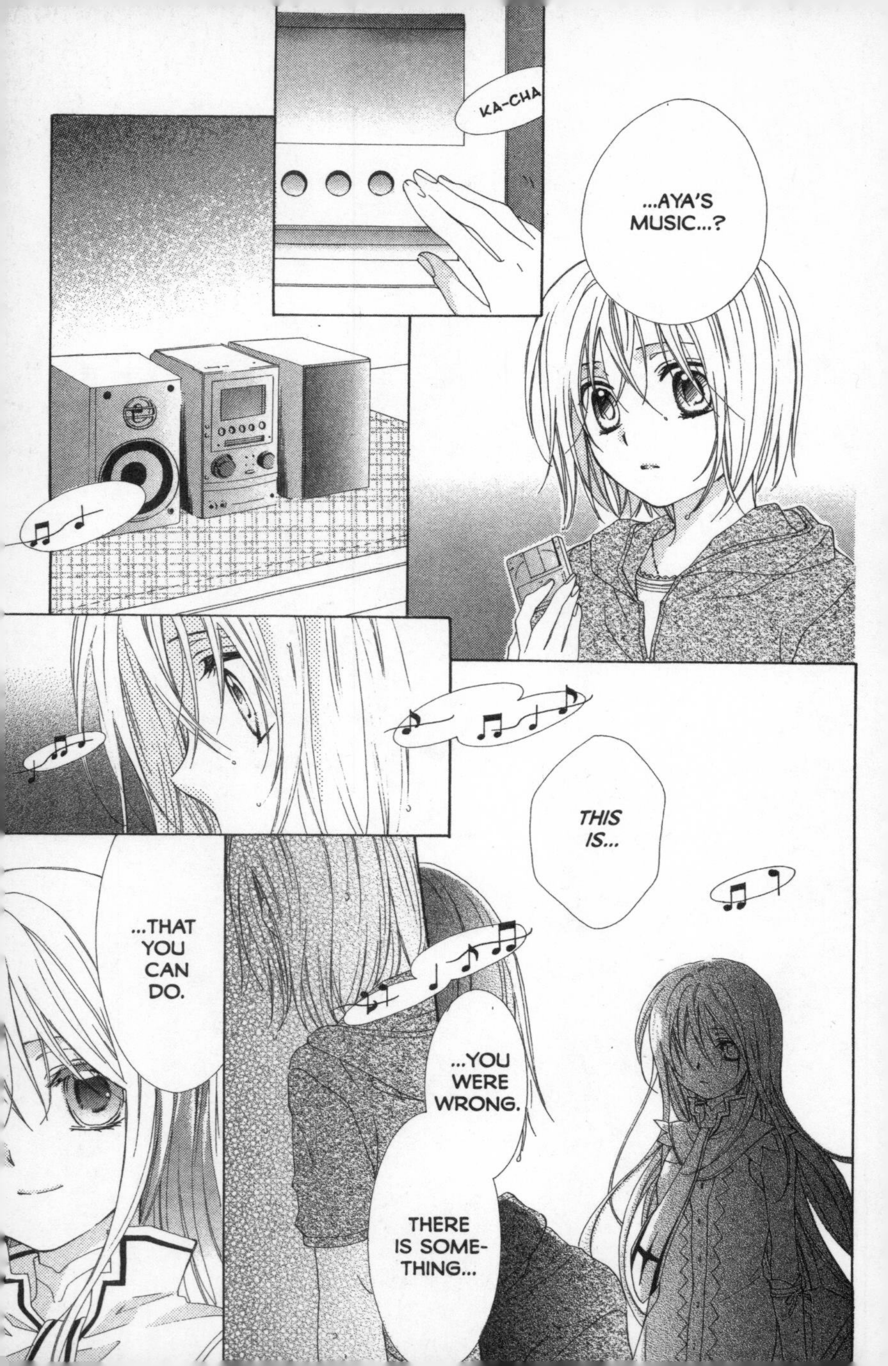
...AYA'S MUSIC...?
KA-CHA
THIS IS...
...YOU WERE WRONG.
THERE IS SOME-THING...
...THAT YOU CAN DO.

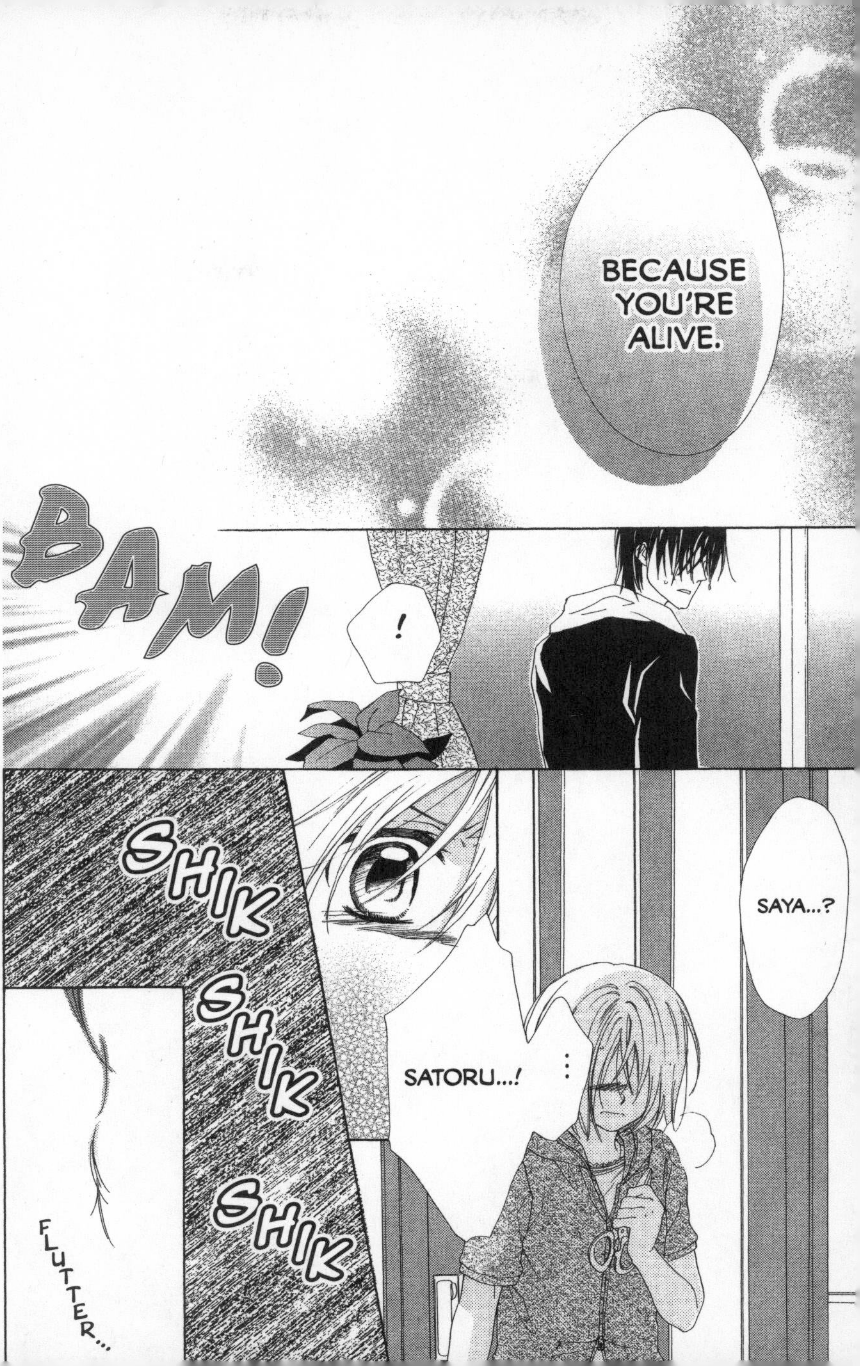
BECAUSE YOU'RE ALIVE.
BAM!
!
SAYA...?
...
SATORU...!
SHIK SHIK SHIK SHIK
FLUTTER...

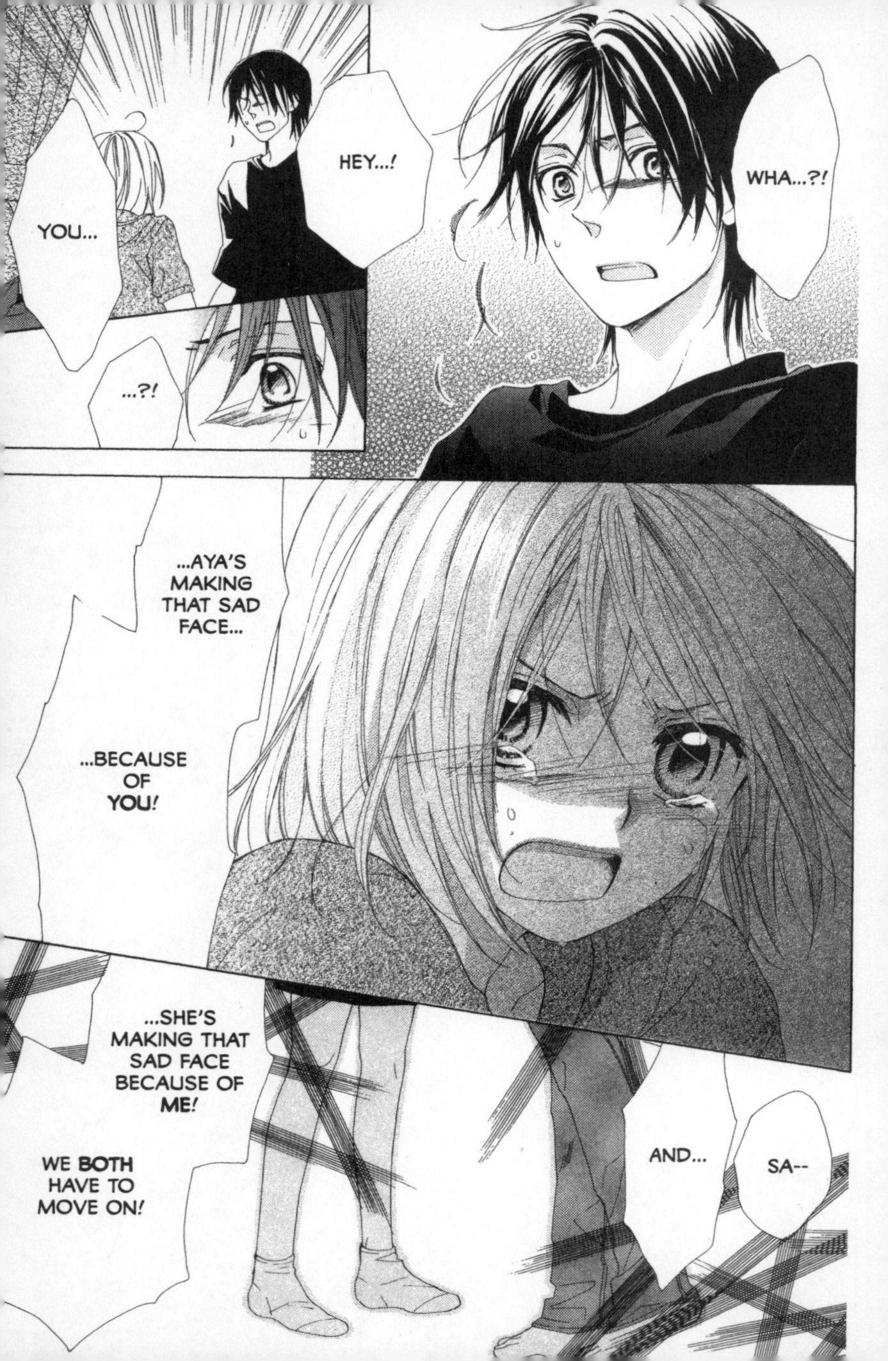
WHA...?!
HEY...!
YOU...
...?!
...AYA'S MAKING THAT SAD FACE...
...BECAUSE OF YOU!
...SHE'S MAKING THAT SAD FACE BECAUSE OF ME!
SA--
AND...
WE BOTH HAVE TO MOVE ON!

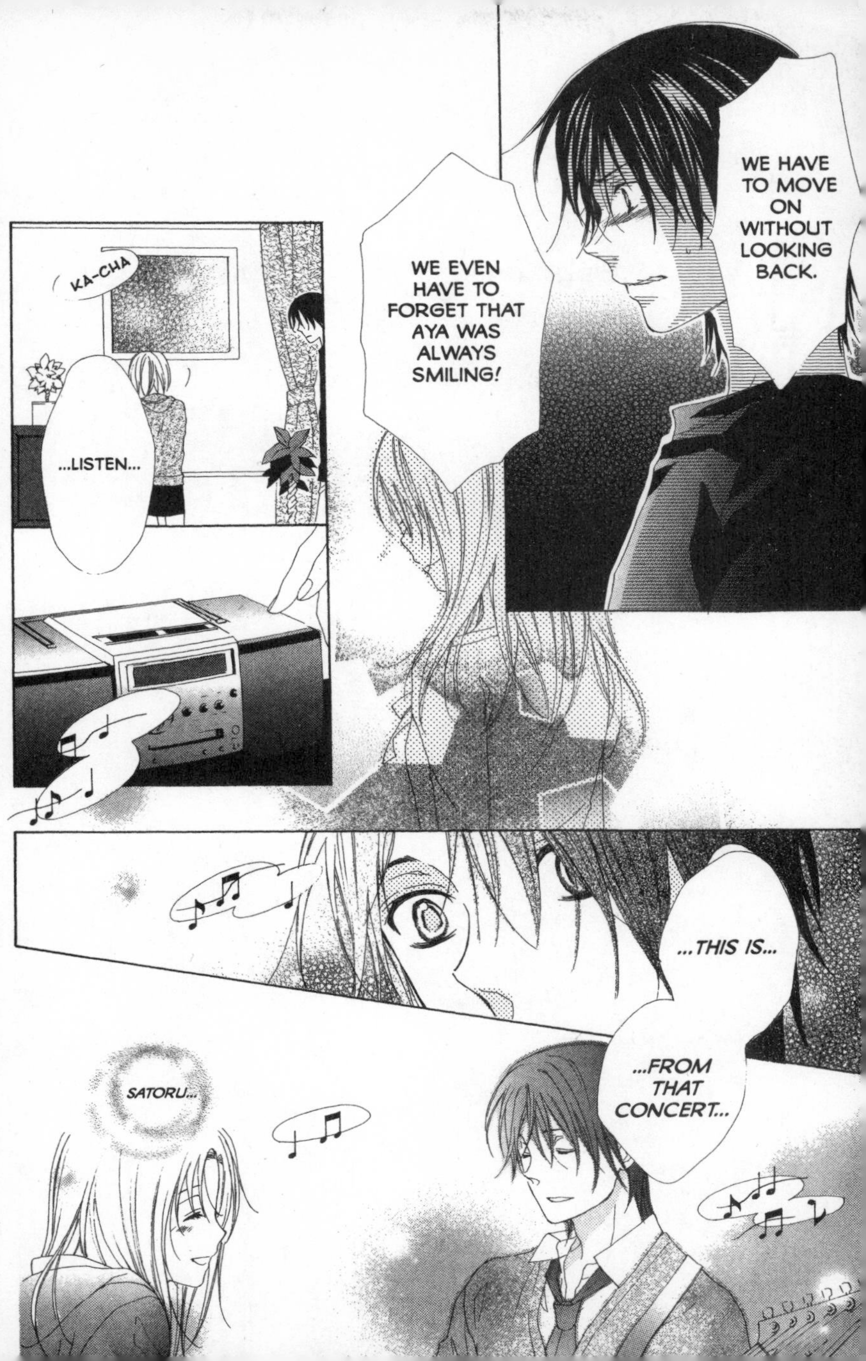
WE HAVE TO MOVE ON WITHOUT LOOKING BACK.
WE EVEN HAVE TO FORGET THAT AYA WAS ALWAYS SMILING!
KA-CHA
...LISTEN...
...THIS IS...
...FROM THAT CONCERT...
SATORU...

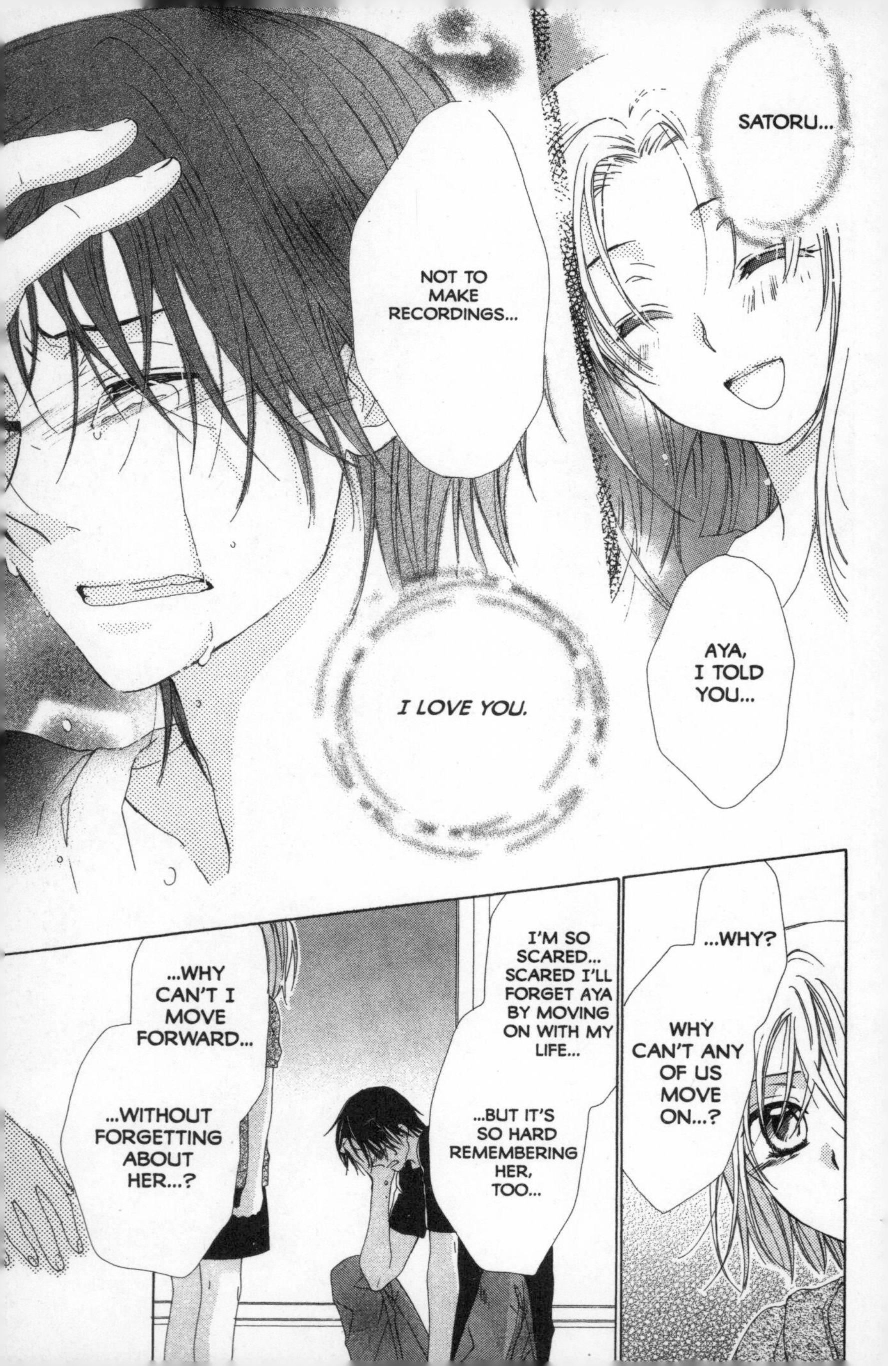
SATORU...
AYA, I TOLD YOU...
NOT TO MAKE RECORDINGS...
I LOVE YOU.
...WHY?
WHY CAN'T ANY OF US MOVE ON...?
I'M SO SCARED... SCARED I'LL FORGET AYA BY MOVING ON WITH MY LIFE...
...BUT IT'S SO HARD REMEMBERING HER, TOO...
...WHY CAN'T I MOVE FORWARD...
...WITHOUT FORGETTING ABOUT HER...?

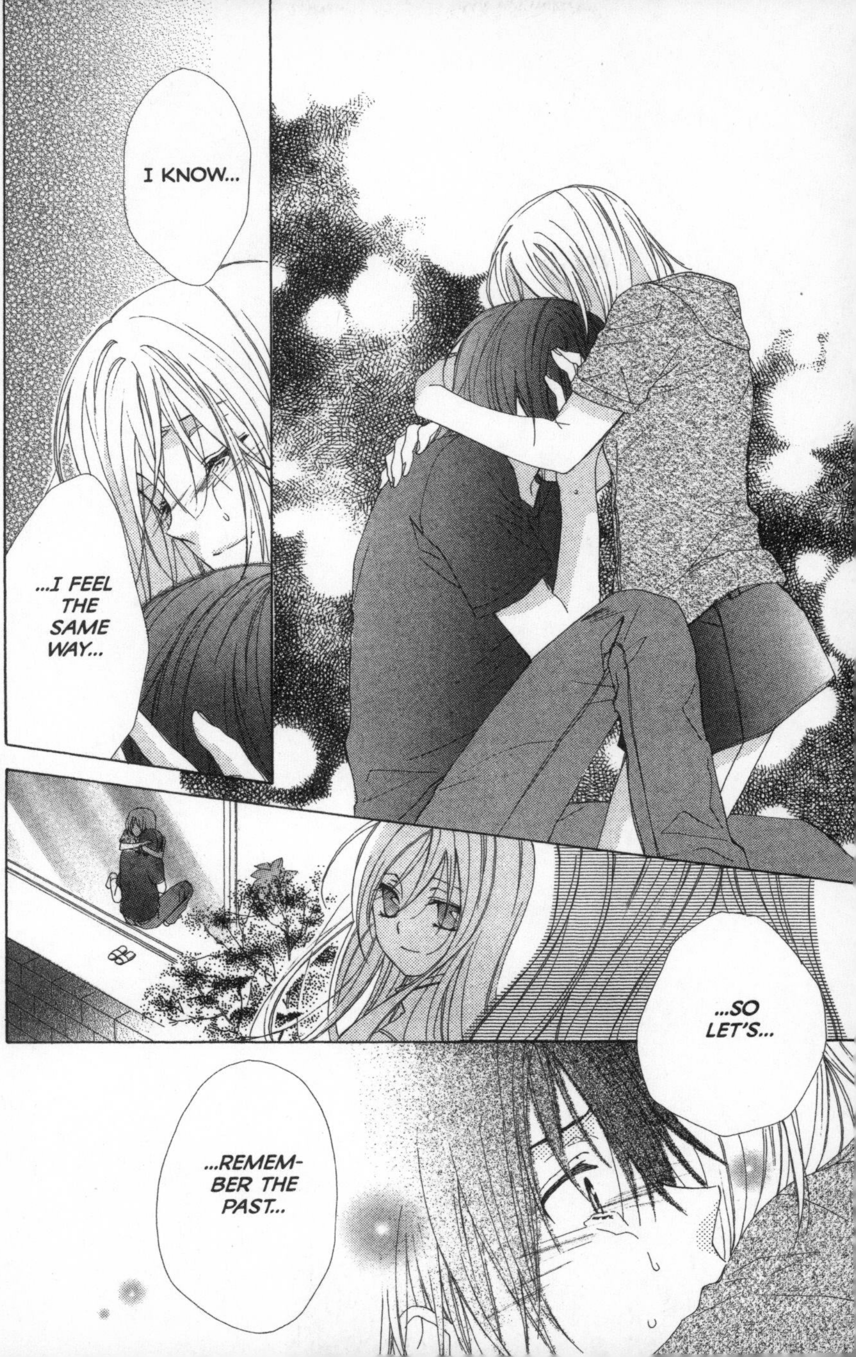

I KNOW...
...I FEEL THE SAME WAY...
...SO LET'S...
...REMEM-BER THE PAST...

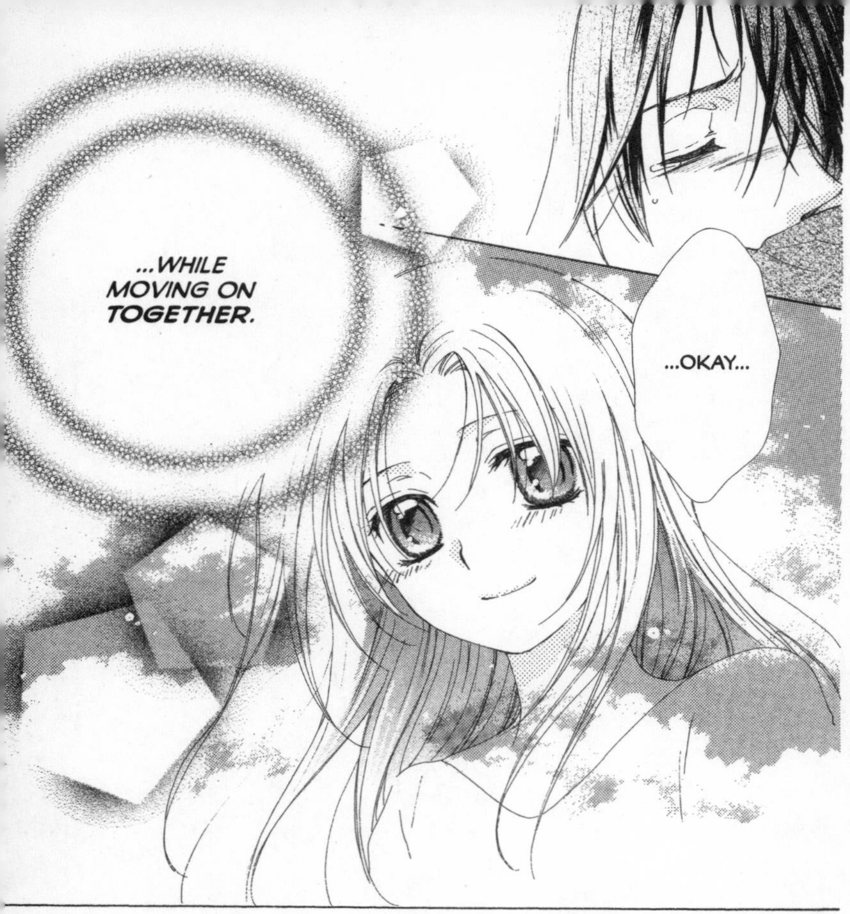
...OKAY...
...WHILE MOVING ON TOGETHER.

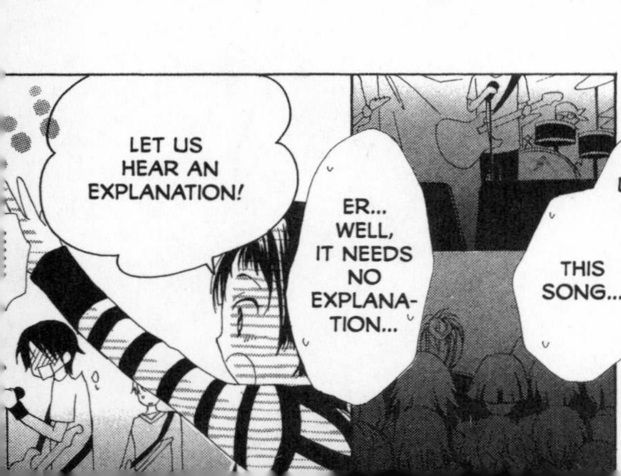
UM...
THIS SONG...
ER... WELL, IT NEEDS NO EXPLANA-TION...
LET US HEAR AN EXPLANATION!

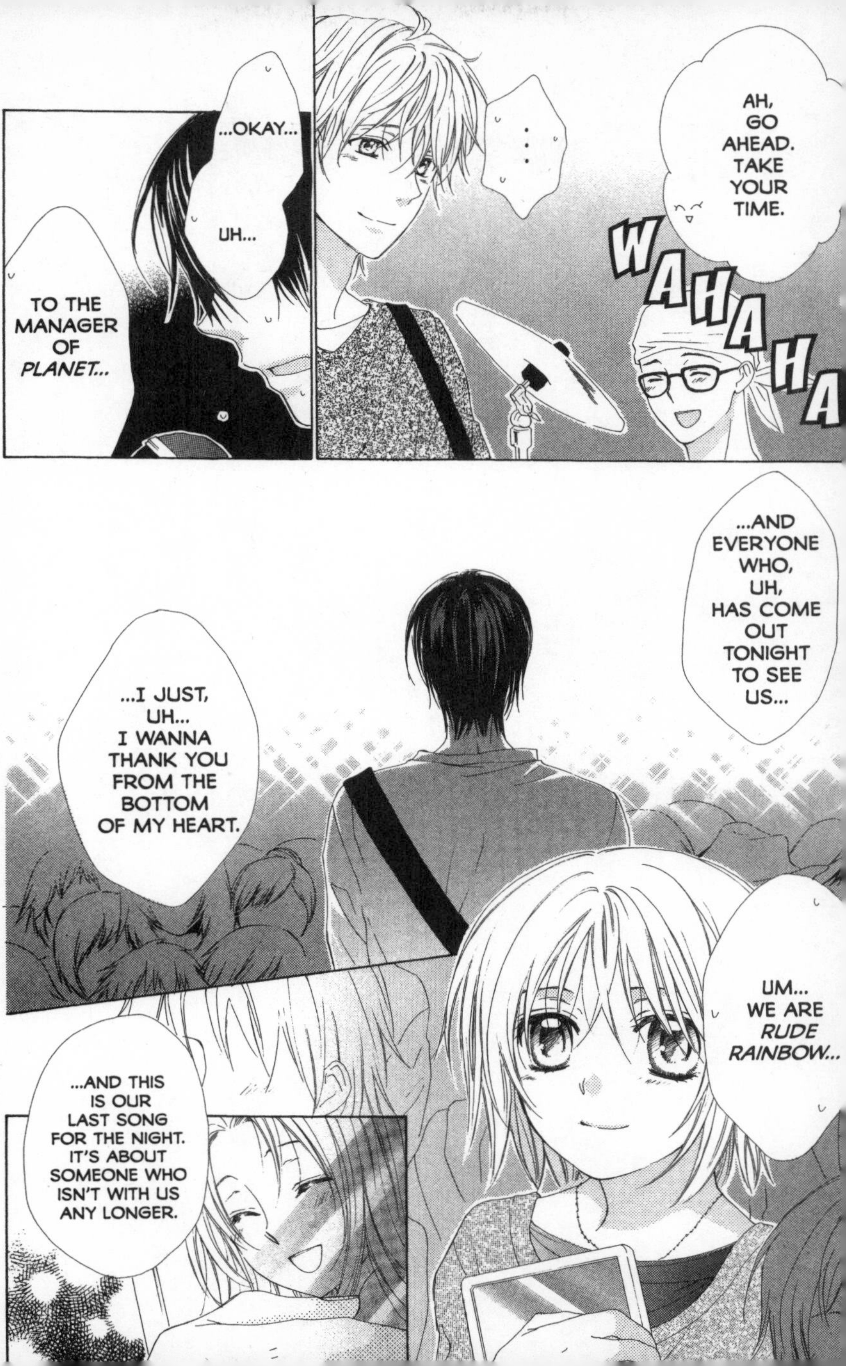

AH, GO AHEAD. TAKE YOUR TIME.
WAHAHAHA
...
...OKAY...
UH...
TO THE MANAGER OF *PLANET*...
...AND EVERYONE WHO, UH, HAS COME OUT TONIGHT TO SEE US...
...I JUST, UH... I WANNA THANK YOU FROM THE BOTTOM OF MY HEART.
UM... WE ARE *RUDE RAINBOW*...
...AND THIS IS OUR LAST SONG FOR THE NIGHT. IT'S ABOUT SOMEONE WHO ISN'T WITH US ANY LONGER.

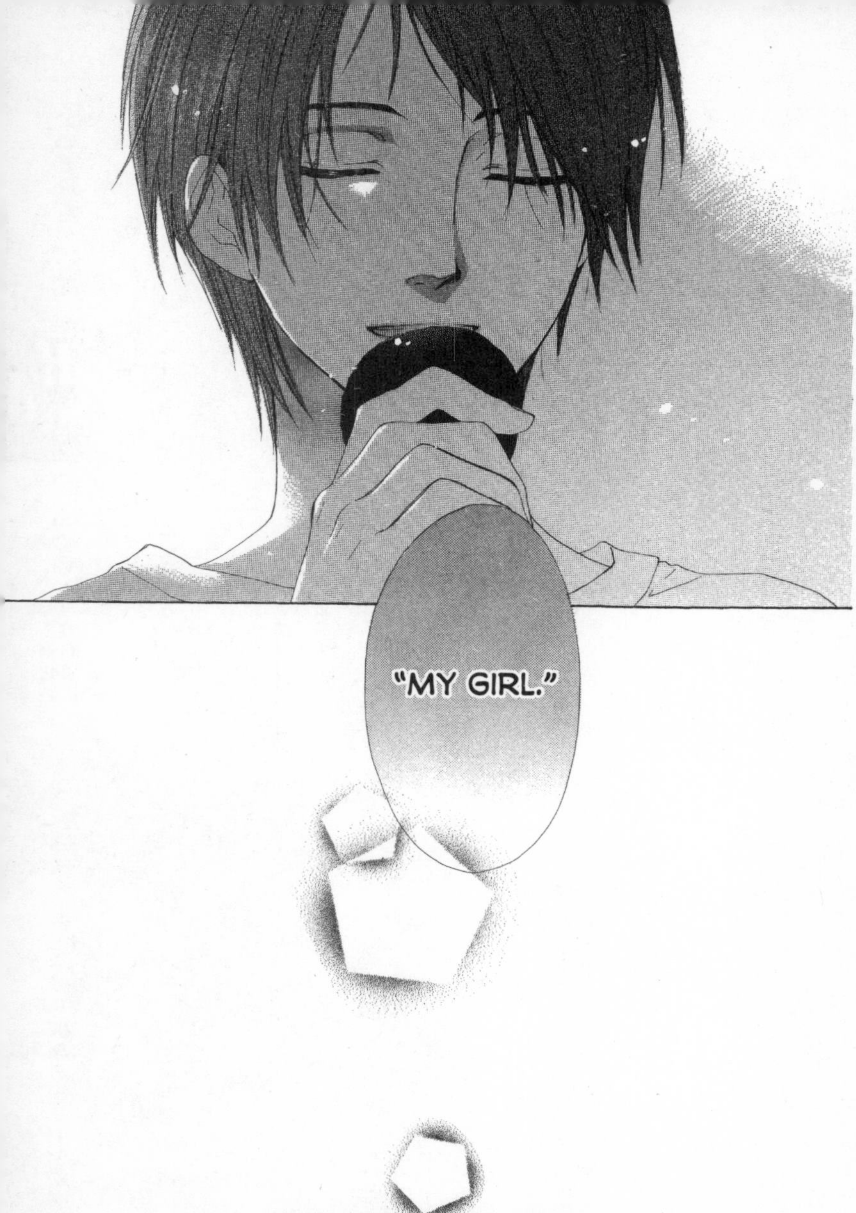
"MY GIRL."

BALLAD OF A SHINIGAMI.
THE END OF THE SUMMER IN WHICH YOU WERE BORN: THE END

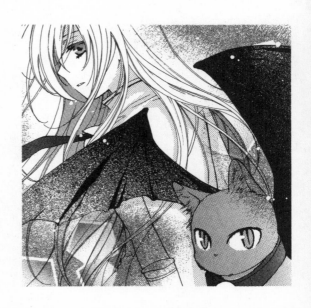

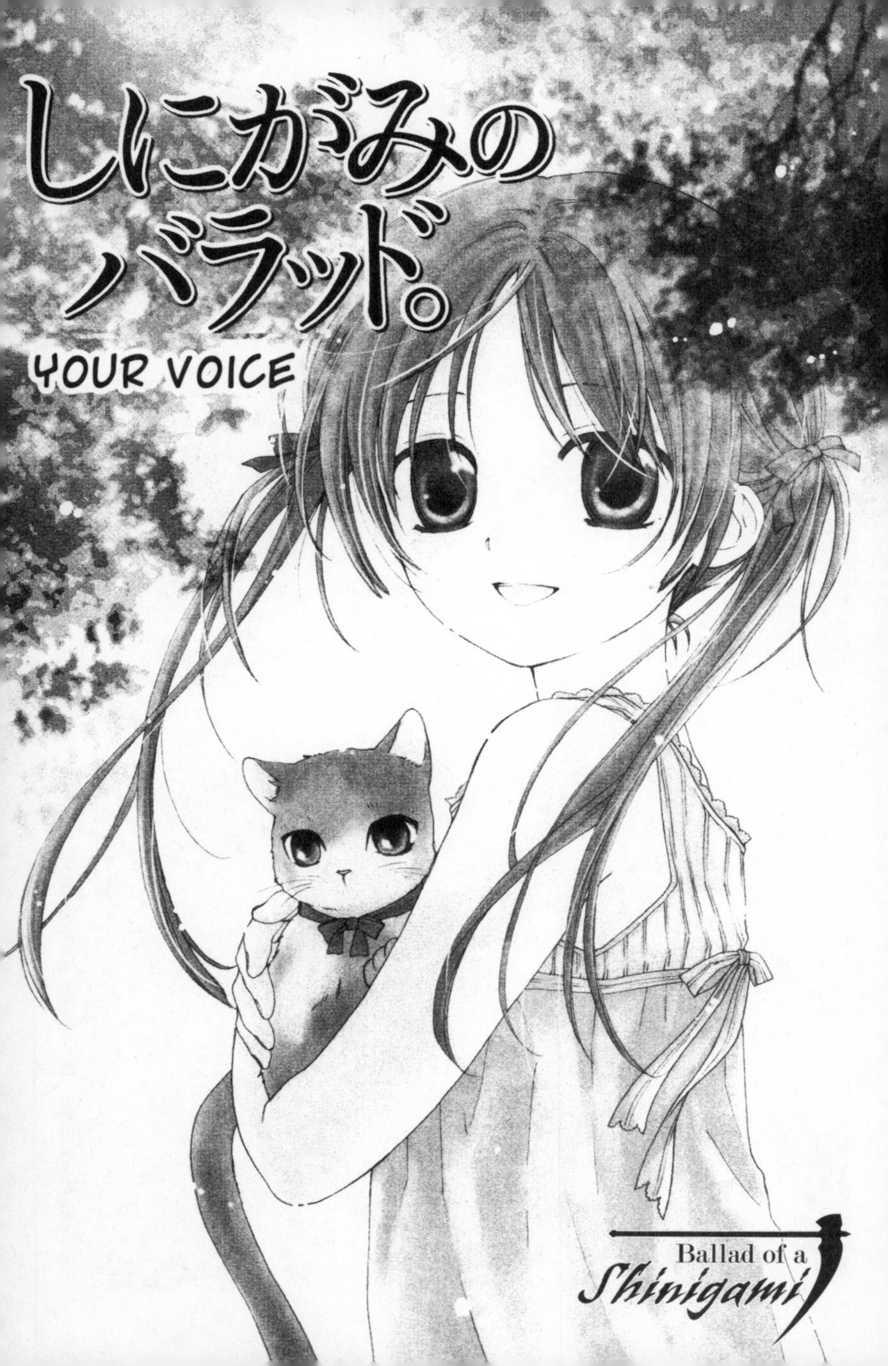
しにがみのバラッド。
YOUR VOICE
Ballad of a Shinigami

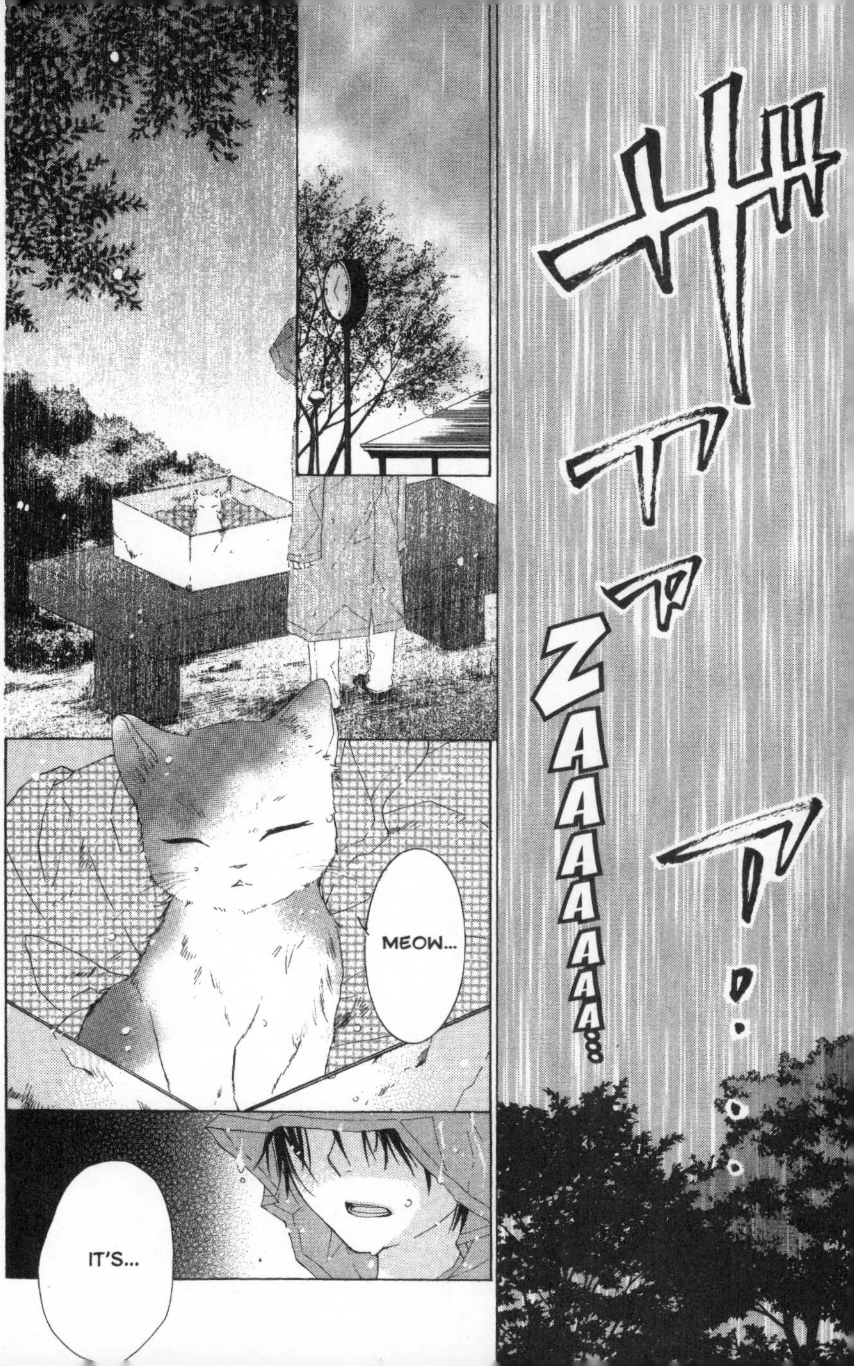
ザァァァァ…
ZAAAAAAA...
MEOW...
IT'S...

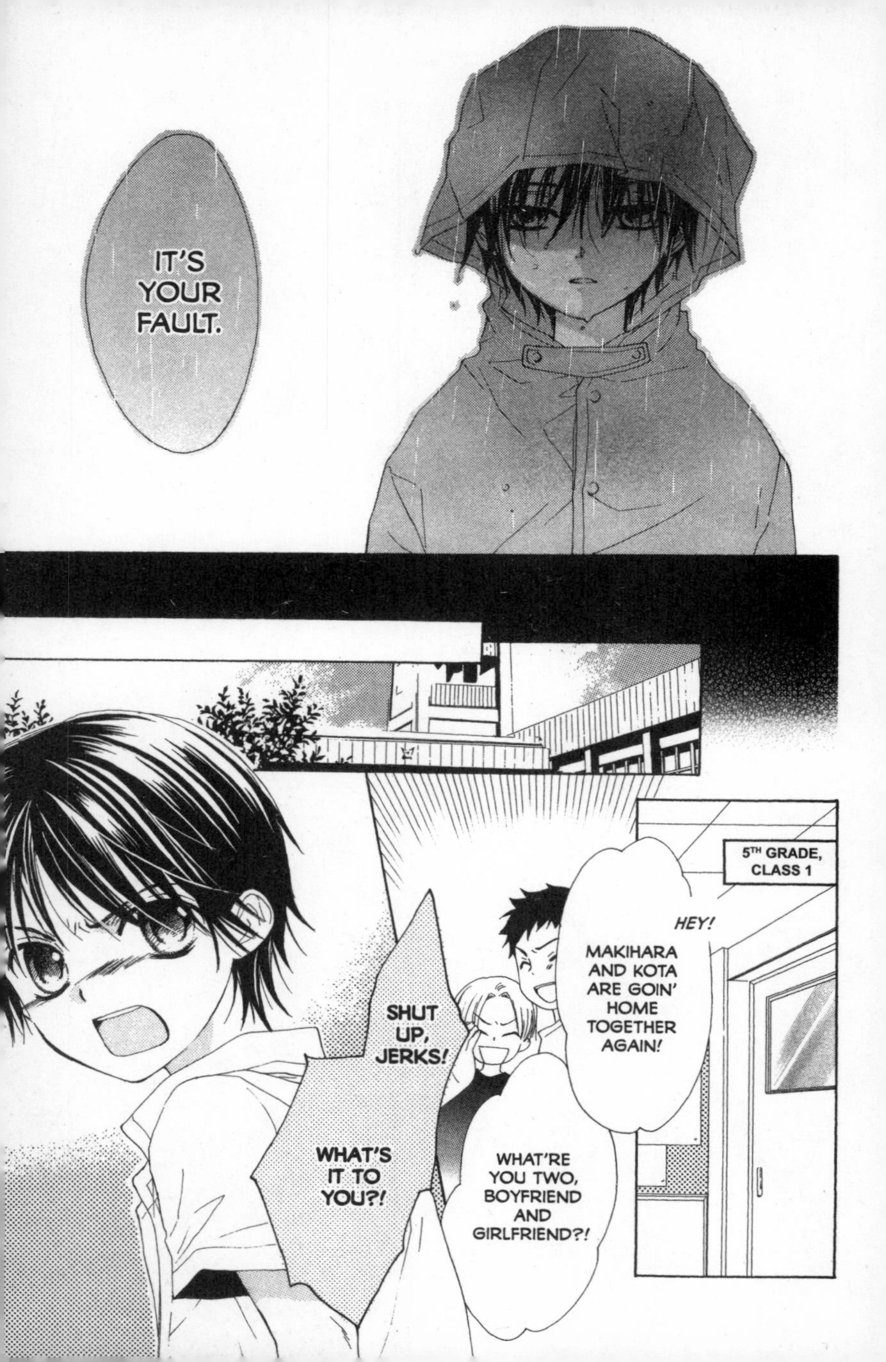
IT'S YOUR FAULT.
5TH GRADE, CLASS 1
HEY!
MAKIHARA AND KOTA ARE GOIN' HOME TOGETHER AGAIN!
WHAT'RE YOU TWO, BOYFRIEND AND GIRLFRIEND?!
SHUT UP, JERKS!
WHAT'S IT TO YOU?!

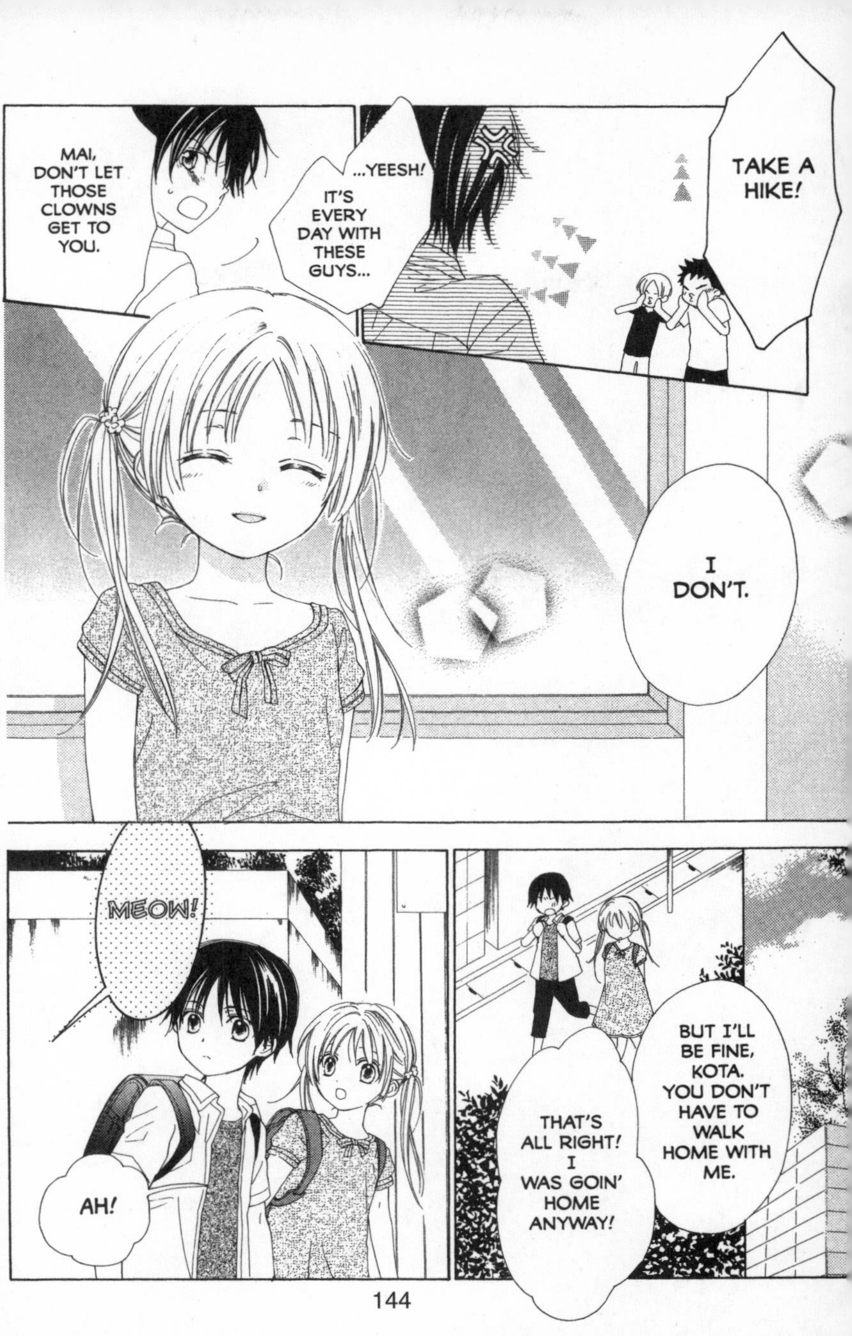
TAKE A HIKE!
...YEESH!
IT'S EVERY DAY WITH THESE GUYS...
MAI, DON'T LET THOSE CLOWNS GET TO YOU.
I DON'T.
BUT I'LL BE FINE, KOTA. YOU DON'T HAVE TO WALK HOME WITH ME.
THAT'S ALL RIGHT! I WAS GOIN' HOME ANYWAY!
MEOW!
AH!

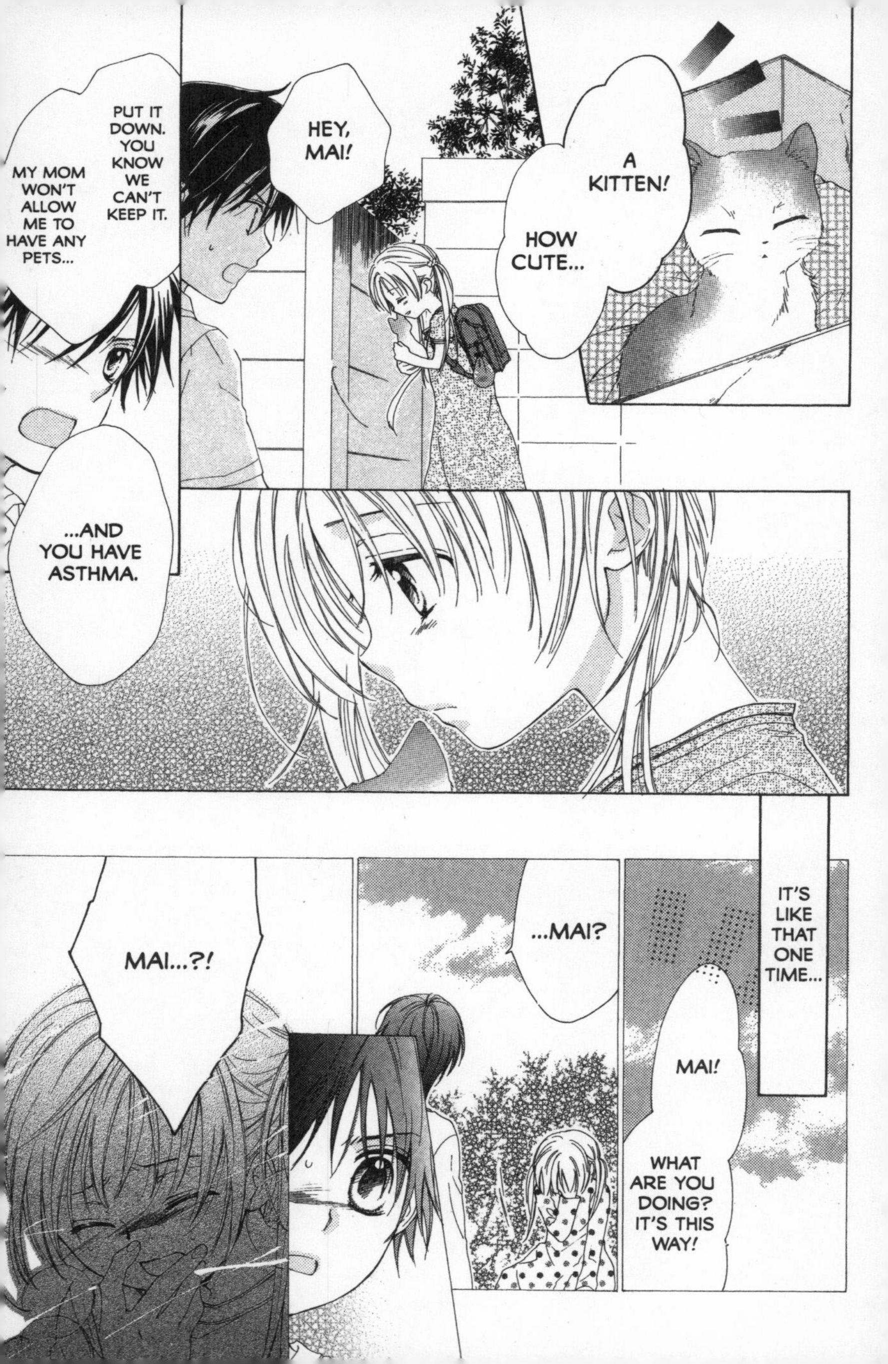
A KITTEN!
HOW CUTE...
HEY, MAI!
PUT IT DOWN. YOU KNOW WE CAN'T KEEP IT.
MY MOM WON'T ALLOW ME TO HAVE ANY PETS...
...AND YOU HAVE ASTHMA.
IT'S LIKE THAT ONE TIME...
MAI!
WHAT ARE YOU DOING? IT'S THIS WAY!
...MAI?
MAI...?!

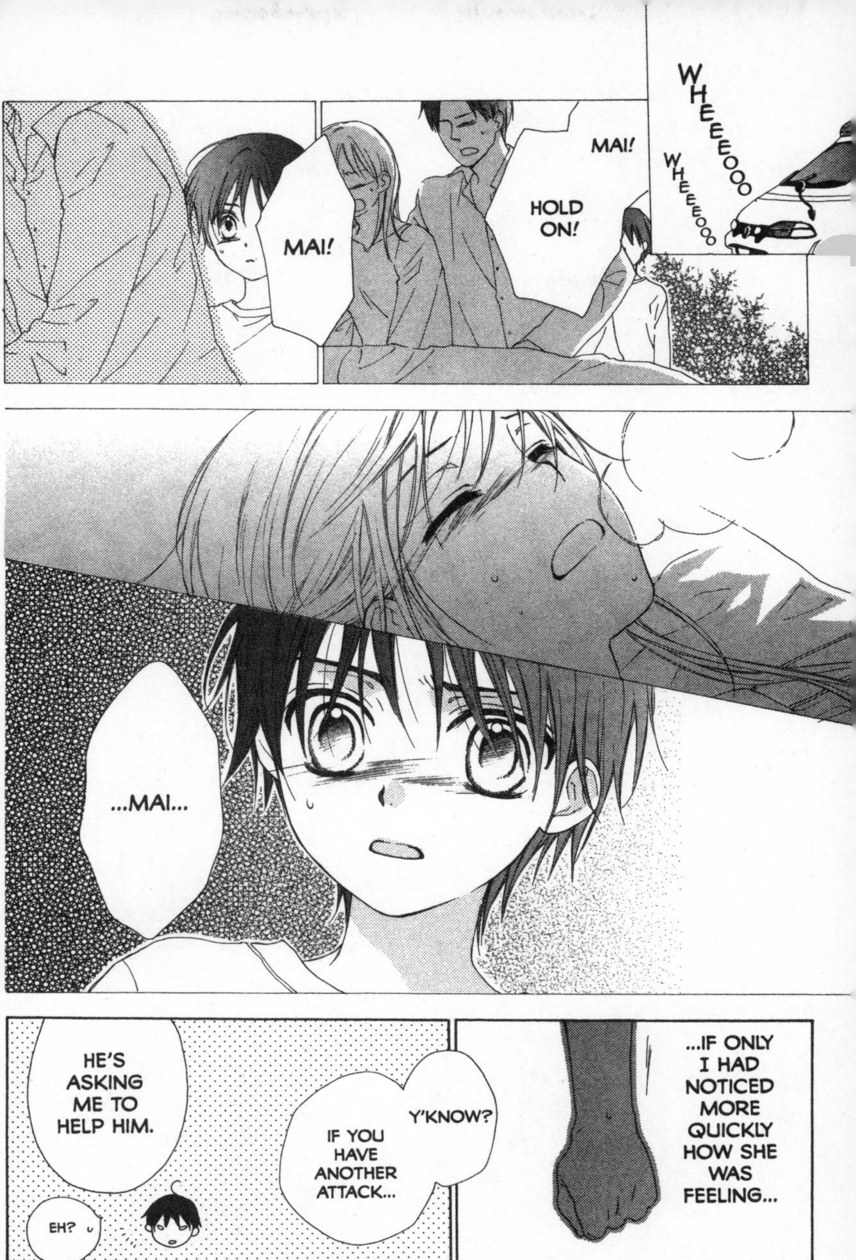
WHEEEOOO
WHEEEOOO
MAI!
HOLD ON!
MAI!
...MAI...
...IF ONLY I HAD NOTICED MORE QUICKLY HOW SHE WAS FEELING...
Y'KNOW?
IF YOU HAVE ANOTHER ATTACK...
HE'S ASKING ME TO HELP HIM.
EH?

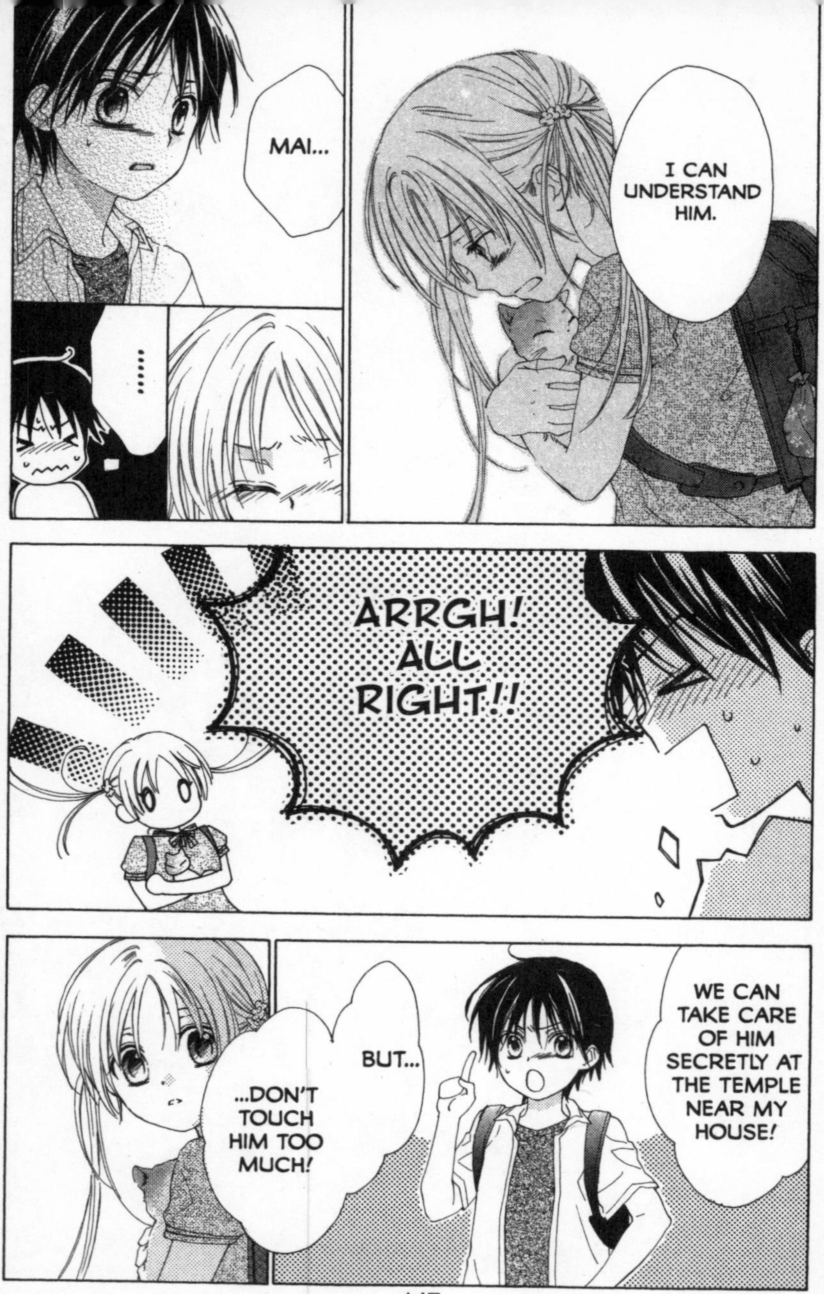
I CAN UNDERSTAND HIM.
MAI...
......
ARRGH! ALL RIGHT!!
WE CAN TAKE CARE OF HIM SECRETLY AT THE TEMPLE NEAR MY HOUSE!
BUT...
...DON'T TOUCH HIM TOO MUCH!

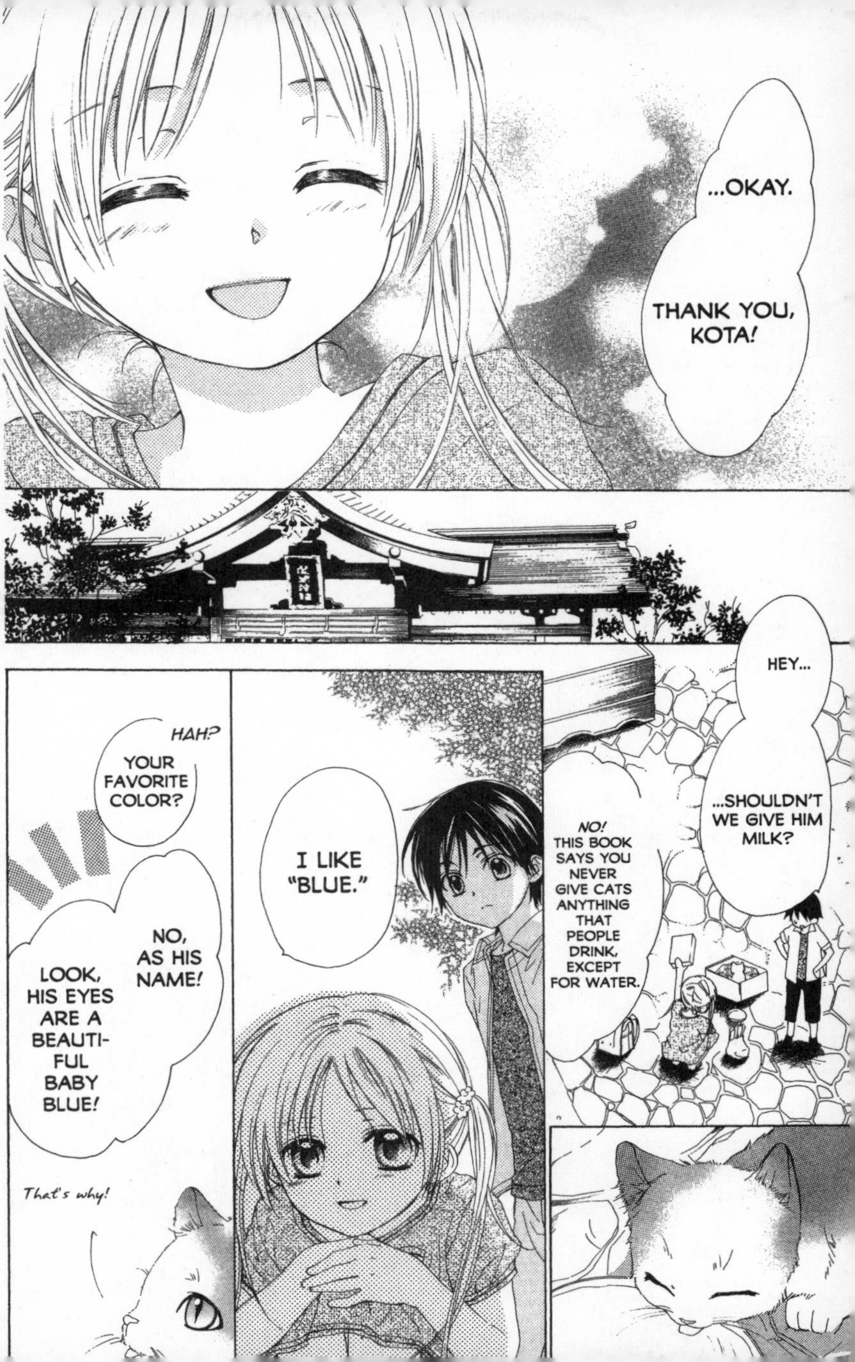
...OKAY.
THANK YOU, KOTA!
HEY...
...SHOULDN'T WE GIVE HIM MILK?
NO! THIS BOOK SAYS YOU NEVER GIVE CATS ANYTHING THAT PEOPLE DRINK, EXCEPT FOR WATER.
I LIKE "BLUE."
HAH? YOUR FAVORITE COLOR?
NO, AS HIS NAME!
LOOK, HIS EYES ARE A BEAUTIFUL BABY BLUE!
That's why!

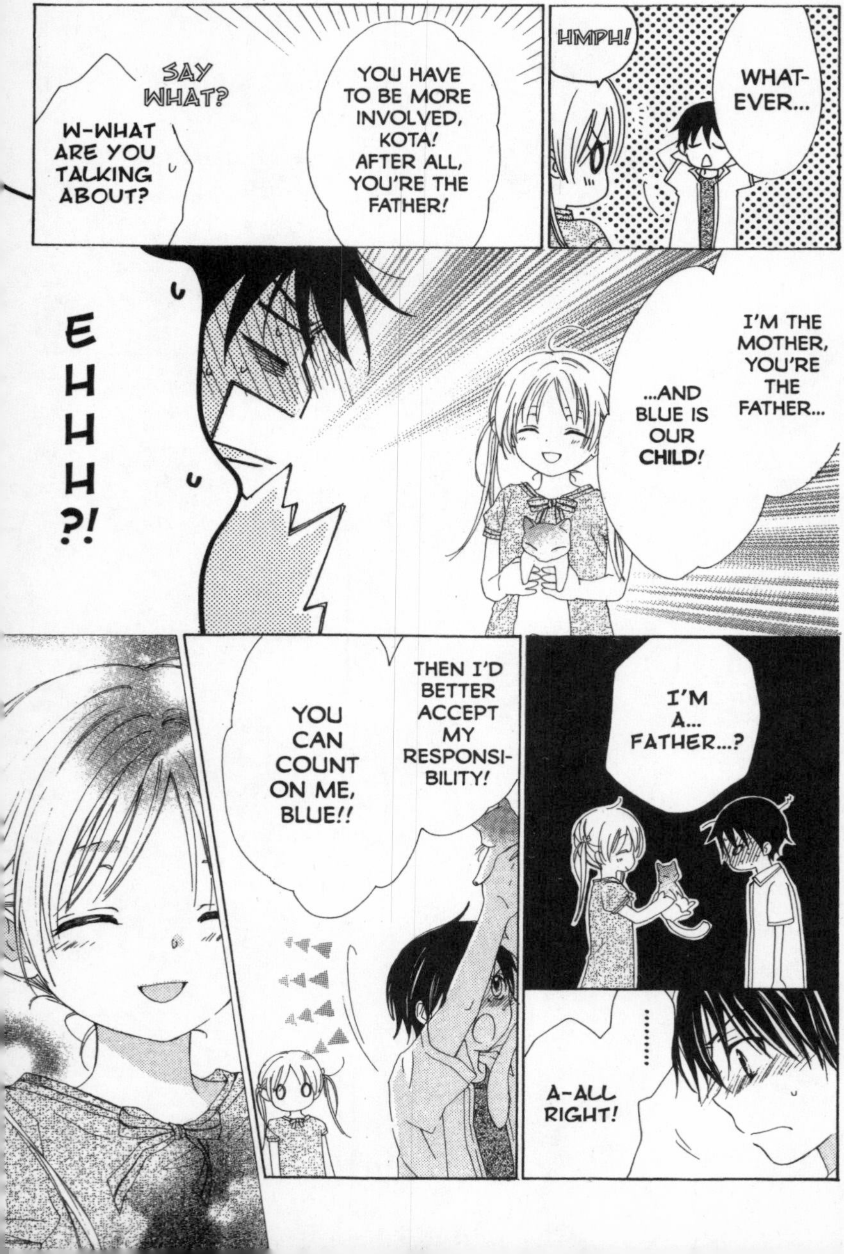
WHAT-EVER...
HMPH!
YOU HAVE TO BE MORE INVOLVED, KOTA! AFTER ALL, YOU'RE THE FATHER!
SAY WHAT?
W-WHAT ARE YOU TALKING ABOUT?
I'M THE MOTHER, YOU'RE THE FATHER...
...AND BLUE IS OUR CHILD!
EHHHH?!
I'M A... FATHER...?
......
A-ALL RIGHT!
THEN I'D BETTER ACCEPT MY RESPONSIBILITY!
YOU CAN COUNT ON ME, BLUE!!

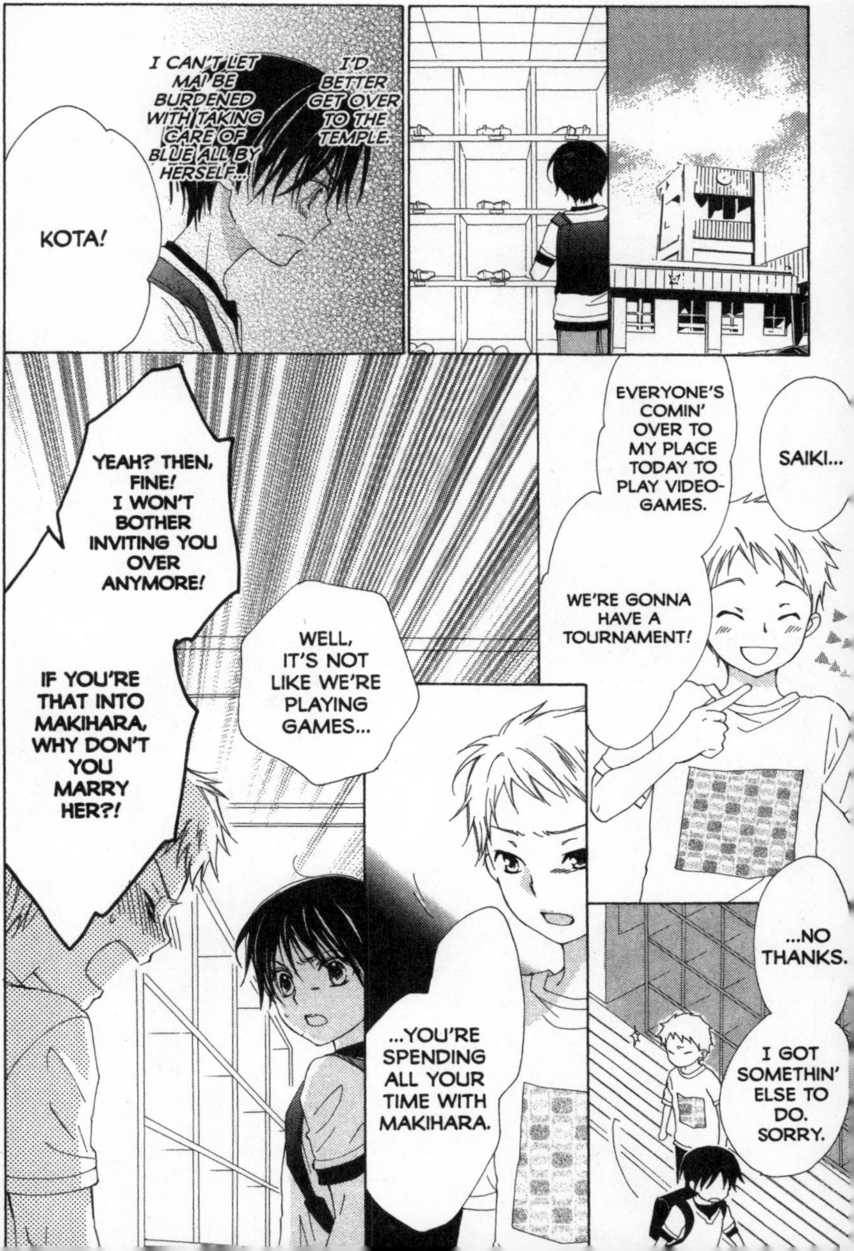
I'D BETTER GET OVER TO THE TEMPLE.
I CAN'T LET MAI BE BURDENED WITH TAKING CARE OF BLUE ALL BY HERSELF...
KOTA!
SAIKI...
EVERYONE'S COMIN' OVER TO MY PLACE TODAY TO PLAY VIDEO-GAMES.
WE'RE GONNA HAVE A TOURNAMENT!
...NO THANKS.
I GOT SOMETHIN' ELSE TO DO. SORRY.
...YOU'RE SPENDING ALL YOUR TIME WITH MAKIHARA.
WELL, IT'S NOT LIKE WE'RE PLAYING GAMES...
IF YOU'RE THAT INTO MAKIHARA, WHY DON'T YOU MARRY HER?!
YEAH? THEN, FINE! I WON'T BOTHER INVITING YOU OVER ANYMORE!

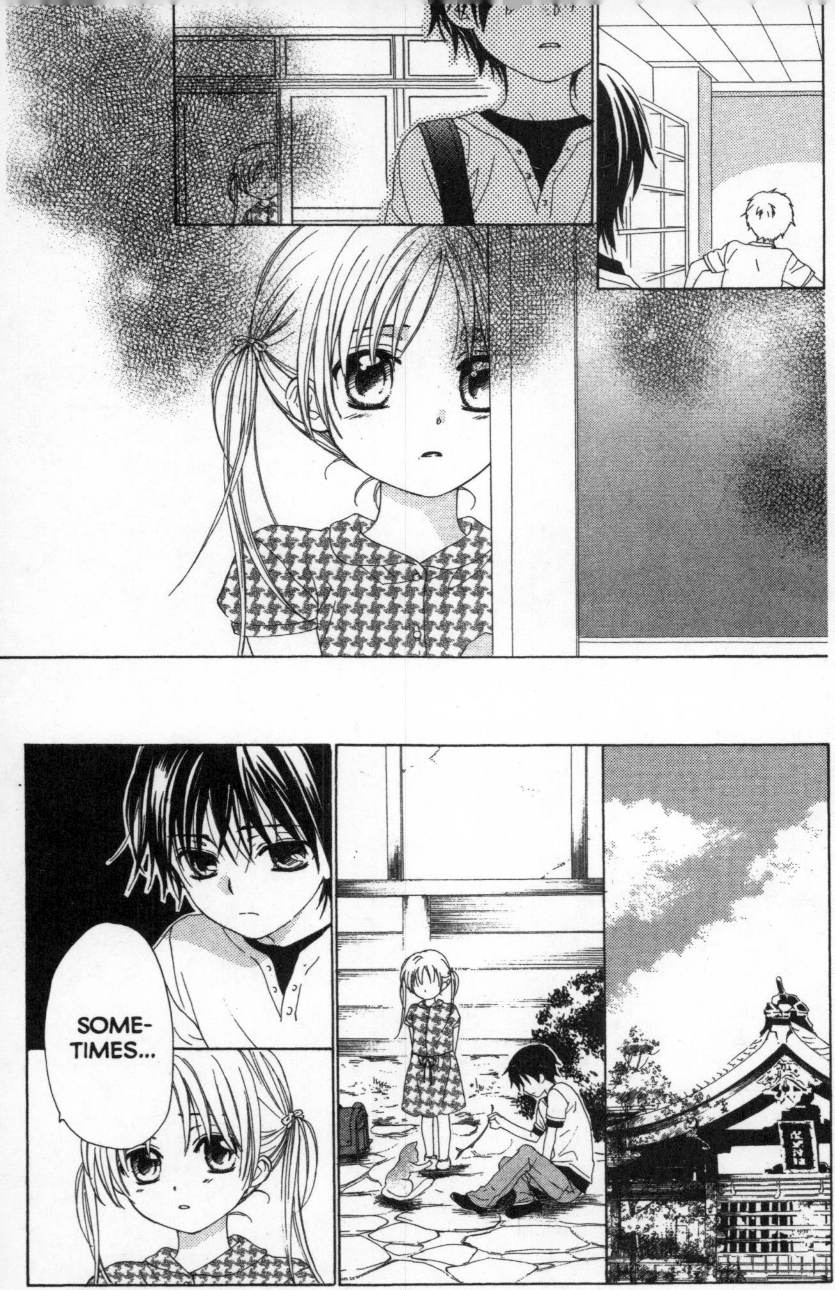
SOME-
TIMES...

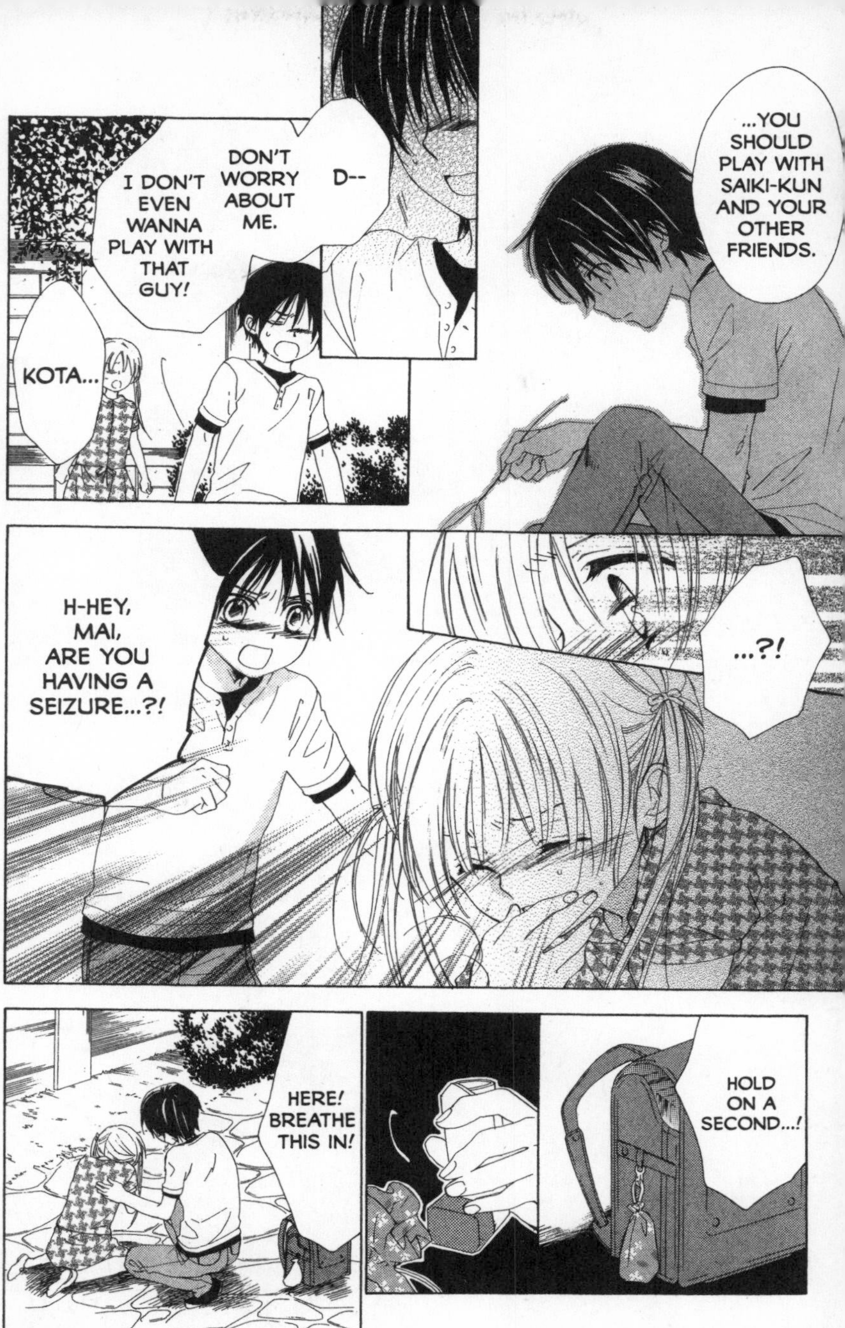
...YOU SHOULD PLAY WITH SAIKI-KUN AND YOUR OTHER FRIENDS.
D--
DON'T WORRY ABOUT ME.
I DON'T EVEN WANNA PLAY WITH THAT GUY!
KOTA...
...?!
H-HEY, MAI, ARE YOU HAVING A SEIZURE...?!
HOLD ON A SECOND...!
HERE! BREATHE THIS IN!

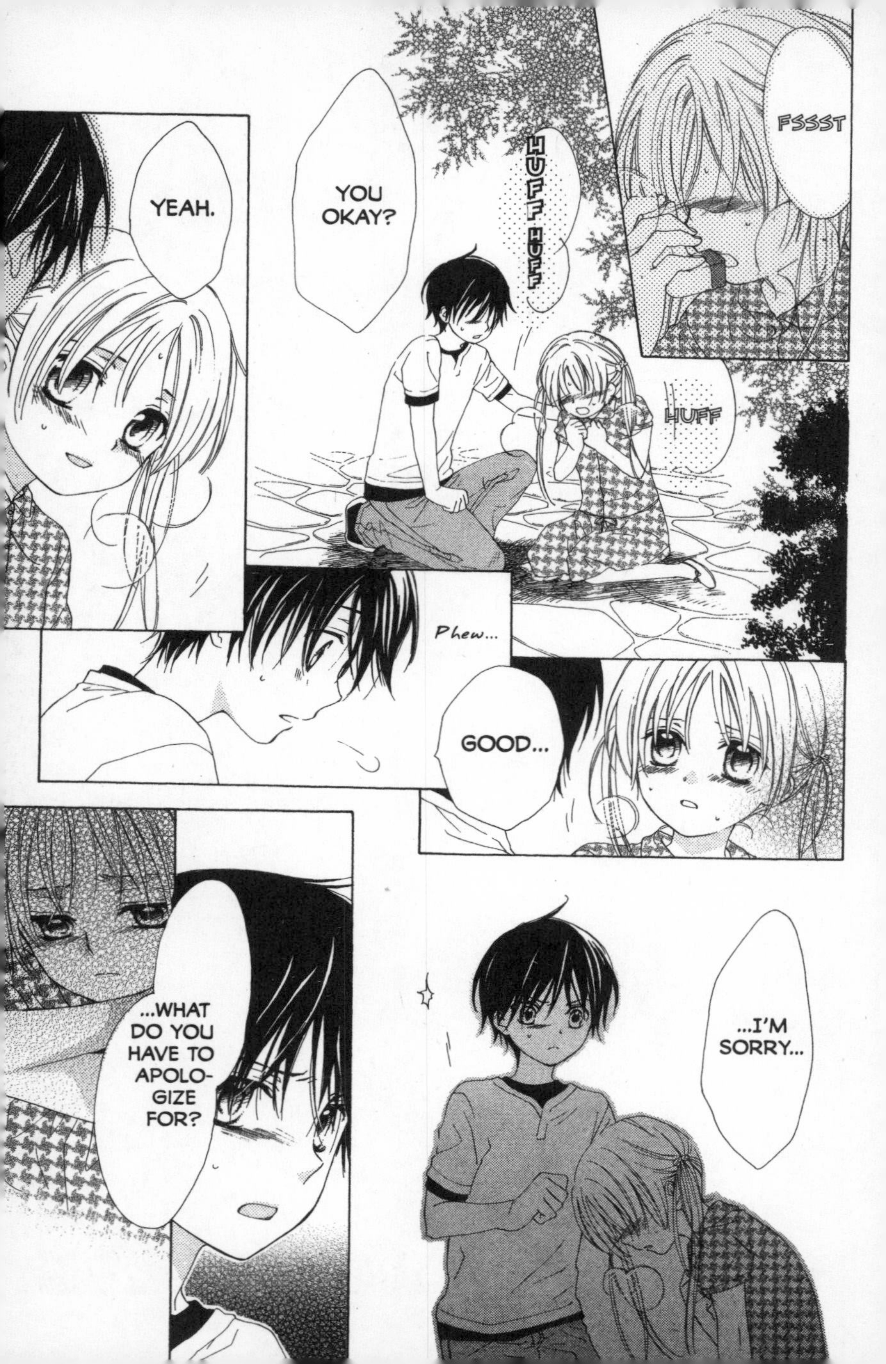

FSSST
HUFF HUFF
HUFF
YOU OKAY?
YEAH.
Phew...
GOOD...
...I'M SORRY...
...WHAT DO YOU HAVE TO APOLOGIZE FOR?

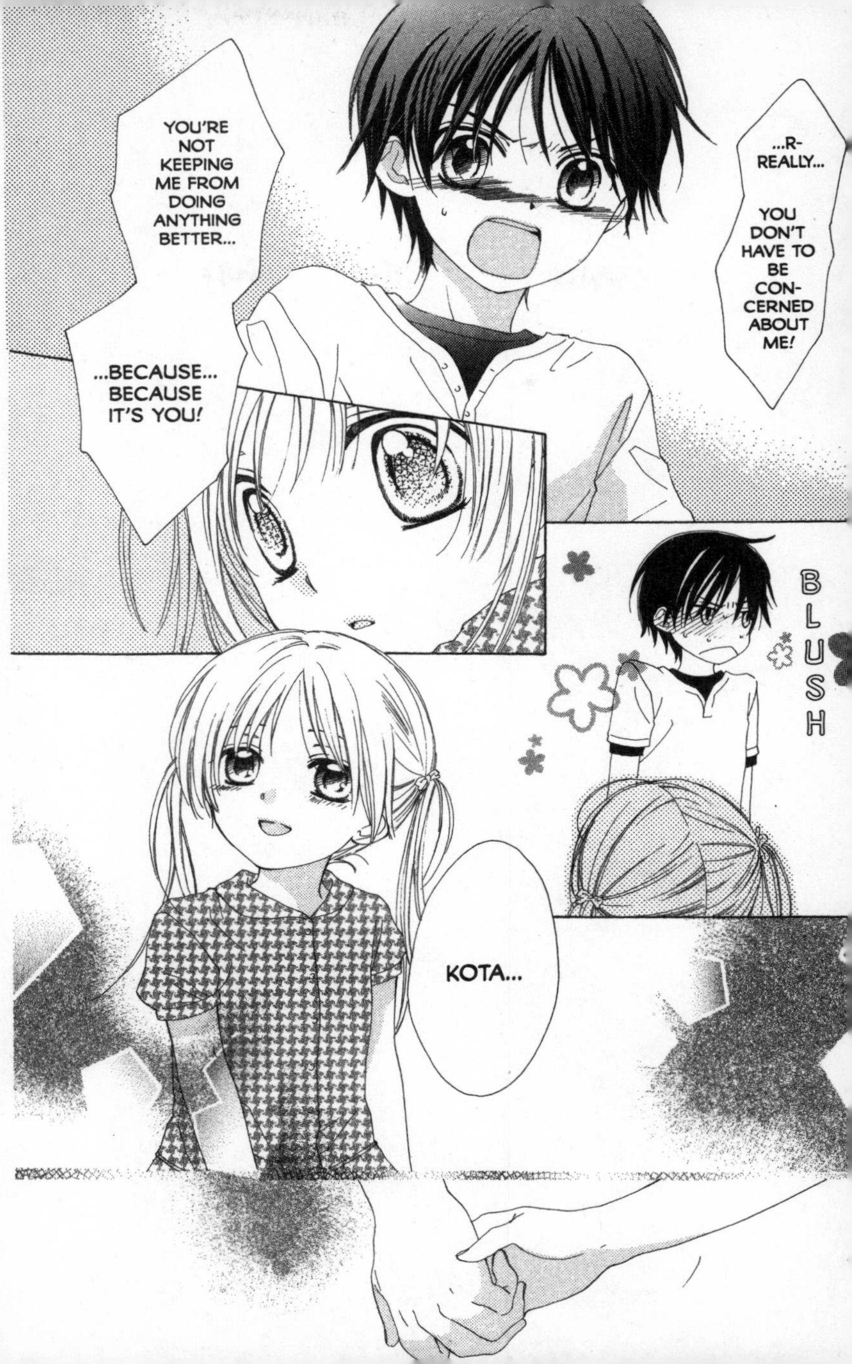
...R-REALLY...
YOU DON'T HAVE TO BE CON-CERNED ABOUT ME!
YOU'RE NOT KEEPING ME FROM DOING ANYTHING BETTER...
...BECAUSE... BECAUSE IT'S YOU!
BLUSH
KOTA...

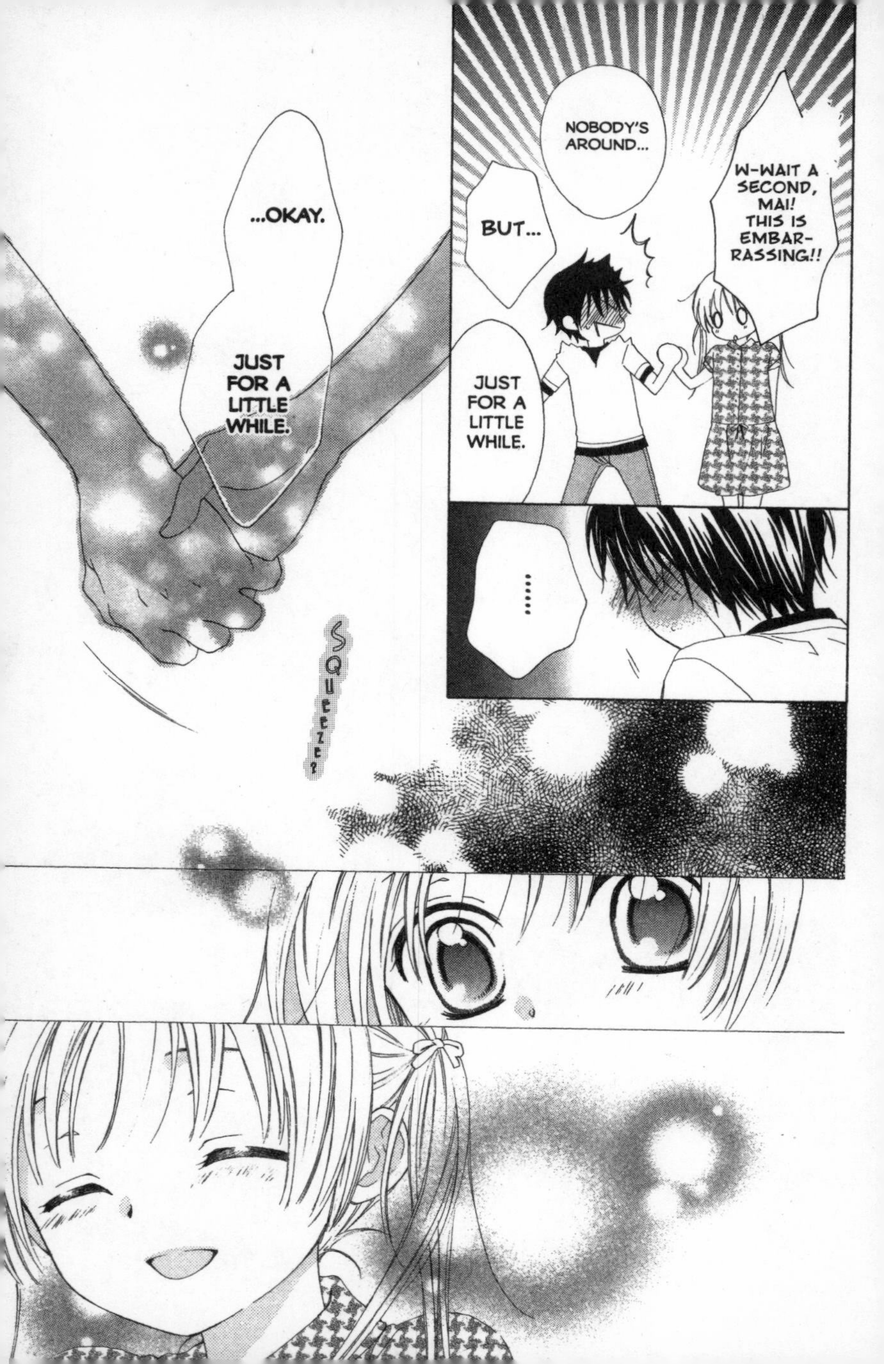

W-WAIT A SECOND, MAI! THIS IS EMBARRASSING!!
NOBODY'S AROUND...
BUT...
JUST FOR A LITTLE WHILE.
......
...OKAY.
JUST FOR A LITTLE WHILE.
SQUEEZE

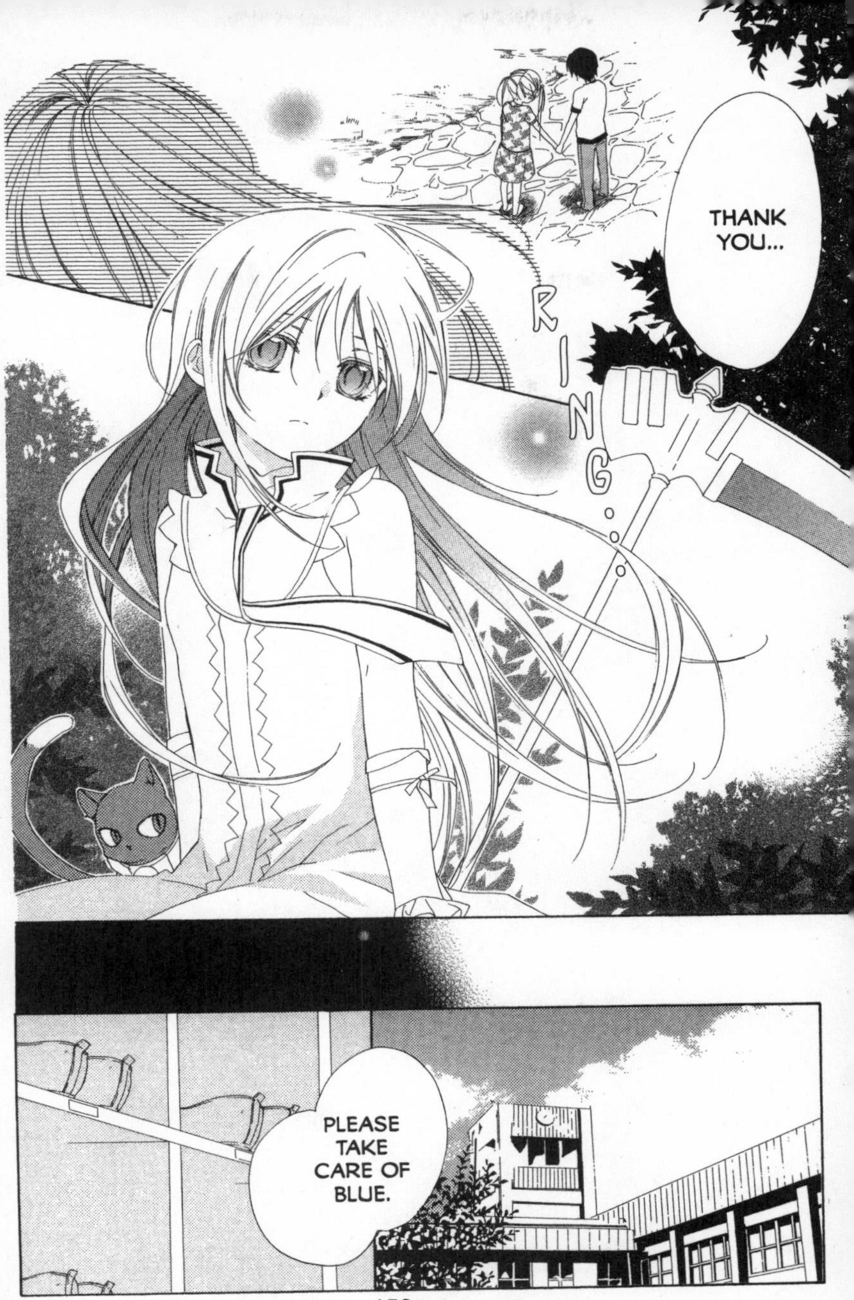
THANK YOU...
RING...
PLEASE TAKE CARE OF BLUE.

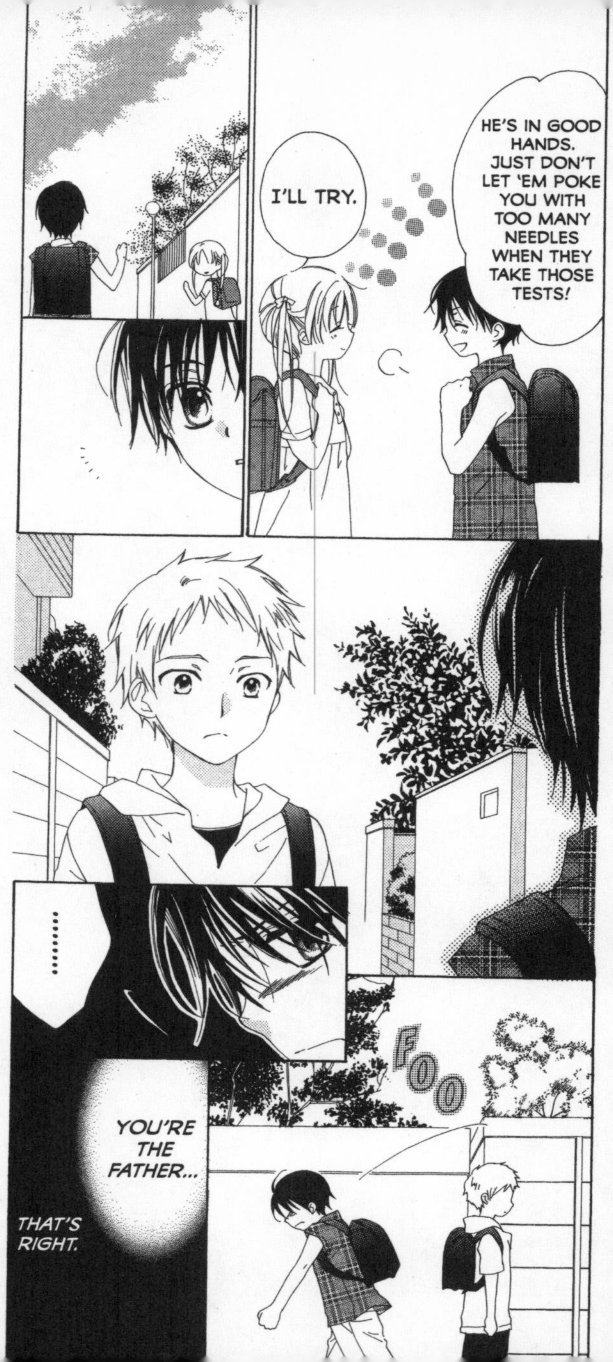
HE'S IN GOOD HANDS. JUST DON'T LET 'EM POKE YOU WITH TOO MANY NEEDLES WHEN THEY TAKE THOSE TESTS!
I'LL TRY.
....
FOO
YOU'RE THE FATHER...
THAT'S RIGHT.

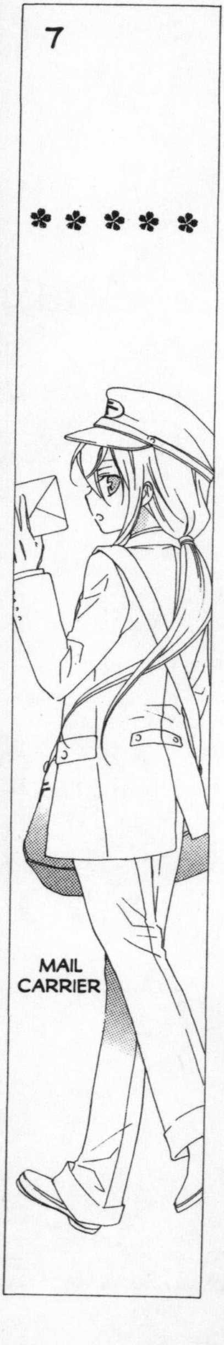
7
✿ ✿ ✿ ✿ ✿
MAIL CARRIER

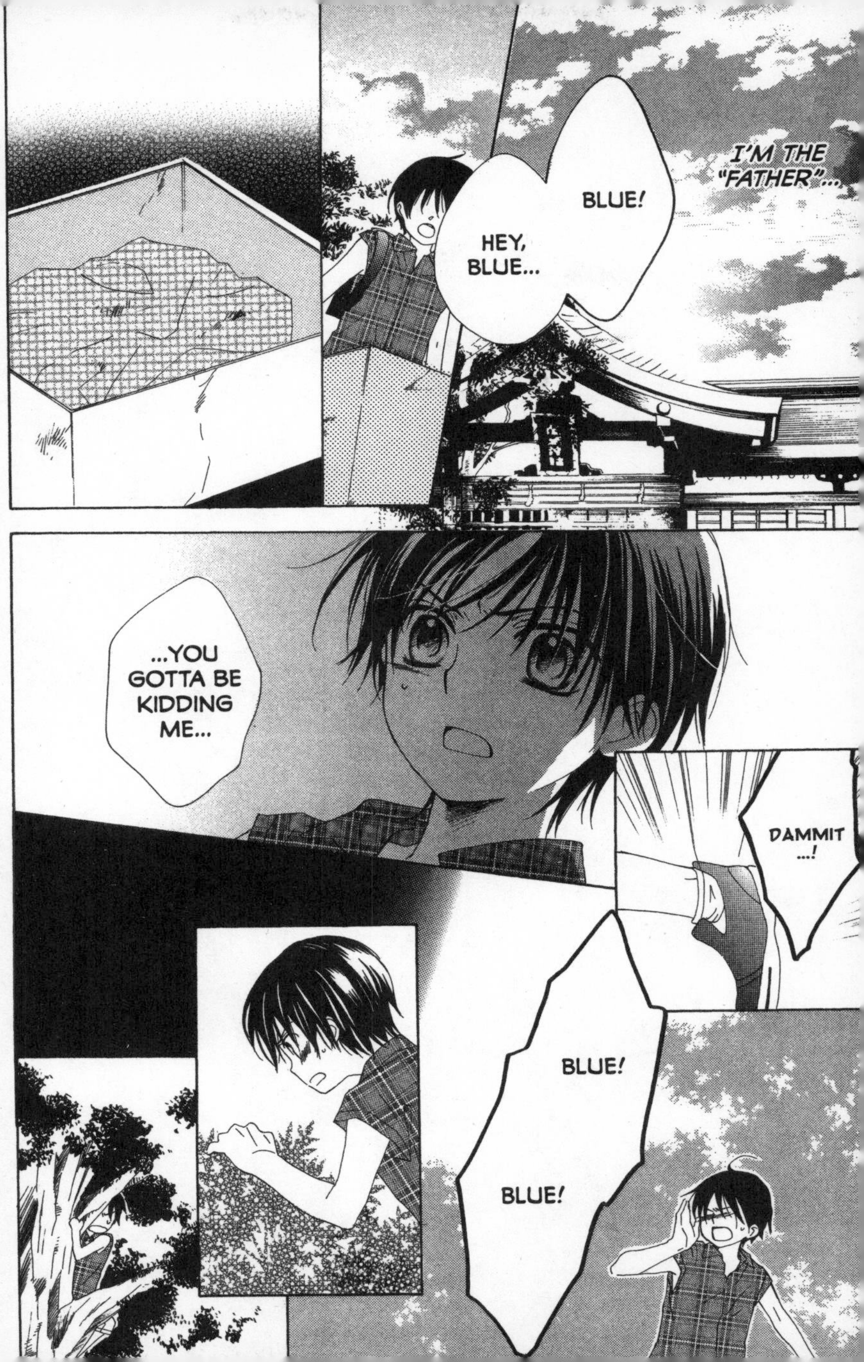
I'M THE "FATHER"...
BLUE!
HEY, BLUE...
...YOU GOTTA BE KIDDING ME...
DAMMIT ...!
BLUE!
BLUE!

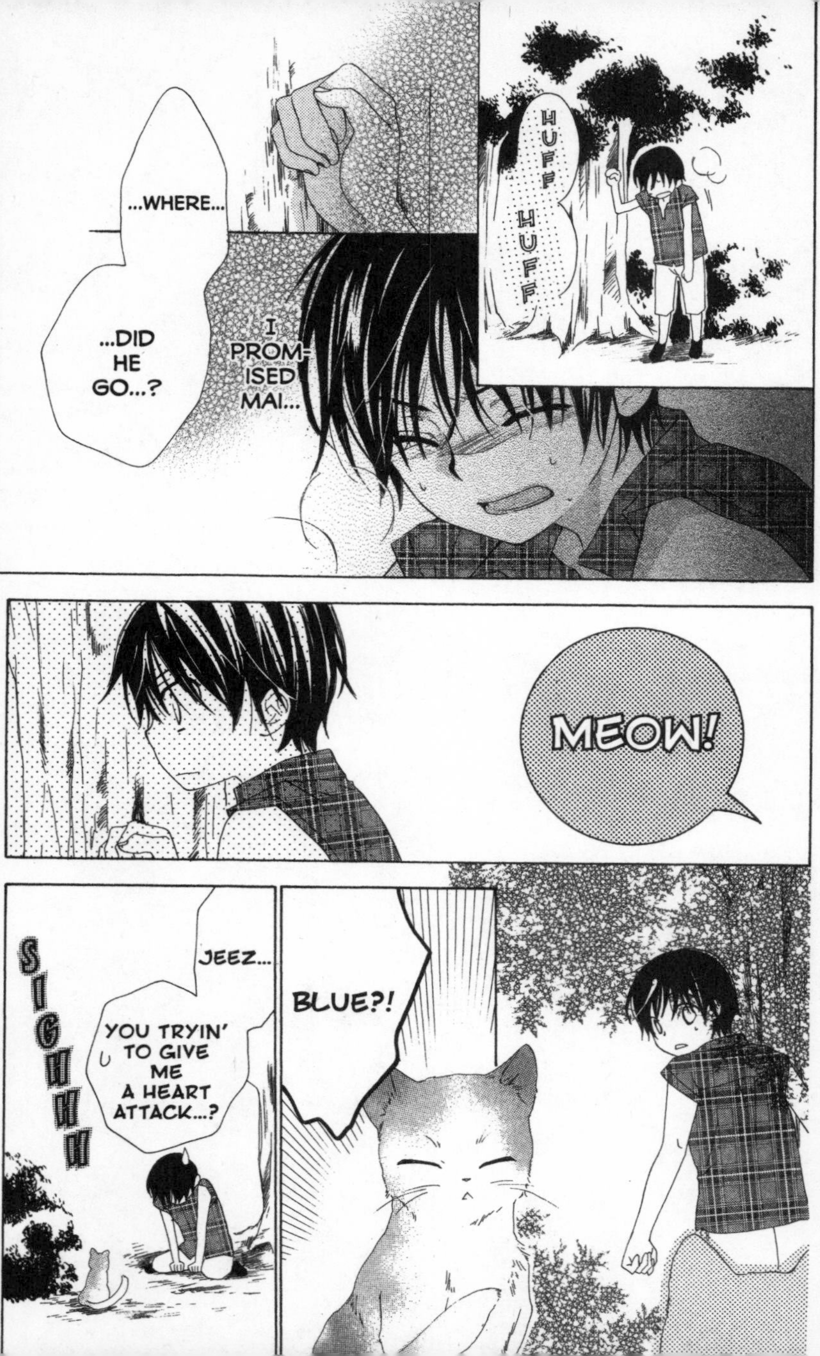
HUFF HUFF HUFF
...WHERE...
...DID HE GO...?
I PROMISED MAI...
MEOW!
BLUE?!
JEEZ...
YOU TRYIN' TO GIVE ME A HEART ATTACK...?
SIGHHH

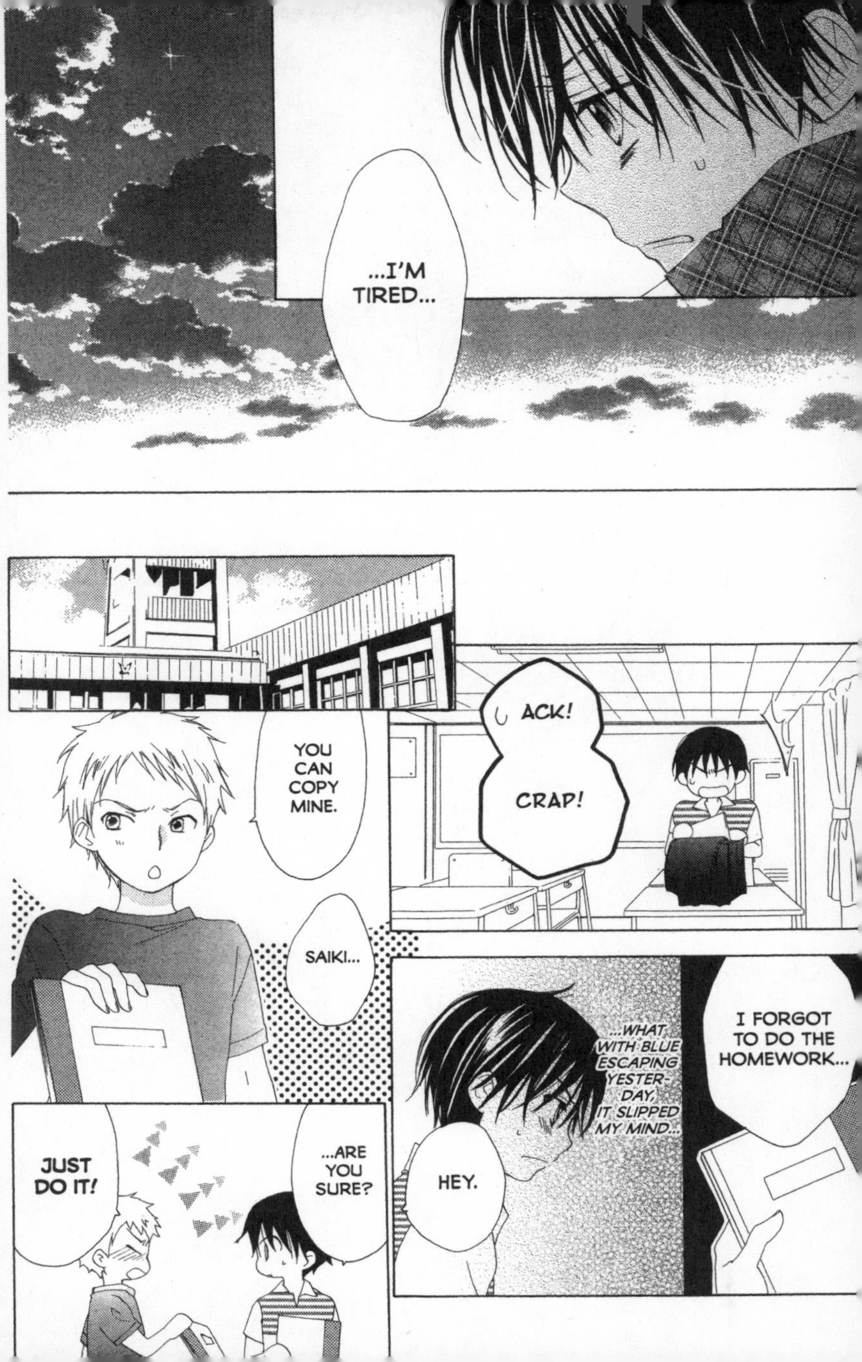
...I'M TIRED...
ACK!
CRAP!
I FORGOT TO DO THE HOMEWORK...
...WHAT WITH BLUE ESCAPING YESTER-DAY, IT SLIPPED MY MIND...
HEY.
YOU CAN COPY MINE.
SAIKI...
...ARE YOU SURE?
JUST DO IT!

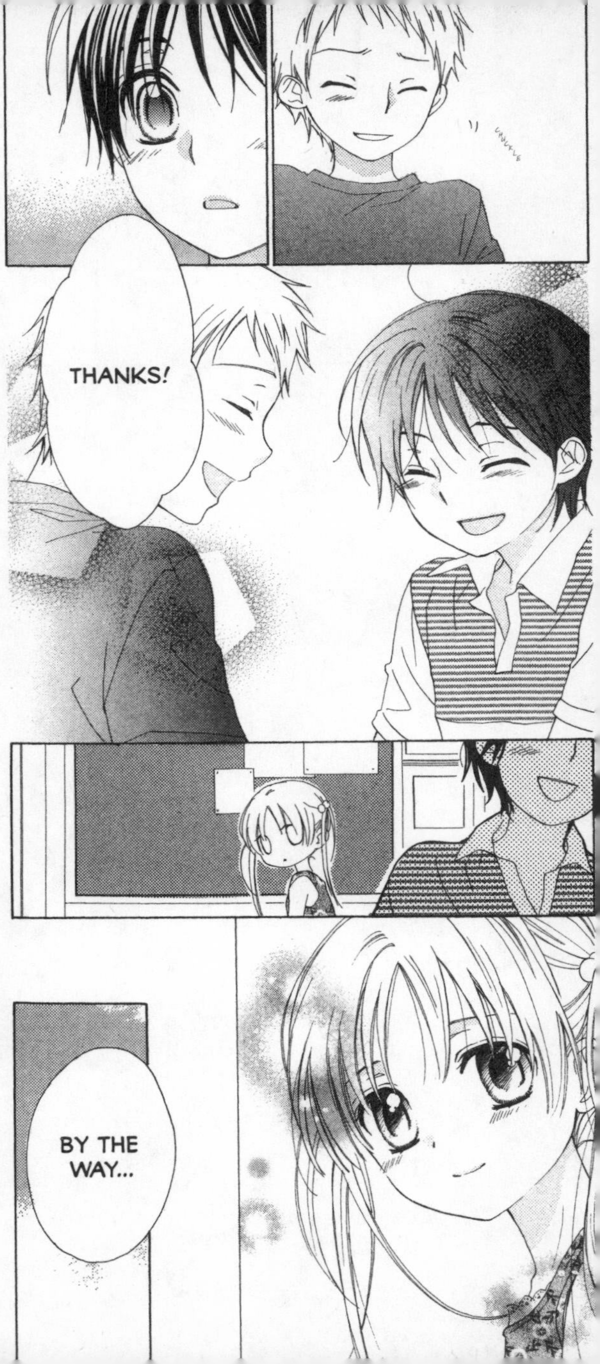
CHUCKLE
THANKS!
BY THE WAY...

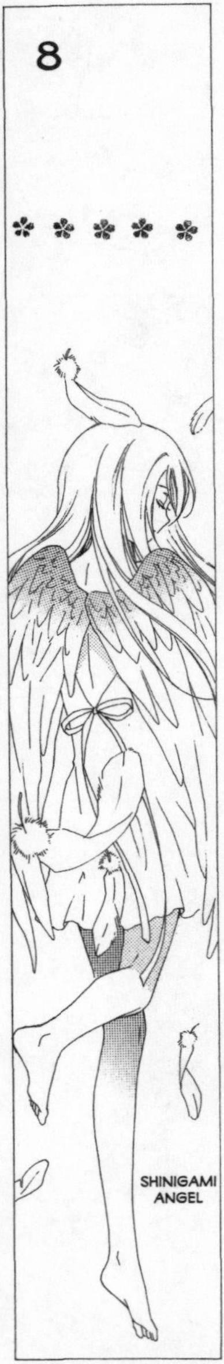
8
SHINIGAMI ANGEL

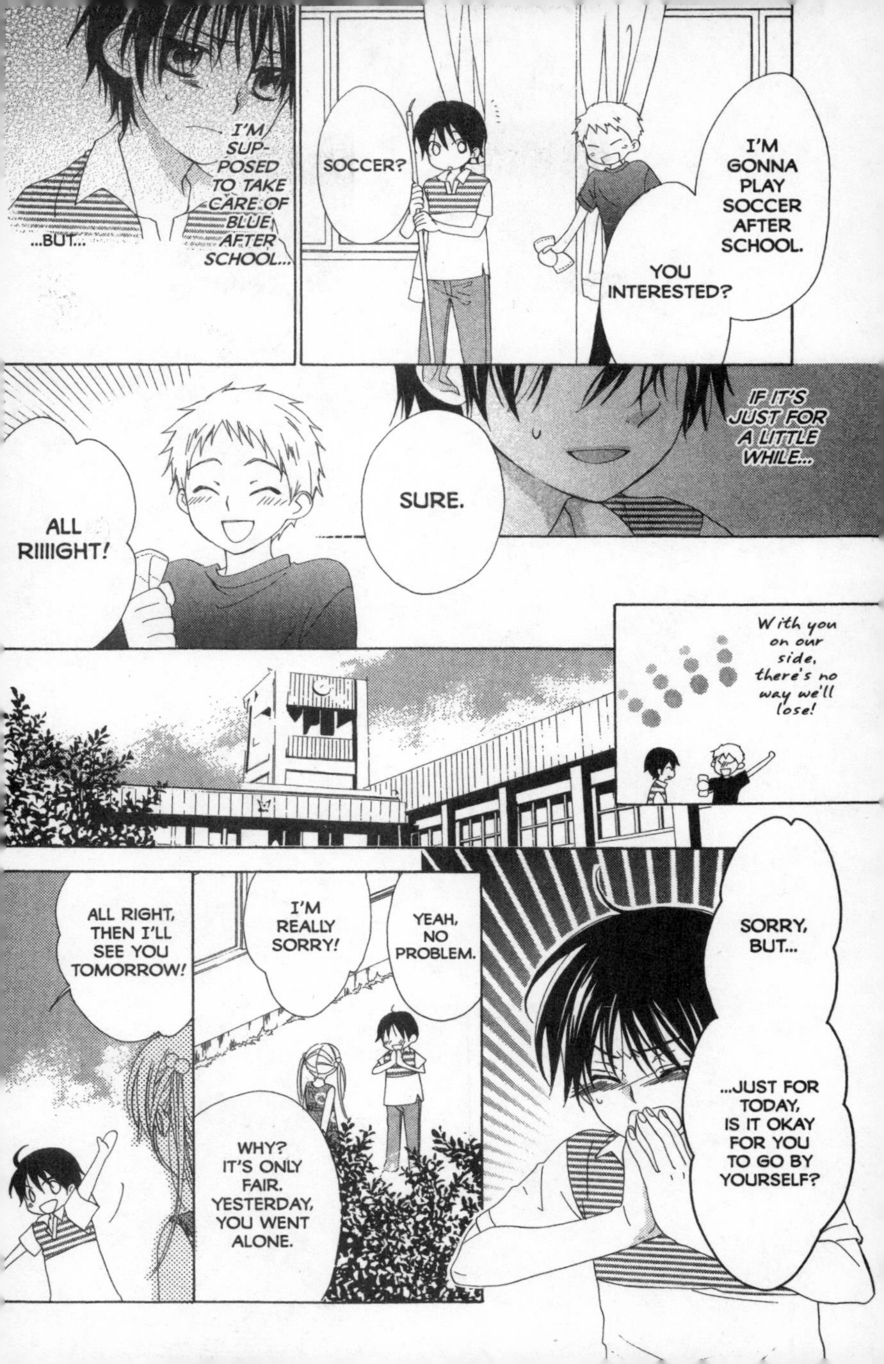
I'M GONNA PLAY SOCCER AFTER SCHOOL.
YOU INTERESTED?
SOCCER?
I'M SUPPOSED TO TAKE CARE OF BLUE AFTER SCHOOL...
...BUT...
IF IT'S JUST FOR A LITTLE WHILE...
SURE.
ALL RIIIGHT!
With you on our side, there's no way we'll lose!
SORRY, BUT...
...JUST FOR TODAY, IS IT OKAY FOR YOU TO GO BY YOURSELF?
YEAH, NO PROBLEM.
I'M REALLY SORRY!
WHY? IT'S ONLY FAIR. YESTERDAY, YOU WENT ALONE.
ALL RIGHT, THEN I'LL SEE YOU TOMORROW!

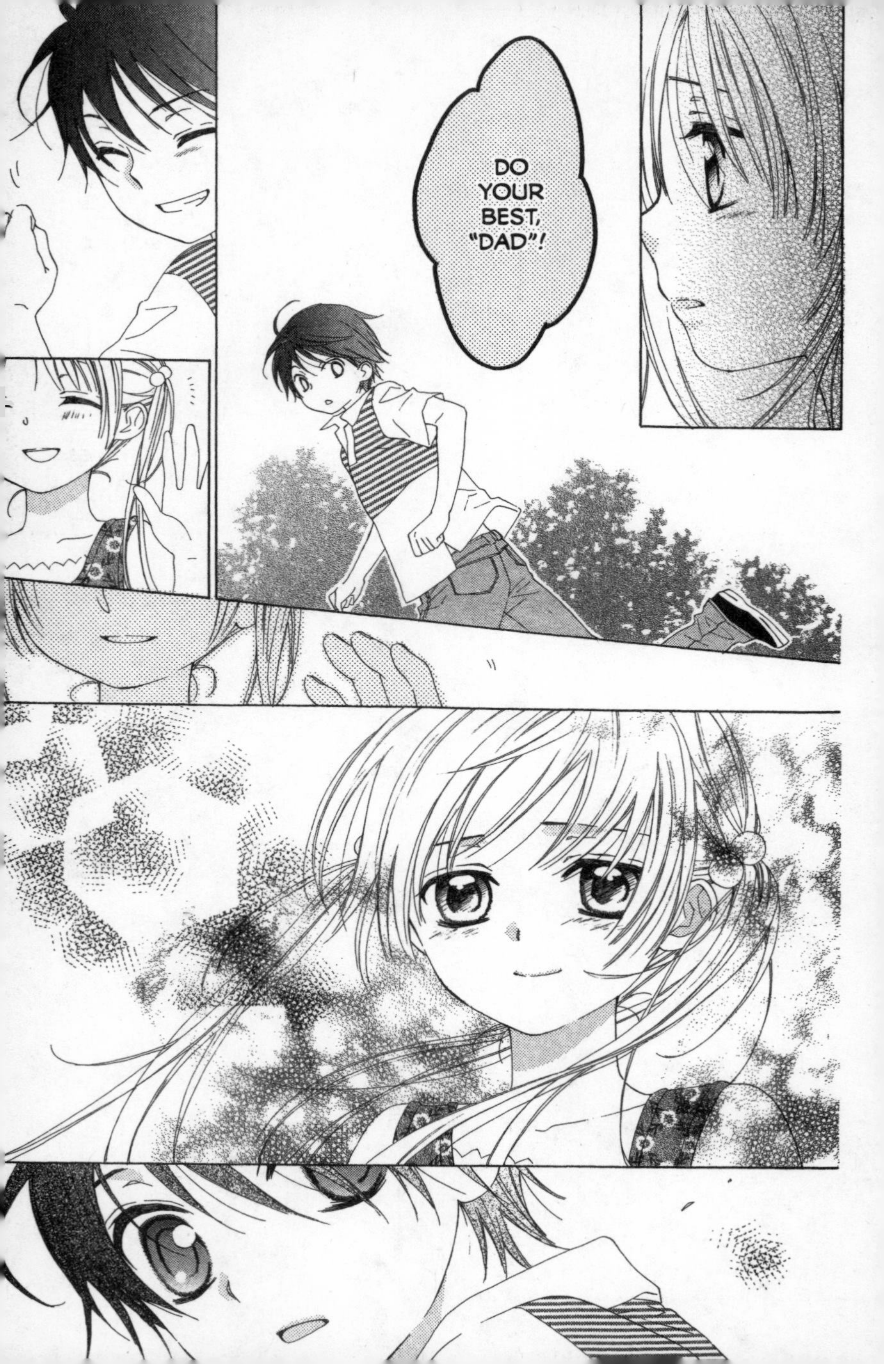
DO YOUR BEST, "DAD"!

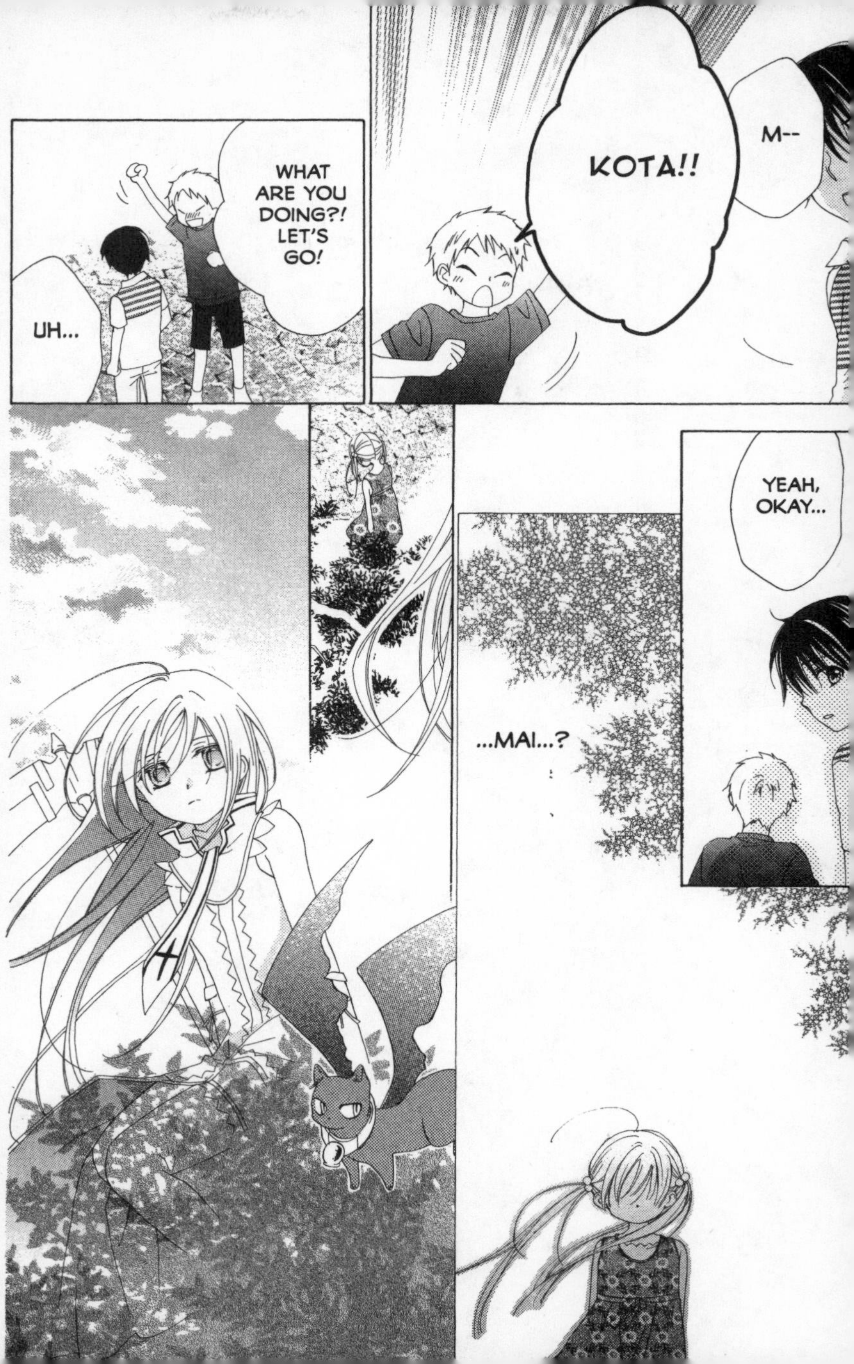
M--
KOTA!!
WHAT ARE YOU DOING?! LET'S GO!
UH...
YEAH, OKAY...
...MAI...?

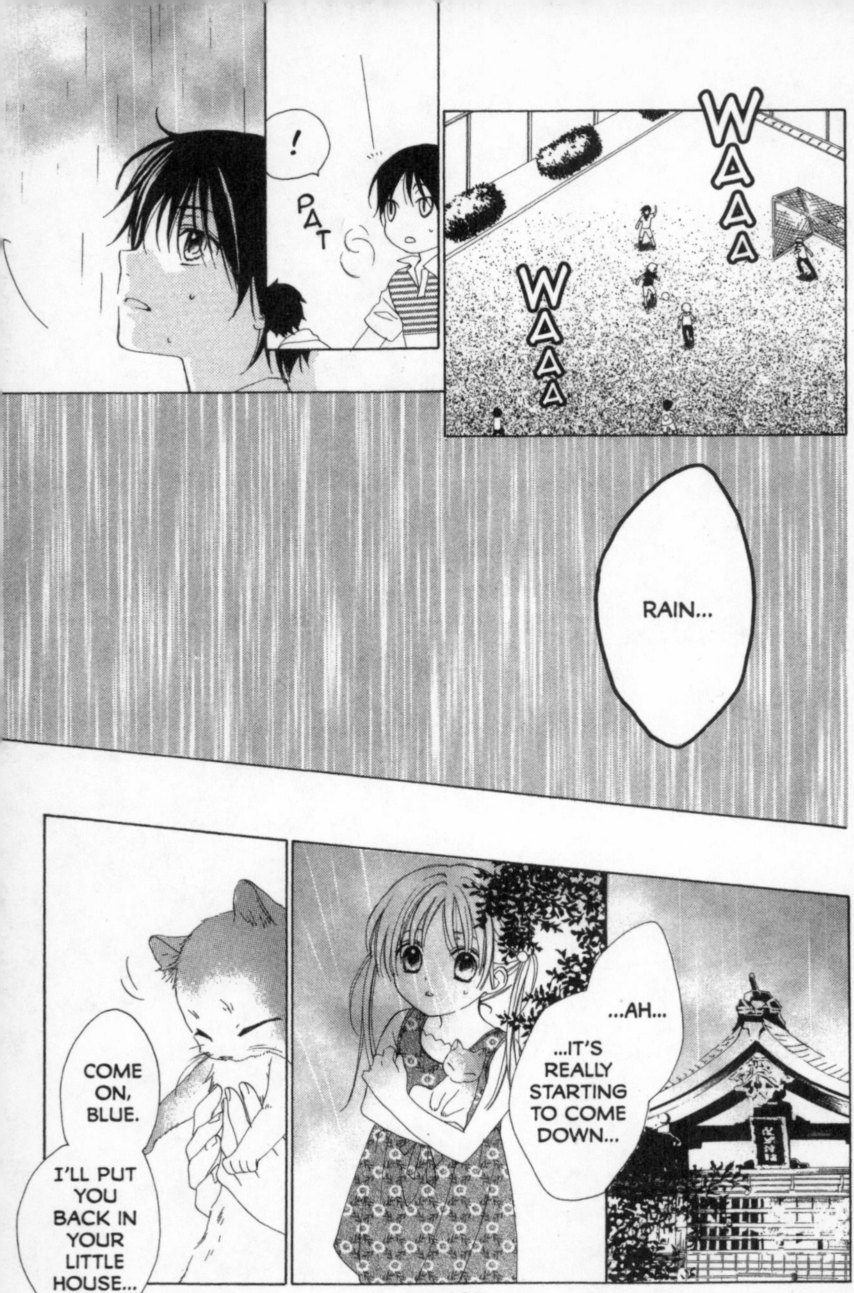
WAAA
WAAA
!
PAT
RAIN...
...AH...
...IT'S REALLY STARTING TO COME DOWN...
COME ON, BLUE.
I'LL PUT YOU BACK IN YOUR LITTLE HOUSE...

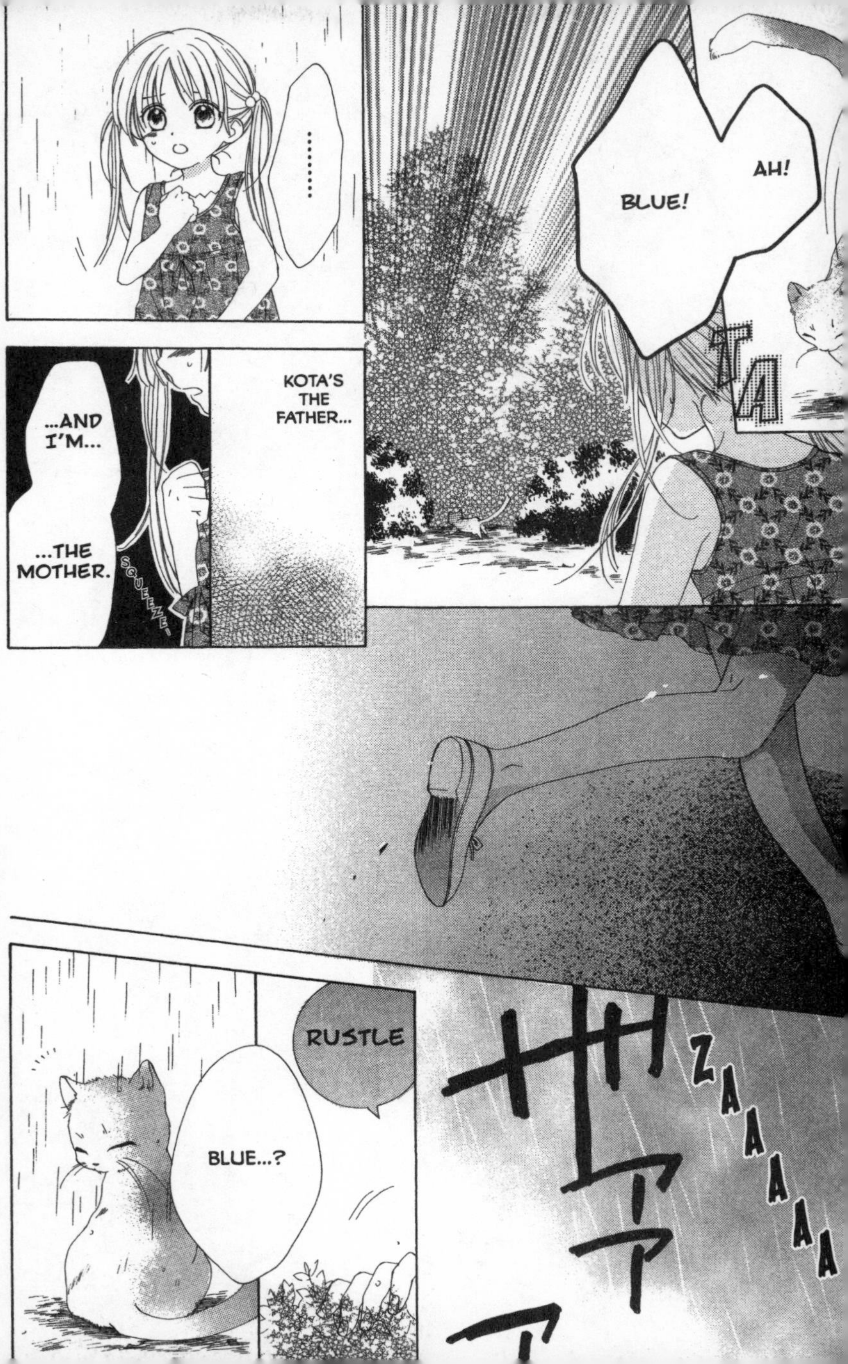
AH!
BLUE!
TA
......
KOTA'S THE FATHER...
...AND I'M...
...THE MOTHER.
SQUEEZE
ZAAAAAA
RUSTLE
BLUE...?

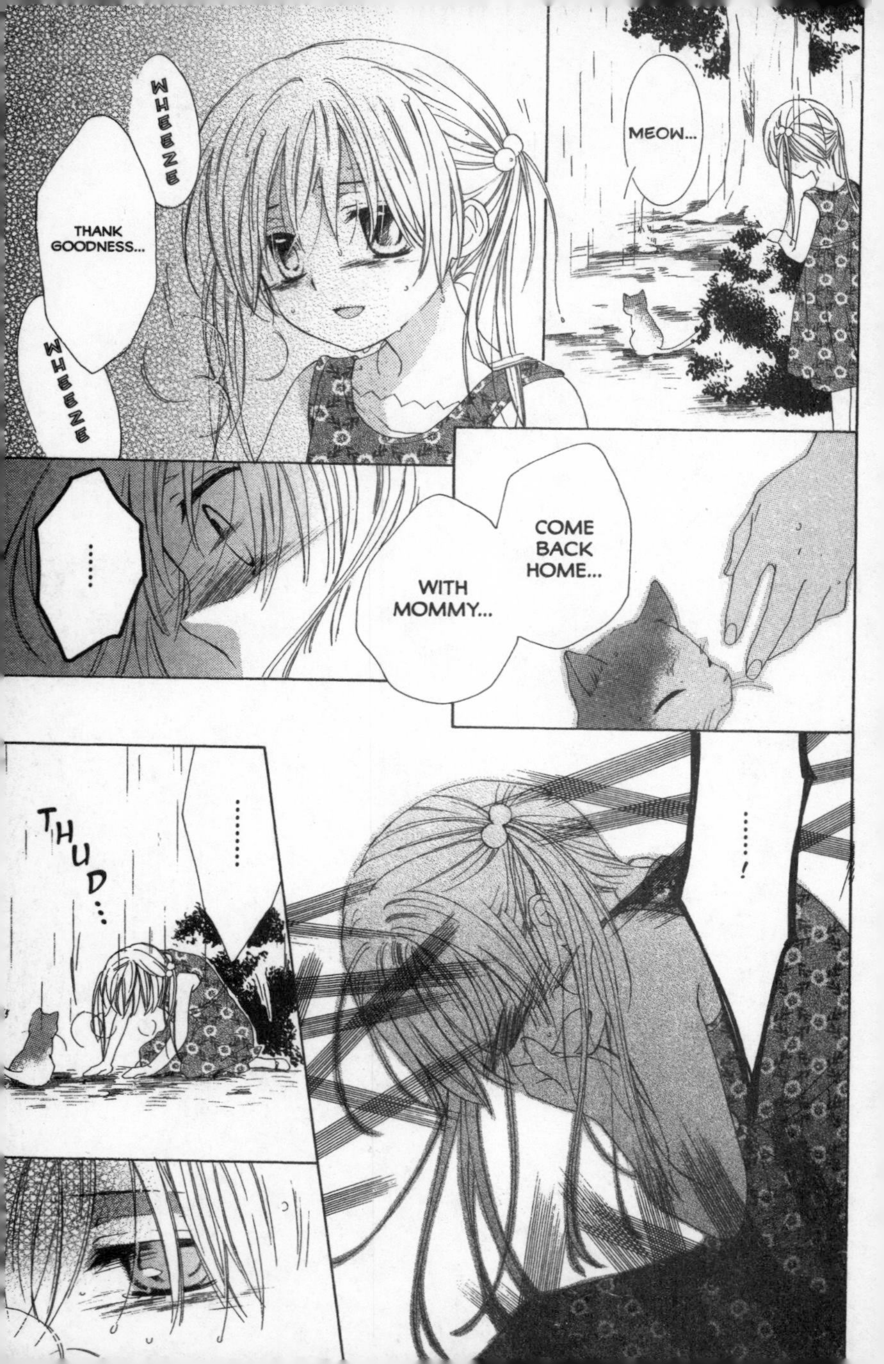
MEOW...
WHEEZE
THANK GOODNESS...
WHEEZE
COME BACK HOME...
WITH MOMMY...
......
......!
....
THUD...

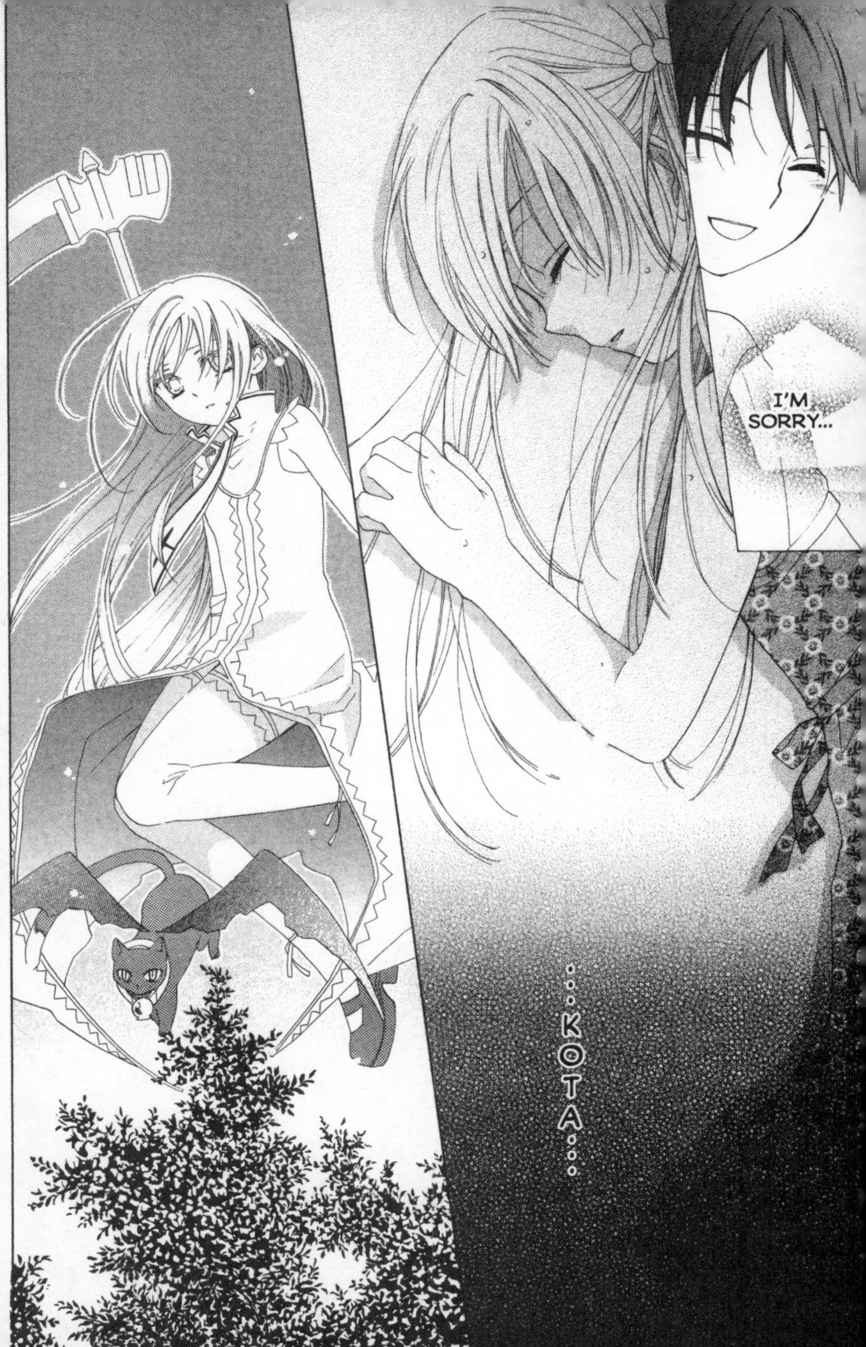
I'M SORRY...
...KOTA...

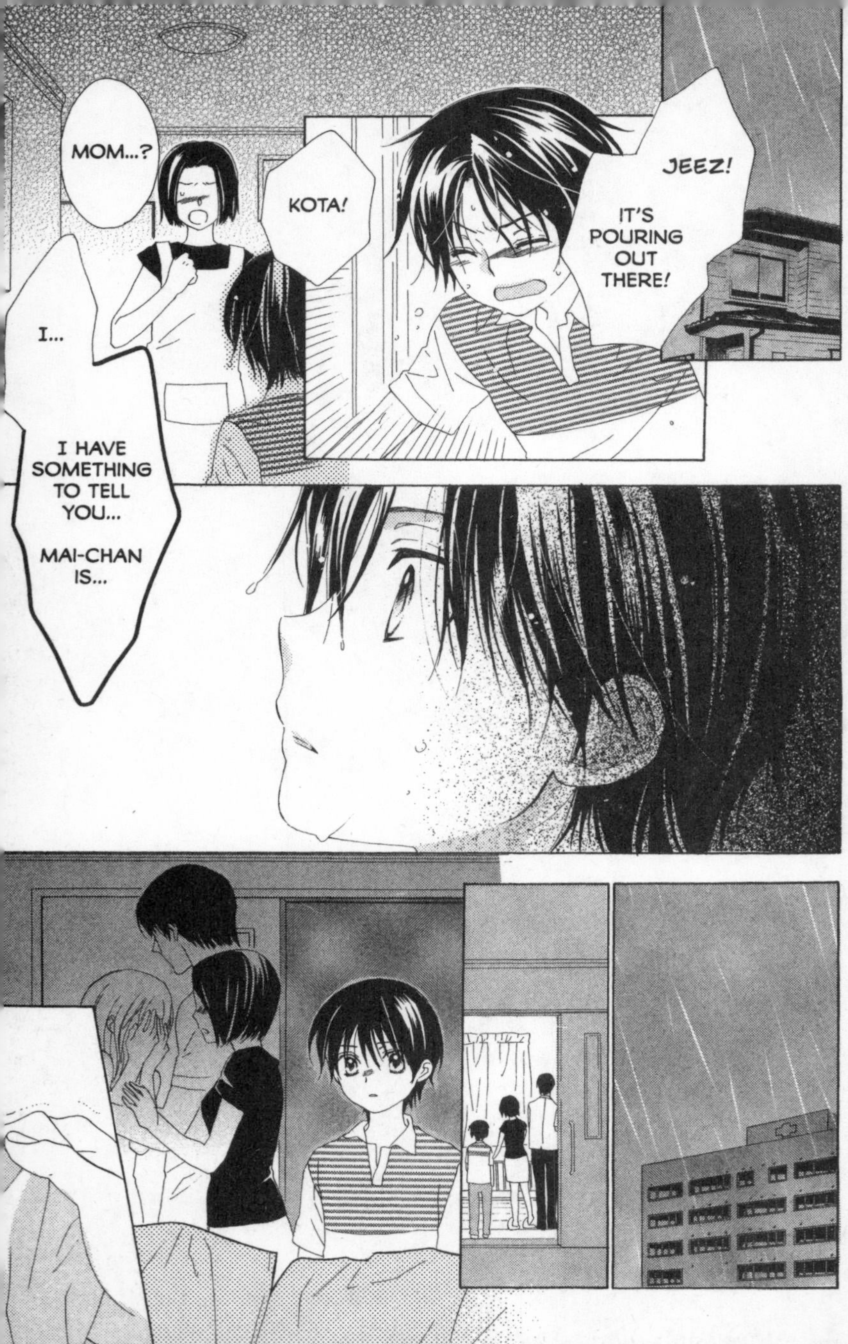
JEEZ!
IT'S POURING OUT THERE!
KOTA!
MOM...?
I...
I HAVE SOMETHING TO TELL YOU...
MAI-CHAN IS...

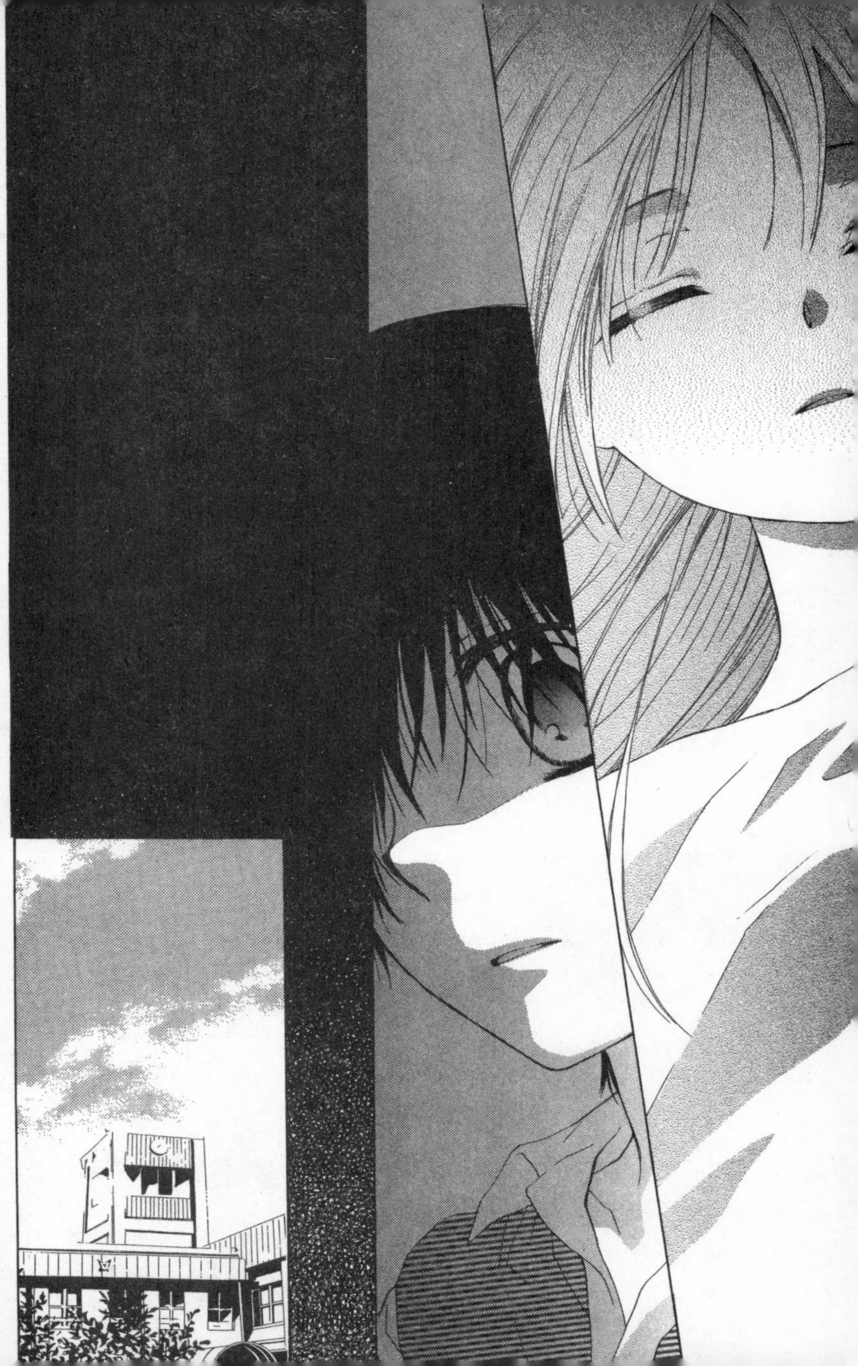

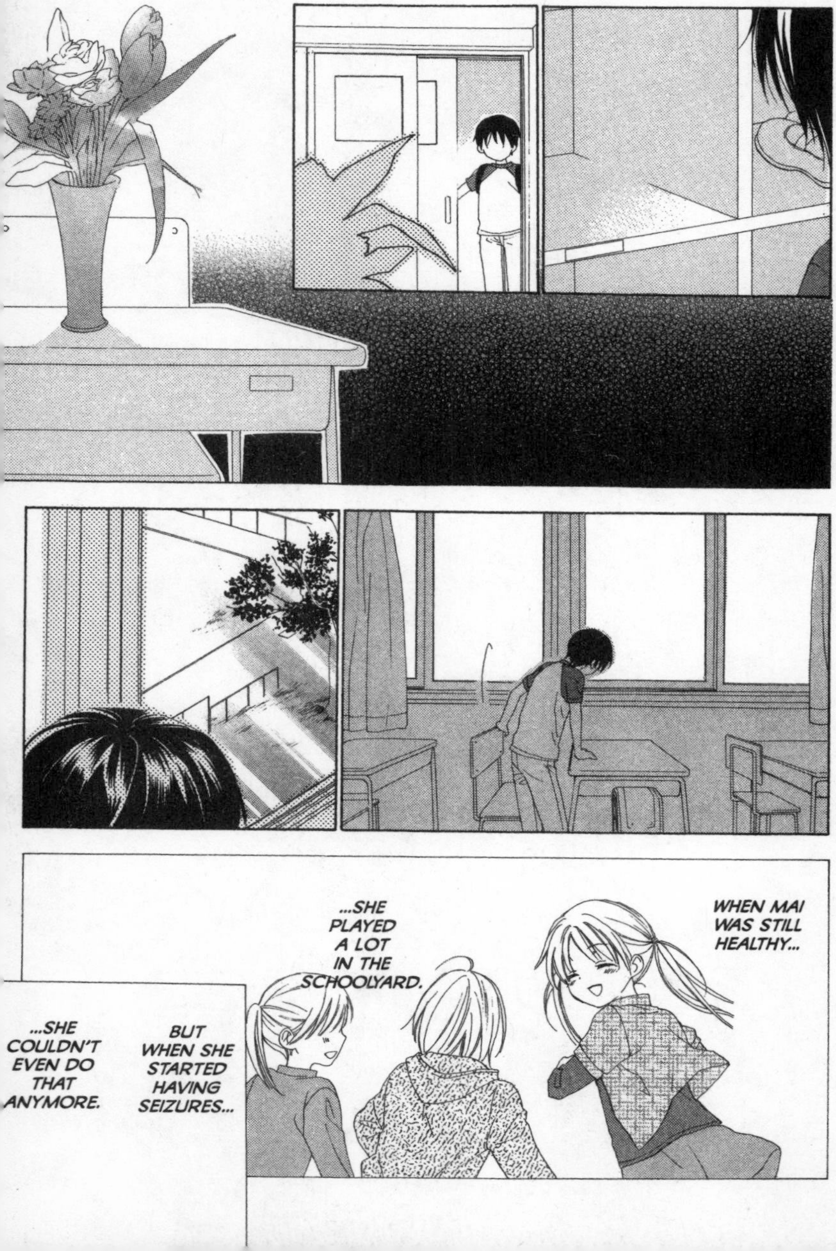
WHEN MAI WAS STILL HEALTHY...
...SHE PLAYED A LOT IN THE SCHOOLYARD.
BUT WHEN SHE STARTED HAVING SEIZURES...
...SHE COULDN'T EVEN DO THAT ANYMORE.

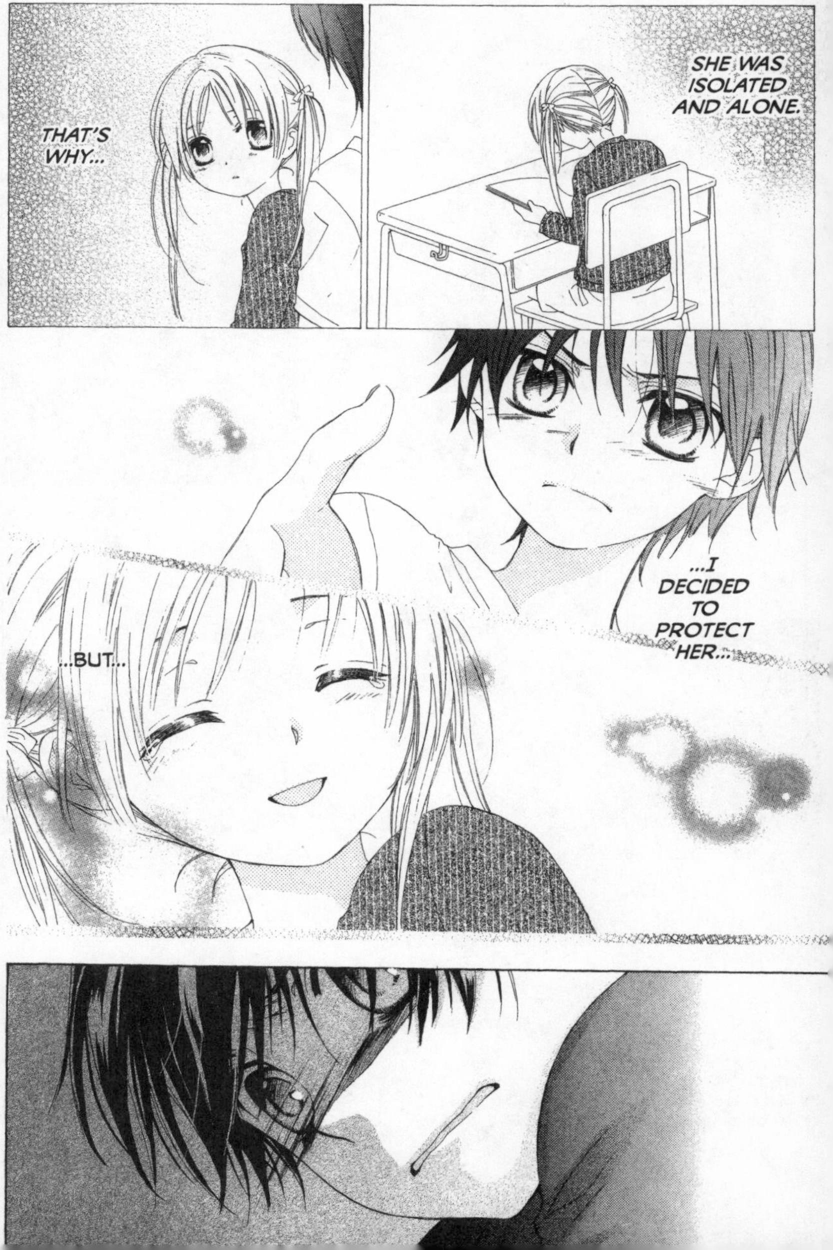
SHE WAS ISOLATED AND ALONE.
THAT'S WHY...
...I DECIDED TO PROTECT HER...
...BUT...

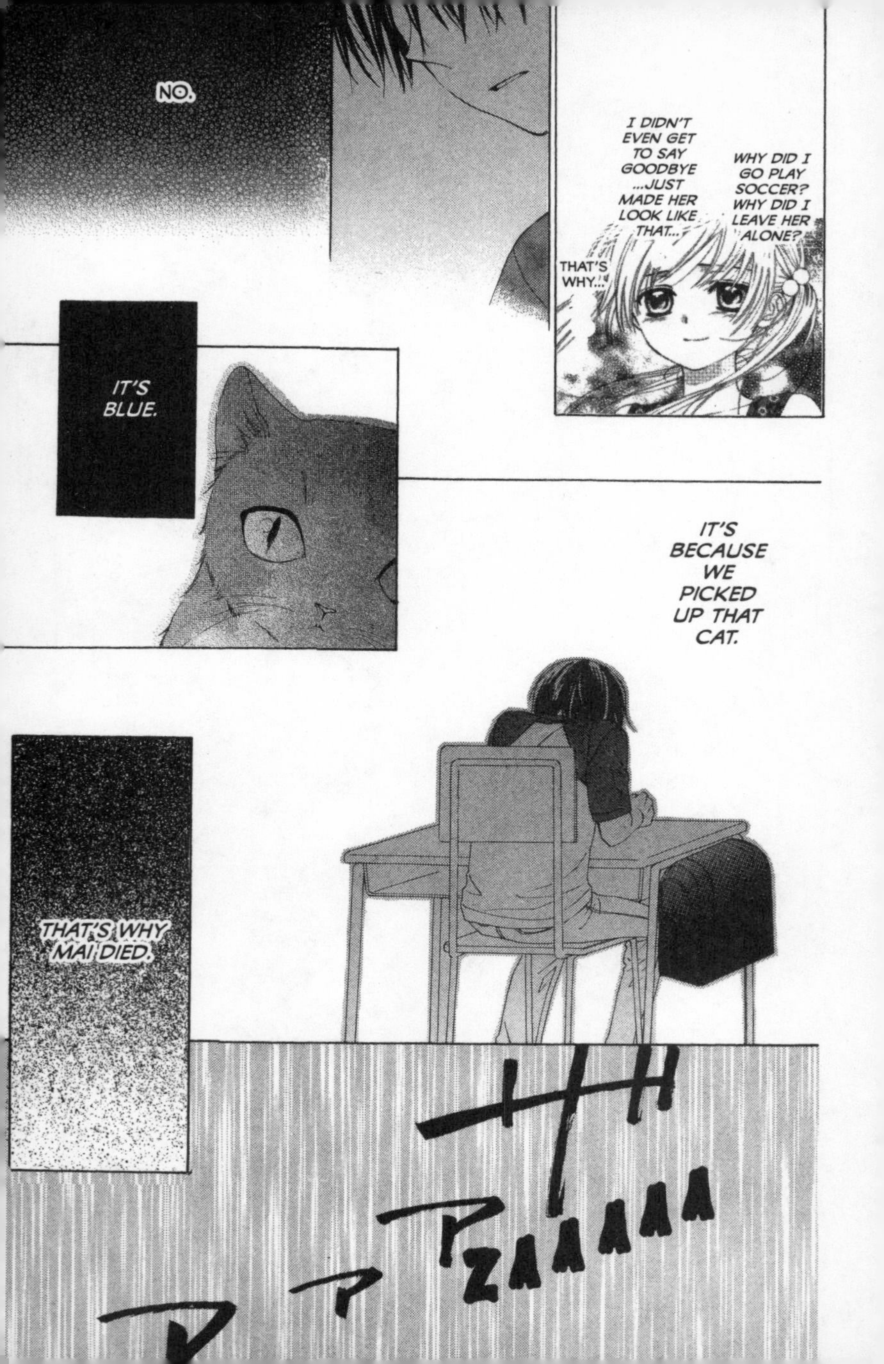
WHY DID I GO PLAY SOCCER? WHY DID I LEAVE HER ALONE?
I DIDN'T EVEN GET TO SAY GOODBYE ...JUST MADE HER LOOK LIKE THAT...
THAT'S WHY...
NO.
IT'S BLUE.
IT'S BECAUSE WE PICKED UP THAT CAT.
THAT'S WHY MAI DIED.
ZAAAAAA

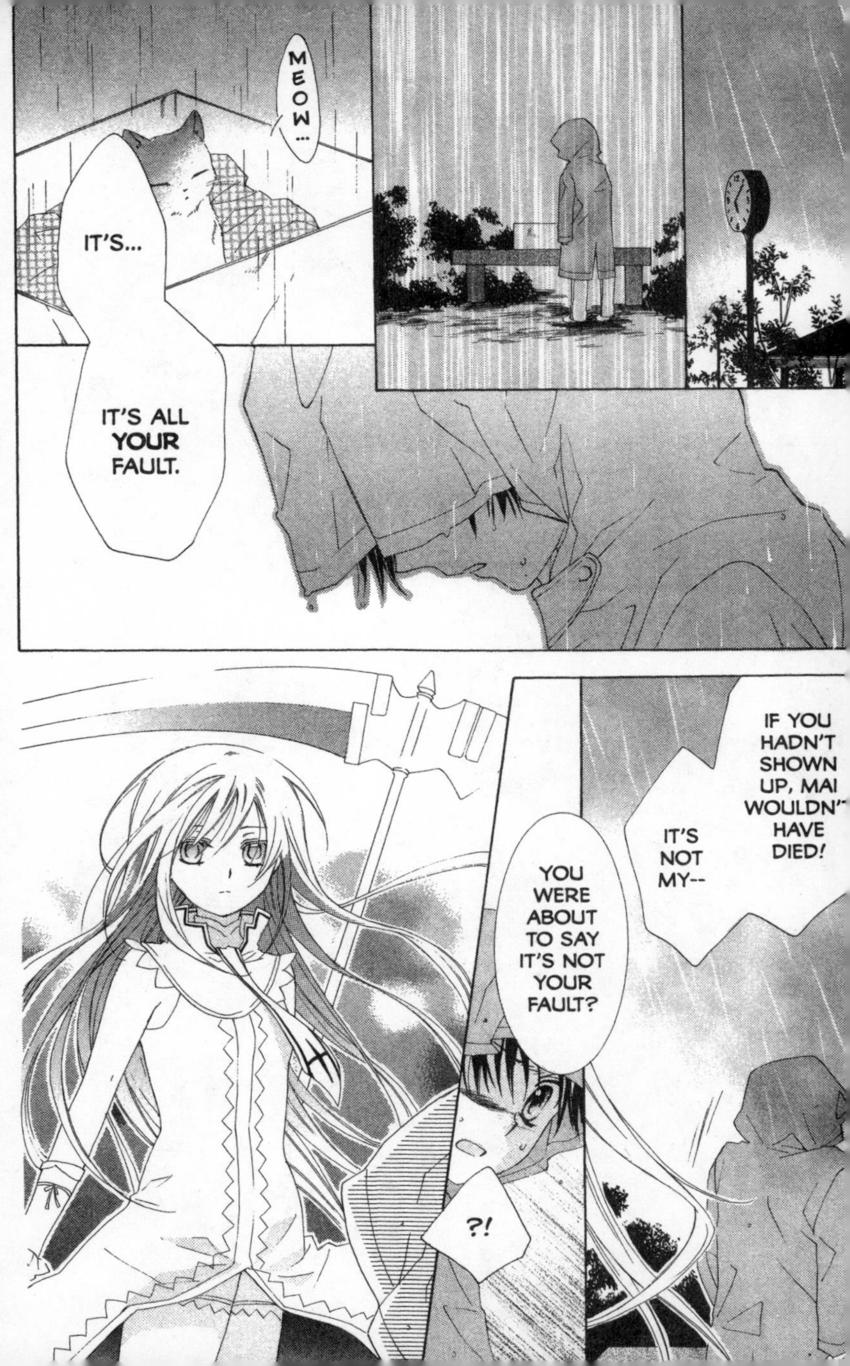
MEOW...
IT'S...
IT'S ALL YOUR FAULT.
IF YOU HADN'T SHOWN UP, MAI WOULDN'T HAVE DIED!
IT'S NOT MY--
YOU WERE ABOUT TO SAY IT'S NOT YOUR FAULT?
?!

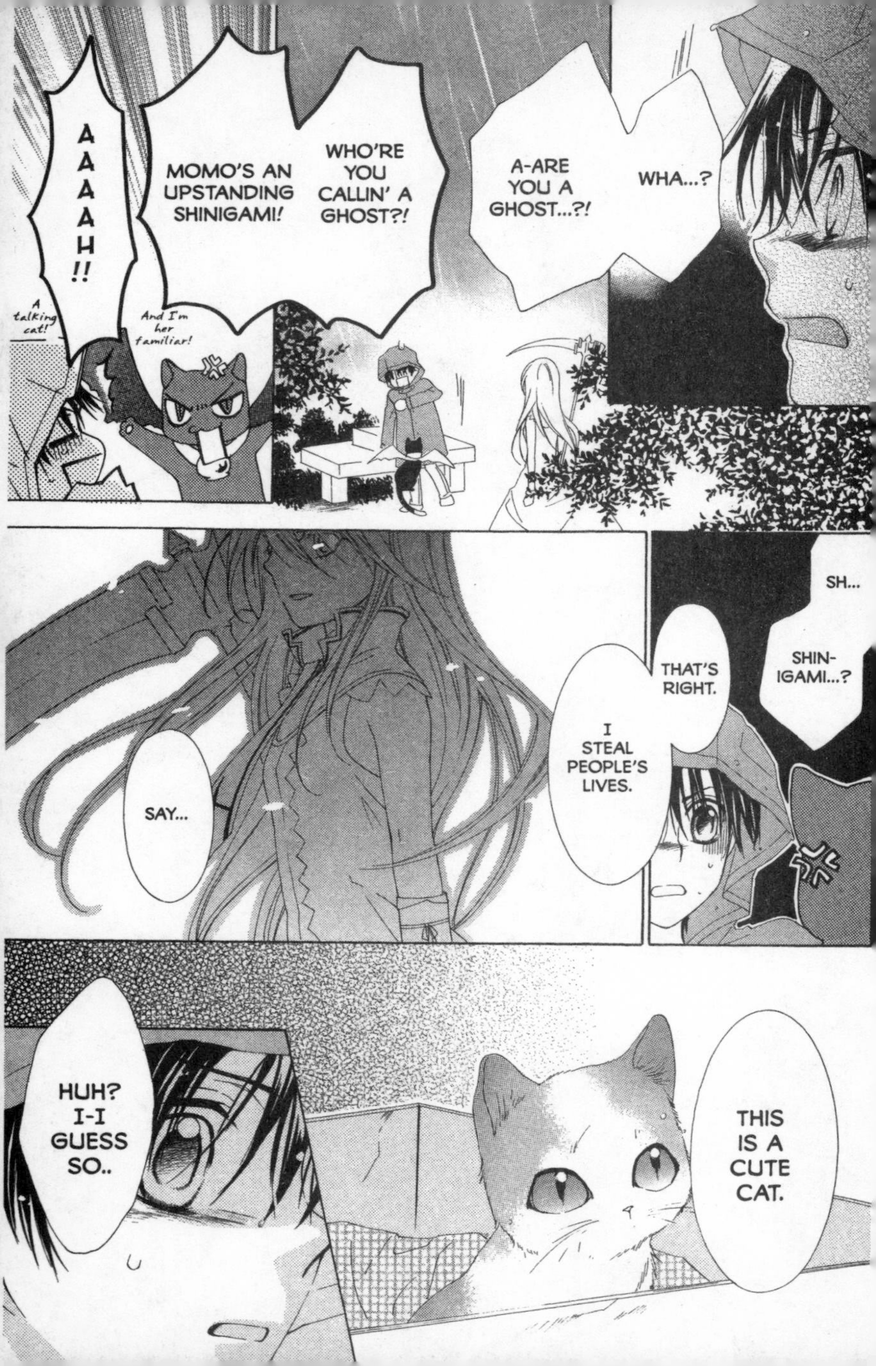
WHA...?
A-ARE YOU A GHOST...?!
WHO'RE YOU CALLIN' A GHOST?!
MOMO'S AN UPSTANDING SHINIGAMI!
And I'm her familiar!
AAAAH!!
A talking cat!
SH...
SHIN-IGAMI...?
THAT'S RIGHT.
I STEAL PEOPLE'S LIVES.
SAY...
THIS IS A CUTE CAT.
HUH? I-I GUESS SO..

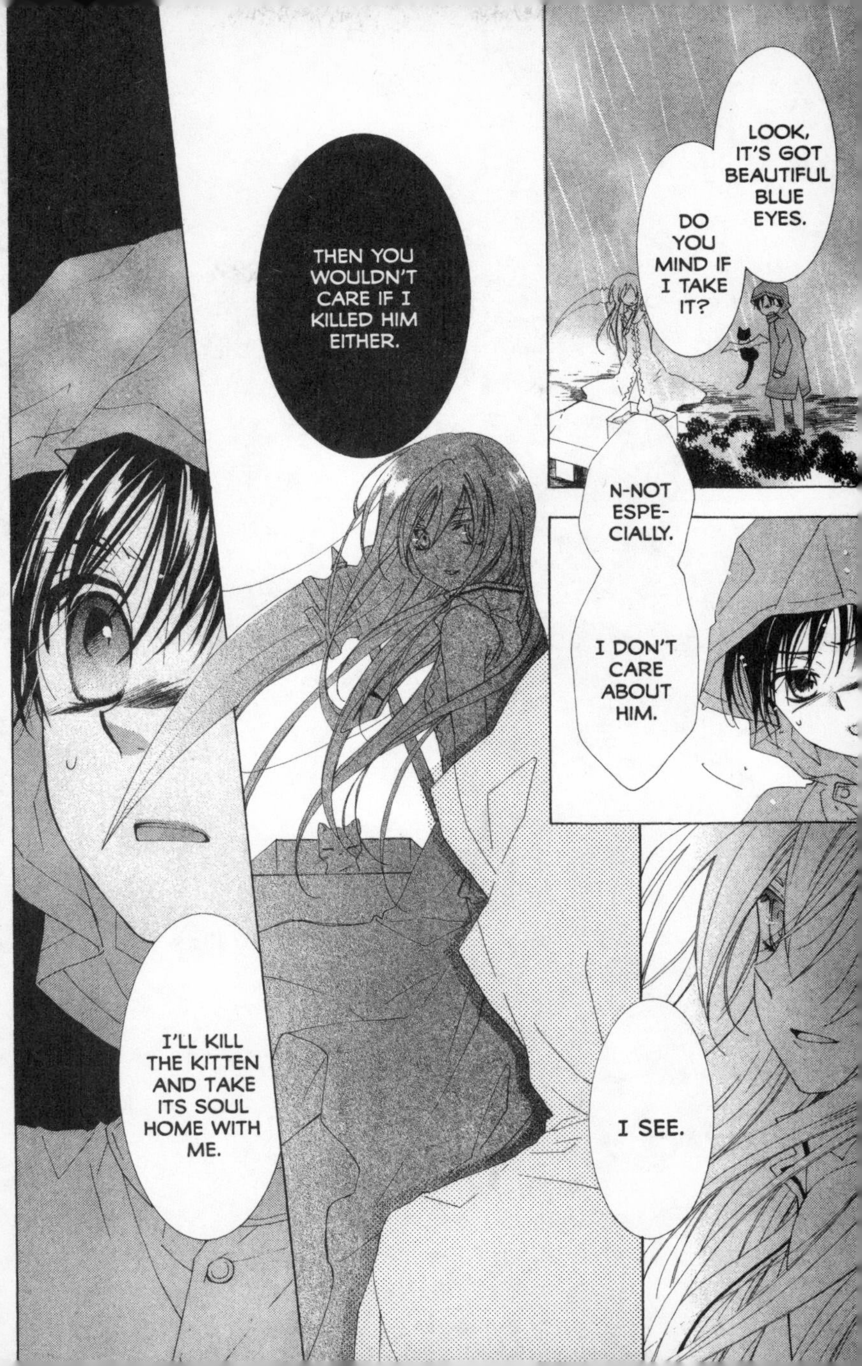
LOOK, IT'S GOT BEAUTIFUL BLUE EYES.
DO YOU MIND IF I TAKE IT?
N-NOT ESPECIALLY.
I DON'T CARE ABOUT HIM.
I SEE.
THEN YOU WOULDN'T CARE IF I KILLED HIM EITHER.
I'LL KILL THE KITTEN AND TAKE ITS SOUL HOME WITH ME.

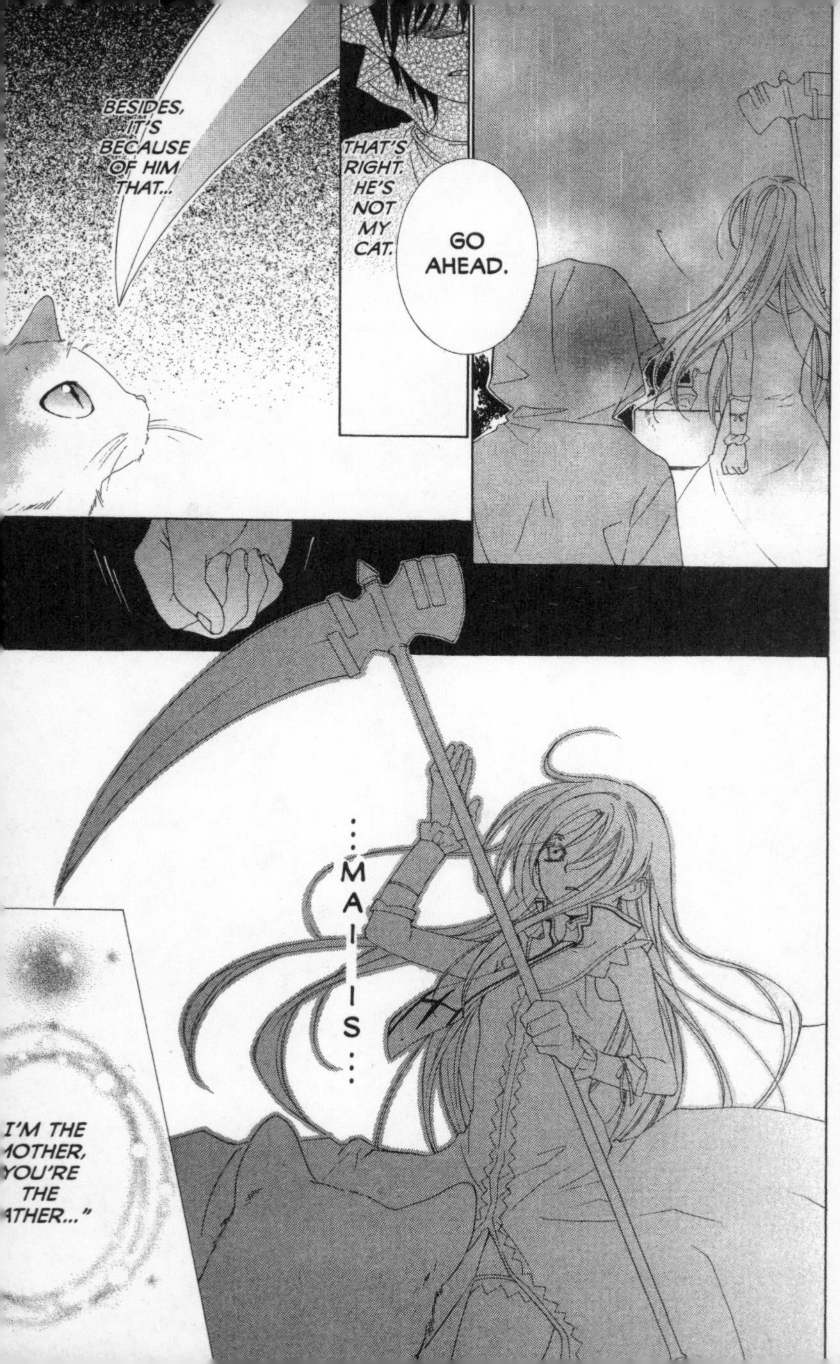
GO AHEAD.
THAT'S RIGHT. HE'S NOT MY CAT.
BESIDES, IT'S BECAUSE OF HIM THAT...
...MAI IS...
I'M THE MOTHER, YOU'RE THE ATHER..."

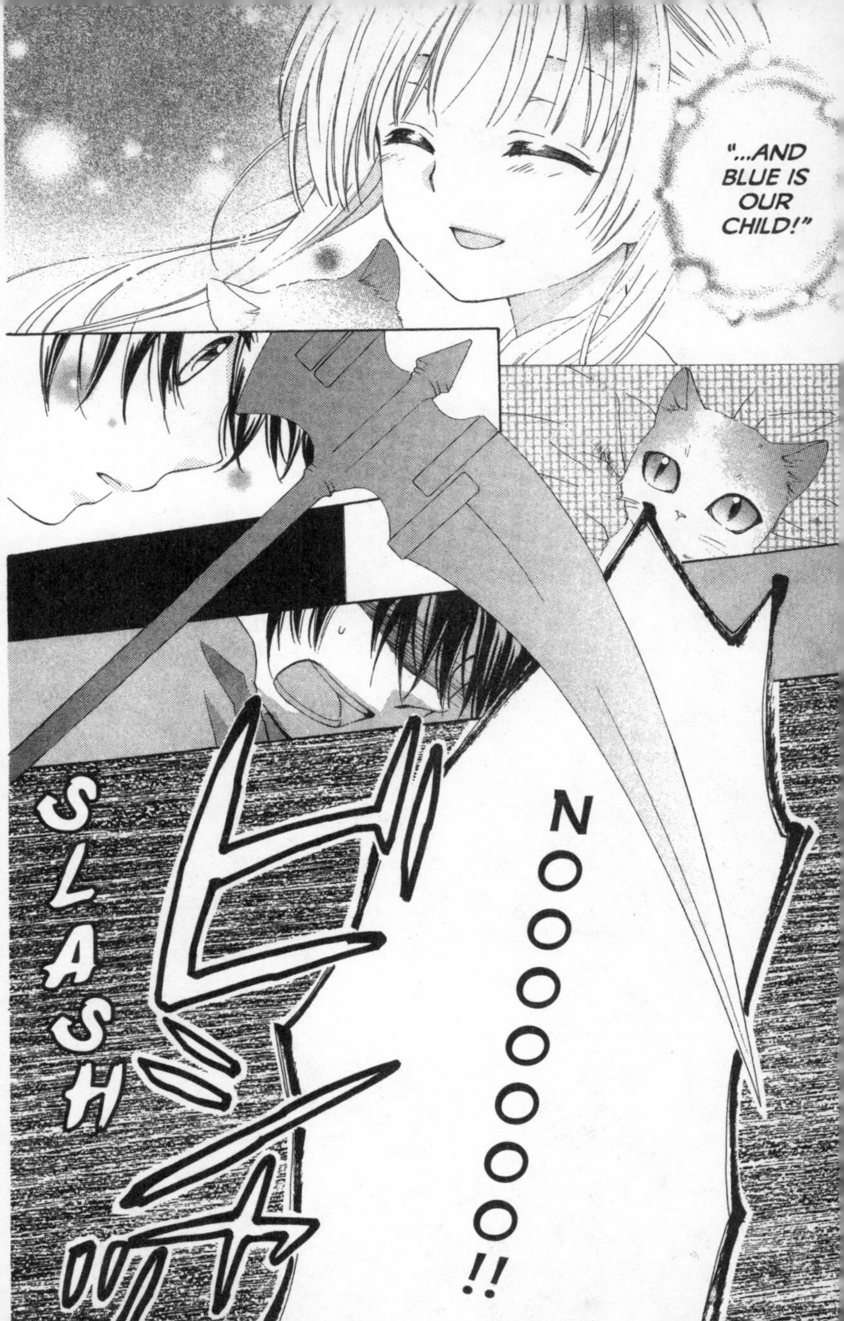
"...AND BLUE IS OUR CHILD!"
NOOOOOOOOO!!
SLASH

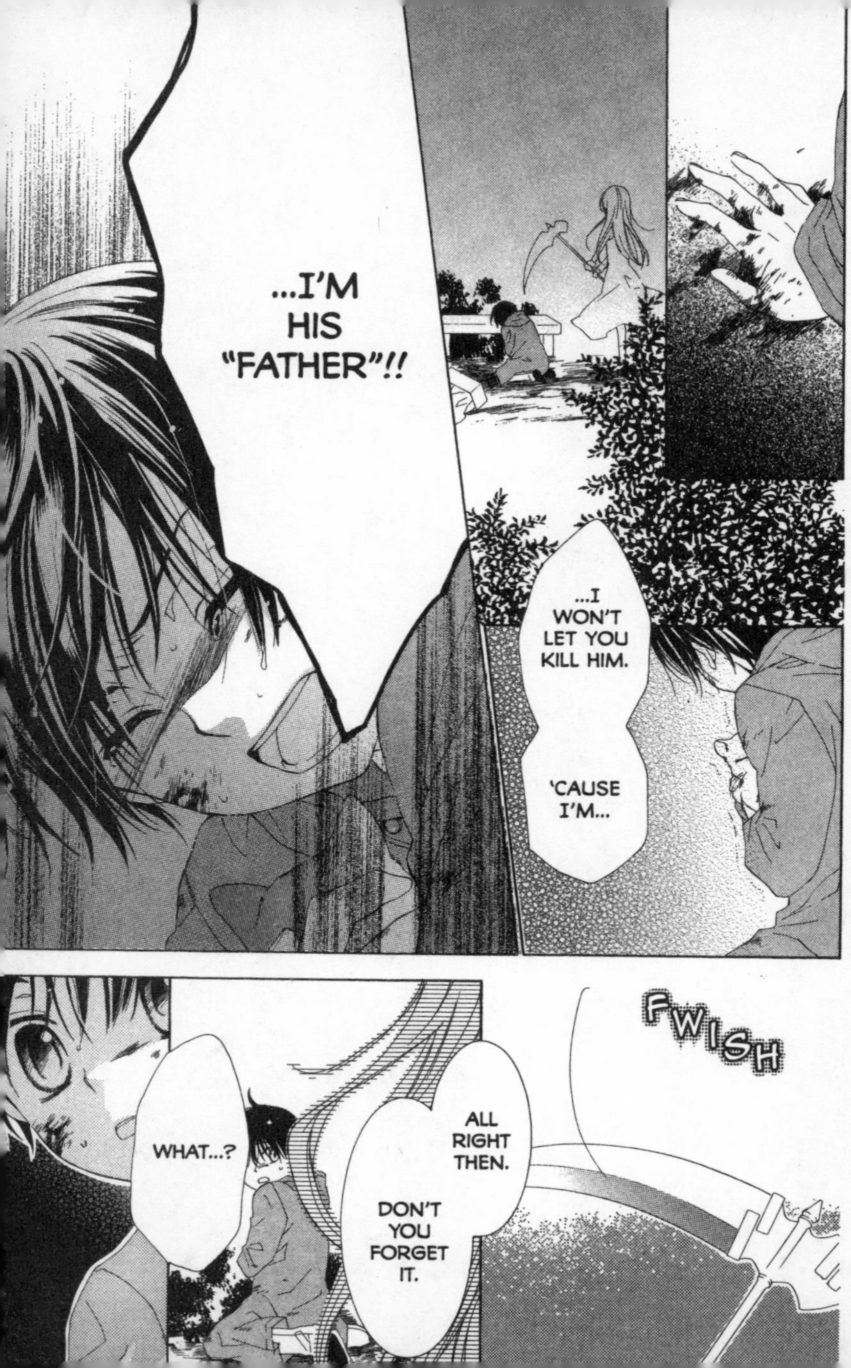
...I WON'T LET YOU KILL HIM.
'CAUSE I'M...
...I'M HIS "FATHER"!!
FWISH
ALL RIGHT THEN.
DON'T YOU FORGET IT.
WHAT...?

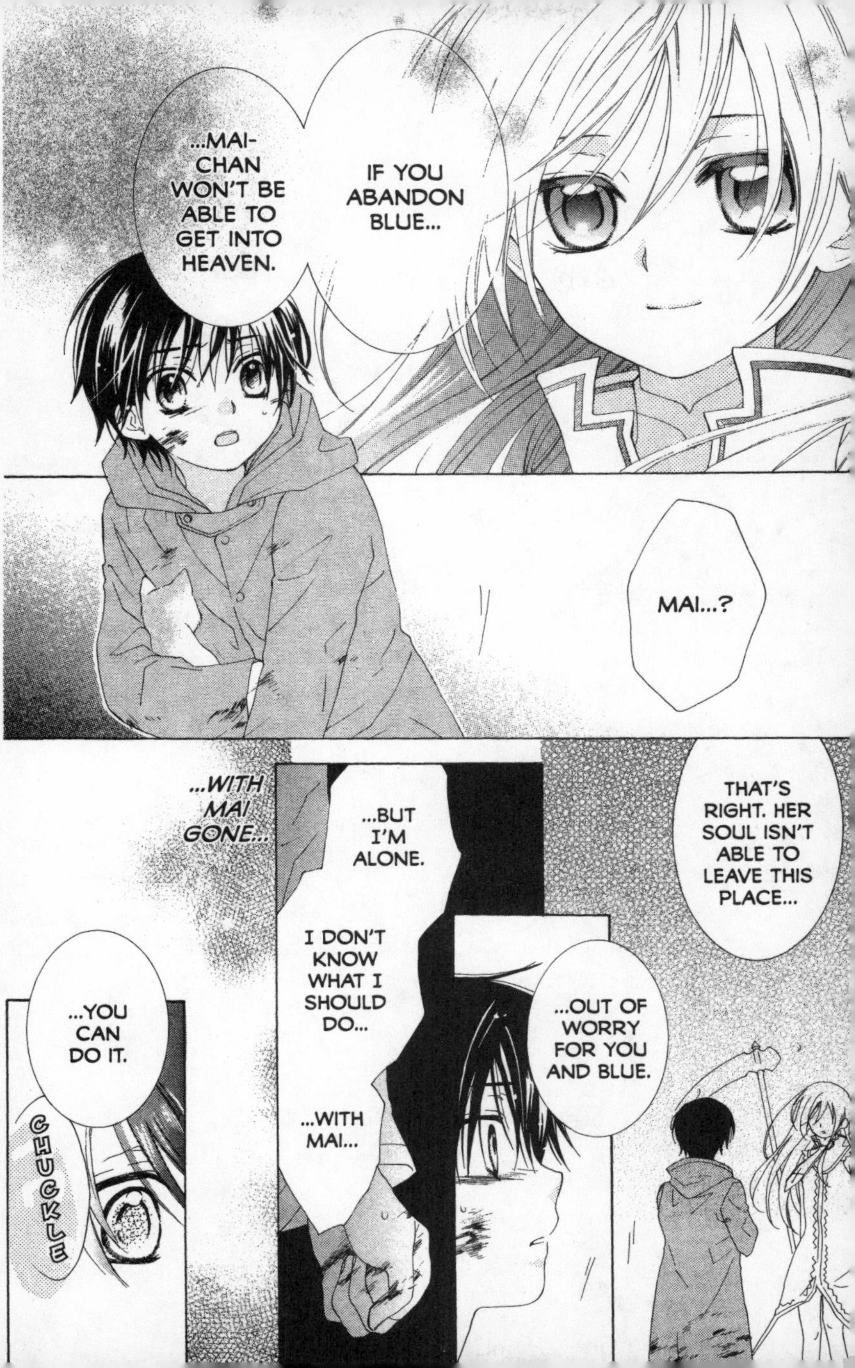
IF YOU ABANDON BLUE...
...MAI-CHAN WON'T BE ABLE TO GET INTO HEAVEN.
MAI...?
THAT'S RIGHT. HER SOUL ISN'T ABLE TO LEAVE THIS PLACE...
...OUT OF WORRY FOR YOU AND BLUE.
...BUT I'M ALONE.
...WITH MAI GONE...
I DON'T KNOW WHAT I SHOULD DO...
...WITH MAI...
...YOU CAN DO IT.
CHUCKLE

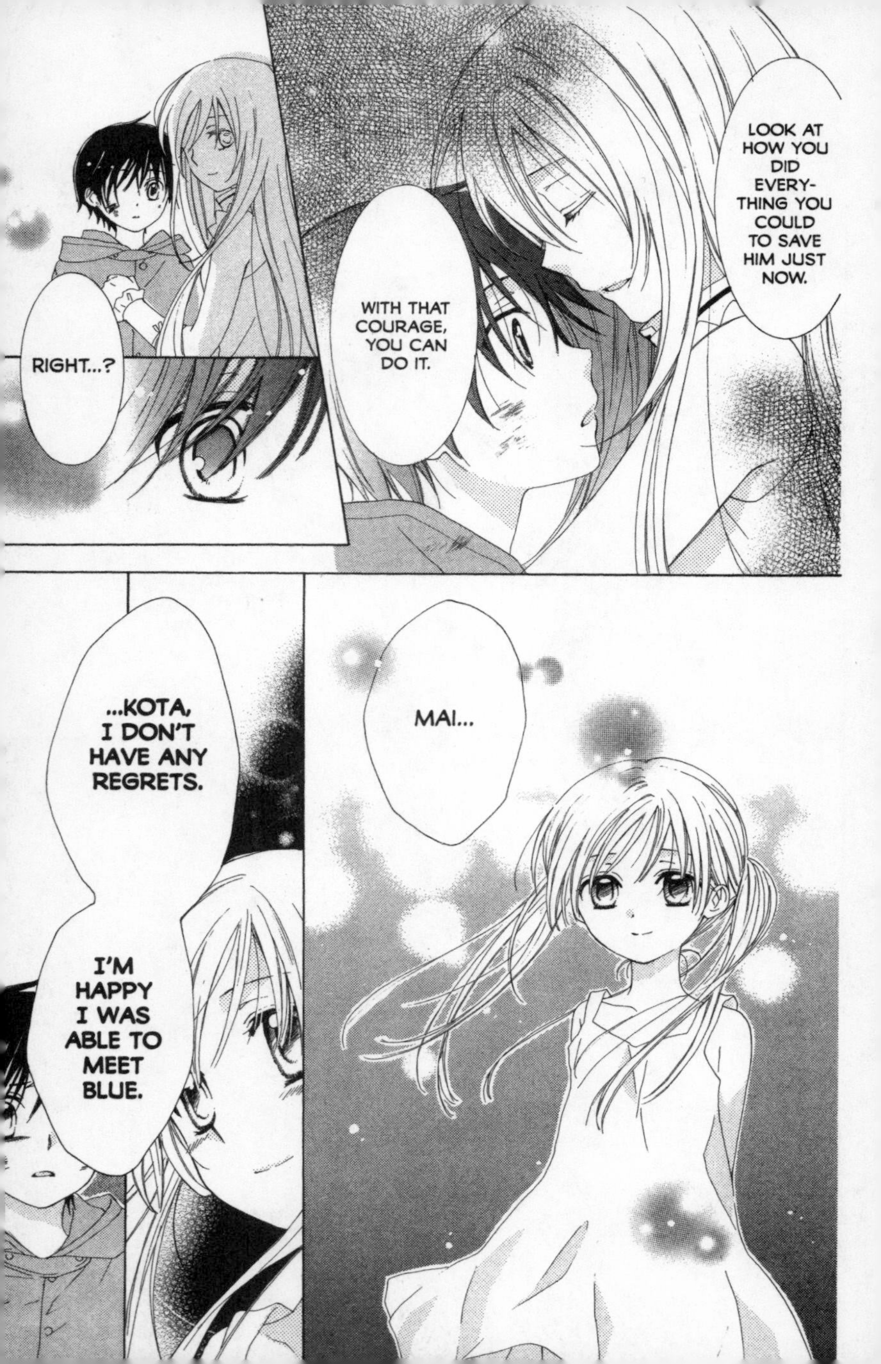
LOOK AT HOW YOU DID EVERY-THING YOU COULD TO SAVE HIM JUST NOW.
WITH THAT COURAGE, YOU CAN DO IT.
RIGHT...?
MAI...
...KOTA, I DON'T HAVE ANY REGRETS.
I'M HAPPY I WAS ABLE TO MEET BLUE.

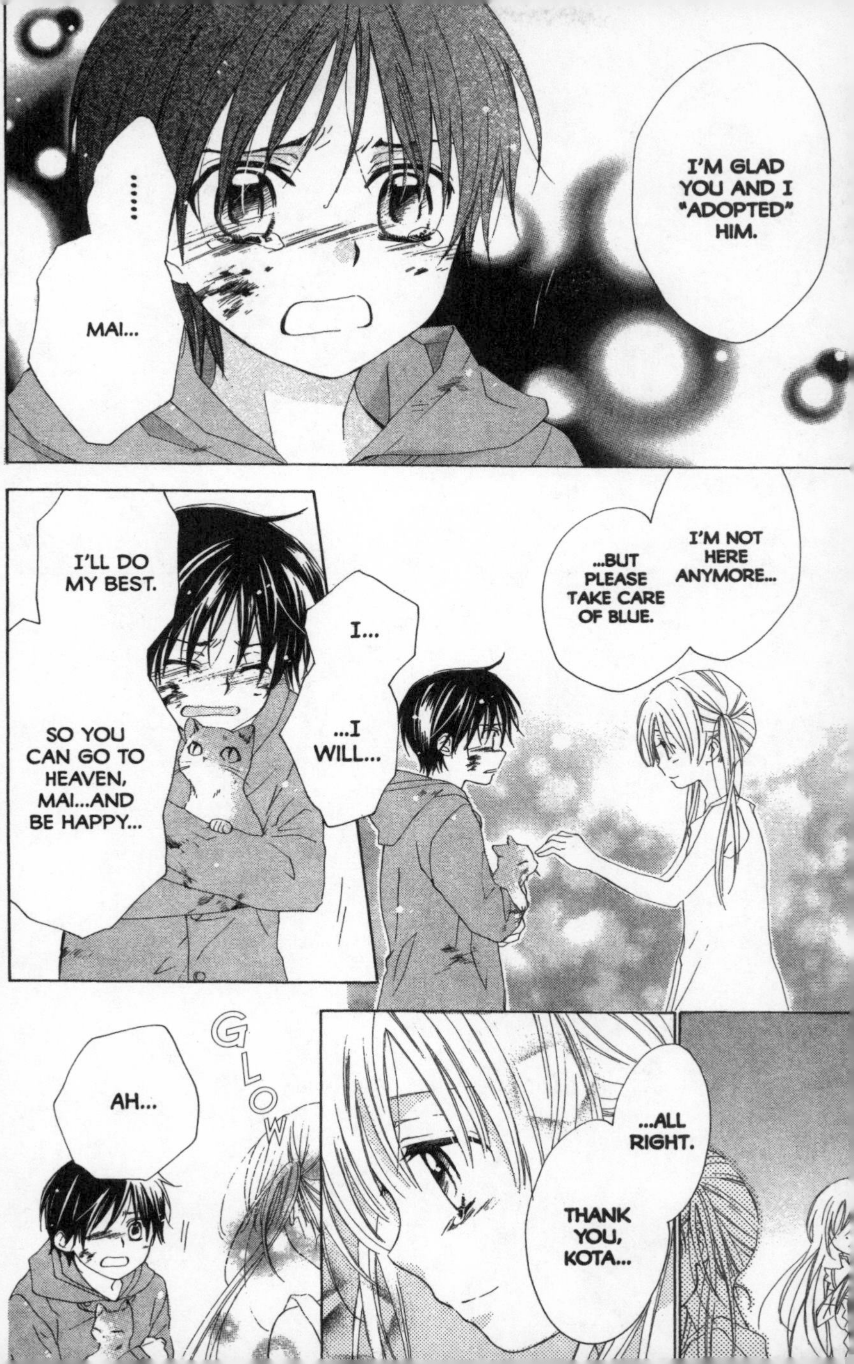
I'M GLAD YOU AND I "ADOPTED" HIM.
......
MAI...
I'M NOT HERE ANYMORE...
...BUT PLEASE TAKE CARE OF BLUE.
I...
...I WILL...
I'LL DO MY BEST.
SO YOU CAN GO TO HEAVEN, MAI...AND BE HAPPY...
...ALL RIGHT.
THANK YOU, KOTA...
GLOW
AH...

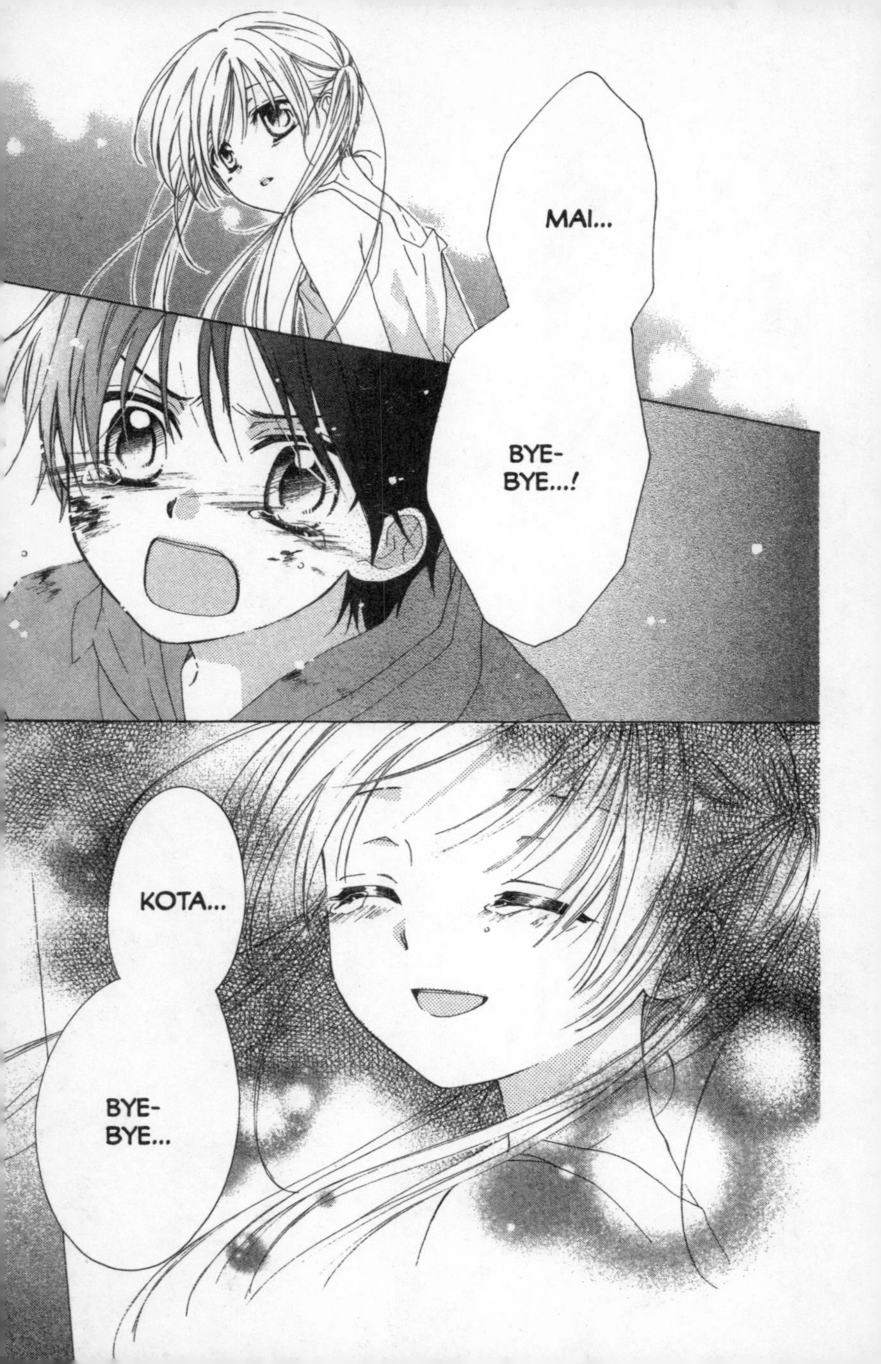
MAI...
BYE-BYE...!
KOTA...
BYE-BYE...

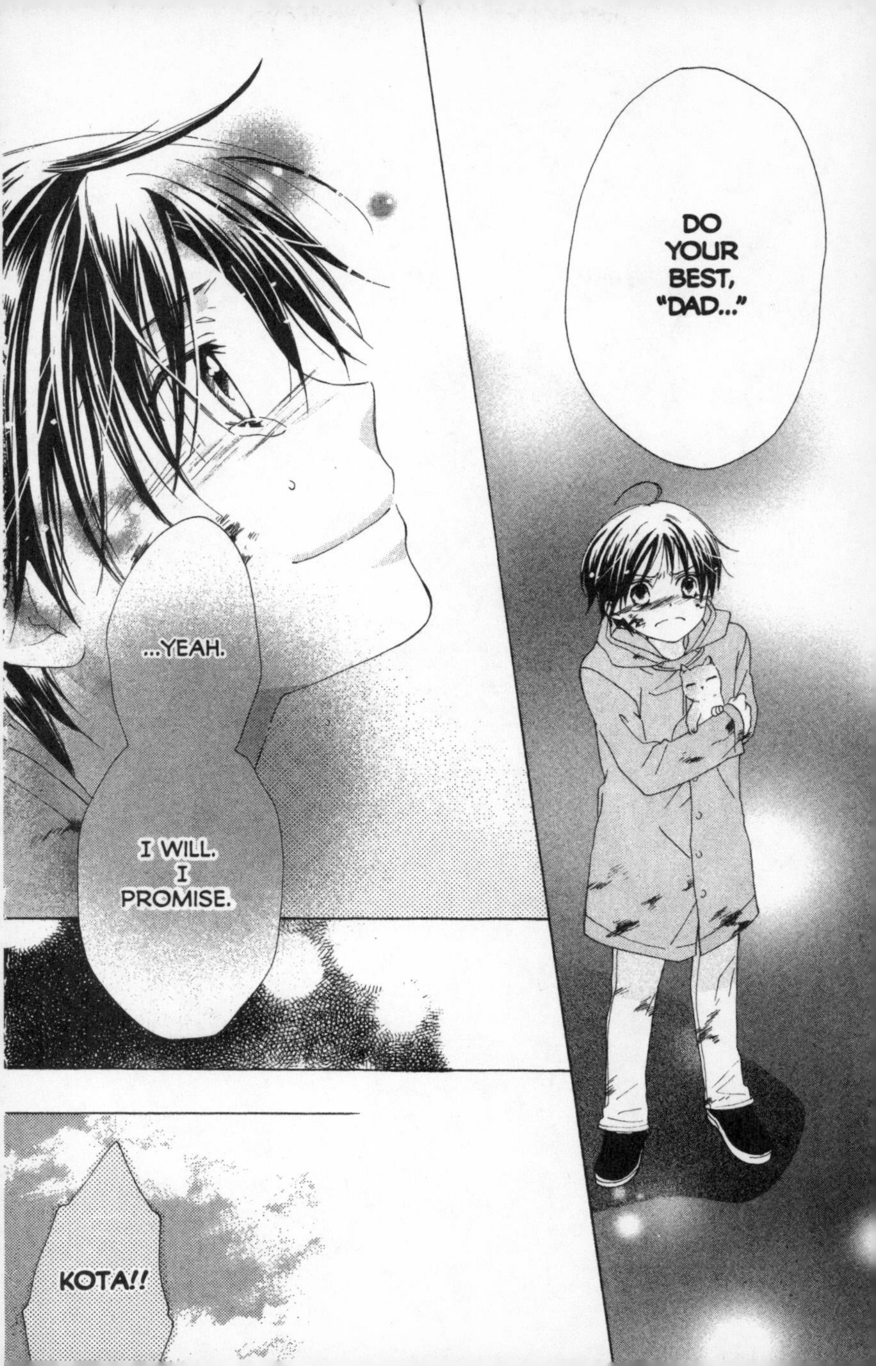
DO YOUR BEST, "DAD..."
...YEAH.
I WILL. I PROMISE.
KOTA!!

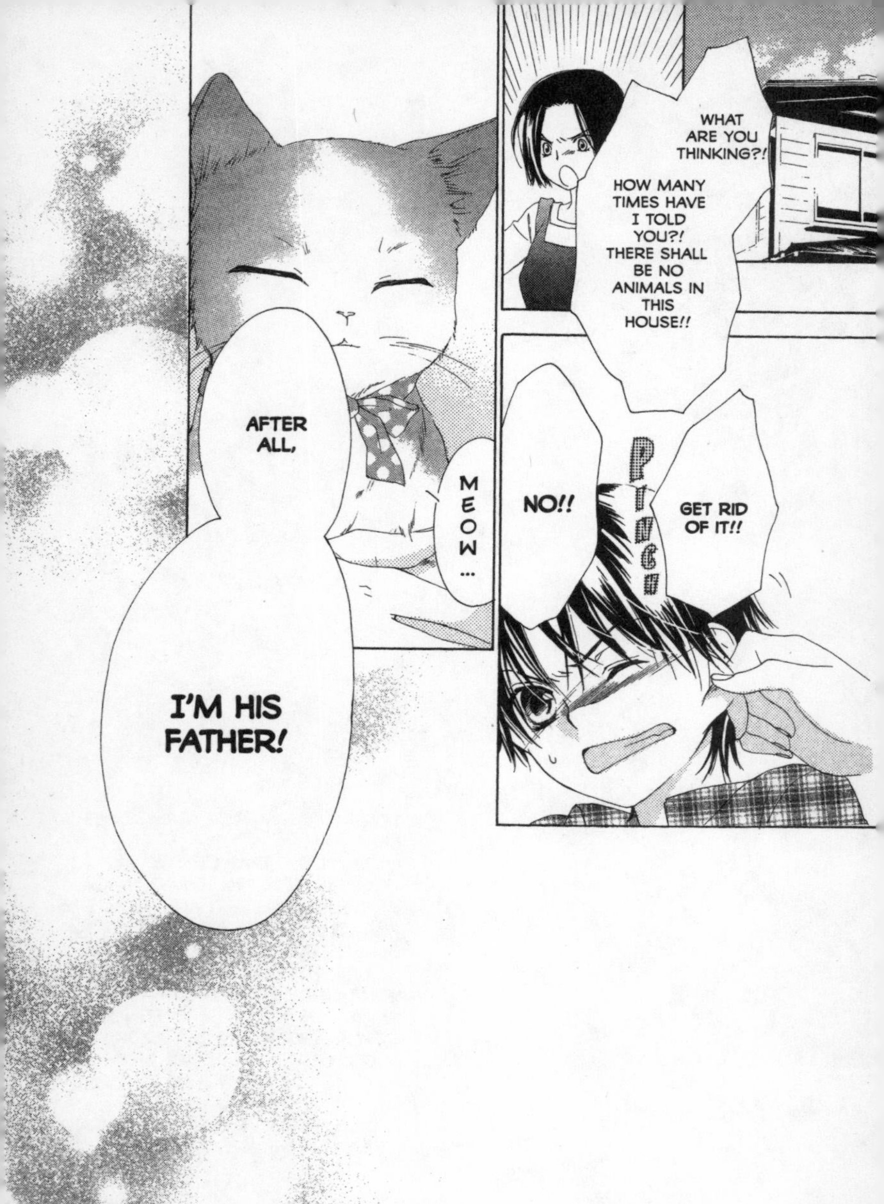
WHAT ARE YOU THINKING?!
HOW MANY TIMES HAVE I TOLD YOU?! THERE SHALL BE NO ANIMALS IN THIS HOUSE!!
GET RID OF IT!!
PINCH
NO!!
MEOW...
AFTER ALL,
I'M HIS FATHER!

BALLAD OF A SHINIGAMI YOUR VOICE: THE END

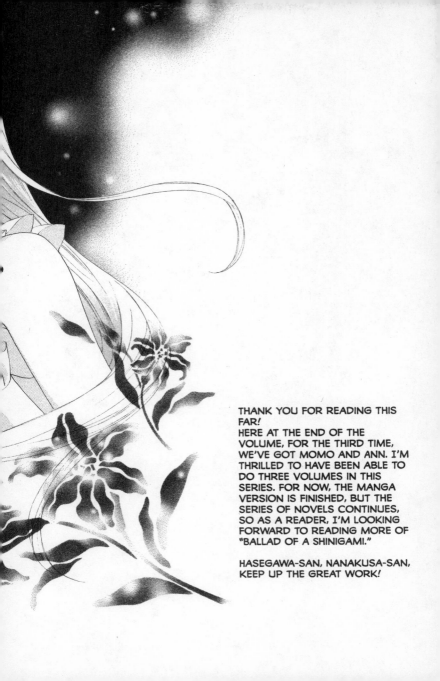

THANK YOU FOR READING THIS
FAR!
HERE AT THE END OF THE
VOLUME, FOR THE THIRD TIME,
WE'VE GOT MOMO AND ANN. I'M
THRILLED TO HAVE BEEN ABLE TO
DO THREE VOLUMES IN THIS
SERIES. FOR NOW, THE MANGA
VERSION IS FINISHED, BUT THE
SERIES OF NOVELS CONTINUES,
SO AS A READER, I'M LOOKING
FORWARD TO READING MORE OF
"BALLAD OF A SHINIGAMI."

HASEGAWA-SAN, NANAKUSA-SAN,
KEEP UP THE GREAT WORK!

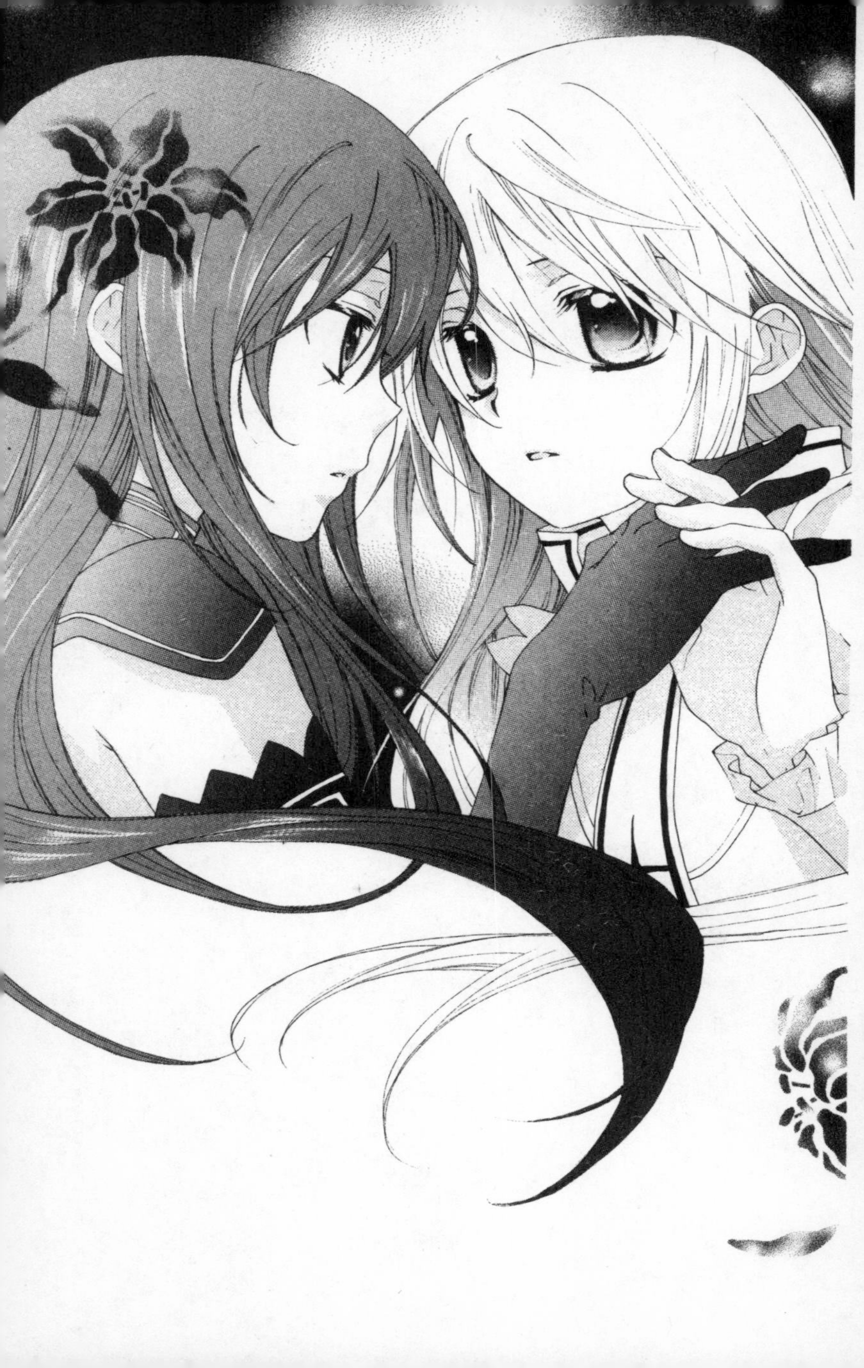

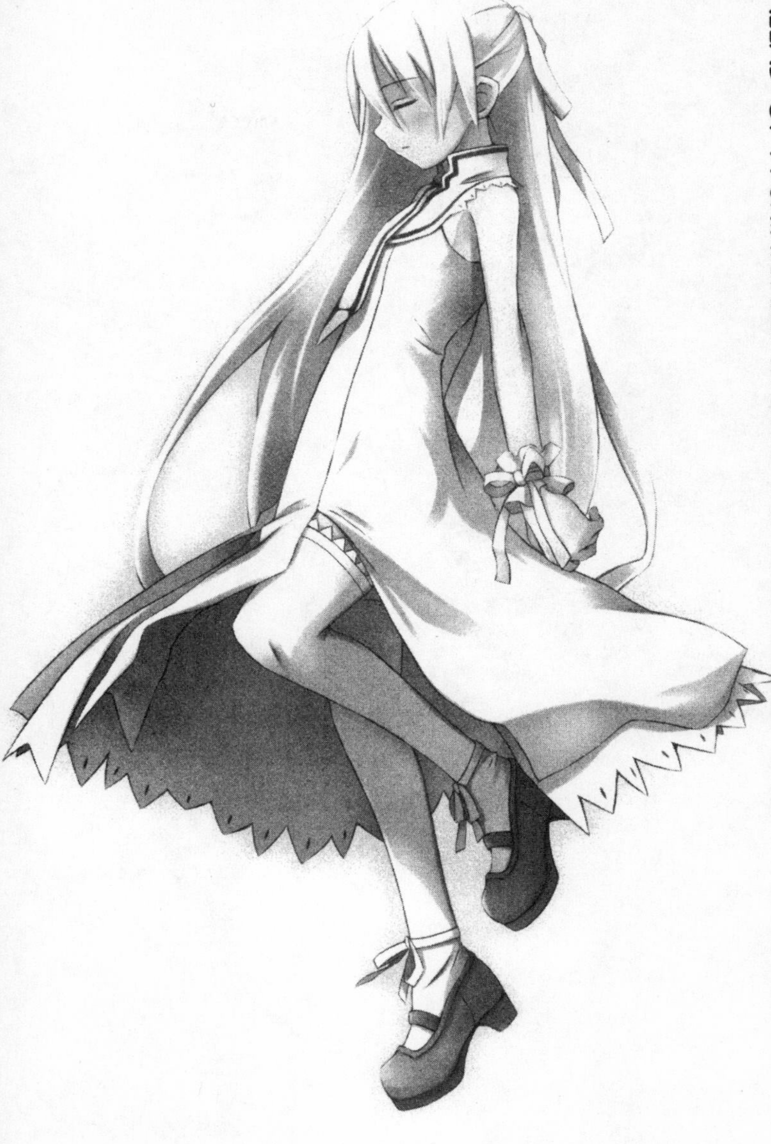

BALLAD OF A SHINIGAMI. MOMO THE GIRL GOD OF DEATH "A COMIC"

MANGA AFTERWORD

HELLO.
I'M K-SKE HASEGAWA.
THIS IS MY SECOND (SHAMELESS) APPEARANCE IN THE BACK PAGES OF
IZUMI-SAN'S COLLECTED MANGA.

EVEN THOUGH I'M SUPPOSED TO BE THE "ORIGINAL AUTHOR" OF "BALLAD
OF A SHINIGAMI," THIS MANGA VERSION BY ASUKA IZUMI-SAN HAS BEEN A
BIG INFLUENCE ON THE NOVEL SERIES. NATURALLY, IT'S NOT A BAD INFLU-
ENCE, BUT RATHER ONE THAT STIMULATES MY IMAGINATION.
ALTHOUGH I'VE NEVER REALLY READ MY OWN SERIES, EVERY TIME I READ
IZUMI-SAN'S "SHINIGAMI," IT'S LIKE LOOKING AT SOMETHING THAT'S
ENTIRELY NEW. AND WHILE READING IT, I OFTEN FIND MYSELF BEING MOVED,
EMBARRASSED, ETC.
THAT ASIDE, ONE OF THE INTERESTING THINGS FOR ME HERE IS DISCOVER-
ING A FACET TO MOMO THAT I DIDN'T KNOW EXISTED. WHEN THAT
HAPPENS, I FEEL PROUD, LIKE A PARENT WHO SEES HIS CHILD GO OFF ON
A TRIP AND THEN RETURN HOME EVEN STRONGER.(LOL)
AND THAT'S WHERE THE INFLUENCE FITS IN, AS I TAKE WHAT I'VE
"LEARNED" AND INSTILL IT INTO THE NOVEL SERIES.
JUST TO GIVE YOU ONE EXAMPLE, TAKE "FLOWERS FROM SCARS" FROM
THE FIRST VOLUME OF THE MANGA SERIES (AND AS IT HAPPENS, VOLUME
ONE OF THE *NOVEL* SERIES AS WELL). THE CHARACTERS IN THAT STORY
REAPPEAR IN THE NOVEL SERIES, IN THE STORY CALLED "MILKY WAY IN THE
PALM OF THE HAND" (VOLUME 8), BUT HERE THEY'VE TAKEN ON THE
PERSONALITY TRAITS AND ACQUIRED BACKGROUND SET-UP THAT
IZUMI-SAN SAW FIT TO GIVE THEM IN THE MANGA. I SHOULD PROBABLY
KEEP THIS KIND OF THING A SECRET(LOL)(SWEAT), BUT IT JUST GOES TO
SHOW HOW MAJOR A PRESENCE IZUMI-SAN'S "SHINIGAMI" IS TO ME. I
FEEL THAT HER WHOLE VERSION IS PERMEATED WITH AN ATMOSPHERE OF
INCREDIBLE, INDELIBLE KINDNESS. I FIND THE SAME VIRTUE IN IZUMI-SAN'S
EARLIER SERIES, "THE LIZARD PRINCE." BOTH TITLES HAVE A VERY WARM,
FRIENDLY AIR ABOUT THEM. AS A READER, I'M DELIGHTED TO SPEND TIME
IN SUCH A COMFORTABLE WORLD AND SO, THROUGH MANY MIRACLES
AND CHANCE ENCOUNTERS, THIS BOOK NOW IN YOUR HANDS HAS COME
TO EXIST, A BLESSED OCCURRENCE IN MY OPINION.
I HOPE THAT YOU HAVE ENJOYED THE TALES WITHIN AS MUCH AS I HAVE
AND THAT THIS SERIES HAS CAPTURED YOUR HEART AS IT HAS MINE.

I'M GRATEFUL TO EVERYONE ASSOCIATED
WITH THIS SERIES AND PRAY THAT WE
CAN MEET AGAIN SOMEDAY, SOMEWHERE.

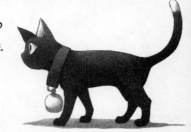

AUTHOR: K-SKE HASEGAWA
ILLUSTRATOR: NANAKUSA

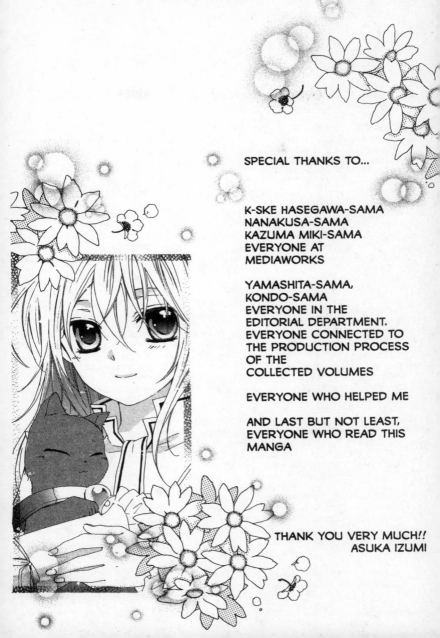

SPECIAL THANKS TO...

K-SKE HASEGAWA-SAMA
NANAKUSA-SAMA
KAZUMA MIKI-SAMA
EVERYONE AT
MEDIAWORKS

YAMASHITA-SAMA,
KONDO-SAMA
EVERYONE IN THE
EDITORIAL DEPARTMENT.
EVERYONE CONNECTED TO
THE PRODUCTION PROCESS
OF THE
COLLECTED VOLUMES

EVERYONE WHO HELPED ME

AND LAST BUT NOT LEAST,
EVERYONE WHO READ THIS
MANGA

THANK YOU VERY MUCH!!
ASUKA IZUMI

Sheldon Drzka
Translation and Adaptation
MPS Ad Studio
Lettering
Larry Berry
Art Director
Chynna Clugston Flores
Assistant Editor
Jim Chadwick
Editor

Jim Lee
Editorial Director
Hank Kanalz
VP—General Manager
Paul Levitz
President & Publisher
Richard Bruning
SVP—Creative Director
Patrick Caldon
EVP—Finance & Operations
Amy Genkins
SVP—Business & Legal Affairs
Gregory Noveck
SVP—Creative Affairs
Steve Rotterdam
SVP—Sales & Marketing
Cheryl Rubin
SVP—Brand Management

This book is manufactured at a facility holding chain-of-custody certification. This paper is made with sustainably managed North American fiber. Printed by World Color Press, Inc. St-Romuald, QC, Canada 2/3/10

DC Comics, a Warner Bros. Entertainment Company.

ISBN: 978-1-4012-2060-0

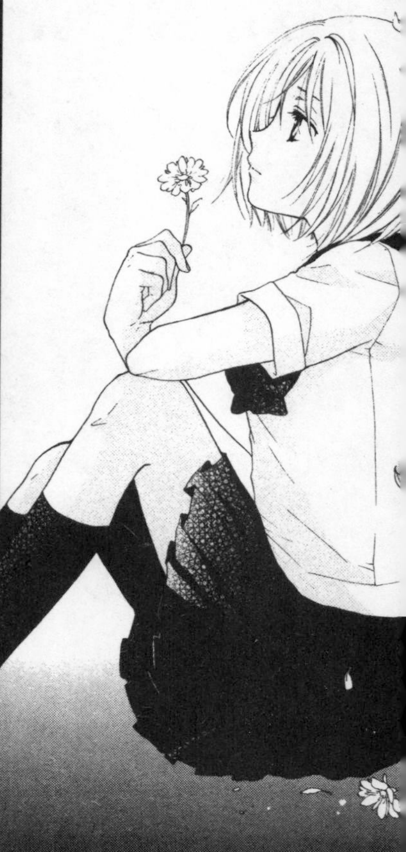

All the pages in this book [...] are printed here—in Japanese RIGHT-to-LEFT format [...] you can read the stories [...].

RIGHT TO LEFT?!

Traditional Japanese manga starts at the upper right-hand corner, and moves right-to-left as it goes down the page. Follow this guide for an easy understanding.

For more information and sneak previews, visit cmxmanga.com. Call 1-888-COMIC BOOK for the nearest comics shop or head to your local book store.

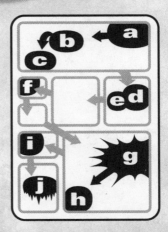